The Roles of Language in CLIL

CAMBRIDGE LANGUAGE TEACHING LIBRARY

A series covering central issues in language teaching and learning, by authors who have expert knowledge in their field.

For a complete list of titles please visit: www.cambridge.org/elt/cltl

A selection of recent titles in this series

Materials Development in Language Teaching (Second Edition)
Edited by Brian Tomlinson

Values, Philosophies, and Beliefs in TESOL: Making a Statement
Graham Crookes

Listening in the Language Classroom
John Field

Lessons from Good Language Learners
Edited by Carol Griffiths

Teacher Language Awareness
Stephen Andrews

Language Teacher Supervision: A Case-Based Approach
Kathleen M. Bailey

Conversation: From Description to Pedagogy
Scott Thornbury and Diana Slade

The Experience of Language Teaching
Rose Senior

Learners' Stories: Difference and Diversity in Language Learning
Edited by Phil Benson and David Nunan

Task-Based Language Teaching
David Nunan

Rules, Patterns and Words: Grammar and Lexis in English Language Teaching
Dave Willis

Language Learning in Distance Education
Cynthia White

Group Dynamics in the Language Classroom
Zoltán Dörnyei and Tim Murphey

Testing for Language Teachers (Second Edition)
Arthur Hughes

Motivational Strategies in the Language Classroom
Zoltán Dörnyei

The Dynamics of the Language Classroom
Ian Tudor

Using Surveys in Language Programs
James Dean Brown

Approaches and Methods in Language Teaching (Second Edition)
Jack C. Richards and Theodore S. Rodgers

Teaching Languages to Young Learners
Lynne Cameron

Classroom Decision Making: Negotiation and Process Syllabuses in Practice
Michael P. Breen and Andrew Littlejohn

Establishing Self-Access: From Theory to Practice
David Gardner and Lindsay Miller

Collaborative Action Research for English Language Teachers
Anne Burns

Affect in Language Learning
Edited by Jane Arnold

Developments in English for Specific Purposes: A Multi-Disciplinary Approach
Tony Dudley-Evans and Maggie Jo St John

Language Learning in Intercultural Perspective: Approaches through Drama and Ethnography *Edited by Michael Byram and Michael Fleming*

The Roles of Language in CLIL

Ana Llinares
Tom Morton
Rachel Whittaker

CAMBRIDGE
UNIVERSITY PRESS

CAMBRIDGE
UNIVERSITY PRESS

University Printing House, Cambridge CB2 8BS, United Kingdom

Cambridge University Press is part of the University of Cambridge.

It furthers the University's mission by disseminating knowledge in the pursuit of education, learning and research at the highest international levels of excellence.

www.cambridge.org
Information on this title: www.cambridge.org/9780521150071

© Cambridge University Press 2012

First published 2012

A catalogue record for this publication is available from the British Library

Library of Congress Cataloguing in Publication data
The roles of language in CLIL / Ana Llinares, Tom Morton, Rachel Whittaker.
    p. cm. – (Cambridge language teaching library)
  Includes bibliographical references and index.
  ISBN 978-0-521-15007-1 (pbk.)
  ISBN 978-0-521-76963-1 (hardback)1.
  Language and languages – Study and teaching.
  I. Morton, Tom, 1958-   II. Whittaker, Rachel.   III. Title.   IV. P51.L588
  2012 418.0071–dc23   2011042630

ISBN 978-0-521-76963-1 Hardback
ISBN 978-0-521-15007-1 Paperback

Contents

Acknowledgements   *page* vi

Introduction   1

Part I   The role of language in CLIL classroom interaction   23

1 *Classroom registers and their impact on learning opportunity*   25

2 *Interaction and dialogue in the CLIL classroom*   52

3 *Interaction patterns and scaffolding in the CLIL classroom*   76

Part II   The language of academic subjects in CLIL   107

4 *Genres in CLIL subjects*   109

5 *Grammar and lexis in CLIL subjects*   154

**Part III   Students' language development and
assessment in CLIL**   185

6 *Focusing on students' language: Integrating form
   and meaning*   187

7 *Students' academic and interpersonal language in CLIL*   219

8 *Developing CLIL students' writing: From oracy to literacy*   244

9 *The role of language in assessment in CLIL*   280

Appendix: Answer key to tasks   316

Glossary   331

Index   338

Acknowledgements

We would like to thank all the teachers and students in Austria, Finland, the Netherlands and Spain whose voices appear in this book. We are also very grateful to Liz Dale, Christiane Dalton-Puffer, Tarja Nikula and Amanda Pastrana for their contributions to the CLIL corpus. The book has benefited greatly from the comments and suggestions from the anonymous reviewers – special thanks go to them. Finally, thanks to Cambridge University Press for permission to reproduce the extracts which appear in Chapters 4 and 5.

Publisher's acknowledgements

The authors and publishers acknowledge the following sources of copyright material and are grateful for the permissions granted. While every effort has been made, it has not always been possible to identify the sources of all the material used, or to trace all copyright holders. If any omissions are brought to our notice, we will be happy to include the appropriate acknowledgement on reprinting.

Cambers, G. and Sibley, S. (2010) *Cambridge GCSE Geography*, Cambridge: Cambridge University Press – p. 127 Text 4.13 and 4.14; p. 128 Text 4.15; p. 130 Text 4.19; p. 148 Text 4.32; p. 149 Text 4.33; p. 150 Text 4.35; p. 182 Text 5.6; p. 183 Text 5.8.

Counsell, C. and Steer, C. (1993) *Industrial Britain: The Workshop of the World*. Cambridge History Programme, Cambridge: Cambridge University Press. (6th printing 2009) – pp. 133–4 Text 4.20; p. 135 Text 4.22; p. 138 Text 4.26; p. 140 Text 4.28; p. 182 Text 5.7.

Edmonds, S. (1993) *Native Peoples of North America. Diversity and Development*, Cambridge History Programme, Cambridge: Cambridge University Press (11th printing 2007) – p. 137 Text 4.25.

Field, R. (1995) *African Peoples of the Americas: From Slavery to Civil Rights*. Cambridge: Cambridge University Press (10th printing 2009) – p. 136 Text 4.26.

Hetherton, G. (1992) *Revolutionary France. Liberty, Tyranny and Terror*, Cambridge History Programme. Cambridge: Cambridge University Press (10th printing 2009) – p. 135 Text 4.23; pp. 149–50 Text 4.34.

Jones, M. and Jones, G. (2002) *Biology,* Cambridge: Cambridge University Press –
 p. 113 Texts 4.1; p. 117–18 Text 4.4; p. 119 Text 4.6; p. 121 Text 4.8; p. 122
 Text 4.9; pp. 122–3 Text 4.10; p. 123 Text 4.11; p. 124 Text 4.11a (= section of
 4.11); p. 157 Text 5.1; p. 160 Text 5.2; p. 173 Text 5.4.
McAleavy, T. (2002) *Twentieth Century History: International Relations since
 1919.* Cambridge: Cambridge University Press – p. 177 Text 5.5.
Mantin P. and Pulley, R. (1992) *The Roman World: From Republic to Empire,*
 Cambridge: Cambridge University Press – p. 136 Text 4.24.

Introduction

Contexts: Defining the scope of CLIL for this book

This book is about a **bilingual educational** approach in which the study of academic content is combined with the use and learning of a foreign language (referred to as FL hereafter). In Europe, this approach is usually known as Content and Language Integrated Learning (CLIL). While the term CLIL was developed in Europe, it can be seen as part of a global trend, especially as regards the use of English as a medium of instruction (Graddol, 2006). The rise in popularity of CLIL in Europe can be seen in the context of the European Commission's white paper (1995) (*Teaching and Learning: Towards the Learning Society*) in which a stated objective was the '1+2 policy', that is, for EU citizens to have competence in their mother tongue plus two Community foreign languages. Even at this early stage, the importance of CLIL or CLIL-like initiatives was envisaged, with the document pointing out that 'it could even be argued that secondary school pupils should study certain subjects in the first foreign language learned, as is the case in the European schools' (p. 47). By 2006, according to a Eurydice Report, CLIL had become 'a fast developing phenomenon across Europe' (Eurydice, 2006: 2). On the whole, though, European CLIL has been mostly a *bottom-up* movement, with many local small-scale initiatives in different parts of the continent. However, as Björklund (2006) suggests, it may be time to move beyond personal experiences, intuition and individual adaptations to 'scientifically justified' and generalisable principles for CLIL. As she puts it, 'the search for common, effective core features must be more intensive than the ambitions for local uniqueness' (p. 194). This book is intended as a step in the direction of establishing generalisable principles about the roles of the first L in CLIL: language.

Many writers on CLIL use a wide definition of the phenomenon, which includes the combination of academic content learning and the learning of heritage and community languages. In CLIL, an **additional language** 'is often a learner's "foreign language", but it may also be a second language or some form of heritage or community language' (Coyle et al., 2010: 1). One way of defining the core features of European CLIL is to distinguish it from other bilingual educational approaches such as Canadian immersion programmes, content-based instruction in the United States or other programmes that involve the use of regional minority or heritage languages as medium of instruction. As

1

Lasagabaster and Sierra (2010) argue, the terms CLIL and **immersion** have often been used interchangeably, and this has led to some confusion and the blurring of important differences between them. These authors describe differences between European CLIL and immersion programmes in the following areas: language of instruction, teachers, starting age, teaching materials, language objectives, inclusion of immigrant students and research. With the aim of clearly identifying the scope of the term CLIL as it is used in this book, in what follows we comment briefly on each of these areas.

In terms of language of instruction, Lasagabaster and Sierra point out that, in CLIL programmes, the language of instruction is a foreign language which, unlike in immersion contexts, is not present in the students' local communities. Nevertheless, even in immersion contexts, exposure to the L2 is largely confined to the classroom (Swain and Johnson, 1997: 7–8). As for CLIL teachers, unlike most immersion teachers, they are non-native speakers of the language used as a medium of instruction. In immersion contexts teachers are usually bilingual or native speakers of the language of instruction. In terms of starting age, CLIL learners often start studying content in the new language later than their immersion counterparts, with the result that there are large differences in the amounts of exposure between CLIL and immersion students. However, this situation is changing as many CLIL students now start learning in English at primary school, or even earlier, and some contexts provide the students with more possibilities of exposure to the target language outside the classroom than others (for example, Northern European countries like Sweden have more exposure than Mediterranean countries like Spain).

Turning to teaching materials, in immersion programmes these are normally the same as those used by native speakers, while in CLIL materials may be adapted or written specifically for a CLIL programme. Regarding the degree of language competence as an objective, Lasagabaster and Sierra claim that immersion programmes aim at native-speaker competence, while in CLIL the expectations are significantly lower. However, this is open to debate, as in most immersion contexts as well as in CLIL the main aim is functional competence. If we take the examples of the roles of French in Quebec and English in Europe, we could argue that, in both cases, the aim for the non-natives would be similar: non-native speakers in Quebec need French in order to participate in the local community and students in European countries need English to participate in the European community, when travelling or doing business, for example. In terms of the role of immigrant students in CLIL programmes, Lasagabaster and Sierra point out that these students might be at risk of exclusion, especially in those contexts where they already have to deal with two additional languages (for example, Spanish and Basque in addition to English in the case of the Basque Country). Finally, these authors acknowledge that there has been a long-standing research effort in immersion programmes, but CLIL is still relatively underresearched. This book will contribute to filling this gap, with a new approach to the roles of language in CLIL and how language is integrated into the teaching and learning of content.

While recognising the very varied realities of CLIL, our focus is on contexts in which a foreign language, English, is used as a medium of instruction. In this book, we draw on a **corpus** of CLIL classroom data from four European countries (Spain, Austria, Finland and the Netherlands). However, the fact that nearly everywhere in the world the target language in content-based language instruction is usually English makes the contents and suggestions presented in this book easily transferable to non-European contexts like China or Latin America.

The core corpus used in this book consists of 500,000 words of secondary CLIL classroom interaction recorded in the aforementioned contexts. This corpus includes data collected by the Universidad Autónoma in Madrid as part of the UAM-CLIL corpus, and data collected by Christiane Dalton-Puffer in Austria, Tarja Nikula in Finland and Liz Dale in the Netherlands. The secondary school corpus is supplemented by a further 200,000 words of preschool and primary CLIL classroom data compiled by the Universidad Autónoma in Madrid, again as part of the UAM-CLIL corpus. These corpora have been used in a wide range of published research studies carried out by the authors and the other contributors. The findings from these studies have played a fundamental role in the development of the ideas about the roles of language in CLIL presented in this book. Throughout the book we use extracts from this database to illustrate these ideas. Because the data extracts are genuine examples of CLIL practice, readers can build a picture of CLIL as it is actually implemented in four European contexts, and can compare what happens in these classrooms with what happens, or may happen, in their own contexts.

The use of this corpus allows us to identify core features within a limited range of variation, something which would be more difficult to do if we included contexts in which community or heritage languages are used as medium of instruction. We can thus identify the broad sociolinguistic and educational parameters of foreign language CLIL initiatives. A very useful instrument for doing this are Cenoz's *continua of multilingual education* (Cenoz, 2009). By using the continua (see Figure 0.1) to more precisely delimit the features of the type of European CLIL that is the focus of this book, readers from other contexts will more readily be able to compare and adapt the ideas we present.

Cenoz's continua of **multilingual education** show how linguistic, sociolinguistic and school factors combine in different ways in different bi- and multilingual education contexts, thus making it possible to compare different situations by seeing them as lying at different points on a range of continua. Although Cenoz uses the term multilingual, she points out that 'bilingual schools can also be considered a type of multilingual school because the term "multilingual" refers to multiple languages and this can be understood as two or more languages' (2009: 33).

Starting at the top of the diagram with school-based factors, schools can be more or less bi- or multilingual depending on how many languages are taught as subjects (*school subject*), how well they are integrated in the curriculum, the age at which they are introduced and the time devoted to them. In most European CLIL contexts, at least two languages (the majority language and one or more regional or foreign languages) will be taught as subjects. There will be differences in the extent to which these languages are integrated into the curriculum. For example, in some primary schools foreign languages can be used in theme-based teaching across different subject areas. In other schools, the second or foreign languages will not be integrated with the rest of the curriculum.

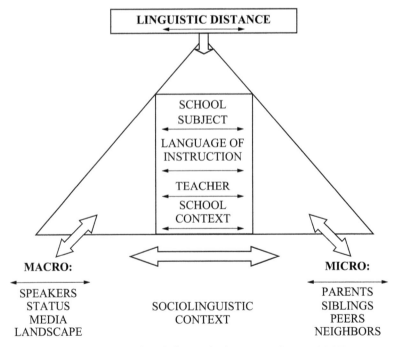

Figure 0.1 The continua of multilingual education (Cenoz, 2009)

4

Schools are more multilingual the more languages are used as the *language of instruction*. In all of the CLIL contexts which we draw on in our European CLIL corpus, at least two languages are used as the medium of instruction: the national or majority language, and English. This would place these schools in the category of what Baker (2006: 216) describes as *strong* bilingual education, that is, mainstream bilingual education in two majority languages. However, the extent of content instruction through the medium of the foreign language also has to be measured. In some contexts, there is a *sampling* approach to CLIL, in which a relatively small part of a subject is taught in the FL, often in collaboration with a language teacher. This *weak* version can be seen as closer to the vision of CLIL that has emerged in foreign language teaching circles. A strong version of CLIL would see a whole subject from the curriculum taught and assessed in the FL. Most of the data from our European corpus are drawn from these strong CLIL experiences, in which the entire subject is taught and assessed in the FL, English. However, in the same way as research on Canadian immersion programmes based on French has influenced many studies and applications to other foreign / second languages throughout the world, the ideas in this book are likewise applicable to other contexts.

The *teacher continuum* refers to whether the teachers in a school have multilingual competences themselves, and to whether they have received training in multilingual education. One of the defining features of CLIL outlined by Lasagabaster and Sierra (2010) is that the teachers are generally non-native speakers of the language of instruction, usually English. Added to this is the fact that many have received little training in CLIL pedagogy. This is the case in the settings in our corpus. Although there are some native speakers of English, most of the teachers are non-native, and many have had little formal training in CLIL methodology. Some of the teachers have a background in language teaching, and all are certified as teachers of their subjects. In some of the contexts in the study, the teachers have the benefit of curricular guidelines which specify content and language objectives, but most do not have this support in integrating content and language.

School context, in Cenoz's model, refers to the use of different languages inside the school for different types of formal and informal communication outside classroom lessons. As the corpus only contains classroom discourse, we do not have transcribed data showing the extent of FL use outside classrooms. This contextual information, where necessary, is provided by informants working in the different contexts. In any case, our focus on the roles of language in CLIL in this book is on the FL in representing subject knowledge and organising the social world of the classroom. This, in many ways, is seen as the main justification for CLIL. Extending FL use outside the classroom, both in terms of oral communication and the *linguistic landscape* (posters, examples of students' work etc.) is, where it is achieved, an extremely useful benefit of CLIL as a context for language use.

In terms of *linguistic distance*, the languages involved in multilingual or CLIL programmes may be closer or more distanced from each other, regarding both the language typology and the amount of contact there has been between the languages in any setting. Two languages may not be related to each other in terms of the language families they belong to, but may have been in close contact, so that one has an impact on the other, for example with the use of 'loan words' (Baker 2006: 51–2). In the CLIL contexts in the corpus, there is of course great variation in the degrees of similarity and difference between the language of instruction, English, and the main languages spoken in the four countries (Dutch, German, Finnish and Spanish). However, English's role as an international language or lingua franca (Graddol, 2006) means that there is, to a greater or lesser extent, an impact of English in these settings, with some people concerned about a possible impoverishing of the local languages, not only due to English loan words permeating them, but also to the influence of English on much wider domains of use, such as business or education.

Sociolinguistic variables can be described at the macro and the microlevels. At the *macrolevel*, it is important to consider the number of speakers of the target languages, the status of the languages in society, their use in the media and their general presence in the local linguistic ecologies, or the way different languages interact with each other in a specific setting (Cenoz, 2009: 37). The more use there is of different languages, the more multilingual the environment will be. In the contexts of the corpus used in this book, English can be seen as having a high status in that it has been chosen as a medium of instruction in the CLIL programmes. This is explained by the shared **sociolinguistic status** of English, which is not like any other foreign language, as it is *the* international lingua franca. However, there are differences in the presence of English in everyday life among the different contexts in the corpus. The Dutch and Finnish contexts can be seen as occupying the high-presence end of the continuum, with Austria somewhere in the middle and Spain at the low-presence end of the continuum. In the Spanish context, the only contact with English for most learners is the classroom. It is true, of course, that technology means that there is easy access to English (through the Internet, easily available DVDs in English etc.) but this does not mean that learners are generally willing to use these resources (Lasagabaster and Sierra, 2010). These features of the Spanish context may be of interest to readers of this book who are planning to implement CLIL in other contexts where there is a low presence of the FL outside the classroom.

The *micro-sociolinguistic level* refers to the students and their local communities of families, friends and neighbours. The context will be more multilingual if more languages are used for everyday communication. In many European countries, there are significant numbers of speakers of co-official regional languages, for example Finland with an important minority of Swedish speakers. Also, in most European countries, and this includes those in our corpus, there have been considerable increases in immigration, with the result that there is much more linguistic diversity in many, mainly urban, local communities. However, as Cenoz says, even if a context is multilingual in terms of the languages used in the local community, it is not so in educational terms if the aim of the school is not to promote multilingualism. In the case of European CLIL, there are clearly issues in introducing a foreign language such as English as a medium of instruction in situations where there are already two languages used in education. And there are also issues in changing the language of instruction in contexts where there are large numbers of students in the classroom who are still learning the majority national language. As we saw in the discussion of Lasagabaster and Sierra's paper (2010), there is a risk of elitism if students who are still learning either the national or regional languages are excluded from CLIL programmes. Thus, it is important that bilingual programmes such as CLIL are inclusive, and that they do no harm to the educational chances of learners who do not speak either of the languages of instruction at home.

By describing how the different CLIL contexts included in the corpus used in this book are located on the continua of multilingual education, we hope to help readers to more precisely describe their own CLIL contexts. This should help CLIL practitioners in situations in which, for example, there are differences along the sociolinguistic, school or teacher dimensions, to make more principled assessments of how relevant the ideas presented in this book are to them. For example, some of the data in the book represent relatively mature CLIL situations, in that practices are quite well developed: they do not, then, represent beginning and/or experimental experiences. As will be seen in the extracts of oral and written language presented throughout the book, both the teachers and the learners in the different classrooms are able to produce at times fairly extended stretches of the L2 for a range of purposes. However, this should not be taken as an indication of homogeneity. The examples used in the book show learners' production of language from a fairly wide range of stages of development, and often the extracts show how learners struggle to make meaning with limited resources. Wherever readers are located along the continua of multilingual education, the framework presented in this book will better equip them to make principled decisions about the roles of language in their local CLIL contexts.

Applying theories of learning and language to a framework for understanding CLIL

Why do we need a book about the roles of language in CLIL? After all, as CLIL stands for content and *language* integrated learning, we could assume that language is already included in the package. However, things are more complicated than that. In spite of the increasing popularity of CLIL across Europe and around the world, there has not always been clarity about key issues such as how language is involved in doing CLIL, what aspects of language should be targeted, how learners' language develops through CLIL, and whether and how language should be assessed along with content. Indeed, much research on CLIL has largely seen language and content as separate issues. As Leung points out, there is a need to bring the two dimensions together:

> [c]urriculum content learning and language learning, which are still generally seen as two separate pedagogic issues, should be consciously taken into account in an integrated way in classroom-based bilingual research.
>
> (Leung, 2005: 240)

Leung's point is that it does not make much sense to argue for bilingual education initiatives such as CLIL without a greater understanding of the ways in which languages are actually used in classroom interaction and activities. Without this understanding, justifications for CLIL tend to be vague, a kind of 'language bath' (Dalton-Puffer, 2007: 3), in which learners, simply by participating in lessons in which they study subject matter in a foreign language, will somehow pick up the foreign language by osmosis. In this view, CLIL classrooms, unlike language classrooms, are a 'natural' environment for language learning in which students can come into contact with the language as it is used in everyday life. In this way, as Dalton-Puffer (ibid.) observes, the CLIL classroom becomes a kind of replacement for the street, especially when the foreign language is not used in the real streets surrounding the classroom.

This book sees the role of language in CLIL rather differently from the language-bath approach. In working with content, students will encounter and have to use a whole range of the language which shapes educational knowledge. This kind of language can be broadly referred to as 'the language of schooling' (Schleppegrell, 2004). It is this language that we focus on in this book. In this sense, the language that can be learned in CLIL classrooms is, in very important ways, unlike the language of 'the street' and the kind of language that is often the focus of communicative language teaching. As Byrnes puts it,

(...) educational knowledge is shaped through language that fundamentally differs from language used to transact life's tasks in, for example, social encounters or to seek or provide information – areas of language use that have dominated communicatively oriented educational practice.

(Byrnes, 2008: 48)

Thus, the focus of CLIL is not to equip learners with the language they need to transact everyday life tasks, such as ordering a meal or buying a train ticket. However, as we will see in this book, in CLIL classrooms learners can and do transact everyday tasks and talk about things which are personally meaningful to them and, therefore, they will find opportunities to develop 'everyday language'. These everyday tasks relate to the organisation of the social world of the classroom, and talk involving personal responses or opinions is generally related to the content-based learning objectives for the subject being studied. In fact, the ability to communicate one's personal experiences and attitudes in a foreign language is fundamental to achieving understanding of complex subject matter taught through that language. The exposure to and practice of the foreign language in different classroom tasks and activities is likely to be transferable to other non-academic contexts.

By giving the book the title *The Roles of Language in CLIL*, we are referring to language in two main ways: that which is involved in representing the meanings which are crucial to any academic subject, and that which is used in organising and orienting the social world of the classroom. In focusing on these two broad roles of language in CLIL, we build on important research carried out in European CLIL contexts. In terms of the social organisation of the CLIL classroom, we draw mainly on work that looks at the pragmatic aspects of CLIL lessons, for example at how students are given opportunities to use language for such functions as issuing requests (Dalton-Puffer, 2007; Dalton-Puffer and Nikula, 2006). As for the language through which educational knowledge is shaped, we build on the large body of work in systemic functional educational linguistics as well as the influential work on CLIL by Do Coyle and colleagues (Coyle et al., 2010), which has already offered frameworks for describing language use in CLIL classrooms. In our own description of the roles of language in CLIL, we acknowledge their distinction between the language *of* learning (language needed to express key aspects of content), language *for* learning (language needed to participate in tasks and activities) and language *through* learning (language which emerges when CLIL students are being stretched to think about and express meanings related to content). Throughout the book, where relevant, we refer to these distinctions, but our own approach draws on a different range of theoretical perspectives, particularly those of **systemic functional linguistics (SFL), sociocultural theory** and **second language acquisition (SLA).** In the next section, we provide a brief overview of these three approaches.

Integrating theoretical approaches

The perspective on the roles of language in CLIL presented here needs a theory of language to sustain it. This theory needs to show in a principled way how, at the same time, social activities such as education shape language use and how language itself constructs knowledge. Theories of language in which language is seen as an abstract system removed from contexts of use will not be adequate to this task. In this book we adopt the systemic functional linguistics framework originated by Michael Halliday (Halliday and Matthiessen, 2004). From its inception, researchers have used this framework to develop understanding of how language and learning are related (Halliday, 1993). Put briefly, systemic functional linguistics or SFL is a *meaning-based* theory of language, in which all choices speakers or writers make from the lexical or grammatical systems of a language are shaped by the social activities, such as education, in which they are involved.

In making these choices, speakers and writers draw on three types of meaning or **metafunctions** of language: **ideational,** interpersonal and textual (see Box 0.1 for an explanation).

Box 0.1: The three metafunctions of language

According to the systemic functional model of language, there are three basic functions of language:

- the **ideational,** through which we construe or make sense of our experience;
- the **interpersonal,** through which we enact our social relationships;
- the **textual,** which facilitates the first two by enabling us to construct sequences of discourse which flow and have cohesion and continuity (Halliday and Matthiessen, 2004: 29–30).

These are labelled 'metafunctions' as they are much more general and intrinsic to language use than the 'functions' of individual examples of language use (ibid.: 31).

It is important to understand that, in using language, we don't jump from one metafunction to another. All three are always active in any use of language. What we say or write is always about some aspect of reality, it expresses some kind of relation with other people, and it is always organised in some way to achieve its effects. The three metafunctions provide a powerful framework for understanding how language is used in CLIL lessons. Ideational meaning is of particular importance in CLIL as it maps onto how content knowledge is represented through talk and other communicative modes in the classroom. The interpersonal metafunction has particular significance in CLIL as it relates to how teachers use the L2 to manage social relationships in the classroom and how differing stances to the content that is being learned are expressed. The textual metafunction is of importance in considering how the texts through which content knowledge is constructed are put together, and how teachers maintain the flow of information and coherence in stretches of discourse and guide the students from spoken to written texts in the L2.

In taking up the challenge to explore the ways in which language can be integrated with curricular content, we not only use a linguistic framework such as SFL, but also make connections to research that has looked at the role of language within education more generally. The systemic functional approach we adopt is in fact very compatible with the **sociocultural theory** of learning developed by Vygotsky (1978, 1986). This is because both Vygotsky and SFL see language and learning as social processes. In SFL, language use is shaped by what kind of activity we are doing and who we are doing it with, and for Vygotsky, such language use with others is the essential mediating tool in our cognitive development. In other words, it is by using language to participate in relevant educational experiences with more competent others that we develop our cognitive abilities. Wells (1999) builds on Halliday's and Vygotsky's ideas to introduce the term dialogic inquiry, which highlights the importance of dialogue between teachers and learners in the construction of knowledge within the different disciplines. As Haneda and Wells (2008) show, such **dialogic inquiry** is not outside the range of learners who are working in an additional or foreign language. In Chapter 3, we bring these ideas to the context of CLIL, by drawing on work such as Alexander's (2008) on the importance of **dialogic teaching**, and Mortimer and Scott's (2003) framework for analysing talk in science classrooms.

Another concept that is central to sociocultural perspectives, that of **scaffolding**, is also an important part of our framework. Broadly, it refers to the ways in which more expert others intervene temporarily to enable learners to achieve learning goals. We apply the concept of scaffolding in two main ways: the first is to the specific spoken interventions during classroom interaction through which teachers and learners can support learning, and the second is to the ways in which CLIL teachers can design learning activity by sequencing the kinds of texts learners need to use *(genres)* and aspects of the language they need to express subject knowledge *(registers)*. Related to the concept of scaffolding, our approach to assessment in CLIL places emphasis on **assessment *for* learning**, that is, the ongoing actions by which teachers and students obtain feedback which can help them make adjustments to their learning or teaching. We extend this notion by applying to CLIL the sociocultural concept of **dynamic assessment**, which focuses on the forms of mediation through which learners can be supported in moving towards more complex content and language goals.

In addressing the fact that European CLIL mainly takes place within a foreign language (FL) learning context, our framework takes into account recent work in second language acquisition. In recent years, there has been a shift from a focus on individual cognitive processes to a much broader social perspective on second language development (Block, 2003; Firth and Wagner, 1997; Hellerman, 2008; Kasper, 2009; Pekarek Doehler, 2010). In these views, second language learning is seen not just as a process that goes on inside the individual's head as he or she is exposed to language, but as one inextricably linked with the social activities learners are participating in and the kinds of identities these activities make possible. This emphasis on second language learning as a social process is very compatible with the views of language and learning we have described above. In fact, there is a very important strand of work in SLA which adopts a sociocultural perspective on second language development (see Lantolf and Thorne, 2006). This more social view of language acquisition can provide a deeper understanding of the links between participation in CLIL classrooms as a social activity, second language use as part of subject learning and the processes of second language development.

Our perspective on second language learning in CLIL classrooms also takes in the important work that has been carried out in immersion contexts, particularly Lyster's (2007) **counterbalanced approach** to learning, language in content instruction. Lyster argues that, in immersion and content-based classrooms in which the prevailing focus is on the expression of content-related meanings, learners will benefit from a form of instruction which pushes their attention towards features of the target language that they may not otherwise notice. This can be done either through a *proactive* approach in which linguistic features are preselected for treatment, or a *reactive* approach in which teachers provide **corrective feedback** to learners' production of language forms. We argue in this book that it is possible to bring about a genuine integration of content and language by helping CLIL learners to attend to language features which are essential for the construction of knowledge in the classroom, either proactively through scaffolding of genre and register features as described above, or reactively as a form of assessment for learning.

An overall sociocultural perspective brings together the various strands in our framework: a **social-semiotic** theory of language as meaning-making activity (SFL), a Vygotskian theory of learning in social interaction, and a view of second language acquisition or development which gives due importance to its socially situated nature. Figure 0.2 graphically represents how the three perspectives overlap.

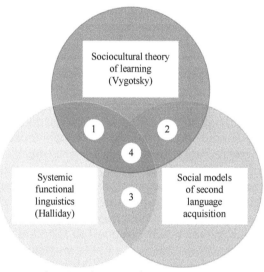

Figure 0.2   Three overlapping theoretical perspectives on CLIL

The overlapping shaded Areas 1 to 3 represent combinations of pairs of these perspectives, and in doing so can throw light on various aspects of language and education. Area 1 represents the merging of Halliday's and Vygotsky's ideas in the work of Wells on dialogic inquiry as described. As such, it is relevant to all educational contexts, whether the language of instruction is the students' L1 or an additional language. Area 2 represents the current sociocultural perspective on second language learning found, for example, in the work of Lantolf and Thorne (2006). As such, it is particularly relevant for second language teaching and learning, but not specifically for content-based instruction. Area 3 represents approaches to language learning that build close connections between the acquisition of higher level linguistic resources and the making of meaning. As such it could account for language development outside instructed contexts. Only Area 4 combines all three perspectives and thus can account for the unique characteristics of CLIL. CLIL students are engaged in the development of higher cognitive functions through schooling (Vygotsky), and in doing so they use language to make the meanings through which school subject knowledge is built (Halliday). By doing that in a foreign language, they develop ever-greater levels of communicative competence through participating in social interaction in the classroom.

A framework for understanding the roles of language in CLIL

Bringing these perspectives together can be seen as an aspect of what Coyle et al. (2010) describe as *convergence*, a process which 'involves the fusion of elements which have previously been fragmented' (p. 4). In this way, our framework for describing the roles of language in CLIL is truly integrated at two important levels: at the level of theory, it integrates the perspectives on language and learning described above; at the level of practice, it shows how, as a consequence of this theoretical integration, CLIL practitioners can attain a more principled integration of language and content in their instruction. Although the book is about the roles of language in CLIL, we hope that by the end readers will see that it is just as much about content. In fact, in the perspective on language we use, it is impossible to imagine any use of language *without* content. Even within language teaching, there is a growing realisation that isolating language from content is not beneficial for the development of either. As Paran (2010) points out in the context of language assessment, we need to abandon the attempt 'to isolate linguistic competence and test it without reference to other competencies and other areas of knowledge' (2010: 5).

In a CLIL context, we can turn Paran's statement around to also make the point that we should not isolate content-based knowledge and skills from the linguistic competences needed for learning. In this book we emphasise the importance of the ways in which language is used in expressing and building knowledge and skills across the subjects. We use the broad term *subject literacy* to refer to the spoken and written language forms and texts through which content knowledge is accessed by CLIL learners. We use the systemic functional term **genre** to refer to the different text types which learners of all subjects have to understand and produce, and the term **register** to refer to the grammatical and lexical resources used in building these genres. We will argue that CLIL teachers need to identify the genres and register features typical of the subjects they teach if they are to help CLIL learners cope with the language demands of accessing subject knowledge.

However, we also argue that in order to help learners move towards mastery of more complex knowledge and skills, and the language needed to achieve this, teachers need to enter into dialogue with students in classroom interaction. It is through this double dialogue – between the learners and the genres and registers through which knowledge is expressed, and between the participants in the classroom – that content and language development occurs. This development can be seen along three dimensions: the learners develop the language needed to express key content ideas (the **field** in functional terms); they develop the linguistic resources to express interpersonal meanings, like stance or evaluation (the **tenor** in functional terms); and they develop the ability to move from more spoken to more written forms of language (the **mode** in functional terms). Each of these dimensions, which are central to the concept of register in Halliday's theory of language, will be explained and demonstrated in the book with examples from CLIL classrooms in the corpus. Throughout the whole process, CLIL teachers will be engaged in **formative** and dynamic assessment, that is, they will be constantly on the lookout for signs of their students' ability to successfully use the different aspects of subject-related literacy, and to provide the mediation and scaffolding they need to move forward.

Our framework for understanding and describing the roles of language in CLIL is depicted in Figure 0.3. We begin in the left-hand box with *subject literacies*, that is, the genres and registers through which content knowledge is realised. According to Love (2009), it is important for all teachers of disciplinary content to have knowledge of how this content is constructed through language and literacy, what she calls 'literacy pedagogical content knowledge' (LPCK).

SUBJECT LITERACIES	ASSESSMENT	CLASSROOM INTERACTION	ASSESSMENT	LANGUAGE DEVELOPMENT
GENRE **REGISTER**	ASSESSMENT	Instructional and regulative registers (focus) Communication systems (approach) Interaction patterns and scaffolding (action)	ASSESSMENT	Expressing ideational meanings (key concepts and understandings) Expressing interpersonal meanings (social relationships, attitudes) Expressing textual meanings (moving from more spoken to written forms of language)

Figure 0.3 A three-part framework for understanding the roles of language in CLIL

In CLIL, the language and literacy needed for content learning should be even more visible, as the fact that the language of instruction is not the students' L1 requires a more explicit approach. In this book, we aim to show how CLIL teachers' understanding of the main text types (genres) and registers (grammar and vocabulary) through which their subjects are realised can enhance CLIL as a context for content learning and language development. CLIL teachers can identify these genre and register features in the materials and activities they use, and highlight them for their learners. The main context in which they do this is through interaction in the classroom. This is the second component of our framework.

In focusing on *classroom interaction*, we highlight the way spoken language is organised for effective learning. To describe the CLIL classroom as an interactive space, we adapt the framework for analysing talk in science classrooms developed by Mortimer and Scott (2003). The key idea that we take from this framework is that of dividing the analysis of classroom talk into the three levels of *focus, approach* and *action*, as shown in Table 0.1.

Table 0.1 *Three levels for analysing classroom talk (after Mortimer and Scott, 2003: 25)*

FOCUS	The content being talked about and its purposes
APPROACH	How the content is communicated about in the classroom. Who talks, and whose ideas get talked about?
ACTION	A 'closeup' view of patterns of interaction, and the specific interventions carried out (mainly) by the teacher

At the *focus* level, we draw a broad distinction between two classroom language varieties, or registers. In the **regulative register**, teachers and students manage and organise the social world of the classroom by, for example, requesting each other to do things. In the **instructional register**, teachers and students talk about key concepts and ideas related to the content being studied. Within the instructional register, we are concerned with what kinds of meanings are being focused on: whether technical or everyday. In doing so, we use the terms **vertical and horizontal discourse**, introduced by Bernstein (1999). These terms distinguish knowledge which has a tightly organised hierarchical structure *(vertical)* and which is learned through schooling, from knowledge which is more loosely organised *(horizontal)*, and which is simply picked up by participation in everyday life. We show, in Chapter 1, how these different ways of constructing content knowledge impact on language use in the CLIL classroom.

Moving to Mortimer and Scott's *approach* level, we shift our attention to the kinds of **communication systems** teachers set up in order to talk about the content. At this level, the important distinctions are between more or less interactive types of talk, and the extent to which there is dialogue (i.e. students' ideas are accepted and worked on). Dialogue is a central component of Mortimer and Scott's framework, and we believe that an understanding of the potential of dialogue is essential for understanding the role of language in classroom interaction in CLIL. As we saw earlier, dialogue is fundamental in sociocultural theories of learning, including in second / foreign language contexts (Haneda and Wells, 2008). International comparative studies of education (Alexander, 2001; 2008) have highlighted the importance of dialogic interaction for effective learning. Scott et al. (2006) show how more or less interactive and dialogic phases in lessons contribute to meeting pedagogic goals.

At the third level, that of *action*, our focus is on the specific interventions that CLIL teachers carry out during classroom interactions to support their learners in acquiring content knowledge and the aspects of language and literacy needed to express it. Here, the concept of scaffolding is important. Scaffolding in this book refers to the variety of ways in which teachers can use talk to provide temporary support for CLIL learners to express meanings in the classroom. At this more 'micro' level, we also focus on how these actions are built into sequences or patterns, such as the **IRF** (initiation / response / follow-up) exchange, in which one speaker (normally the teacher) initiates by (usually) asking a question, a second speaker (usually a student) responds, and the first speaker follows up by (often) evaluating the second speaker's response.

Returning to the structure of our framework for understanding the roles of language in CLIL, the third component is that of CLIL students' *language development*. Understanding the roles of language in CLIL in this sense means gaining an appreciation of the ways in which CLIL learners' linguistic competences can be expected to develop through classroom interaction and engagement with the genres and registers through which content knowledge is expressed. This development can be seen as having three dimensions. First, CLIL learners will need to acquire the lexical and grammatical forms which are necessary for expressing the key ideas related to their subject (in Halliday's terms, ideational meanings). Second, as the classroom is a social space, they will also need to develop linguistic resources for expressing interpersonal meanings (e.g. for coordinating actions in the classroom, getting on with classmates, meeting social needs). Interpersonal meanings are also relevant to the content being learned. CLIL learners need not only to express the knowledge and facts relating to their subjects, but to articulate a range of attitudes and judgements relating to this knowledge (e.g. how true or trustworthy it is, aesthetic responses, gauging of importance etc.). Third, CLIL learners will need to move from more spontaneous, spoken forms of language to the written language which is typical of academic school subjects, especially as students move through the secondary curriculum. CLIL students, just as any students, need to acquire these more prestigious written forms as a part of their linguistic capital (Bourdieu, 1991). In some L1 educational contexts, there has not always been sufficient explicit focus on more advanced literacy, with the result that learners may fail to achieve academically at expected levels. CLIL is a magnificent opportunity to remedy this situation, as the fact that the language of instruction is everyone's L2 calls for a particularly explicit treatment of these issues. CLIL students' language and literacy development cannot be taken for granted. As will be seen in this book, we advocate an explicit, interventionist approach to language which meets CLIL students' developmental needs, but which is always integrated with the relevant subject-matter content objectives.

As can be seen in Figure 0.3, *assessment* is crucial to our approach to understanding the roles of language in CLIL. Assessment appears in every component and throughout the teaching process. In deciding how learners are going to be assessed in any subject or topic, CLIL teachers need to take into account the language and literacy practices through which students will demonstrate knowledge, skills and understanding. In this sense, we advocate what Wiggins and McTighe (2005) call **backward design**. This is a process in which desired content goals are first identified, and then the assessment tasks through which students will demonstrate their knowledge and skills are chosen. Finally, the specific learning experiences and activities through which learners will be guided towards attaining the desired goals are planned. In CLIL, and in fact in all educational contexts, it is necessary to identify the language and literacy (genres and registers) that learners will use in attaining these goals. Another crucial aspect of assessment is that of the formative, or ongoing, assessment through which CLIL teachers and learners collect information that will allow them to check on progress towards learning goals, and to adjust learning and teaching practices if necessary. This assessment *for* learning is, in fact, the main focus of our approach to assessment in CLIL. Indeed, we take this further by suggesting that the sociocultural concept of dynamic assessment can be extremely fruitful for CLIL. As well as seeing assessment in CLIL as obtaining feedback on performance, we can see assessment as a form of mediation in which the assessor intervenes not just to check previous learning but to offer the kinds of mediation that will help the learners improve their performance. As will be seen in the final chapter of the book, with assessment we come full circle. Assessment is not a stage or separate component of the framework; it pervades our whole understanding of the roles of language in CLIL.

The structure of this book

The book is divided into three parts, each of which focuses on one of the three main components of the framework depicted in Figure 0.3. Given the importance of the classroom as the setting for CLIL as an activity, and the fundamental role of social interaction in our approach, we begin the book in the CLIL classroom. This first part explores the CLIL classroom as a space for learning, and focuses on the interactions between teachers and learners and between learners themselves. Using Mortimer and Scott's (2003) framework as a broad lens, we begin in Chapter 1 by exploring how language is used in organising the social world of the classroom and in constructing content knowledge. We also introduce some key concepts from the functional model of language which is used throughout the book. In Chapter 2 we describe the **communication systems** through which teachers and students talk about content in CLIL classrooms, emphasising the importance of dialogue. Chapter 3 takes us to the most detailed level of Mortimer and Scott's framework, in which the focus is on the interaction patterns which emerge in CLIL classrooms and specific actions carried out by teachers in scaffolding learners' contributions.

In Part II, the focus changes to the left-hand component of Figure 0.3, that of the linguistic model based on the key systemic functional concepts of genre and register. We explore the language through which educational knowledge is shaped in the texts learners need to understand and produce in the academic subjects studied through CLIL. In Chapter 4, we introduce the key concept of genre as it has been used to study literacy across academic disciplines. The chapter describes the main text types, or genres, typical of some common CLIL subjects, showing how they are structured, and giving examples of written and spoken work from our corpus. Chapter 5 analyses in detail the language which CLIL learners need to use when understanding and producing these genres. It shows how grammar and vocabulary work in CLIL can be integrated with the learning of subject-specific literacies.

Part III shifts the focus to the right-hand section of our framework, the development of CLIL students' foreign language competence. Each of the four chapters explores a different dimension of the ways in which learners' language can be expected to develop in CLIL. Chapter 6 focuses on ways in which CLIL learners can be encouraged to produce more appropriate language in CLIL classrooms, both in terms of form and meaning. The chapter describes some of the different types of corrective feedback provided by CLIL teachers to offer opportunities for the development of learners' language. Chapter 7 examines the connection between CLIL learners' academic and interpersonal language development. Drawing on the role of interaction presented in Part I and that of academic language in Part II, this chapter explores the role of interpersonal language in the CLIL classroom, and the types of activities that generate the use of interpersonal language features in the L2. In Chapter 8, we examine how CLIL students' language production moves along a continuum from more spoken to written forms of language as they approach mastery of the literacies of the disciplines. Here, the concept of scaffolding presented in Chapter 3 acquires a new dimension with the notion of **register scaffolding** in CLIL. The final chapter, Chapter 9, focuses on assessment in CLIL, with the aim of providing a coherent framework for content and language-integrated assessment. The chapter brings together key themes of the book, including the role of genre in integrating content and language objectives, and the role of interaction in formative assessment.

Finally, at the end of each chapter there are questions for critical reflection and tasks, some of which involve working with data from the CLIL corpus. Many of the tasks allow readers to apply the models presented in the book to the analysis of real data. By the end of the book, we hope that the reader will have a deeper understanding of the roles of language in CLIL, and will be able to apply and adapt the ideas in the book in a principled way in their own contexts. While – as Cenoz's continua make clear – there is considerable variation among contexts of multilingual education, we hope that our exploration of the roles of language in European foreign language CLIL classrooms will help readers in various contexts to more clearly assess the benefits and possible limitations of combining content and foreign language learning. In particular, we would hope that our approach, based on a functional model of language, and the forging of links with the work on language in the wider world of education, will contribute to a more principled integration of content and language wherever CLIL or CLIL-like initiatives are implemented.

References

Alexander, R. J. (2001) *Culture and Pedagogy: International Comparisons in Primary Education*, Malden, MA: Blackwell Publishers.

Alexander, R. J. (2008) *Towards Dialogic Teaching: Rethinking Classroom Talk* (4th ed.), York: Dialogos.

Bernstein, B. (1999) 'Vertical and horizontal discourse: An essay', *British Journal of Sociology of Education*, 20, 2, 157–73.

Baker, C. (2006). *Foundations of Bilingual Education and Bilingualism* (4th ed.), Clevedon: Multilingual Matters.

Björklund, S. (2006) 'Content and language integrated approaches: What lies ahead?', in Björklund, S., Mård-Miettinen, K., Bergström, M. and Södergård, M. (eds.), *Exploring Dual-Focussed Education. Integrating Language and Content for Individual and Societal Needs*, Vaasa, Finland: Centre for Immersion and Multilingualism, University of Vaasa, pp. 189–99.

Block, D. (2003) *The Social Turn in Second Language Acquisition*, Edinburgh: Edinburgh University Press.

Bourdieu, P. (1991) *Language and Symbolic Power*, Cambridge: Polity.

Byrnes, H. (2008) 'Assessing content and language', in Shohamy, E. and Hornberger, N. H. (eds.), *Encyclopedia of Language and Education* (2nd ed.), volume 7: *Language Testing and Assessment*, New York: Springer, pp. 37–52.

Cenoz, J. (2009) *Towards Multilingual Education: Basque Educational Research from an International Perspective*, Bristol: Multilingual Matters.

Coyle, D., Hood, P. and Marsh, D. (2010) *CLIL: Content and Language Integrated Learning*. Cambridge: Cambridge University Press.

Dalton-Puffer, C. (2007) *Discourse in Content and Language Integrated Learning (CLIL) Classrooms*, Amsterdam and Philadelphia: John Benjamins.

Dalton-Puffer, C. and Nikula, T. (2006) 'Pragmatics of content-based instruction: Teacher and student directives in Finnish and Austrian classrooms', *Applied Linguistics*, 27, 2, 241–67.

European Commission. (1995) *Teaching and Learning: Towards the Learning Society*. White paper on education and training. COM (95) 590. Brussels.

Eurydice. (2006) *Content and Language Integrated Learning (CLIL) at School in Europe*, Brussels: European Commission.

Firth, A., and Wagner, J. (1997) 'On discourse, communication, and (some) fundamental concepts in SLA research', *The Modern Language Journal*, 81, 3, 285–300.

Graddol, D. (2006) *English Next. Why Global English May Mean the End of 'English as a Foreign Language'*, London: The British Council.

Halliday, M. A. K. (1993) 'Towards a language-based theory of learning', *Linguistics and Education*, 5, 2, 93–116.

Halliday, M. A. K. and Matthiessen, C. M. I. M. (2004) *An Introduction to Functional Grammar* (3rd ed.), London: Arnold.

Haneda, M. and Wells, G. (2008) 'Learning an additional language through dialogic inquiry', *Language and Education*, 22, 2, 114–36.

Hellerman, J. (2008) *Social Actions for Classroom Language Learning*, Clevedon, UK: Multilingual Matters.

Kasper, G. (2009) 'Locating cognition in second language interaction and learning: Inside the skull or in public view?', *IRAL – International Review of Applied Linguistics in Language Teaching*, 47, 1, 11–36.

Lantolf, J. P. and Thorne, S. L. (2006) *Sociocultural Theory and the Genesis of Second Language Development*, Oxford: Oxford University Press.

Lasagabaster, D. and Sierra, J. M. (2010) 'Immersion and CLIL in English: More differences than similarities', *ELT Journal*, **64**, 4, 367–75.

Leung, C. (2005) 'Language and content in bilingual education', *Linguistics and Education*, **16**, 2, 238–52.

Love, K. (2009) 'Literacy pedagogical content knowledge in the secondary curriculum', *Pedagogies: An International Journal*, **5**, 4, 338–55.

Lyster, R. (2007). *Learning and Teaching Languages through Content: A Counterbalanced Approach*, Amsterdam and Philadelphia, PA: John Benjamins.

Mortimer, E. F. and Scott, P. (2003) *Meaning Making in Secondary Science Classrooms*, Maidenhead and Philadelphia, PA: Open University Press.

Paran, A. (2010) 'More than language: The additional faces of testing and assessment in language learning and teaching', in Paran, A. and Sercu, L. (eds.), *Testing the Untestable in Language Education. New Perspectives on Language and Education*, Bristol: Multilingual Matters, pp. 1–13.

Pekarek Doehler, S. (2010) 'Conceptual changes and methodological challenges: On language, learning and documenting learning in conversation analytic SLA research', in Seedhouse, P., Walsh, S. and Jenks, C. (eds.), *Conceptualising Learning in Applied Linguistics*, Basingstoke: Palgrave MacMillan, pp. 105–26.

Schleppegrell, M. (2004). *The Language of Schooling: A Functional Linguistics Perspective*, Mahwah, NJ; London: Lawrence Erlbaum.

Scott, P. H., Mortimer, E. F. and Aguiar, O. G. (2006) 'The tension between authoritative and dialogic discourse: A fundamental characteristic of meaning making interactions in high school science lessons', *Science Education*, **90**, 4, 605–31.

Swain, M. and Johnson, R.K. (1997) 'Immersion education: A category within bilingual education', in Johnson, R. K. and Swain, M. (eds.), *Immersion Education: International Perspectives*, Cambridge: Cambridge University Press, pp. 1–16.

Vygotsky, L. S. (1978) *Mind in Society: The Development of Higher Psychological Processes*, Cambridge, MA: Harvard University Press.

Vygotsky, L. S. (1986) *Thought and Language* (Kozulin, A. ed., trans.), Cambridge, MA: MIT Press.

Wells, G. (1999) *Dialogic Inquiry: Towards a Socio-cultural Practice and Theory of Education*, Cambridge: Cambridge University Press.

Wiggins, G. P. and McTighe, J. (2005) *Understanding by Design* (2nd ed.), Alexandria, VA: Association for Supervision and Curriculum Development.

Part I

The role of language in CLIL classroom interaction

1 Classroom registers and their impact on learning opportunity

1.1 Introduction

The talk and interaction that take place in CLIL lessons would seem to be an obvious place to look if we want to understand how participating in CLIL can have an impact on students' opportunities to learn both subject matter and language. Dalton-Puffer, in her detailed study of the discourse of CLIL lessons, comes to the conclusion that, 'The event in which teachers and learners are participating (in the CLIL lesson) is never brought into focus as an important ingredient and condition for the learning process' (Dalton-Puffer, 2007: 276). As she goes on to argue, the result of this is that CLIL teachers may lack the terminology or **metalanguage** to discuss the different kinds of talk that they use in the classroom and its purposes, and how this relates to what their students can achieve in terms of learning and communication. This chapter, together with Chapters 2 and 3, aims to provide CLIL teachers with a clearer understanding of the roles and functions of talk (both between teachers and learners and among learners) in their classrooms. The chapters introduce a framework and metalanguage which will help CLIL teachers build and share their understandings.

In this chapter we begin to use the framework that we adapted from Mortimer and Scott (2003) and explained in the Introduction. We explore the level of **focus** by looking both at the nature of the content that is being talked about and at the notion of teaching purpose. Mortimer and Scott identify six broad purposes in science teaching:

1. Opening up the problem;
2. Exploring and probing students' views;
3. Introducing and developing the scientific story;
4. Guiding students to work with scientific ideas and supporting internalization;
5. Guiding students to apply, and expand on the use of, the scientific view and handing over responsibility for its use;
6. Maintaining the development of the scientific story.

(Mortimer and Scott, 2003: 25–6)

It is clear that these pedagogical goals can readily be applied to other subjects, not just science. This is because, as Mortimer and Scott point out, they are 'based on the basic tenets of the Vygotskian perspective on teaching and learning' (2003: 26), that is, learning is seen as a process in which **intermental** activity mediated by social interaction becomes **intramental** activity as the learner acquires new concepts and skills. It is crucial that the notion of purpose is considered at the level of focus. This allows teachers to plan for teaching more effectively by not just thinking about which aspects of a topic they are going to teach, but also about their purposes for teaching this topic. It makes a big difference to the role of spoken language in the CLIL classroom if the teacher is, for example, exploring and probing the students' views, or introducing and developing the scientific (or historical, geographical etc.) story.

In CLIL, we could also add to the level of focus any language points (either *of* or *for* learning) that can be prespecified. Thus, at the level of focus in CLIL, a teacher could ask herself these questions at the planning stage:

- What specific content knowledge and skills am I going to focus on? Is the knowledge clearly related to everyday life or is it more 'scientific' or 'technical'?
- What is my purpose in focusing on this knowledge and these skills? For example, is my purpose to get the students' ideas about a topic, or to apply ideas already learned to a new situation?
- What language will the students need in order to access the knowledge and skills? This could be language *of* or *for* learning.

Apart from these questions, the teacher may also need to think about how she will set up activities, for example by giving spoken instructions. In CLIL classes, the focus of interaction may be on this *organisational* aspect of learning, sometimes for quite extended periods of time. The level of focus, then, shows the close relationships between the content being taught, the purposes in teaching it, and the language used to express its meanings. As we show in the rest of this chapter, the systemic functional concept of register is a useful tool for capturing the role of language in enacting these relationships in the CLIL classroom.

1.2 The concept of register

The concept of register is used to look at how language varies according to the social situation, as explained in Box 1.1. The boxed examples show how the concept of register and the three variables of *field, tenor* and *mode* can provide an extremely useful framework for understanding how language is used in CLIL classrooms. In any CLIL classroom, field will be of crucial importance, as it will refer to the knowledge and skills that participants have as well as the types of classroom activity they are involved in. The tenor variable helps to highlight the importance of the ways CLIL teachers and learners use language to establish closeness or distance, solidarity or authority. Mode alerts us to the need to see language in the CLIL classroom as just one resource among others for expressing meaning.

Box 1.1: Register

Register is the concept which is used in systemic functional linguistics to describe how the different dimensions of a social situation impact on language use. According to Halliday and Hasan (1989), there are three dimensions of social situations: *field*, *tenor* and *mode*. They are described as follows:

Field refers to the kind of activity that the participants are engaged in, in which language figures as some essential component.

Tenor refers to who is taking part, i.e., to the nature of the participants, their statuses and roles.

Mode refers to what part language is playing, what it is that the participants are expecting language to do for them in the situation.
(Halliday and Hasan, 1989: 12)

In any social situation, these three dimensions, or 'variables', combine in different ways, depending on the nature and purpose of the activity, the relationships established between participants, and the role that language is playing. The following two examples from CLIL lessons illustrate the three register variables:

Example 1
In a biology lesson, the teacher is at the blackboard speaking and writing words and drawing a diagram on the board about the relationships between DNA sequences and mutation.

Field: Biology (genetics and mutation)
Tenor: A person in authority, the teacher, informing the learners about science
Mode: Spoken language used by the teacher to explain the blackboard diagram, with what the teacher says referring to the diagram. Language constitutes most of what is going on.

(cont.)

27

Example 2

In a design and technology lesson the teacher is helping a group of students saw a piece of wood to make the legs of a wooden toy.

Field: Design and technology (materials + making a wooden toy)
Tenor: Teacher–student, but more equal than Example 1 as the teacher works with the students at their table, kneeling down and sawing as one girl holds the piece of wood steady
Mode: Language is only a small part of the overall activity, which is sawing the wood; spoken language often refers (or 'points') to things and places that everyone can see (move *that* over *there*).

In terms of describing actual language use in CLIL classrooms, each of the register variables relates to one of the metafunctions of language described in the Introduction (Figure 0.3). Table 1.1 shows this relationship.

Table 1.1 *The three register variables and the metafunctions of language*

REGISTER VARIABLE		METAFUNCTION	
Field	activity taking place	ideational	making sense of experience
Tenor	relationships between participants	interpersonal	enacting social relationships
Mode	the role language is playing	textual	organising spoken and written language

We can see, then, that in any CLIL classroom situation, language will be used to make sense of experience (*ideational*), whether it is of students' or teachers' 'everyday' experience or more technical matters. It will also be used to enact the relationships between the participants, for example whether the atmosphere is informal and friendly, or perhaps more strict or distant (*interpersonal*). Whatever is being said will be linked to other utterances, often to build up a coherent 'story' of whatever topic is being taught (*textual*). Language will also be used and understood in connection with other forms of communication, such as diagrams or demonstrations. The exact ways in which this happens will depend on the configuration of the situation, in terms of field, tenor and mode, and this will also reflect the teacher's purposes in dealing with any topic.

1.3 The regulative and instructional registers

The concept of register can be used to distinguish two main ways in which language reflects the social situation in the classroom. Based on earlier work by the British sociologist Basil Bernstein (e.g. 1990), Christie (2002) describes two main classroom registers – the *regulative* register, which refers to the role of language in managing the social world of the classroom, and the *instructional* register, which refers to the role of language in building the knowledge and skills relevant to the subject being studied. Within the instructional register, we focus on the variable of field, drawing on Bernstein's (1999) description of two broad orientations to knowledge: everyday or **horizontal knowledge**, and scientific or **vertical knowledge**. We use examples from the CLIL corpus to show how these registers emerge in classroom talk, and how teachers and learners use the L2 to manage shifts between the different kinds of knowledge.

The two registers operate, of course, in any classroom, regardless of whether the language of instruction is a first or an additional language, or any combination of languages. However, in CLIL, they help us gain a clearer understanding of the opportunities and challenges for language use in the classroom. For example, Dalton-Puffer (2007) shows how each register offers different possibilities for learners to use such pragmatic aspects of language as making requests. Thus, we see how language is used for two main purposes, or functions, in the CLIL classroom: organising the social world and building content knowledge. In the rest of this chapter, we look at the roles of language in the CLIL lesson through the lens of these two registers.

The regulative register in CLIL lessons

When teachers give instructions for activities, explain classroom procedures or maintain order, they are creating and maintaining the conditions in which subject-related knowledge and skills can be learned. In other words, they are *regulating* the social (and moral) world of the classroom, and so working in the regulative register. According to Christie (Christie, 2002), the regulative register *projects* the other main register, the instructional, in which teachers and students work together on content-relevant knowledge and skills. In other words, the instructional register (i.e. productive work on knowledge and skills) can only take place through the regulative register. The proper conditions for productive classroom activity need to be set up and maintained, mainly by the teacher, but of course the students play an important role in this, as we shall see in the extracts from the corpus below. These extracts show the regulative register being used in L2 by both teachers and learners to manage classroom activity. The examples show the complexity and some of the challenges and opportunities when the regulative register is in operation in CLIL classrooms. The main focus in the analyses is on **directives**, that is, the kind of interpersonal language which people use to get other people to do things, such as requests for action and information.

Extract 1.1 shows how the teacher uses the regulative register to organise a group activity. It is taken from a lower secondary (grade 7, ages 12–13) CLIL history lesson. In this lesson, the class has been doing a group activity on megalithic monuments. Each group has become an expert or 'specialist' in one monument by doing some research on it. In the extract, the teacher is giving instructions to change groups, so that in each new group there will be one expert on each monument. Her method for forming groups is to give each student a bracelet with a different colour (green, blue, red, brown and purple). To form new groups, students with bracelets of the same colour have to sit together.

Extract 1.1	
1	T: OK listen to me. What are we going to do now?
2	Something different.
3	Now we are going to change the teams.
4	We are going to change and everyone who's got the same
5	colours are going to sit together, right?
6	Right? So for example you have to stand up, right?
7	And change your places.
8	So please try to do it as quietly as possible and as quickly as
9	possible.
10	First listen to me, first listen to me.
11	Here these five people with the green bracelets here.
12	Green bracelets blue bracelets red bracelets brown and purple
13	((children start moving)).

The teacher's overall purpose is to get the students to change groups, but in order to get that action done, she has to carry out a range of more specific moves, to which the students need to respond. These moves include getting the students' attention (line 1), announcing a change in activity (lines 1 and 2), telling students what is going to happen (lines 3–5), checking that they understand (use of *right* at line 6), giving an example of what they have to do (lines 6 and 7), telling them how they have to do something (lines 8 and 9), repeating (line 10) and showing and telling them where they have to go (line 11).

In terms of the register variable of tenor, the teacher is in a role of authority, controlling the physical movements of the students. The interpersonal language used to do this is mostly in the form of imperatives, but she also uses questions and declaratives. We can also see how she uses the textual metafunction in two ways to organise the instructions. She uses *now* (line 3) and *first* (line 10) to show how the instructions are organised in time, and *so* (line 8) to show how the next instruction is a consequence of what has been explained before. The extract shows the kinds of linguistic competences required by CLIL teachers as they use the L2 to manage the classroom. As for the learners, CLIL students with some experience of bilingual education seem to handle this regulative aspect of classroom language quite easily and comfortably. Particularly where CLIL is introduced at primary level, students get plenty of experience of having the social world of the classroom managed in the L2. Well before they reach secondary level, they are comfortable with this use of the L2, and are easily able to respond to requests for action and do the activities planned by the teacher.

It is not only the teacher who can use this kind of interpersonal language in the regulative register. It is also possible, under certain conditions, for students to have opportunities to produce, as well as respond to requests, and so expand the functions in their linguistic repertoire. However, for this to happen, at least two contextual factors need to be considered. First, the object of a request – whether it is for information or action – plays a crucial role. In classrooms it is not frequent that students ask teachers to carry out actions, but it is quite normal to ask for information about procedures in the regulative register (Dalton-Puffer and Nikula, 2006: 259–60). Second, the format of the activity – whether whole-class or group work – will have an impact. As Dalton-Puffer and Nikula point out, group work allows opportunities for students to issue directives for action to each other (2006: 260). Take the following example of group work which took place a bit later in the same history lesson described above:

Extract 1.2
1   S1: Okay this is er Stonehenge that is in the United Kingdom er 2   S2: Loud voice please. 3   S1: It is a crom- a megalithic monument that is a Greek word 4   that in English ...

Here, S2 issues a request for action (line 2), which in a more pragmatically developed form might be something like, *Can you speak up, please?* Although the student may be at an early stage in his L2 pragmatic development, he is taking on a 'teacher's' role in ensuring that everyone can be heard above the inevitable noise of an activity taking place in a classroom where a number of groups were speaking at the same time. We can see here that students in CLIL classrooms may operate with a somewhat limited lexical and grammatical repertoire, but that does not prevent them from carrying out important pragmatic functions, if they are given the opportunity to do so. Without such opportunities, it will be difficult for them to develop the use of these functions. Through time, they will be able to expand their repertoires of linguistic realisations of functions such as requests, especially if this kind of language is modelled by the teacher.

In this next example from a technology lesson (grade 7, ages 12–13) we can find further evidence of the regulative register in group work. The students are in the technology workshop beginning a project in which they have to make a wooden toy with moving parts:

Extract 1.3
1   S1: Boys, look I think the ins – say we do three ... 2   but can we do one? 3   S2: Okay *claro* (Sp. of course). 4   S1: Because three is very ... a lot. 5   S2: We make one but not three or four. 6   S1: Okay A. Do you like my opinion? My idea? 7   C ((the teacher)) gave us a box ... 8   Please A speak in English! 9   S2: But D, look! We only do one ... only one!

In this extract, we can see various examples of requests (*look!; Please A speak in English!*). Students take on various teacher's roles such as getting attention (*Boys*) and policing the use of the L2 (line 8). They are also sorting out the procedural aspects of what they have to do, working from written instructions and materials given to them by the teacher (line 7). Together, they reach a decision about the number of parts of the wooden toy they will make – only one instead of three or four. This decision is in their hands and they manage the decision-making process by offering ideas and checking that others in the group find them acceptable (line 6).

The implications for CLIL teachers are clear here. In terms of learning the different subjects, there are of course very good reasons for allowing students to take more control of classroom activities. Learner autonomy is also developed, particularly at the level of managing learning. From the point of view of language development, the potential of CLIL lessons as a context for the development of a wider range of interpersonal language functions will only be realised if students have the opportunity to manage their own activities (see Chapter 7 for further discussion of the interpersonal function in CLIL). When CLIL students have more control over the management of activities, they will need to interpret instructions, refer each other to materials, make decisions not only about the content of learning, but about procedures, and make efforts to keep each other on task and keep communication channels open. Of course, the effect on their range and accuracy of L2 use will not be immediate, but this can be pushed along by the teacher 'feeding in' appropriate ways of carrying out these functions, either before or during activities.

There is a general expectation that in CLIL lessons, these regulative aspects of the classroom should be carried out in the L2. However, this is not the case in all CLIL contexts. Dalton-Puffer (2007) found in her study of Austrian CLIL classrooms that, in pair and group work, directives concerning actions or material things were expressed 'almost without exception' in the L1. In contrast, in a comparative study between Austrian and Finnish CLIL classrooms, the Finnish students were much more likely to use the L2 in pair and group work (Dalton-Puffer, 2007: 203; Dalton-Puffer and Nikula, 2006). In the extracts discussed here, there is evidence of the students' willingness to conduct small-group work in the L2 and thus gain experience in using directives in the regulative register.

If the L2 is increasingly used by the teacher in the regulative register, the likely result is that students will have opportunities to develop a range of pragmatic features of the L2 through their participation in the activity of the CLIL classroom. As argued above, this potential becomes even greater if students are given opportunities to manage their own actions in small-group work in the L2. However, this observation should not imply any negative attitude towards the use of the students' L1. Increasing use of L2 can take place in an environment where the teacher is also positive about the use of the L1, and encourages its use for clearly defined purposes. The important thing is for CLIL teachers to have clear goals: how much the L2 can and should be used, and for what purposes. In the light of the evidence from the corpus extracts and the research findings discussed here, we believe that it is a very worthwhile goal that the management of the social world of the classroom, both in whole-class situations and in small-group work, be carried on in the CLIL target language. As Dalton-Puffer puts it, 'In the interest of foreign language development it can therefore be said *without reservation* that the regulative register should be conducted in the target language' (Dalton-Puffer, 2007: 203; italics added).

As we have seen in the classroom extracts above, there is evidence that CLIL students can use the target language in the regulative register even when the range of linguistic resources at their disposal is restricted. Of course, especially at lower levels, many CLIL learners will use their L1 to carry out these actions. However, with gentle persistence, and explicit attention to useful language for managing their activities, it is possible to gradually shift the classroom culture towards more use of the L2 in the regulative register. A sign that this is being achieved is when the regulative register spills out of the CLIL lesson and into the corridor or office, and students approach teachers with procedural questions about homework or exams in the L2.

The instructional register in CLIL lessons

In many ways it could be claimed that the instructional register is at the heart of CLIL pedagogy. After all, one of the main arguments put forward in favour of CLIL is that cognitive engagement with meaningful content is a driver of both linguistic and conceptual development. As Coyle et al. point out, effective CLIL instruction can 'have an impact on conceptualisation (literally, how we think), enriching the understanding of concepts, and broadening conceptual mapping resources' (2010: 11). In terms of language development, van Lier (2005) argues that it is only in the context of dealing with meaningful content, tasks and projects that the 'authentic communicative conditions' to become an effective language user exist (p. 20). In engaging with meaningful subject matter content, students get the opportunity to use language *of* learning by coming into contact with subject-specific terminology. They use language *for* learning by participating in a range of activities which are typical of the subject. And they get to learn language *through* learning by activating thinking processes necessary to understand and apply the knowledge of the subject (Coyle et al., 2010).

In analysing classroom talk in the instructional register, the register variable of field is especially important. As we saw earlier, this register variable relates broadly to the area of activity or experience one is involved in. In terms of the metafunctions of language, in engaging in activities in which they talk about subject knowledge, teachers and students will largely be using ideational language, that is, using language to make sense of experience of the world. It is ideational meaning that is used to express knowledge, or, as Martin puts it, 'knowledge is by and large realised through, construed by, and over time reconstrued through ideational meaning' (2007: 34). The ideational metafunction can be further broken down into two components: the experiential and the logical. The experiential component includes who or what is being talked about, what they are doing (to whom) and in which circumstances. The logical component makes explicit links between these participants, processes and circumstances in terms of such relationships as time, consequence, comparison and addition (Schleppegrell, 2004: 54).

In a CLIL classroom, in the instructional register, teachers and students will be using the L2 to identify participants (both people and abstract concepts), processes, circumstances, and causal and other logical links between them. It is in this sense that the kind of language used in CLIL classrooms can be very different from that used in the language classroom. As was pointed out in the Introduction, it is also quite different from the kind of language used to carry out everyday tasks or express everyday knowledge. For example, in Extract 1.4 from a CLIL history lesson (grade 8, ages 13–14), the teacher and students are talking about something that is not very familiar to the students, especially since the school is in an urban area:

Extract 1.4
1   T: Why can't you use the same land without leaving it to rest?
2   S: Because you plant different things.
3   T: Good. By planting different things which need different
4   substances from the earth. Do you know in Spanish?
5   Does anybody know the Spanish word for when the land rests?
6   S: erm
7   T: *La tierra esta en ...* (Sp. The land is in ...)
8   S: *ba-?*
9   T: *en?*
10   S: *Barbecho* (Sp. Fallow).
11   T: *Barbecho* good good.
12   *Esta es la palabra española* (Sp. This is the Spanish word)
13   that many of you don't know but you have to learn it too.
14   Spanish words OK?

It is clear that the teacher does not expect the concept of land lying fallow to be part of her urban students' everyday knowledge (lines 12–13), although one student is able to come up with the term in Spanish (line 10). This class was studying agriculture in feudal Europe, and was thus dealing with a field of knowledge far removed both in time and space from the world of experience of most of the students. It is interesting that, in this CLIL classroom, the teacher highlights the importance of also learning the L1 terms for the concepts introduced.

Using the functional linguistic concepts of field and ideational metafunction provides us with tools for describing more precisely the nature of the language that shapes educational knowledge in CLIL classrooms. Field is closely related to the ways that knowledge can be constructed in terms of activity types, pedagogical purposes and, importantly, how it is organised. As we will see in more detail in Chapter 4, knowledge in all subjects, irrespective of their level of technicality, is organised according to taxonomies of classification and composition. Classifications refer to different types and subtypes of a phenomenon, and they are typically organised in a hierarchical fashion (*hyponymy*) with more general classes on top and subclasses below. Composition refers to part–whole relations (*meronymy*) in which a phenomenon is seen as consisting of a structure made up of various components, often consisting of labelled diagrams. In the two extracts below, we see how the different ways of classifying knowledge interrelate with the use of the ideational metafunction in secondary CLIL history lessons.

In Extract 1.5, from a student presentation in a CLIL history lesson on prehistory (grade 7, ages 12–13), we can see how a student classifies different prehistoric humans and related species of hominids:

Extract 1.5
1 S: Then there was the Homo sapiens
2   who appeared a hundred thousand ye- years ago
3   and is divided into two sub-types:
4   the Homo sapiens neanderthalensis
5   and the Homo sapiens sapiens.
6   The Homo sapiens neanderthalensis started living
7   in the northern part of Asia and Europe,
8   in Oceania and in the western coast of America.
9   The Homo sapiens sapiens appeared thirty-five thousand
10   years ago and is the species we belong to.
11   He lives in all the world because he arrived into America.

This extract shows how a student can use linguistic resources to classify knowledge. She has classified *Homo sapiens* according to a hyponymic relationship, with *Homo sapiens* as the superordinate term and *Homo sapiens neanderthalensis* and *Homo sapiens sapiens* as the two co-hyponyms. She uses the ideational metafunction to do this by producing appropriate language to express this kind of relationship (*is divided into two sub-types* – line 3). She then goes on to build on this classification by providing descriptions of the two species she has identified. Such descriptions would make less sense if they did not occur in the context of this prior classification.

In Extract 1.6, from a history lesson on Romanesque churches (grade 9, ages 14–15), the students have been looking at a picture of a church on a website and have been filling in the different parts on a ground plan:

Extract 1.6
1   T: Tell me the name of the different parts of the ground plan.
2   　　All the different parts of the ground plan.
3   　　OK, tell me, what are the names of these pictures here?
4   　　Three ondulations. These chapels here.
5   　　What are the names of that?
6   S: Apses.
7   T: Apses, that's right. And this one? So we enter here.
8   　　So what's the name of this central part?
9   S: Nave.
10 T: You are doing very well. M, do you remember the name
11 　　of these two corridors at the sides? What was the name
12 　　of this?
13 S: Aisles ((non-standard pronunciation))
14 T: Aisle ((standard pronunciation)). That's right, the aisles
15 　　here. Good.

In this example the taxonomic relationship is one of meronymy, as the students identify the different parts on a labelled ground plan of a Romanesque church. Together with the teacher, they build up a description of the features of a Romanesque church, with the teacher explicitly signalling the compositional relationship by her use of lexis referring to parts and labelling (*Tell me the name of the different parts of the ground plan; What are the names of these pictures here?; What's the name of this central part?*). Thus, the classroom talk in these two examples consists not only of the ideational content in terms of the specialised terminologies used (*Homo sapiens neanderthalensis, Homo sapiens sapiens, apse, nave, aisle*) but also consists of the lexis and grammar which express the taxonomic relationships through which knowledge in different subjects is organised. In the instructional register, CLIL teachers and learners need not only to use the language *of* learning, but will need to use language *for* and *through* learning, as they do the various tasks required of them in different subjects and use language as a tool for expressing the different structures through which knowledge in the disciplines is built. In Chapter 4, we will return to the topic of knowledge structures when we analyse the generic structure of texts in different academic subjects.

Vertical and horizontal discourses

When teachers and students are talking about content in the instructional register, they can do so in two ways. The content can be looked at from a more *commonsense* point of view in which students' and teachers' knowledge and experience of everyday life are used. Or it can be seen from a more *uncommonsense* perspective, in which concepts from the subject being studied are used to describe or explain phenomena, thus bringing in knowledge that is not in the pupil's experience. This is similar to Vygotsky's well-known (1994) distinction between everyday and scientific knowledge in his work on concept development in adolescence. For example, children may explain a natural phenomenon in terms of their everyday needs:

Extract 1.7
1 I: So the question is very simple.
2   Could you explain me why we have day
3   and why we have night?
4 A: Okay, because we need day to play
5   and we need night to sleep.
6   And then if we don't have day we don't have light
7   and we can bump to something or something.
(adapted from Roth, 2008: 31)

The child's explanation of why we have day and night does not use any *scientific* ideas, but instead uses the needs of everyday life such as playing, sleeping and avoiding danger to explain why there is day and night. Of course, these ideas are not inferior or less useful than a scientific explanation of why there is day and night. They are extremely useful ideas that we employ to get on with the normal business of everyday life. However, one of the purposes of schooling is to expand children's knowledge, introducing them to the explanations of phenomena typical of the different subjects in the curriculum. They need to get to know the scientific or historical story as well as the everyday one.

In CLIL classrooms, as in all classrooms, there is a double 'bridging' process going on. One is between the ideas themselves, from the everyday to the more scientific, and the other is between the two types of language used to talk about these ideas. In terms of language, Gibbons (2006) describes this process as one in which

> [t]he talk of teachers and students draws together – or bridges – the 'everyday' language of students learning through English as a second language, and the language associated with the academic registers of school which they must learn to control.

(Gibbons, 2006: 1)

This distinction between everyday and scientific knowledge and the associated language is a very useful one for helping us think about what is being focused on in CLIL lessons. Because many different subjects are taught in CLIL, we need a framework for describing the level of focus that is not specific to any one subject. It is useful to classify CLIL subjects, topics within subjects and even classroom talk in terms of the knowledge focus, whether everyday or more scientific. This would give us a more principled way of describing the role of language in CLIL in the instructional register. A useful way of doing this is to use the distinction between horizontal and vertical discourses introduced by Bernstein. According to Bernstein (1999), vertical discourses relate to the kind of uncommonsense knowledge which is learned through formal education. In vertical discourses, such as the physical sciences, knowledge is organised in tightly hierarchical taxonomies, with concepts and constructs building on one another in superordinate structures to construct one overarching theory. Within vertical discourse there is some variation in the hierarchical nature or verticality of knowledge structures. Some subjects, such as physics, have a much more hierarchical structure, while others, such as the social sciences, are more loosely structured, and allow a wide number of competing theories, or 'languages' as Bernstein terms them.

Horizontal discourses, on the other hand, are more related to the kind of commonsense knowledge that is acquired through participation in local practices, such as the family or friendship groups. Bernstein gives as examples of horizontal discourse such tasks as learning to tie shoelaces or doing errands. This kind of knowledge is only loosely organised into taxonomies or classificatory systems. For example, in everyday life, the ways in which we classify certain foods such as tomatoes as fruit or vegetables is purely a practical matter, and, as anyone who learns other languages discovers, does not necessarily reflect any biological classification.

Turning to CLIL, we can see that the knowledge structures associated with different subjects will be closely related to the kinds of language that students will be exposed to and have to use in the instructional register. And, of course, even within subjects, and individual topics and lessons, there will be shifts from horizontal to vertical knowledge structures and back again as teachers build on students' everyday knowledge and experience in order to introduce curricular content. Taking a more temporal point of view, as students move up through the grades of secondary schooling, the types of knowledge they come into contact with become more vertical, even in subjects such as history, which are seen as having less hierarchically organised knowledge structures. As we will explore in Chapters 4 and 5 of this book, the 'language of schooling' (Schleppegrell, 2004) becomes more abstract and distanced from everyday experience as students move more deeply into 'scientific' or 'historical' forms of reasoning. For example, in late primary and early secondary history lessons, much of the language will consist of chronological narratives relating to concrete historical personalities and events, while in the later secondary years, students will be expected to deal with texts in which the participants are abstract concepts, and which are organised in terms of causes and consequences (Coffin, 2006).

However, it may be too simple to see some subjects as more vertical or horizontal than others. From the point of view of understanding communication in CLIL classrooms, we can consider how shifts between horizontal and vertical knowledge structures occur within one subject, or within one topic or piece of curricular content. In the following extract from a CLIL biology lesson (grade 10, ages 15–16), the teacher and students are using horizontal knowledge as they talk about a famous sporting personality and their own personal experience:

Extract 1.8
1   S: If you have if your parents have a good ((searches for words))
2   T: Strong.
3   S: If they have a good physical –
4   T: Sorry? What do you mean? Physical conditions?
(cont.)

5	S:	If they have good physical conditions
6		you are going to have physical conditions
7	T:	Do you think so? I mean for instance if your father is
8		who's this swimmer ... very famous
9	S:	Phelps. Michael Phelps.
10	T:	Michael Phelps. So do you think that the children
11		that Phelps might have
12		they're gonna be from the very beginning that strong?
13	S:	No.
14	S:	( ) *cuadrado* (Sp. square, beefy build)
15	T:	Why is he so strong, *cuadrado*? Why is he so strong?
16		Because of the genes? Is it because he exercises a lot?
17	S:	I have two friends that they are brothers
18		and they are the same strong.
19	T:	Well I have two daughters and one of my daughters is very
20		strong and the other one is very thin.
21		And they have been brought up in the same way. Absolutely.

This exchange takes place in the context of a lesson on genetic variation, in which students and teacher are deciding whether certain characteristics or traits are inherited or have more to do with environmental factors. In this extract, we can see that both students and teacher recruit horizontal knowledge gained from their own experience of everyday life (watching the Olympic Games, relationships with family and friends) to provide warrants for their assertions.

Typical of these horizontal exchanges is the sense that one person's knowledge is as good as another's, and no 'right' answer is imposed. A student may know more about Michael Phelps than the teacher. And, as in ordinary conversation, personal experience can be used to support or refute another's assertion. In Chapter 7 we explore how having the opportunity to talk about personal experience impacts on students' language production. Here, from the point of view of knowledge construction, we see that the teacher's example about her daughters does not represent 'official' biology knowledge but is another example to put alongside the experiences of the students. Of course, the teacher has more power to impose her points, and may use the ideas as 'thinking tools' to push her students along towards *official* or vertical knowledge, in this case, perhaps towards the idea that physical strength and fitness may be the outcome of complex interrelationships between inherited and environmental factors.

As a striking contrast with this example of horizontal discourse, the following extract from earlier in the same lesson clearly shows vertical knowledge structures in action:

Extract 1.9
1   T: What does to be dominant mean? For an allele?
2   S: One gene is more important than the other.
3   T: It's more important in what sense?
4   S: It dominates the other allele.
5   T: Exactly. It dominates the other allele,
6   so that when we see the characteristic
7   that particular gene expresses to the outside,
8   what we really see, whether you have blue or dark eyes for
9   instance, okay, it's because of what combination of alleles
9   that individual has for that particular genotype, right?
10   So, if he's got two copies of the dominant allele, what
11   happens?
12   What is the phenotype like? What do we see?
13   S: Dark eyes.
14   T: Did you say eyes?
15   S: Yes eyes.
16   T: If we see the double recessive allele, what phenotype do
17   we see? What type of eyes does that individual have?
18   S: Blue eyes.
19   T: Absolutely. Blue eyes.

In this sequence, the teacher and her class are going over material on genetics that they have previously covered. The teacher skilfully draws out the contrast between what can be observed in everyday life (individuals can have blue or dark eyes) and the scientific explanation for these phenomena. In the scientific version, knowledge is tightly structured and terms have very specific meanings (*dominant, allele, genotype, double recessive allele, phenotype*) which have to fit into current theories of genetics as explained in textbooks. It is clear, then, that within the same subject, and within the same lesson, or even interactional sequence, there can be shifts between more horizontal and vertical knowledge structures. However, it is usually also clear that a classroom episode will have an overall vertical or horizontal orientation, as can be seen in the two extracts above.

It would be misleading to assume that vertical knowledge structures only exist in the physical sciences. In social science subjects like history and geography, as students move up through the curriculum, they come into contact with more vertical forms of knowledge. In Extract 1.10, we can see a discussion from what may be considered to be a less vertical subject – geography. The extract is from a geography lesson (grade 9, ages 14–15), and the class is discussing the concept of development.

Extract 1.10
1 T: Can you tell me why birth rate and death rate
2   are elements to talk about development?
3 S: ( )
4 T: Yes?
5 S1: Because if a country develops the death rate would be less
6   and the birth rate will grow higher.
7 T: Excellent. Okay, and so we are talking about what
8   if the birth rate increases?
9 S2: That is more life expectancy ... no, that it is a good
10   country to live.
11 T: That it's a good country to live. That's a good answer. Yes?
12 S3: That there are good medicines and education.
13 T: Excellent. So, can you say that again please?
14 S3: That there is more education.
15 T: More education, excellent. What else?
16 S3: More health.
17 T: More health.
18 S3: The country is better – more services.
19 T: More services, excellent.
20   As you can see, not only GNP is an element to consider,
21   but the health services people have, OK? And education.

In this extract we can see that the teacher and students are discussing concepts which are more towards the vertical or uncommon-sense end of the scale. One indication of this is the considerable use of **nominalisations** (see Box 1.2). Examples are *birth rate, life expectancy, development* and *GNP*. These concepts have already been presented and discussed in previous lessons on development, and it is now taken for granted that students have access to the meaning of the terms, and can elaborate on them if they have to. These are all quite abstract terms, and the teacher and students are using these abstractions as participants in the discourse, rather than, for example, specific people or groups of people. Thus, for instance, at lines 5–6, a student relates birth and death rates to development, and it is these abstract entities which grow or decrease, rather than individuals or groups.

Box 1.2: Nominalisation

Nominalisations are noun phrases which express meanings which could be 'unpacked' as actions with people as participants. For example, 'birth rate' in Extract 1.10 could be expressed as 'the number of babies born in a place for every 1,000 people in a certain period of time'. Nominalisations are typical of the academic registers of school subjects, and as such are strongly associated with vertical discourse (Martin, 2007). For Schleppegrell (2004: 143), using these prepackaged meanings allows teachers and students to take an idea that 'has already been presented and elaborated at length and present it again as a technical term representing knowledge which is now held in common (...)'. Nominalisation and the related concept of grammatical metaphor are discussed in more detail in Chapter 5.

The examples in this section show how the functional linguistic concepts of field and ideational metafunction can allow us to get a better grasp of the complexity of communication in CLIL classrooms when teachers and students interact in the instructional register. However, from the point of view of language development, we should be cautious about what exactly can be achieved, and where some of the limitations might lie. Dalton-Puffer and Nikula are quite clear about the limitations of the instructional register in terms of the possibility of learning pragmatic uses of language. As they put it, 'The instructional register is much more uniform and offers a much narrower scope for exposure and active use of highly context-dependent language on the part of the students (...)' (Dalton-Puffer and Nikula, 2006: 264).

If communicating about content in the CLIL classroom becomes limited to the transmission of factual information and checking of what the students are already supposed to know, then it will indeed be a very limiting context for language development, and, for that matter, for learning the subject in question. Unfortunately, this may be the case in some CLIL contexts. Dalton-Puffer, in her research on Austrian CLIL classrooms, rather worryingly stated that, 'The bread and butter of Austrian CLIL classrooms is obviously facts, facts, and facts' (Dalton-Puffer, 2007: 125). However, this may not always be the case in other

CLIL contexts. The extracts from the corpus in this section provide evidence that secondary CLIL teachers and students are able to use the L2 to shift skilfully between the different types of knowledge structure. Sometimes they are talking about highly structured 'facts', but at other times students' (and teachers') own everyday opinions and experience can form the content that is being talked about. The interesting aspect of this is that, even when everyday knowledge is used, it is used for the pedagogical purposes of advancing the learners towards the more scientific or geographical versions.

1.4 Convergence of regulative and instructional registers

Christie (2002) points out that as schooling continues into the higher secondary grades, explicit use of the regulative register becomes less frequent. Students become more familiar with the range of activities they have to do and can carry them out with a minimum of control and management. On the scale of a single lesson or sequence of lessons on a topic, if the regulative register has been used effectively by the teacher in setting up an activity, the resulting work by students will show a preponderance of the instructional register. The regulative register will of course be running tacitly in the background, ready to be invoked if there is any deviance from the prescribed activity. For example, in the extract we saw earlier, in which students worked in small groups on an activity about megalithic monuments, after the short regulative intervention from S2 at line 2, the activity continues in the instructional register:

	Extract 1.11
1	S1: Okay this is er Stonehenge that is in the United Kingdom er
2	S2: Loud voice please.
3	S1: It is a crom- a megalithic monument that is a Greek word
4	that in English er
5	S3: Greek war?
6	S1: Yes in Greek.
7	S3: Yes, yes.
8	S1: Yes the er the word er megalithic ...
9	S3: Ah yes, yes I understand that this was a war a war a fight
10	S1: Ah no no word word
11	S1: The translation in English of 'megalithic monument' will be
12	'a big stone'.

(cont.)

13	S2: What?
14	S1: The translation of megalithic monument in English
15	will be big stone and the stones of the (stone) circle
16	that I (think about) weigh 25 eh tone ...
17	S3: Tons.
18	S1: Tons yes. Er this monument er they build about eh five
19	S3: Thousand.
20	S1: Yes five thousand years ago and this is a cromlech
21	but there are other types of megalithic monument
22	that are menhirs and dolmens.
23	S3: Okay.

In this small-group interaction the students maintain some verticality in the discourse, with the use of the technical terms *megalithic, cromlech, menhir* and *dolmen*. The student who presents the information (S1) attempts a description of some of the features of the monument such as its weight and age (lines 16–20) as well as a classification of types of megalithic monument (lines 20–22). It is noticeable how the students try to keep the communication channels open by repairing a mishearing of *Greek word* as *Greek war* (lines 5–10). The extract is also rich in teacher-like behaviour on the part of S3, as she steps in (perhaps too quickly) to 'help' her colleague with the words he needs to complete his turns (lines 17 and 19).

For this type of small-group work activity to produce any kind of sustained interaction in the instructional register, there needs to be quite intensive previous work in the regulative register by the teacher. It is significant that, in the lesson from which this extract is drawn, the teacher's contributions are practically all in the regulative register, while all the classroom talk in the instructional register is carried on by the students in small groups. Extract 1.1, in which the teacher gives instructions to change groups, is also from this lesson. It is only one example of several intensive regulative phases in the lesson, at moments when students had to change activity or group formation.

Extract 1.11 provides evidence that, in a CLIL context, it is possible for small groups of students to work together to maintain the instructional register in classroom talk. However, the interaction is fairly limited, and consists more of the presentation of some previously learned facts, than of any exploration of ideas or use of language for 'thinking together' (Mercer, 2000). For example, there is no evidence of the student presenting the information having to justify or defend his ideas in the face of questions. This of course is related to the type of activity the students were doing: the presentation of previously learned material. If the students were doing a problem-solving activity in which they had to reach an agreed outcome, there would be much more room for this kind of joint exploration of ideas, or thinking together. However, this would require an even greater amount of energy and training in the regulative register on the part of the teacher, in which she would have to present 'ground rules' for carrying on such 'exploratory talk' (Mercer and Dawes, 2008). In other words, just like learners using their first language, CLIL learners would need to be trained in the use of language as a tool for thinking together. This would seem to be a very worthwhile aim for CLIL, as it would meet the double objective of encouraging the use of higher-level thinking skills, and helping CLIL students to extend their linguistic repertoires. If, as Christie explains, the regulative register *projects* the instructional register, it will not be possible to achieve worthwhile communication in the more vertical aspects of the instructional register, if we do not equip CLIL learners with the *social* language they need to reach this aim.

1.5 Conclusion

The focus of this chapter has been on the *what* of communication in CLIL classrooms, that is, the content that is being communicated about and the teacher's purposes in doing so. We have argued that the notion of register helps us get a clearer, more detailed grasp of the communicative possibilities of the CLIL lesson at this level. At any point in a CLIL lesson, the main focus may be on regulative aspects, and, indeed, there is some evidence from the corpus that CLIL lessons require more of this than lessons in students' L1. When the focus is on subject-matter content, this may be treated as a more horizontal type of discourse, in which learners' and teachers' everyday experience is highlighted. This of course raises its own issues for CLIL, as learners (and indeed teachers) may have limited access to the language needed to talk about a wide range of everyday experience. In appealing to students' everyday experience, the teacher enters a realm where the unpredictable can come up, and where the students may know, or want to know, as much as the teacher. This in turn may provide opportunities for genuine negotiation of meaning, which has been strongly associated with second language acquisition, and is something that has been claimed to be lacking in content-based classrooms (Musumeci, 1996; Pica, 2002). Such flexibility places demands on both teachers and learners, and at times their communicative competence can be stretched to its limits as they attempt to express unexpected or unprepared-for meanings.

Because CLIL teachers are responsible for their students' content learning, the use of horizontal discourse usually has a clear pedagogical purpose. It is normally used as a springboard towards the more vertical aspects of the content. In terms of the metafunctions of language, this ideational content will be expressed in less everyday language, notably with the use of grammatical metaphors such as nominalisations. In terms of content learning, this may be seen by some CLIL teachers as the real purpose of their teaching, which is of course to ensure that their students have acquired the concepts and skills of the subject they are teaching at the appropriate grade level. Expressing this content with the appropriate terminology and producing the text types typical of the subject may also be seen as a part of this (see Chapter 4 on genre).

However, from the point of view of CLIL lessons as a context for language development, the other types of language use (the regulative register and horizontal discourse within the instructional register) are equally important, and challenging. It is hoped that this chapter has provided the reader with a metalanguage to think about these aspects of communication in CLIL classrooms, and with a clearer understanding of their possibilities and limitations. However, in this chapter we have necessarily looked at the CLIL classroom from the fairly static perspective of *focus* by broadly describing the two registers and structures of knowledge. In the next, we move to the level of *approach* in which we consider the dynamics of interaction in the CLIL classroom, particularly the communication systems which teachers are largely responsible for setting up and maintaining.

Questions and tasks for reflection and discussion

1. Look at Extract 1.12 from a CLIL science lesson (grade 7, ages 12–13). Make a list of all the features of the regulative register you can find.

Extract 1.12
1   T: Okay, so can we just stop stop here for a minute.
2   Okay, listen. Can you put your pencils down now and listen.
3   Put your pencils down now and what I want you to do next
4   is you are going to choose another pair, at the most two
5   other pairs and you're going to ask them about their
6   answers.
7   So for instance this group over here, this pair over there.
8   And you're going to compare your answers
9   and you're also going to do it with this other group.
10   So just compare your answers and three no more groups OK?
11   Right?
12   And check your answers and you can complete a little bit your
13   own answer. And then we'll put it all together on the board OK?
14   And I will help you to summarise it OK?

2. Think of an activity you would normally use in teaching a topic in a CLIL subject. How would you set it up in the classroom using the regulative register? Make a list of some language (vocabulary and grammar structures) you would need to use.
3. Look at Extract 1.13 from a higher secondary CLIL physics lesson. Identify examples of the regulative and instructional registers in the extract.

Extract 1.13
1   T: K diverging lines don't intersect in infinity,
2   just parallel lines, but, this situation ...
3   K, K leave that problem for now,
4   you can return to the problem later on erm,
5   I still can use this situation in with this lens for something else,
6   because imagine, imagine that someone is sitting over here
7   looking with an eye and the eye is, through a nerve, connected
8   to the brain, ((laughter)) yeah these light rays ((laughter))
9   it's hard to keep up the attention (yeah it's the weather outside)
10   erm I think I need I need five more minutes
11   please be concentrated for five more minutes
12   and then you can go to work by yourselves erm,
13   but if you keep talking, if you keep talking then I need
14   more than five minutes.
15   The light rays hit the eye, an eye connected to the brain,
16   well, brains can think, and a brain well, it's a little bit stupid
17   because this brain doesn't know that this light ray is
18   refracted over here.
19   A brain always thinks that light rays just travel in a straight line,
20   so his brain thinks that this light ray comes from this
21   direction ...

4. Think of a specific topic from the subject you teach (or may teach) in CLIL. Make a list of some everyday or horizontal knowledge that it would be useful to activate in teaching this topic. To what extent do you think the learners would be able to use this language? How could you help them?
5. Using the same topic as in 4, list the main concepts and skills the students would have to be introduced to. Identify some vertical language they would need. Are there any particularly important nominalisations? Would it be necessary to 'unpack' them as actions with human participants? How would you do this?

References

Bernstein, B. B. (1990) *The Structuring of Pedagogic Discourse*, London: Routledge.

Bernstein, B. B. (1999) 'Vertical and horizontal discourse: An essay', *British Journal of Sociology of Education*, **20**, 2, 157–73.

Christie, F. (2002) *Classroom Discourse Analysis: A Functional Perspective*, London: Continuum.

Coffin, C. (2006a) 'Learning the language of school history: The role of linguistics in mapping the writing demands of the secondary school curriculum', *Journal of Curriculum Studies*, **38**, 4, 413–29.

Coyle, D., Hood, P. and Marsh, D. (2010) *CLIL: Content and Language Integrated Learning*, Cambridge: Cambridge University Press.

Dalton-Puffer, C. (2007) *Discourse in Content and Language Integrated Learning (CLIL) Classrooms*, Amsterdam; Philadelphia: John Benjamins.

Dalton-Puffer, C. & Nikula, T. (2006) 'Pragmatics of content-based instruction: Teacher and student directives in Finnish and Austrian classrooms', *Applied Linguistics*, **27**, 2, 241–67.

Gibbons, P. (2006) *Bridging Discourses in the ESL Classroom: Students, Teachers and Researchers*, London: Continuum.

Halliday, M. A. K. and Hasan, R. (1989) *Language, Context, and Text: Aspects of Language in a Social-Semiotic Perspective*, Oxford: Oxford University Press.

Halliday, M. A. K. and Matthiessen, C. M. I. M. (2004) *An Introduction to Functional Grammar* (3rd ed.), London: Arnold.

Martin, J. R. (2007) 'Construing knowledge: A functional linguistic perspective', in Christie, F. and Martin, J. R. (eds.) *Knowledge Structure: Functional Linguistic and Sociological Perspectives*, London: Continuum, pp. 34–64.

Mercer, N. (2000) *Words and Minds: How we use Language to Think Together*, London: Routledge.

Mercer, N. and Dawes, L. (2008) 'The value of exploratory talk', in Mercer, N. and Hodgkinson, S. (eds.) (2008) *Exploring Talk in School*, London: Sage, pp. 55–71.

Mortimer, E. F. and Scott, P. H. (2003) *Meaning Making in Secondary Science Classrooms*, Buckingham, UK: Open University Press.

Musumeci, D. (1996) 'Teacher–learner negotiation in content-based instruction: Communication at cross-purposes?', *Applied Linguistics*, **17**, 3, 286–325.

Pica, T. (2002) 'Subject-matter content: How does it assist the interactional and linguistic needs of classroom language learners?', *The Modern Language Journal*, **86**, 1, 1–19.

Roth, W.-M. (2008) 'The nature of scientific conceptions: A discursive psychological perspective', *Educational Research Review*, **3**, 1, 30–50.

Schleppegrell, M. J. (2004) *The Language of Schooling: A Functional Linguistics Perspective*, Mahwah, NJ; London: Lawrence Erlbaum.

van Lier, L. (2005) 'The Bellman's Map: Avoiding the "Perfect and Absolute Blank" in Language Learning', in Jourdenais, R. and Springer, S. (eds.) (2005) *Content, Tasks and Projects in the Language Classroom: 2004 Conference Proceedings*, Monterey, CA: Monterey Institute of International Studies, pp. 13–21.

Vygotsky, L. S. (1994) 'The development of academic concepts in school aged children', in van der Veer, R., and Valsiner, J. (eds.) (1994) *The Vygotsky Reader*, Oxford: Blackwell, pp. 355–70.

2 Interaction and dialogue in the CLIL classroom

2.1 Introduction

Chapter 1 looked at how teachers and learners use classroom talk to represent different types of knowledge and to organise the social world of the classroom. In this chapter, in terms of our adaptation of Mortimer and Scott's framework, we are moving from the level of focus to that of *approach*. That is, from looking at how knowledge is represented in classroom talk, we start to look at the interaction and dialogue through which teachers and learners communicate about this knowledge. We will see that CLIL teachers set up different types of *communication systems* in order to achieve their pedagogical purposes in teaching content topics. There is a very close relationship between different ways of talking about content and learning opportunity. As Barnes (2008: 2) points out, 'The communication system that a teacher sets up in a lesson shapes the roles that pupils can play, and goes some distance in determining the kinds of learning that they engage in.'

In a CLIL context, this is likely to be true both for content learning and language development. Overuse of a communication system which consists largely of question-and-answer chains, in which the teacher already knows the answer, is going to be limiting both for what students can do with the ideas being talked about, and their L2 skills. It would be similar to the CLIL classrooms we commented on in Chapter 1, which Dalton-Puffer described as existing on a diet of 'facts, facts, facts'. Or it could be like this rather vivid description of the content-based classrooms researched by Diane Musumeci:

> The teachers (...) speak more, more often, control the topic of discussion, rarely ask questions for which they do not have answers, and appear to understand absolutely everything the students say, sometimes even before they say it! One might conclude from these findings that teachers are a loquacious, manipulative, power-hungry bunch of know-it-alls.
>
> (Musumeci, 1996: 314)

Of course, Musumeci was not accusing teachers of being a bunch of know-it-alls, but her analysis of classroom communication shows how easy it is to fall into a routine in which the talk flows along smoothly without anyone having to push themselves to make their meaning clear or demand clarification from others. The CLIL classroom is a familiar environment for teachers and students, and the knowledge of the routines enacted within it can allow them to get by with a minimum of explicitness (Dalton-Puffer, 2007). This is of course true for most classrooms, not just CLIL ones, and it may have more to do with the social constraints of classroom learning than any particular methodology, or the language used as a medium of instruction. For example, one of the teachers of the classes recorded in the corpus claimed that she never asked her students to give long answers because they wouldn't do it in their L1 either. She pointed out that students of this age (15–16) always give short answers.

However, there are good arguments, from the points of view of both content and language learning, for students to be encouraged to make the effort to express their meanings with greater clarity, and even to allow a certain amount of struggle for this to happen. From the point of view of using language as a tool for 'thinking together' (Mercer and Dawes, 2008), it is important that reasoning processes and justifications for ideas be made available for all on the social plane of the classroom. This is something that is taken up strongly in this chapter, in which we argue for the importance of a dialogic approach in CLIL. From the perspective of L2 development, students need opportunities to produce language which stretches their current levels of competence. As Ortega (2009) points out, 'Optimal L2 learning must include opportunities for language use that is slightly beyond what the learner currently can handle in speaking or writing' (p. 63). CLIL offers unique opportunities for synergies between the dual aims of content and language learning, and for this reason, it is important that teachers seize these opportunities by communicating and interacting in ways that can bring these joint goals about.

In this chapter we introduce Mortimer and Scott's (2003) concept of *communicative approach* as a tool to describe different communication systems in the CLIL classroom. We argue that, for the purposes of both content and language learning, there is a need for CLIL teachers to ensure that the full range of communication systems is used in their classrooms. We then build on this in the second half of the chapter to present an argument for a greater use of what Alexander (2008) describes as *dialogic talk* in CLIL classrooms. Our aim is to show that dialogic teaching is both possible and necessary in CLIL. We use examples from the corpus to show aspects of dialogic teaching in action in CLIL classrooms, and point out some of the features of this type of talk. The chapter also aims to raise CLIL teachers' awareness of the features of different interactional formats in CLIL classrooms, and of the role of dialogic talk in these communication systems. The hope is that a greater awareness of the CLIL classroom as a communicative space will enable teachers to use a wider range of interactional formats and strategies to meet the twin goals of content learning and L2 development.

2.2 Communication systems in the CLIL classroom

Once teachers have decided what content is to be taught and for what purposes, they need to think about the specific ways this content will be presented and talked about in the classroom. Will they simply 'tell' the students the new information? Or will they try to elicit students' own ideas about the topic? Who will do most of the talking? Mortimer and Scott (2003) consider these questions at the level of *approach.* They identify two dimensions along which talk between teachers and students (and indeed between students) can be described: interactive / non-interactive and dialogic / authoritative. When talk is interactive, a number of people contribute, and when it is non-interactive only one person intervenes. The dialogic / authoritative dimension refers to whose ideas get talked about in class. If the talk is dialogic, students are encouraged to contribute their own ideas and points of view on a topic. In authoritative talk, only the teacher's or the 'official' point of view is recognised. This system yields, according to Mortimer and Scott (2003: 34–40), four classes of communicative approach. Their use of the term is thus very different from the way it is used in second and foreign language teaching, and it is Mortimer and Scott's meaning that we use here. The four classes of communicative approach are shown in Table 2.1.

Table 2.1 *Four types of 'communicative approach'* (*Mortimer and Scott, 2003: 35*)

	INTERACTIVE	NON-INTERACTIVE
DIALOGIC	A. Interactive / Dialogic	B. Non-interactive / Dialogic
AUTHORITATIVE	C. Interactive / Authoritative	D. Non-interactive / Authoritative

The continuum of authoritative or dialogic discourse overlaps with the concepts of vertical or horizontal knowledge introduced in Chapter 1. Vertical knowledge is likely to be seen as harder to call into question, and thus more authoritative, while more horizontal or 'everyday' knowledge may be open to a wider range of points of view, and therefore more dialogic. As Mortimer and Scott show, all four communicative approaches have their importance in classroom talk. It will depend on the nature of the content and the teacher's purpose in teaching it. They describe classroom talk as shifting between more dialogic and authoritative phases as, for example, teachers engage with students' ideas in more dialogic interaction before introducing the 'scientific story' in more authoritative fashion.

This concept of communicative approach is crucial for CLIL classrooms, for, if students are to gain communicative competence in their L2 through studying academic content, they will need opportunities to participate in all four types of communication system. A CLIL classroom in which the vast majority of interaction is of the authoritative / non-interactive type would obviously present an impoverished context for language development, especially if we see language production as essential to this process. In contrast, in a CLIL classroom in which there is wide use of the interactive / dialogic communicative approach, students will have opportunities to express their own ideas or points of view on a topic, and there will be a toing and froing of interaction between students and teacher or between the students themselves. In order to participate in this type of interaction, CLIL students will need to have both the language resources to talk about everyday knowledge and experience, and the interactive skills to manage turn taking. In CLIL in foreign language contexts (which is the situation in the classes in this corpus), there may not be a great deal of contact with the L2 outside school, so it cannot be taken for granted that students will find it easy to talk about everyday experiences and participate in this kind of interaction.

In order for the CLIL lesson to fully realise its potential as a communicative space for both subject learning and language development, teachers need to use the four types of communicative approach, matching them effectively with their pedagogic purposes in dealing with content (as they are identified at the level of focus in our framework). In doing so, they can take advantage of the nature of these communication systems to provide richer environments for language use. To begin to do this, CLIL teachers can gain a clearer understanding of how these communication systems work. This is our aim in presenting and discussing the examples in the next section.

2.3 Communication systems in action in CLIL classrooms

In this section we use examples from the CLIL corpus to highlight some ways in which the choice of communicative approach has an impact on both content- and language-learning opportunity. The first five extracts come from two CLIL biology lessons on the topic of genetics (grade 10, ages 15–16). By focusing on one class and topic, we can show how the different communication systems operate at different stages in teaching, according to the focus on either horizontal or vertical knowledge, and the teacher's pedagogic purposes. In Extract 2.1 the teacher introduces the idea of mutation.

	Extract 2.1
1	T: What do you think a mutant is?
2	Have you ever seen a mutant anywhere?
3	S: (in films)
4	T: In films? Can you give me an example of a mutant?
5	What is a mutant?
6	S: In plants.
7	T: In plants? Do you have any mutant plants at home?
8	A mutant. It sounds like something that happens in films.
9	S: A Doberman.
10	T: But actually it doesn't, it happens in nature.
11	S: The Doberman.
12	T: The Doberman. Is that a mutant? A Doberman?
13	It looks weird, yes, but it's not a mutant, actually.
14	S: It's a mixture.
15	T: It's a mixture, yes. Of what?
16	S: Of races of dogs. Of dogs races.
17	T: Different breeds you say. *Razas* (Sp. breeds)
18	Yeah, they've been mixing different dogs throughout time.

In this extract the teacher's purpose is to open up the problem of mutation, and explore the students' views. She does this by directly asking them what they think a mutant is, or by appealing to their experience, *Have you ever seen a mutant anywhere?* (line 2). The talk is interactive, as both the teacher and individual students are participating, and it is dialogic, as the students' own ideas are elicited and commented on. Different students contribute possible candidates for mutant status, with the one that is taken up by the teacher being that of a Doberman dog. This develops into a discussion of whether a Doberman is a mutant or not, and the talk moves into authoritative mode when the teacher gives the 'official' version, that is, a Doberman is not a mutant:

	Extract 2.2
1	T: But this is not mutation, you see this is something else.
2	So a Doberman is not a mutant.
3	((pause))
4	So, what is a mutant then, for you? What do you think?

However, this authoritative moment is embedded in an overall dialogic stretch of discourse. Its parenthetical status can be seen in the pause at line 3, after which the teacher switches back to the dialogic mode by asking the students for their views on what a mutant is (line 4). We can see here that even in short sequences of classroom interaction, the teacher manages shifts between two distinct types of classroom talk.

Later in the same lesson, there is a very clearly authoritative / non-interactive stretch of discourse, as illustrated in Extract 2.3:

Extract 2.3		
1	T:	So, listen, this is the way it is.
2		I'll write something on the board for you, okay?
3		Okay, proteins are over. Have you studied at all?
4	SS:	(yes)
5	T:	Okay, listen, you all know this?
6		You know this, don't you?
7		Okay, now okay, a compound A,
8		that's going to turn into a compound B, okay?
9		Chemical reaction, catalysed by an enzyme one, right?
10		Enzyme one, okay?
11		Enzymes are proteins, are they not? Yes.
12		So, there must be one gene, gene one,
13		that codes for this enzyme one.
14		Do you agree?
15	SS:	Yes.
16	T:	Yes. Now, okay, now.
17		Compound B turns into compound C.
18		This chemical reaction must be catalysed by enzyme two,
19		which in turn would be coded for by gene two.
20		Do you agree? Yeah?
21		Well that's the way it is.

In this sequence, the teacher is introducing the scientific version of how a mutation occurs. After exploring the students' views on mutation by discussing Doberman dogs and plants, she decides it is time for some authoritative discourse. She reinforces this by going to the board, and starting to clean it in preparation for writing. Her voice quality changes as the phrases become sharper and more emphatic. There are clear signals of authoritative talk in the extract, for example her use twice (at lines 1 and 21) of *this / that is the way it is*. The language also changes from the more everyday or horizontal (*Doberman, scary, weird, films*) to the scientific or vertical (*compound, chemical reaction, enzyme, codes for, catalysed*). The ideas are no longer the students', but the 'official version' or scientific story, and there is very little interaction. When the teacher does ask questions, she hardly expects an answer, and indeed answers her questions herself, as at line 11 (*Enzymes are proteins, are they not? Yes.*).

Nearer the end of this lesson, there is an example of the authoritative / interactive communicative approach:

Extract 2.4
1   T: This is a DNA sequence of bases, okay?
2   Now how does this translate into a protein?
3   S: You have first the ...
4   T: First you need to do ...
5   S: The messenger.
6   T: Good, you need to do the messenger RNA,
7   to transcribe this into – messenger RNA.
8   So what would the transcribed sequence of bases be?
9   SS: ((different students)) A, E, C.

Here, the teacher is guiding the students as they work with and internalise the scientific ideas. The information being talked about is 'official' scientific content; however, the students are not just listening, but are able to contribute by building up the knowledge together in the public space of the classroom. Thus, one student was able to supply the idea of messenger RNA (line 5), and collectively they were able to provide the transcribed sequence of bases. In a post-lesson interview, the teacher confirmed that the students were able to help her build this process on the board as they had already studied the relevant background.

In these three extracts from one biology lesson, we can see evidence from a CLIL context of what Scott et al. (2006) refer to as a 'tension' between authoritative and dialogic discourse in science teaching. It is not that one is better than the other, but that each is suited to different teaching purposes. Thus, when we are exploring students' points of view and personal experiences on a topic, the communicative approach is likely to be dialogic / interactive, but when we are concerned to get the scientific (or historical, or geographical) story across clearly, we are likely to use an authoritative / non-interactive approach. Dialogic and authoritative phases will arise out of each other within and across lessons, as teachers first explore students' views, introduce the subject-matter story, and then move back into dialogic mode to explore the application of the new ideas.

Successful interaction, particularly if it is of the dialogic / interactive kind, is unlikely to be trouble-free and free-flowing, as in the classrooms described in the quote from Musumeci (1996). When teachers and students are making real efforts to understand one another, the resulting discourse is, according to Walsh (2006) 'jagged, with a lot of interruption, back-tracking, and requests for clarification'. As he puts it, 'smooth-flowing interaction does not necessarily equate with uninhibited learning' (p. 135). In Extract 2.5, from the previous lesson, the teacher and students are discussing whether certain physical characteristics are inherited or may be caused by environmental factors. The discourse proceeds smoothly with the students providing correct answers which are filled in on a table. However, we can see that the smooth flow is interrupted and the discourse becomes rather 'jagged' when a student insists that hand size can be affected by the environment:

Extract 2.5
1   T: So we have hair colour, mouth shape,
2   we have obviously nose shape.
3   It's the same idea, eye colour.
4   We've got a lot on this side.
5   S: Hand size.
6   T: Hand size.
7   S: No.
8   T: What is it?
9   S: No, it can be inherited or environmental.
10   T: Okay! Let's see. Okay J. Do you mind.
11   Okay what does he want to know? J.
12   What is he saying? Have you heard his question?
13   Or his statement. He has only just said something,
14   very interesting by the way.
15   S: Doesn't have to be inherited
16   T: Sorry? What did you say?
17   S: That the hand size can be inherited or environmental.
18   T: Can you go a little bit further?
19   S: That if you make er the basketball or ...
20   T: Play.
21   S: ... your hands will grow
22   T: ... grows bigger. How about if you play the piano?
23   S: If you play the piano your fingers are bigger and strong.

It is noticeable here how the teacher, rather than continuing with the smooth filling in of the table with one-word suggestions, makes real efforts to establish joint understanding by making sure that the student's contribution can be heard, for example at line 12 (*What is he saying? Have you heard his question?*). She also encourages the student's contribution by mentioning that it was *very interesting* (line 14). Two lines further on, when she is not clear about what he said, she asks him to clarify by saying, *Sorry?*, something that is not too common in the kind of 'smooth-flowing' classroom talk described by Musumeci. Having established the floor for the student and enabled him to express his idea, she pushes him to be more explicit by saying, *Can you go a little bit further?* (line 18). This requires more 'pushed output' (Swain, 2005) from the student, and we can see the pressure on his linguistic competence from his error, *if you make er the basketball* (line 19). However, the student is able to continue, and by introducing the idea of playing the piano, the teacher scaffolds the student to produce the longer, and more appropriate, though not quite accurate, last utterance in the extract.

The communication systems set up by CLIL teachers to meet their purposes in dealing with content need not be ones in which the teacher dominates, or even participates in, the classroom talk. In our corpus of CLIL classroom talk, there were several examples of occasions where the students engaged in interaction with each other with only minimal or indeed no involvement at all by the teacher. This could be small-group activities in which students completed a task set by the teacher, or whole-class presentation, discussion or question–answer sessions. In most of these contexts, students were able to sustain interaction in the L2, and, as in the examples of teacher–student talk, switch between more authoritative and dialogic communication systems. In the following extracts from a CLIL geography lesson (grade 9, ages 14–15), we see how students manage the interaction by switching from a dialogic / non-interactive communication system to a dialogic / interactive one. In this class, a group of students have completed a project on land use in which they have designed a skateboarding park to occupy a piece of disused land in their local area. In Extract 2.6, the group is presenting the project:

Extract 2.6
1 S1: So this is our project ...
2   It's about eh to build a skateboard park in C ((name of city)).
3 S2: And we are start uh ...
4   by explain pros and the cons of the project.
5   The pros of eh building a skateboarding park in C
(cont.)

6	is that has a good accessibility.
7	For example, you can access the skateboarding park
8	by train, bus, car, bicycle or by skateboard or walking.
9	Also it's near to high schools and our school,
10	so children after classes can go to skate.
11	It's near to a shopping centre
12	and guys can buy meals and drinks if they're hungry.
13	Uh ... it's in a very big place and you can be there
14	skateboarding or just sitting there and watching all the
15	people.
16	It's near a ur- urbanisation of flats so people can access
17	there easily.
18	And it's very near and is in the middle of C, so it's very good.

In this extract, the communication system is clearly non-interactive, as it is only the presenters who have the floor, and it is dialogic in that they state that their intention is to describe the pros and cons of their proposal (as they go on to do). The ideas are not official or vertical knowledge from the geography curriculum, but their own ideas which are to be debated with those who may disapprove of the project, as we see in the next extract just a little bit further on in the same session:

	Extract 2.7	
1	T:	You have to come okay? It's a nice area very green ...
2	S3:	No.
3	T:	... with this rain.
4	S3:	But it's green now in winter but in summer ...
5	S1:	Uh it doesn't matter because we are going to build on it
6		and so I think that the grass doesn't matter.
7		((laughter))
8	S3:	But this year have been many rain season
9		but the normally it's a desert uh area with uh
10	S1:	I repeat you that we are going to build on it.
11		So uh if it's a green area it doesn't matter
12		because in the future it will be cement.
13		((makes 'covering' gesture with hands))
14	S3:	Very good progress yes. Taking out a green area to put uh-
15	SS:	((laughter))

(cont.)

16	S1:	Yes I destroy an area
17		because uh there are a lot of parks
18		with green areas in C not just one.
19	S3:	No. One question.
20		You said that there you keep all the vegetation that is there?
21	S1:	I don't think that it's a very good place ...
22	S3:	No but in the presentation ...
23	S1:	... for vegetation because you can see
24		that there are grass but bad grass.
25	S3:	In the presentation you have said
26		that it's a green area with animals and trees and uh-
27	S1:	There aren't trees and there aren't animals and plants.
28	S3:	So if you are arguing for one side that there are animals
29		and trees
30		uh why in the other side you say that
31		uh you are going to take it out to put cement?
32	S1:	There are insects not animals.

The teacher is only minimally involved at the beginning of this episode (lines 1 and 3) but her evaluative comment about the nice green area provides the spark for a lively debate between S1 and S3 about the wisdom of building a skateboard park and cementing over an area which seems to be, at least to some extent, a green space. The communication system is clearly interactive in that there is a rapid exchange of turns, with plenty of overlap and interruption. It is also extremely dialogic in that students are using evidence from their own knowledge of living in the area to make assertions and counter-assertions about the relative merits of building the skateboard park or conserving the green space. This kind of interaction seems to encourage the use of all kinds of rhetorical tactics such as sarcasm (line 14), throwing back to speakers what they said earlier (lines 20, 22, 25, 28, 29) and backing down from previous assertions (lines 24 and 32). Thus we have seen how, in one classroom activity, students themselves can manage the interaction as they move from one communicative approach (non-interactive / dialogic) to another (interactive / dialogic).

We hope to have shown with the corpus extracts in this section the wide range of communicative situations that can emerge in even one CLIL classroom, or even within one activity, as in the geography example. Each of the communication systems has its purpose, particularly from the point of view of curricular content learning outcomes. From a CLIL point of view, we have seen how each may provide different challenges and opportunities for language use and development. For CLIL teachers, we see one main benefit from gaining a better understanding of communication systems in the classroom: CLIL teachers can be enabled to make conscious decisions about what types of approach are best for dealing with different types of content and the purposes in teaching it, and which will afford more opportunities and perhaps fewer restrictions for language use. This means that, in terms of Mortimer and Scott's framework, planning in CLIL should go beyond the focus level, to also include approach. CLIL teachers, then, would need to not only identify the content topic (including whether the ideas are more horizontal or vertical), and the purpose in dealing with it, but also the communication system best suited to dealing with these.

While all the communication systems that can emerge in classrooms have their uses, we have argued that the overuse of one may have negative effects for both content and language learning. This is the case with the heavy use of an authoritative / non-interactive (or minimally interactive) approach in which the main objective seems to be the recitation of facts. Other types of communication may be hardly used at all. This may be the case with what can be called *dialogic teaching*. Dialogic teaching goes beyond the description of one or two types of communicative approach, rather identifying a more wide-ranging philosophy of how talk should be used in classroom teaching and learning. We believe that the concept of dialogic teaching has important implications for CLIL, and it is thus the topic of the next section.

2.4 Dialogic teaching in CLIL classrooms

In this section we argue that dialogic teaching can be an extremely effective instrument for encouraging cognitive and language development in the CLIL classroom. Alexander (2008) describes dialogic talk as that which achieves 'common understanding, through structured, cumulative questioning and discussion which guide and prompt, reduce choices, minimise risk and error, and expedite "handover" of concepts and principles' (p. 30). Based on a large corpus of video-recorded lessons from around the world, Alexander and his colleagues found this kind of classroom talk to be the rarest of all. Much more common was *recitation* talk in which teachers ask questions to stimulate recall of what has already been learned, often by providing clues to allow students to answer, in many ways like the CLIL classrooms described by Dalton-Puffer.

The relative rarity of dialogic talk may not be surprising because, as Alexander puts it, dialogic teaching challenges both teachers' and students' understandings by demanding that we have 'a secure conceptual map of a lesson's subject matter, and that we give children greater free-dom to explore the territory which that map covers' (2008: 31). Taking this into the CLIL context, we can easily imagine the linguistic chal-lenges which emerge both for teachers and learners when we leave the safer shores of rote and recitation classroom talk. As we have seen in some of the extracts in Chapter 1 and in this chapter, studying subject matter in L2 requires handling of both horizontal (everyday) and verti-cal (scientific, technical) types of concepts, and opening up the class-room to more dialogic communication will place a heavier linguistic load on all concerned. It will also create challenges at the level of class-room management, as it opens up the classroom to more student par-ticipation, and perhaps less centralised control by the teacher. This, too, has its linguistic dimension, as non-native CLIL teachers may find their linguistic repertoires for using the regulative register stretched.

However, these challenges should not be seen as a justification for not using dialogic teaching in situations such as CLIL where the students are learning content in an additional language. Alexander's work, which we will discuss in more detail later, was carried out in contexts where teachers and learners were using their L1. However, the importance of dialogic teaching has also been highlighted in con-texts where the learners are additionally learning the language of instruction. Haneda and Wells (2008) give three main reasons why dialogic teaching is vitally important for students learning content in an additional language. These three reasons are summarised here (based on Haneda and Wells, 2008: 118–19):

1. By encountering the additional language in use, students not only receive **comprehensible input** in terms of understanding messages in L2 (Krashen, 1985) but also have opportunities to produce **com-prehensible output** (Swain 2005), in the form of longer and more complex contributions as they participate actively in discussions.
2. By using their language resources to contribute to the ongoing dia-logue, they also learn appropriate social and communicative strat-egies (for example, when and what to contribute, how to express their ideas appropriately) for accessing academic content and being recognised as legitimate members of the classroom community.
3. By taking part in dialogic interaction, language learners come into contact with alternative perspectives on different topics, in the voices of students as well as the teacher. They learn different ways of expressing ideas and using language for negotiation, such as when they agree or disagree with someone. This contact with different voices creates linguistic redundancy as students encounter different ideas and the same ideas expressed in different ways.

Dialogic teaching, then, can be doubly beneficial for learners studying through an additional language. In terms of content learning, Alexander claims that it is the most 'cognitively potent' element in a teacher's repertoire of communication systems. In terms of language learning, as Haneda and Wells show, it provides an optimum environment for the development of a range of capacities in the L2. Therefore, for CLIL to be successful in providing the richest possible context for language development, there needs to be a concerted effort to introduce more dialogic teaching. In order to show how this might happen, we here outline the main characteristics and benefits of dialogic talk as described by Robin Alexander, and then show how they emerge in two samples of talk from our corpus of CLIL lessons.

According to Alexander, dialogic classroom talk is:

- *collective*: teachers and children address learning tasks together, whether as a group or as a class;
- *reciprocal*: teachers and children listen to each other, share ideas and consider alternative viewpoints;
- *supportive*: children articulate their ideas freely, without fear of embarrassment over 'wrong' answers [or language errors]; and they help each other to reach common understandings;
- *cumulative*: teachers and children build on their own and each other's ideas and chain them into coherent lines of thinking and enquiry;
- *purposeful*: teachers plan and steer classroom talk with specific educational [and language development] goals in view.

(Alexander, 2008: 38;
references to language in square brackets added)

Of course, Alexander's proposals for the benefits of dialogic teaching apply to all classrooms and subjects, not just CLIL. However, when seen through the prism of CLIL, they take on a special meaning. In a CLIL classroom in which there is dialogic teaching, students will be using the L2 to do learning tasks together, to share ideas, help each other to common understandings without fear of making mistakes (of content or language), and build on each other's ideas. In effect, it is only in this kind of classroom that the benefits of dialogic teaching for second language learning highlighted by Haneda and Wells will be found. Such a classroom will clearly be a much richer environment for language development than one in which the recitation of facts is prevalent.

The following extract, from a geography lesson on development (grade 9, ages 14–15), which we have already visited in Extract 2.10, shows some key features of dialogic classroom talk. The class is going over an activity in which students were asked to identify signs of development in countries. In the middle of this quite teacher-controlled activity, S1 gives reasons why she thinks health is particularly important as an indicator of a country's development:

Extract 2.8
1   S1: I think the wealth is the most important
2   because if you don't have …
3   T: Wealth or health?
4   S1: Health.
5   T: Health? Yes –
6   S1: Because if you don't have doctors that help you
7   you don't know if the water is clean or not.
8   T: Ah.
9   S1: And then if you don't have any doctor, you can't –
10   T: Hey, excuse me are you listening?
11   SS: Yes.
12   T: Mm hm very important points yeah.
13   S1: You can't erm ((long pause)) erm clean the water
14   or see that this water is doing is affecting you.
15   T: Mm hm so you need a doctor as a supervisor
16   for loads of activities, in order to be healthy.
17   Okay that's a good point. Yes?

In this extract, which is a clear example of a dialogic / interactive communicative approach, the students and teacher are addressing the learning task (deciding on main factors indicative of development) together as a whole class. The teacher supports the student in making her contribution by intervening to repair *wealth* to *health* (lines 3–5) and by making sure that the students are listening to each other and sharing viewpoints (lines 10–12). At lines 15 and 16 she helps the class to achieve a common understanding and steers the talk towards her goal of building knowledge about development by reformulating S1's ideas. She ends the sequence in a supportive fashion by positively evaluating the student's contribution.

However, as the activity goes on, alternative points of view emerge:

Extract 2.8 (continued)
18   S2: But you can know if water is clean or is not clean
19   but if you know it you are not going to have clean water and –
20   T: Sorry, sorry can you explain?
(cont.)

21	S2:	That – you can know if you have clean water or not
22	T:	You may know yeah.
23	S2:	What does it – erm for what do you want to know
24		if you haven't got clean water because you are going to die?
25	S1:	No you can get sick because of –
26	S2:	Yeah but you don't have the clean water.
27	S1:	No no no you can get an illness with the not clean water
28		and then the doctor can tell to you what have ...
29		you *que tienes* ((Sp. what you have))
30	S:	What have you got.
31	S:	What do you have to do.
32	S1:	And the doctor can tell you what do you have to do.
33	T:	E, E okay. Can we let E give her idea?
34	S2:	*¿Cómo se dice 'aún así'?* ((Sp. How do you say 'even so'?))
35	T:	Even though.
36	S2:	Even though you don't have clean water to drink.
37	T:	Ah hah. Why not?
38	S2:	Because you don't find clean water.
39	T:	Wait wait wait wait. Yeah okay excellent. D, your point.
40	S3:	You have a high GNP you have some money
41		and you can buy clean water and you –
42	S2:	But how can you ... If you don't have water
43		you can't do the products.
44	T:	Ah hah. Okay so. Okay last thing. Your point of view?
45	S2:	Unless you develop something
46		you haven't got any money to buy water.
47	T:	Ah okay. Remember that we spoke about
48		sustainable development using the local area okay?
49		That means having the suitable simple technology to
50		make water clean, and to have access to clean water
51		with the local resources. Remember that?
52		Okay that was the important thing
53		about sustainable development.
54		Okay, well you are right because everything is important.
55		There is not one good or bad,
56		but obviously if we think of the main element in life
57		which is ...
58	SS:	Water.
59	T:	Water. Okay so the right okay to have clean water
60		is a main issue and that really marks a difference among
61		countries.

When S2 makes her contribution at line 18, she begins an exchange of ideas that lasts until the teacher closes the sequence with, *Ah okay*, at line 47. The liveliness of the exchange shows clearly that the students are not embarrassed about making mistakes (whether conceptual or linguistic ones), and they help each other out when they need the language to express an idea (as at lines 29–32). Throughout the exchange, ideas are built on and chained together as the students put forward a series of identifying factors for development. In exchanging their ideas about clean water, students S1, S2 and S3, while disagreeing, build logically on each other's arguments. As this is a whole-class activity, the teacher is clearly present, but she physically steps into the background when the students start to become the main protagonists of the discussion.

Perhaps the most important piece of purposeful intervention by the teacher is in her two longer turns which close the sequence (lines 47–61). In these turns, she reviews what has gone before, bringing together the different points made and leaving the students with an upshot of the conversation – in this case, the importance of clean water to sustainable development. However, at lines 54–55 she herself signals the dialogic nature of what has gone before by accepting the students' ideas as well. Thus, the official curricular knowledge about one important factor in indicating development has been built up by taking into account the students' contributions, and, where necessary, the students have been supported in making these contributions in the L2.

This, then, is an example of how dialogic interaction can emerge in a CLIL context. It depends both on CLIL teachers' planning of what kind of talk is necessary to achieve their pedagogic goals, and their 'steering' of the talk as it is produced. There are many skills which are important for CLIL teaching in evidence here. First, even before teaching this class, the teacher may have envisaged the best type of communication system for meeting her content-learning goal of getting students to work on and extend their understanding of the concept of development. In the classroom, she needed to keep control of the activity by using the regulative register where students' attention or participation was flagging. She also kept up a positive affective tone by praising the students' contributions. She had to know when to step back and let the students take over the interaction, but to be available to help, for example by feeding in language as it was needed. And finally, she took on a more authoritative voice to tie everything together in terms of the official geography content, although in doing so she also valued the students' contributions. These actions are only a part of the 'interactive toolkit' that CLIL teachers need to use in order to make the most of communication in the CLIL classroom. We have looked at some aspects of it here in the context of describing dialogic teaching. In Chapter 3, we provide a more detailed description of this toolkit when we explore the level of specific interventions or actions.

The example of dialogic talk we analysed in Extract 2.8 took place in a whole-class teaching situation. However, there is clear potential for dialogic teaching in each of the other interactional formats available in the classroom: whole-class teaching, teacher-led group work, pupil-led group work, and one-to-one pupil pairs. If, as Alexander points out, this potential 'needs to be thought about carefully in the planning of talk' (2008: 40), it will be all the more necessary in CLIL, where we have the added complexity of planning talk in a language which is itself an object of learning. In order to plan for the kind of talk that may emerge, it is important for CLIL teachers to have an awareness of the kinds of language typical of whatever interactional format they have chosen to use to meet their teaching purposes.

As an example, we can look at the kind of language that may be found in one of the formats mentioned above, one-to-one teacher–pupil interaction. In this type of interaction, the teacher works intensively (perhaps for a short time) with one student, and enters into a dialogue about what he or she is doing and justifications for it. On gaining a better understanding of the student's work, the teacher may offer feedback on how it can be improved (something we will look at in more detail in Chapter 9, where we explore formative assessment in CLIL). In the following extract, from a higher secondary physics lesson on optics (grade 10, age 15–16), the dialogue is about a student's drawing used in solving a mirror image problem set by the teacher.

Extract 2.9	
1	S: Is this the same as this one?
2	T: But now my question. Compare the length of the mirror
3	with the length of the person.
4	S: It's not exactly the same. Well, I haven't drawn it to scale.
5	T: No but you can see it from the sketch as well
6	and use some thinking skills.
7	S: It will probably be because this is also sitting half way. Why?
8	T: This is half way, the person's eyes and feet and this point is
9	half way. The person's eyes and probably the head.
10	S: Yeah, but I don't know why.
11	T: You don't know why because these light rays divide er this
12	distance.

(*cont.*)

13	Can I use your pen?
14	Because the angles the incident and reflected angle are the same,
15	this distance will be divided exactly in two
16	and this distance will be divided by two as well.
17	S: Yeah.
18	T: Yeah? Okay. Then you can do the problems in your book.

The talk here shows the features of dialogic teaching as described by Alexander. Even though only two people are involved, the talk is collective as the teacher and student address a learning task together, with an emphasis on the student's performance of the task. It is clearly reciprocal, as the teacher and student listen to each other, share their ideas and consider alternative viewpoints. For example, at line 5, the teacher offers an alternative perspective signalled by the way she begins the turn with *No*. At lines 8–9, different explanations for phenomena are offered, and the student is active in eliciting alternative perspectives from the teacher by asking questions (line 7) or claiming not to know (line 10). The atmosphere is clearly supportive, in that the student articulates his ideas freely, and is not afraid or embarrassed to own up to some 'failings', as for example at line 4 where he admits he didn't do the drawing to scale, or at line 10 where he claims a lack of knowledge. The teacher is also clearly supporting the student to reach a common understanding, by asking him to do things (lines 2–3 and 6). It is interesting that the teacher encourages this process by even suggesting *how* he can reach a common understanding (by using *some thinking skills*). She also supports this process by offering alternative explanations, as at lines 14–16, and even directly intervening by adding to the drawing (line 14). The talk is cumulative as the eventual explanation at lines 14–16 is built on the preceding turns. The teacher begins the sequence by focusing the student's attention on a discrepancy (between the length of the mirror and the person in the drawing) and from there, through a question-and-answer sequence (with two of the turns being in effect questions from the student), a coherent line of inquiry is built. Throughout the sequence, there is a clear sense of purposefulness, as it seems clear that the teacher had a clear goal at the outset in focusing the student's attention on the discrepancy in the drawing.

2.5 Conclusion

In this chapter we have argued that in CLIL classrooms, as in any other classrooms, there is a dynamic relationship between pedagogical goals, the communication systems set up to achieve them, language use and successful learning outcomes. We hope to have shown that, in CLIL, this takes on even more importance given that language development is a desired learning outcome. The aim of the chapter has been to deepen understanding of and provide a metalanguage for talking and thinking about how CLIL teachers and students interact in the classroom, and how this may impact on their learning opportunities. A fundamental concept has been that of dialogue, or dialogic teaching, as we have seen in the work of Robin Alexander. We firmly believe that dialogic teaching must form an essential part of all CLIL teachers' repertoires in all the different interactional formats, both because of its cognitive potency and the opportunities it provides for exposure to and use of rich language in the classroom. However, as we argue, dialogic teaching, or in fact any of the communication systems mentioned in this chapter, do not just 'happen'. They need to be planned and prepared for ahead of teaching, and skilfully navigated in the act of teaching. This means that CLIL teachers need to go beyond planning the types of tasks and activities they will get their students to do and the subject-specific language they need ('language *of* learning' in Coyle's terms). They also need to identify the interaction formats and communication systems through which these activities will come into being, and prepare students for the language they need to participate in these (Coyle's 'language *for* learning'). It is hoped that the ideas and examples presented in this chapter will encourage CLIL teachers to see the need to expand the repertoires of communication systems they use to achieve their teaching purposes, and within these, to consider the benefits of dialogic teaching for both content-learning outcomes and language development.

In this chapter we have focused on the level of communicative approach in Mortimer and Scott's framework. At this level, our descriptions of classroom talk are still rather broad, as it is our intention that CLIL teachers can plan for the kind of interactional format and communication system they will use in teaching their particular content topic. Once teachers are aware of the general characteristics of each format and the different communication systems, they can make choices about which to use, without having to predict the exact details of the language that will be used. For example, if the teacher's purpose is to elicit students' views on a topic as a bridge to introducing the more subject-specific knowledge, the choice is likely to be a dialogic / interactive communicative approach, with perhaps a whole-class interactional format.

As we have seen, some communicative approaches are more dialogic than others. Indeed, for some very specific teaching purposes and phases of lessons it may not even be appropriate to use dialogic talk.

However, within an overall dialogic approach to teaching, as we advocate here, CLIL teachers will need to develop a host of interactive skills and strategies, as we have begun to sketch out in our analyses of the last two extracts from the corpus. Although it is more difficult to plan consciously for the use of strategies at the level of single turns or utterances, it is possible for teachers to deliberately use certain strategies if they become aware of them. Such specific interventions can create different opportunities for learning in the ways they build up shorter sequences of interaction. Within Mortimer and Scott's framework, this is the level of action, that is, the specific interventions or utterances used by teachers in order to support their students' learning. This is the topic of the next chapter, the last of the three which explore the CLIL classroom as a communicative space.

Questions and tasks for reflection and discussion

1. Look at this extract from a CLIL biology lesson (grade 7, ages 12–13). The students had been asked to think in groups about whether bacteria were helpful or harmful, and are reporting back on their ideas to the whole class. Think back to Mortimer and Scott's framework of four communicative approaches, and use them to comment on the interaction in the extract.

Extract 2.10	
1	T: So let's see what do you think.
2	What do you think, what's your answer.
3	S: My answer ...
4	T: Your group's answer.
5	S: It's the two things, helpful and harmful
6	because it's good for some foods like bread has a bacteria no?
7	((looking at teacher))
8	T: Do you think bread is made with bacteria?
9	S: Yes, but ... ((makes 'not sure' gesture))
10	T: So they are helpful because they make bread?
11	S: But also it has- it can be harmful to other organisms
12	like animals or persons.
13	T: Good, good. It can be harmful do you agree?
14	SS: Yes.
15	T: Hold on, do you agree with this– the first idea?
	(cont.)

16	SS:	Yes.
17	T:	So you all think that bread is made with bacteria?
18	SS:	Yes yes.
19	T:	Yeah? All of you are you sure?
20	SS:	Yes yes.
21	SS:	No no.
22	T:	What do you think? ((pointing to one student))
23	S:	That if if the bread is making with eh eh how do you
24		say *harina* (Sp. flour)?
25	T:	Flour.
26	S:	Flour ... *levadura* (Sp. yeast)
27	T:	*Levadura* how do you say *levadura* in English?
28		I don't think you know. I can tell you that okay?
29		*Levadura* is ((writing on board)) yeast ok?
30		Yeast yeast *es* (Sp. is) *levadura* but *levadura* is not a
31		bacteria okay?
32		I'm telling you that right now.
33		I know you don't know it but this is something new for
34		you okay?
35		Yeast *levadura* are not bacteria. But they are microbes too.
36		They are a sort of fungi okay? Microscopic fungi.
37		We'll be teaching these things in further lessons
38		but not today okay?
39		So you need to know that what you first said is
40		not correct,
41		because bread is made with a living being.
42		But it's not a bacteria it's a yeast which belongs to the
43		kingdom of fungi. And we'll talk about that later okay?
44		Not today because today we're focusing on bacteria
45		and yeast is a fungi ((writing on board)).
46		It's a fungus, it's a type of fungus – microscopic one.
47		It makes br- we make bread with it okay, and we make
48		beer with it

2. Look again at Haneda and Wells's three reasons for using dialogic teaching with students who are learning English as an additional language (on page 64). Can you find any evidence of these in the extract below from a CLIL secondary lesson (grade 8, ages 13–14) on mediaeval history? The class is discussing the causes and consequences of the Plague.

	Extract 2.11	
1	S1:	Yes. The rat, or some things that are animals invade the cities,
2		and after they, they, the people can, no can eat
3		because they don't have anything for eat,
4		because the rat eat all the things.
5	T:	Yes.
6	S2:	Other name for the Plague is Black Death.
7	T:	The Black Death. Very good.
8	S3:	The Black Death was caused by the dirty of the people.
9		They don't wash very much and they threw the,
10		the rubbish and the things to the street.
11		And that brings rats and other, other diseases.
12	T:	((to student)) You do want to say something?
13	S4:	And the ones who had the Black Death, they were, eh,
14		let alone for not to, eh, contage, the eh, the disease.
15	T:	Mm. Okay. And?
16	S5:	And the Black Death was, eh, passed by the rats
17		because the rats were, in the streets, walking like a normal
18		animal, for example a dog, and they pass it to the people
19		and the people ...
20	T:	Yes. Very good. Yes C.
21	S6:	That the person that suffered the Black Death, eh, didn't
22		live more than three years, three days, sorry.
23	T:	Three days. A?
24	S7:	Eh, the Black Death reduced, eh,
25		about one third of world's population.
26	T:	Mm. Of Europe's population. And?
27	S3:	And, was a, a disease that expand to all Europe. And if
28		you were infected by the Black Death, the people of the, of
29		your family left you apart, to die, because if not you passed
30		the Black Death to another member of the family.

3. Think of a topic from a CLIL subject you teach or may teach in the future. Choose an idea that is key to the students' understanding of the topic. Identify three main purposes in dealing with the idea (if you like, use Mortimer and Scott's list of purposes on page 25). For each purpose, decide on the communicative approach you would use. Record your ideas in Table 2.2. Can you identify any opportunities for teaching the topic in a dialogic way?

Table 2.2 *Planning communicative approaches to lessons*

Key idea	Teaching purpose	Communicative approach

References

Alexander, R. J. (2008) *Towards Dialogic Teaching: Rethinking Classroom Talk* (4th ed.), York: Dialogos.
Barnes, D. (2008) 'Exploratory talk for learning', in N. Mercer and S. Hodgkinson (eds.) (2008) *Exploring Talk in Schools: Inspired by the Work of Douglas Barnes*, London: Sage, pp. 1–16.
Dalton-Puffer, C. (2007) *Discourse in Content and Language Integrated Learning (CLIL) Classrooms*, Amsterdam; Philadelphia: John Benjamins.
Haneda, M. and Wells, G. (2008) 'Learning an additional language through dialogic inquiry', *Language and Education*, 22, 2, 114–36.
Krashen, S. (1985) *The Input Hypothesis: Issues and Implications*, London: Longman.
Mercer, N. and L. Dawes. (2008) 'The value of exploratory talk', in Mercer, N. and Hodgkinson, S. (eds.) (2008) *Exploring Talk in School*, London: Sage, pp. 55–71.
Mortimer, E. F. and Scott, P. H. (2003) *Meaning Making in Secondary Science Classrooms.* Buckingham, UK: Open University Press.
Musumeci, D. (1996) 'Teacher-learner negotiation in content-based instruction: Communication at cross-purposes?', *Applied Linguistics*, 17, 3, 286–325.
Ortega, L. (2009) *Understanding Second Language Acquisition*, London: Hodder Education.
Scott, P. H., Mortimer, E. F. and Aguiar, O. G. (2006) 'The tension between authoritative and dialogic discourse: A fundamental characteristic of meaning making interactions in high school science lessons', *Science Education*, 90, 4, 605–31.
Swain, M. (2005) 'The output hypothesis: Theory and research', in Hinkel, E. (ed.) (2005) *Handbook of Research in Second Language Teaching and Learning*, Mahwah, NJ: Lawrence Erlbaum Associates, pp. 471–83.
Walsh, S. (2006) *Investigating Classroom Discourse*, London: Routledge.

3 Interaction patterns and scaffolding in the CLIL classroom

3.1 Introduction

So far, in this first part of the book, we have used Mortimer and Scott's (2003) framework as a broad outline for the exploration of how classroom talk is used as a tool for learning in CLIL classrooms. In Chapter 1, we presented the first level, focus, by analysing pedagogical purposes and how knowledge is represented in classroom talk, in the regulative and instructional registers. In Chapter 2, we looked at the second level, that of approach, by describing different communication systems in the CLIL classroom, and the potential of dialogic talk for providing greater opportunities for language and content learning.

In this chapter, we turn to the third level of Mortimer and Scott's framework, that of *action*. At this level, the analysis moves down to the details of classroom interaction, that is, the discourse patterns which emerge, and specific interventions that take place, which reveal teachers' and students' interactional competence in CLIL classrooms. CLIL teachers' work at this level is of great importance if active student learning is to be enhanced. According to Coyle et al. (2010: 29), two conditions are necessary in order to create this kind of learner-centred scenario:

- social interaction between learners and teachers, and
- learning that is scaffolded (that is, supported) by someone or something more 'expert' – such as the teacher, other learners or resources.

In this chapter we focus in more detail than in the two previous chapters on the teachers' and learners' specific interventions (e.g. types of questions asked by teachers, students' initiations) as they unfold moment by moment in the classroom, and how they are built into recurring patterns. It is through these specific interactions and the patterns built around them that we can see, at a microlevel, how teachers can scaffold CLIL learners in achieving content and language-learning goals.

3.2 Interaction patterns in the CLIL classroom

Studies of L2 classroom interaction (e.g. Seedhouse, 2004) have shown that there is a close relationship between different pedagogical purposes and the ways in which interaction is organised into patterns.

We would expect patterns of interaction in a classroom in which the teacher's main purpose is to transmit knowledge to be different from those in a more student-centred classroom which uses the kind of dialogic teaching we described in Chapter 2.

In many classrooms, the main pedagogical purpose is to exchange already known information and check students' knowledge, this being one of the main distinctions between 'classroom communication' and 'communication outside the classroom'. This distinction has often led to the assumption that classroom communication is not genuine, as 'real communication' normally involves the transfer of new information. Some research has claimed that the acquisition of a second language in childhood seems to be more effective in natural contexts than in the classroom. In this view, the classroom is considered an artificial context from the point of view of communication, with the result that children fail to learn the L2 as efficiently as adults (Foster-Cohen, 1999).

Leaving aside the fact that every interactional context can be said to be genuine in that it has its own purposes and business, the classroom does offer opportunities for 'genuine communication', such as exchanging opinions, making requests or asking for clarification. Geekie and Raban (1994) found patterns in the interactions of children with their teachers in the classroom which also appeared in interactions between mothers and children. Studies such as this would seem to provide support for the idea that any classroom context (including CLIL) has the potential to provide opportunities for more 'natural / genuine communication', if teachers can create the types of interaction which encourage it. This is interesting for any type of classroom, but even more in CLIL, where it is crucial for the students to be provided with different interactional opportunities, which allow them to use the foreign language in different ways and for different purposes.

We argue, then, that CLIL classrooms should aim at allowing both for exchanges in which students provide the teacher with known information as well as others that enable 'more genuine' communication. In the following sections of the chapter we analyse the interaction patterns generated by different types of teacher intervention and student participation. We begin by looking at the interaction pattern that has most commonly been described in classrooms, the IRF exchange.

3.3 The IRF pattern in CLIL classrooms

The most frequent interaction pattern in classroom contexts is the IRF pattern (Sinclair and Coulthard, 1975), or triadic dialogue (Lemke, 1990). This pattern is made up of the teacher's Initiation, the student's

Response and the teacher's Follow-up or Feedback. The third move, the follow-up, can be a type of evaluation or serve as an extension of students' answers (Scott and Mortimer, 2005; Wells, 1999).

Box 3.1: The IRF pattern

The Initiation–Response–Follow-up (IRF) pattern is a type of interaction where the teacher initiates some form of action, usually through a question, the student responds, and the teacher acknowledges the student's response (Sinclair and Coulthard, 1975).
 	
 Example:
   T: Is the whale a mammal?
   S: Yes.
   T: Good.

Some scholars have criticised the restrictive nature of the IRF pattern as it does not encourage students' initiations and repair (van Lier, 1988) and does not leave enough space for students' development of their own ideas or participation in extended talk (Nikula, 2007). Others have supported the use of this pattern as long as teachers are clear about its purposes and goals (Christie, 2002; Schleppegrell, 2004; Wells, 1993). The following exchange from a science CLIL class at the pre-primary level (kindergarten, ages 5–6) shows the teacher's control of the task through the use of the IRF pattern:

Extract 3.1	
1	T: Okay now ... Let's see. Milk. Does milk come from plants
2	or animals?
3	S1: Animals.
4	T: From animals. That's right. From the cow or the goats. So
5	cut up the pictures, cut up the pictures from the milk. Em,
6	have you cut up the picture ... ?
7	S1: Yes.
8	T: Good! Let's see, S. You've got a lot of things that come
9	from plants now. Let's find something else. Some other
10	food that comes from animals. Yes, where does the bread
11	come from: plants or animals? You remember what it's
12	made from? It's made from wheat.
13	S2: Plants.
14	T: From plants. Good boy! So stick it where it says plants.

In this extract, the teacher clearly controls the activity and is successful in eliciting the students' correct and expected responses. However, in this exchange the students are not encouraged or expected to use extended responses which would require more complex language and higher cognitive engagement. According to Coyle et al. (2010: 29), for CLIL teaching to support effective learning, it has to take into account not only the knowledge and skills base, but also cognitive engagement by the students.

Although studies such as Nikula's (2007) have found that the IRF pattern is more frequent in EFL than in CLIL contexts, it is certainly a common pattern in every kind of classroom setting, including CLIL classrooms (Dalton-Puffer, 2007). In the previous chapter, we saw how effective dialogic / interactive talk is. In this chapter, we would also like to argue that the potential of the IRF pattern in triggering CLIL students' participation (in both dialogic and authoritative talk) is not directly linked to the structure of the pattern itself but to the role of the participants in it and the purpose it is used for. Some studies highlight the importance of student-initiated IRF exchanges (Nikula, 2007; Sunderland, 2001) and the positive effects, for language use and expansion, of those tasks that trigger young learners' initiated interactions (Llinares, 2007a, 2007b). Similarly, as suggested by van Lier (1988), the third move, the feedback or follow-up, can also be taken as an opportunity for the teacher to expand on students' responses, which in turn might encourage further participation by the students. These two variants of the IRF pattern will be described and exemplified in the next two sections.

Student-initiated interactions

The dominance of teachers in classroom talk is an unavoidable outcome of their obligations to control the classroom, and therefore they almost always initiate interactions. However, in certain activities such as group work there is frequent opportunity for student-initiated interactions. The following extract (grade 7, ages 12–13) shows an exchange during a group work discussion on the topic of 'Natural disasters':

Extract 3.2
1	S2: Now floods ... floods.
2	S1: When the water, eh-.
3	S4: It's a lot of rainfall. A lot of precipitation.
4	S3: When there are lot of water in the ...

(cont.)

5	S1: When the river precipitates.
6	S2: No because it's rainfall.
7	S3: When there are a lot of ... when there are a lot of
8	precipitations and the river
9	((tosses her hands about))
10	S2: Precipitation no, because it's rainfall.
11	S4: A precipitation is when the water ...

In this exchange, S2 sets up the topic of the discussion: *floods*, her turn being followed by three other students' initiations (S1, S4 and S3). The discussion turns into a metalinguistic debate on the terms *precipitation* and *rainfall* that shows high interactional involvement by different students (a total number of four). This discussion has a dual positive effect on the students' content and language engagement: different students use the L2 to discuss both content and language issues, and there also seems to be high cognitive involvement by the students, as they are trying to solve a conceptual problem in a group-work environment.

Student-initiated patterns may also happen in 'teacher-fronted whole class situations' (Nikula, 2007: 197). In fact, in her analysis of young learners' use of communicative functions across different classroom tasks, Llinares (2007a) found that certain activities, such as show-and-tell sessions, triggered students' initiations in the L2. One example of this type of session can be seen in the following exchange (kindergarten, ages 5–6) in an arts and crafts session:

Extract 3.3	
1	S1: Eh ... this ... this ... this Saturday I was in Madrid. I go ...
2	I was to Madrid. On Saturday I went to the Thyssen.
3	T: Oh! Good.
4	S1: And I saw the portrait of Henry the Eighth.
5	T: Uh! That famous one. Yes.
6	S1: Yes. And it's like that ((indicating very small)).
7	T: Yes A? We expect portraits, don't we? To always be
8	very big.
9	SS: ((several)) Yes.

In this interactive / dialogic extract, the student takes the role of the initiator and is also in charge of providing feedback. Again, the students' linking of the subject content to their own experiences (horizontal knowledge) allows for interaction patterns that are rarely found in classroom contexts but are key for students' participation and involvement.

Expanding feedback

In IRF exchanges, the feedback or follow-up move has an important role in encouraging students' participation and extended production. If the objective of the teacher is to acknowledge the students' response by providing a positive or negative evaluation, the students' opportunities for interactional participation are limited (Nikula, 2007; van Lier, 1988). However, there seems to be space for the teacher's evaluation to be followed not necessarily by another teacher initiation. This evaluation could also be followed by students' reactions, as shown in the following extract from a CLIL geography class (grade 6, ages 11–12), where the teacher's evaluative feedback in line 6 is followed by a turn initiated by the student, which is, in fact, the longest student turn in the extract.

Extract 3.4
1 T: This is the harbour yes, okay, and in front of the harbour
2   what can you see? This yellow cabs
3 S1: Taxis.
4 T: It's not New York huhu this yellow cabs
5 S2: Taxis.
6 T: It's a taxis yes okay good.
7 S2: What do they drive like, what are the drivers like, are
8   they crazy?
9 T: Yes, yes.

An alternative pattern of interaction occurs when, instead of making an evaluation of a student's response, the teacher gives feedback to the student in order to prompt further elaboration of a point of view and thereby to sustain the interaction (Mortimer and Scott, 2003). With this type of elaborative or expanding feedback, the student is supported in elaborating and making the ideas explicit. Even sequences that start with questions for known information can develop into what Nassaji and Wells (2000: 400–401) call 'more equal dialogue' if the teacher requests justifications or counter-arguments, instead of evaluating the students' response. This triggers students' elaboration, as in the following example from a CLIL history class (grade 7, ages 12–13).

Extract 3.5
1   T: ((asking about where the first civilisations appeared))
2   OK, D?
3   S1: That ... eh ... Egypt, along the Nile.
4   T: OK. Yes. Along the Nile ... Why along rivers? Think
5   about that. OK? So, develop that idea.
6   S2: Eh ... that they placed in the banks of the river because
7   they were the only fertile lands.

In this example, the elaboration is provided by a different student (S2) from the one participating in the first response.

One way of prompting the students' further elaboration is by asking **metacognitive** questions, defined by Dalton-Puffer (2007: 98) as those questions that 'engage the learner in an extended dialogue in which s/he has to explain or argue a particular position'. This is exemplified in Extract 3.6 (grade 10, 15–16):

Extract 3.6
1   T: So now we are successful because there is the European
2   Union. Do you think the European Union is positive ... ?
3   S1: Yes.
4   T: Why?
5   S1: Because the European Union is very good for everything.
6   For example, now for travelling we have to do less things
7   and ... about ... mmm ... buying products because it is
8   much better and the money,
9   you have the same coin and is very easy ...

The student's short response to the teacher's yes/no question is followed by the teacher's metacognitive question *Why?*, which triggers an elaborated response by the student, in which he uses the language needed for argumentation (see Chapter 4 on history genres), employing exemplification (*For example*) and giving reasons that support his argumentation (*because it is much better and the money, you have the same coin and is very easy ...*).

In her analysis of teacher feedback in CLIL and EFL pre- and primary bilingual classrooms, Llinares (2005) divided feedback into two main types: pedagogic and interactional. As expected, pedagogic feedback was the most frequent in classroom contexts and consisted of follow-up or feedback turns with the purpose of correcting or evaluating the children's performance. In the CLIL classes studied, this type of feedback mainly focused on content and, occasionally, on language form. Interactional feedback refers to that provided by the teacher with no evaluative or corrective purpose. These two types of feedback (pedagogic and interactional) match, respectively, Cullen's (2002) distinction between evaluative and discursive follow-up moves. Cullen (2002: 122) argues that discursive feedback plays a fundamental role in giving support for learning, with the teacher 'providing a rich source of message-oriented target language input as s/he reformulates and elaborates on the students' contributions and derives further initiating moves from them.' This is very important for CLIL as it involves students' cognitive, content and language engagement. Here we focus on interactional or discursive feedback. The role of pedagogic or evaluative feedback in CLIL will be addressed in Chapter 6.

Interactional feedback has been shown to be successful in triggering students' follow-up / feedback moves (Llinares, 2005). This is exemplified in Extract 3.7. from a section of a preschool show-and-tell session (kindergarten, ages 5–6):

Extract 3.7
1	T: What's the matter with the saw?
2	S1: because the battery's finished
3	T: Oh, you need to get new batteries
4	S1: I can take this one.

In this example, the teacher's reformulation of the student's problem leaves the problem unsolved and encourages the student to think of a possible solution, which he then formulates in the foreign language.

Both interactional feedback at a conversational level and Mortimer and Scott's notion of elaborative feedback in academic interactions at higher levels of schooling (two sides of the same coin) should be practised in any classroom context as they enhance students' participation. In the CLIL class, they become particularly useful as they both trigger further elaboration by the students and, respectively, help develop their **Basic Interpersonal Communication Skills (BICS)** and their **Cognitive Academic Language Proficiency (CALP)** (Cummins, 1979). We will return to these concepts in Chapter 7.

3.4 Questions in the CLIL classroom

Asking questions is the function of language through which we investigate reality and access knowledge. According to Halliday and Matthiessen

(2004), 'demanding information' is one of the four key speech roles in language. This heuristic function (the use of language to enquire about the world) even appears in the protolanguage of the child; this happens at about 16 months of age (Halliday, 1975). However, as Dalton-Puffer (2007) highlights, learning in educational contexts does not necessarily depend on the satisfaction of learners' needs or solutions to their problems. Instead, the students are usually confronted with scientific or social problems which have already been solved before, and it is the role of the teacher to check that knowledge, often through the formulation of questions. This leads us to the well-known typology of classroom questions introduced by Mehan (1979), who distinguished between display and referential questions.

Display and referential questions

Display questions are those whose answer is known by the questioner, while *referential questions* seek information unknown to the teacher. Research in different types of language-learning contexts shows that, as can be expected, display questions are more frequent than referential questions, and the quantity and quality of students' responses are directly related to the type of question asked by the teacher (Long and Sato, 1983; Romero and Llinares, 2001). Referential questions tend to trigger more complex and longer answers from the students, since they are 'real' questions, formulated to demand unknown information. It has then been suggested that classrooms would be more effective environments if more referential questions were asked (Brock, 1986; Long and Sato, 1983).

However, display questions in the classroom do have, in fact, a real purpose, and are genuine questions in the educational context. As Dalton-Puffer argues, when asking display questions the teacher is interested in obtaining new information not on the subject matter but on what and how much the students know. 'Additionally, display questions also aim at putting a topic or a knowledge item centre stage, thus making it available for collective access and reference' (2007: 95). The use of display questions is, then, part of the 'naturalness' of any learning context (including CLIL), as in most cases classroom interaction needs to revolve around content that the teacher (as an expert) already knows.

In spite of the fact that, generally speaking, referential questions tend to trigger longer and more complex responses, this is not always the case. Some referential questions trigger short and simple responses, even when the questions are open, while display questions, depending on how they are formulated, may trigger / produce long and complex answers. This can be seen in Extracts 3.8 (kindergarten, ages 5–6) and 3.9 (grade 10, ages 15–16), which provide examples of CLIL teachers' use of referential and display questions, respectively:

Extract 3.8 Referential question
1   T: What colour are you going to colour that fish?
2   S: Pink.

Extract 3.9 Display question
1   T: Ok, so can you explain why the Second World War
2   was even worse than the first one? L, yes?
3   S: Because they were ... the army was still more powerful
4   and there were more contrasting points and it was even
5   worse.
6   The ... Germany just want the revenge because they were
7   kind of angry because they had lost the world before
8   because they ... they weren't too supported as the other
9   countries.

As these extracts show, there are other distinctions, apart from that between display and referential questions, which may determine whether the students produce long and complex responses and, therefore, whether they are engaged cognitively and communicatively in the task. In fact, as Schleppegrell (2004: 15) argues, 'The level of cognitive demand of a particular question depends on what the teacher's goals are, what the students have already learned, and the point in the lesson at which the question is asked.'

These three aspects (goals, previous knowledge and classroom task or activity), related to the specific context in which learning takes place, will be developed in the next section.

Questions: Goals, previous knowledge and class activities

According to Dalton-Puffer (2007: 94), one of the most important aims when studying teachers' questions is to identify their function or goal in order to determine what type of contribution they make to the process of students learning the subject content. In her analysis of CLIL classes in Austria, Dalton-Puffer (2007: 98) identifies five categories of questions:

- questions for facts (asking for objective happenings)
- questions for explanation (asking for how something happened)
- questions for reasons (why something happened)
- questions for opinion
- metacognitive questions (which engage the learner in extended dialogues).

This author noted that there were many factual questions in the CLIL classrooms she investigated, which usually made the interaction cognitively undemanding for the students (Dalton-Puffer, 2007: 126). Schleppegrell (2004) argues that the level of the cognitive demand is sometimes found in the form of elicitation, but other times it is also negotiated in the interactive task or activity. The following extracts show the students' responses to a question for opinion in two different classroom activities. The first example (Extract 3.10) comes from a history class on World War I (grade 10, ages 15–16) and the second extract (Extract 3.11) is from a geography class on natural disasters (grade 7, ages 12–13). These are two contrasting examples of the students' degree of success in their responses to a teacher's question for opinion:

Extract 3.10

1	T:	We today, have learned lessons from this war, can you
2		think of any situations that are happening now, maybe we
3		want to act in a certain way, but if we look at the war, if we
4		look at what happened, maybe we understand we should do
5		it in a different way? You know what I'm saying?
6	S1:	Yes.
7	T:	What are some conflicts or what are some issues that you
8		think we might be able to learn from today?
9	SS:	((no response))
10	T:	Ok, let's talk about the crisis, right? People are saying
11		there is a crisis, right? So ... for example, we know that
12		there were economic problems, economic issues with
13		Germany that caused it to act in the way it did in the war,
14		right? So ... what's something that we can learn as Spain,
15		or something that another European country could learn,
16		to try and not make the same mistake again? Can you
17		guys think of anything?

(cont.)

18	SS: ((no response))
19	T: What was it that happened? What was the economic
20	situation that caused either the First World War or the
21	Second World War?
22	S2: They were fighting for the ... the best ... the best
23	economy.

In Extract 3.10 the students had worked in groups on a number of questions on World War I previous to a whole-class discussion run by the teacher. The question in the prompt that was being discussed was 'Why did WWI come to an end?', which is a question asking for a reason in Dalton-Puffer's typology. However, the teacher moves into a question for opinion, *can you think of any situations ... ?*, embedded in a long turn, which ends in the teacher's formulation of a comprehension check (*You know what I'm saying?*). The students do not seem to understand the teacher's goal and one student surprisingly responds to the comprehension check with *yes* but does not answer the main question posed by the teacher. The teacher tries again in his next turn with a simplified formulation of the same question but the students keep silent. This might show that the lack of response by the students is not only related to the complexity of the question asked by the teacher but also, possibly, to the fact that this idea brought up by him was not activated before in the students' group discussions. Therefore, in this case the students' potential for developing 'language through learning' (Coyle, 2007) has not been enhanced. It is only when the teacher asks a factual question related to the content the students had activated in the previous group discussion (*What was it that happened? ...*), that the students seem able to respond (lines 19–23). The second example is in Extract 3.11:

	Extract 3.11
1	T: And what do you think? S?
2	S1: That is false because some disasters that ... like the
3	earthquakes eh ... occur because of the plac- tectonic
4	plates.
5	T: Mmm.
6	S1: And this is not our fault.

This extract shows a different situation regarding the students' response to a question for opinion. Again, previous to a whole-class discussion, the students had worked in groups, in this case on some statements provided by the teacher, and had to decide whether they thought they were true or false and explain why. As in Extract 3.10, the teacher asks a question for opinion but here the student responds with a complex answer that includes subordination (*because some disasters that ... like the earthquakes eh ... occur*). This subordinate clause includes a complex nominal group (*some disasters that ... like the earthquakes*) and a prepositional phrase to express cause (*because of the plac tectonic plates*). The complexity of the student's response to the teacher's question for opinion in this extract (compared to Extract 3.10) might be the result of the focus of the previous group-work task, in which the students were explicitly asked to give a justified opinion on a number of statements.

In sum, CLIL students' cognitive and communicative engagement does not seem to depend on the type of question alone, but also on the students' previous learning and experience with the topic and the type of activity designed by the teacher. These factors need to be taken into account by CLIL teachers when planning their lessons and in their own teaching practice. The type of activity also plays an important role in students' formulation of their own questions, as the next section illustrates.

Students' questions

Students are aware that their role in the classroom is that of a non-expert who is expected to follow the teacher's instructions and is rarely expected to initiate interactions. As Dalton-Puffer (2007) indicates, most of the students' questions in the classroom are 'real' referential questions and, the majority (around 40%) tend to happen within the regulative register, that is, that part of the lesson which is devoted to the organisation of the pedagogic activity (see Chapter 1), as exemplified in Extract 3.12 (grade 7, ages 12–13):

Extract 3.12
1   T: ... OK. So, now we're going to work in groups. You have
2   to ...
3   S1: How many people?
4   T: Four ... people in each group. Right?

In Dalton-Puffer's data, students rarely ask questions to obtain specific information on the content, let alone obtain explanations or arguments.

However, certain activities such as project work seem to trigger students' real engagement in interaction and their formulation of different types of questions, also within the instructional register, as can be seen in the examples below, from the same geography class (grade 9,

ages 14–15). These extracts show the students' performance in the formulation of different types of questions during a class discussion of
their own projects:

Extract 3.13
1 S1: One question. You said that you have to come to the ...
2   green area or to the skate park?
3 S2: You have to come to the skateboarding park. It's obvious!

Extract 3.14
1 S1: Yes, but you want that the people eh ... the foreign people
2   came to C to see our vegetation? In C vegetation!?
3 S2: And you like to be twenty metres square ... you like to ... to
4   build a ... skate park in twenty metres eh ... of square that is ...
5   that in this green area keep all the animals and vegetation.

Extract 3.15
1 S1: eh ... eh I think I think is a very expensive project because
2   L said is five thousand euros. I think is really really
3   expensive to ... do a skateboarding park of this price.
4 S2: Eh ... what do you mean with that? That is very expensive?

The questions asked by the students in Extracts 3.13, 3.14 and 3.15 are
not typically found in classroom contexts and, if they are, they usually
appear in teachers' turns. In Extract 3.13, S1 is making a clarification
request appear (*You said that you have to come to the ... green area or
to the skate park?*), classified by Long and Sato (1983) within the group
of echoic questions, characteristic of the language used in foreigner talk
(Ellis, 1985). In Extract 3.14 the student is using a rhetorical question,
which helps her reinforce her point of view (*you want that the people
eh ... the foreign people came to C to see our vegetation? In C vegetation!?*). Finally, Extract 3.15 shows an example of a metacognitive
question (*What do you mean with that?*), which requires S1 to develop
his point of view more.

These examples show that some activities like project work provide
students with more opportunities to play an active role in the classroom.
In this section, we have seen that this has an effect on the variety of

questions used, some of which are not usually asked by students in the classroom. This type of activity, then, provides opportunities for 'language *through* learning', where students spontaneously use unplanned language to articulate their meanings and advance their thinking process while acquiring new knowledge (Coyle et al., 2010). Although language through learning can be challenging for students, as they sometimes lack the necessary linguistic resources, project work seems to provide opportunities for CLIL students' use of this type of language.

3.5 Repair in the CLIL classroom

Conversational repair refers to the ways in which speakers deal with communication breakdown or miscommunication. In a CLIL classroom, the type of repair used by the teacher is usually expected to have a pedagogic aim, to solve some possible difficulty that the students might have in their language or content performance. In this sense, compared to informal conversation, teachers' repairs can be considered 'not real', as the teacher usually knows, and is offering or triggering 'the answer'. On the other hand, teachers' repairs are also for the benefit of the other students – a purpose which is normally absent from informal conversation but genuine and legitimate in the classroom. As we will see in Chapter 6, teachers' pedagogic or evaluative repair or feedback has an important role in improving students' language and content learning in CLIL.

In contrast to teacher repair, student-initiated repairs in CLIL reflect the type of repair that happens in everyday conversations. In Extract 3.16 (which we previously looked at in Chapter 1, Extract 1.11), S3 uses a clarification request in line 5, *Greek war?*, which pushes S1 to look for the corresponding English term for the word *megalithic*. This is, once again, a clear example of student cognitive involvement in the task:

Extract 3.16
1   S1: Okay this is er Stonehenge that is in the United Kingdom er
2   S2: Loud voice please.
3   S1: It is a crom- a megalithic monument that is a Greek word
4   that in English er
5   S3: Greek war?
6   S1: Yes in Greek.
7   S3: Yes, yes.
(cont.)

8	S1: Yes the er the word er megalithic
9	S3: Ah yes, yes I understand that this was a war a war a fight
10	S1: Ah no no word word
11	S1: The translation in English of 'megalithic monument' will
12	be 'a big stone'.
13	S2: What?
14	S1: ((emphasising each word)) The translation of megalithic
15	monument in English will be big stone and the stones of
16	the (stone) circle that I (think about) weigh 25 eh tone ...
17	S3: Tons.
18	S1: Tons yes. Er this monument er they build about eh five
19	S3: Thousand.
20	S1: Yes five thousand years ago and this is a cromlech but
21	there are other types of megalithic monument that are
22	menhirs and dolmens
23	S3: Okay.

It is noticeable, then, how the students in this extract try to keep the communication channels open by repairing a mishearing of *Greek word* as *Greek war*. Discussions of repair in classroom discourse often confuse this term with the 'normal' activity (for classrooms) of providing corrective feedback on student utterances (Hall, 2007). However, in this example we see a case of genuine repair, as two students work together to troubleshoot a misunderstanding and keep the activity on track.

These examples show that repair is more than 'negotiation of meaning' with the aim of providing feedback. It offers opportunities for learning in a broader sense, in that it allows the building of mutual understanding by keeping the channels of communication open.

3.6 The role of interactional scaffolding in CLIL classrooms

Gibbons (2002: 10) defines scaffolding as 'the temporary assistance by which a teacher helps a learner know how to do something, so that the learner will later be able to complete a similar task alone'. In any classroom situation, teachers need to provide access to the content as well as the language features necessary to express that content. In CLIL contexts, teachers' scaffolding is even more necessary as students need to process and express complex ideas in a foreign language. Following Llinares and Whittaker (2009), in this book we use the term scaffolding in two ways. The present chapter focuses on scaffolding as the type of assistance provided in classroom interaction, and seeks to outline types of scaffolding that can be used to cognitively engage students at different parts of the lesson. Chapter 8 will deal with **task scaffolding** which allows for the appropriate sequencing of content and language in relation to genres and registers. These two approaches to scaffolding could be mapped onto the distinction between 'contingent or interactional' and 'designed in' scaffolding (Gibbons, 2002; Hammond and Gibbons, 2005; Sharpe, 2006). This section focuses on the former, the type of scaffolding that becomes spontaneously necessary at a specific point in classroom interaction, across different types of activities and subjects, as well as on samples of **peer scaffolding.**

Gibbons (2006) identifies a number of stages in which learning and teaching activities take place:

- review and orientation
- setting up of new task
- carrying out a task
- reflection on task
- written work

In this section we will illustrate the role of teacher scaffolding in the CLIL classroom in the first four of these stages together with two other stages that we propose, which are characteristic of teacher-fronted interactions and the most pervasive types in CLIL classes, mainly at secondary level:

- topic introduction
- end-of-topic discussion

We will first address the role of scaffolding in those stages characteristic of teacher-fronted sessions and then move on to learner-centred, task-based sessions.

Review and orientation stage

New learning is necessarily based on learners' previous experience. The following example from a biology lesson (grade 10, ages 15–16) shows the teacher's discourse aimed at building a bridge between the students' prior experience with the topic in previous classes and the learning aims of the next task.

Extract 3.17
1   T: What are we talking about lately?
2   S: Alleles.
(cont.)

3	T: Sorry?
4	S: Alleles.
5	T: Alleles yeah we talked about alleles yesterday only
6	yesterday. Have you have you gone through the information
7	I gave you yesterday about alleles? Can anybody tell me
8	what an allele is? Or alleles are? What do you think alleles
9	are, F? I didn't clean the board for you so we've got on the
10	board- it's yesterday's information okay?
11	S: The allele ... Different versions of the same gene
12	T: Different ... ?
13	S: Versions.
14	T: Versions right of the same gene okay so those are alleles.

In this extract, the teacher uses a clarification request (*Sorry?*) to help the students focus on the key word *allele*. Once she has made sure that the students have activated the topic under study, she asks a referential question about their homework (lines 6–7) followed by a much more specific display question searching for a definition (lines 7–8). She gives some clues to the students, referring them to the information on the blackboard and reminding them of the fact that they had worked on that same content the day before. This is, therefore, a clear example of an orientation stage based on the activation of the students' previous knowledge, which is fundamental for their subsequent comprehension and participation in this classroom session. In fact, in spite of one student providing the right definition, the teacher encourages the students to co-construct with her the definition of *allele* (lines 12–14), making sure that the concept is clear to everyone. The building of shared context (Edwards and Mercer, 1987) needs to be carefully constructed in CLIL settings where classroom interactional competence (Walsh, 2011) needs to be enhanced; this is especially true when teachers and learners are non-native speakers.

Topic introduction and end of topic discussion

Both in traditional content classes as well as in CLIL classes the introduction of a topic is usually teacher-fronted and based on the teacher's delivery or lecturing of the content, occasionally interrupted by comprehension checks (*ok?*, *do you understand?* etc. ...). However, in the following extract from the topic introduction stage in a biology lesson (grade 10, ages 15–16) the teacher scaffolds the students in both the conceptual and the linguistic aspects of the topic.

	Extract 3.18
1	T: So listen, you all have seen a lot of mutants around. Do you
2	know anyone who is ... for instance albino?
3	S: Yes.
4	T: Or have they ever seen an albino? What is that? What is to
5	be albino?
6	S: Well, they can be ( ) skin colour, and they can't be
7	exposed too much to sun.
8	T: What is their skin colour like?
9	S: Very white.
10	T: Yes, why is it so white?
11	S: Because they haven't got, in the nucleus, they haven't
12	got ... a lot of thing ...
13	T: What makes our skin, what makes our skin be ...
14	S: ( )
15	T: Yeah, brown, so white as your T-shirt, because there are
16	pigments. Actually there is one pigment in our skin, do you
17	know the name? You do
18	S: So ...
19	T: You do, the name? Me ... la ...
20	S: Melanine.

In this biology lesson about genetic codes, the teacher uses an example that bridges the students' spontaneous knowledge with new academic knowledge on the topic (see Chapter 1 on horizontal and vertical knowledge). She also scaffolds the linguistic demand by asking an easy, closed, referential question related to the students' personal experience: *Do you know anyone who is ... for instance albino?* In her next turn (line 4), the teacher uses a pronoun (*that*) in a question asking for a definition, which she next substitutes for the content word (*albino*), again. While pronouns are used naturally to avoid repetition, CLIL teachers need to make sure that the key content word is activated.

Gradually, the teacher leads the students into the academic content, first asking a factual question (*what is their skin colour like?*) and then moving to a question for reason: *why is it so white?* (line 10), which also requires a more complex response from the students. In addition, instead of providing the terms for the key concepts herself, the teacher asks the students to complete a word (*You do, the name? Me ... la ...*) or to complete a sentence with a keyword (*What makes our skin, what makes our skin be ...*).

The next extract (grade 8, ages 13–14), this time from an end-of-topic discussion (included in Llinares and Whittaker, 2009), shows some similar patterns:

Extract 3.19

1	T: OK. Good. And what about the obligations of the
2	peasants? What did they have to do, A?
3	S: They have to work the lands of the, of the lords, but they
4	can't leave.
5	They could go to another, eh, to the land of another, of
6	another lord if they want.
7	T: OK. And B, the same. What about their rights? What were
8	the rights of the peasants?
9	S: Eh, the, the, the free peasants, eh, they were free. They could
10	do-. They work, attending the lords and things like that. And
11	the serfs were similar to slaves. They, they have few rights.
12	T: And, why, em, eh, was there a rebirth of cities?
13	S: In the Late Middle Ages.
14	T: In the Late Middle Ages. Do you remember why?

Here, the teacher provides a reformulation of an abstract noun (*obligations*) into a clause with a modal verb which is taken up by the student in her response. As in Extract 3.18, the teacher reformulates a question including a referring possessive adjective (*What about their rights*) with another one, where the antecedent is provided (*What were the rights of the peasants?*). The antecedent is again taken up by the student at the beginning of his response (in a fronted position): *Eh, the, the, the free peasants ...* The teacher again scaffolds the cognitive and linguistic demand of the questions by asking a factual question followed by questions for reason.

These two examples show the potential of teacher-fronted sessions in developing students' language and content engagement by using interactional modification strategies (reformulations), by co-constructing the knowledge with the students and by formulating a sequenced variety of questions.

Setting up a new task

In this stage, the teacher's role is that of facilitating the understanding of the task. This is illustrated in Extract 3.20 (grade 7, ages 12–13), where the teacher works in the regulative register to make sure the task is organised and the students know what to do, and in Extract 3.21

(grade 7, ages 12–13), where the teacher works in the instructional register, to introduce key vocabulary necessary for the completion of the task (see Chapter 1 on instructional and regulative registers):

	Extract 3.20
1	T: Four ... people in each group. Right? We're going to work,
2	um, in groups, eh, with these, small sentences. Right?
3	These sentences you have to, eh, see in groups, if they are
4	true, or if they are false. Right? You have to talk
5	and you have to explain why, they are false or why they are
6	true. Right?
7	S: We can do it now?
8	T: Yes. Of course. Then, afterwards, we will have to explain
9	for the whole group. Right? So first we're going to work in
10	small groups. So, you divide, ok? ((teacher gives out some
11	handouts.))

In Extract 3.20, the teacher uses a long turn with four instances of the comprehension check *Right?* and she constantly uses 'message abundancy' (Gibbons, 2006), reformulating her message to make sure that the students follow her instruction. For example, she changes the position of the phrase *in groups* in the sentence, *We're going to work, um, in groups, eh, with these, small sentences,* to the end of the following sentence (*These sentences you have to, eh, see in groups*), where it will have more prominence for the students.

In Extract 3.21 the teacher makes sure the key vocabulary is understood before the students start working on the task.

	Extract 3.21
1	T: Listen listen listen: does everybody understand the words
2	helpful?
3	SS: Yes.
4	T: Harmful?
5	SS: Yes.
6	T: Can anybody tell me what to be harmful means?
7	S: That damage
8	T: It damages yeah produces damage. Ok? How do you say
9	harmful in Spanish?
10	SS: *Dañinas* (Sp. harmful).

(cont.)

11	T:	*Dañinas o perjudiciales* (Sp. harmful). How about helpful.
12		Can anybody tell me what helpful means?
13	S:	That helps the body to
14	T:	Yes. It is something good, good ok? So how d'you say
15		helpful in Spanish?
16	S:	*Bueno* ((Sp. good)).

Interestingly enough, the students provide definitions of *helpful* and *harmful* in English but the teacher asks them for the translation of those words into the students' L1 (Spanish) as she considers this necessary for them to perform the task properly. This is a good example of the effective use of the L1 to reinforce the meaning while maintaining the focus of the interaction on the L2.

Carrying out a task

When students work in groups the teacher has an important mediating role. There are certain school subjects that may require more intervention by the teacher during task performance. This can be seen in the Extract 3.22 from a technology class (grade 7, ages 12–13), where task performance involves activities that the students are just learning to carry out:

	Extract 3.22
1	T: Where's the screwdriver? Not very tight, not very tight. Try
2	to find, try to find longer screws, longer screws, all right?
3	S: *¿Hay que pintarlo?* (Sp. Do we have to paint it?)
4	T: You have to put something ... I don't know, use your
5	imagination.

The language used by the teacher in this extract has interesting features. In his first turn, the teacher repeats the keywords and phrases for the learner to complete the task properly, mainly focusing on descriptive adjectives, using verbless clauses (*Not very tight, not very tight*) or simple directives consisting of a verb in the imperative followed by a noun phrase (*try to find longer screws*). The role of the teacher's instruction is not so important in the second turn, where he is trying to get them to work on their own and finish their task in time, and this is reflected in his language in that, in contrast to the previous turn, he does not use strategies such as repetition or comprehension checks (*all right?*).

Reflection on the task

Reflecting on a task is one of the stages that require more mediation by the teacher (Gibbons, 2006). We see this in Extract 3.23 (grade 6, ages 11–12), where a physics teacher tries to make the students compare the results of an experiment done in this class with another one carried out in a previous class. This requires a great cognitive effort by the students, regarding both content and language:

Extract 3.23

1	T: Okay A, can you tell me now what's what the difference is
2	to the experiment we did last lesson because you said we
3	did that already!
4	S1: The holes were ... at the bottom ... round the
5	T: Yes.
6	S1: *Flasche?* (Ger. bottle)
7	T: Bottle ((SS laughing)) the holes were at the bottom of the
8	bottle and around the bottle and what did the experiment
9	show?
10	S1: ... Mhm
11	T: What did it show about water pressure?
12	S1: ( )
13	T: That water pressures ... good that water pressures spreads
14	in equal
15	S: Distances.
16	T: Into all direction in equal distances okay! ... and now ...
17	what did the experiment now show? L! ... A! that water
18	pressure
19	S1: ( )
20	T: That water pressure increases ... with the ... what does "to
21	increase" mean? ... shhhh ...
22	S: ((whispering)) D is unemployment!
23	T: D is unemployed, yes! ((SS laugh))
24	:::
25	T: Yeah water pressures increases with the
26	S: Water level.
27	T: With the water level, with the depths of the water ... the
28	further you come down, the bigger the pressure. ... okay?
29	S: *Ich weiß es ...* ( ) (Ger. I know it ...)
30	T: On this place quite a role were ... role? Part ... did anybody
31	of you oh try to dive already?
	(cont.)

Interaction patterns and scaffolding in the CLIL classroom

32	S:	Try to die?
33	T:	Dive!
34	S:	*Wie* to die? (Ger. How to die?)
35	T:	Diving!
36	S1:	(?) Diving!
37	S:	*Also tauchen* (Ger. so diving)

Aware of the difficulty of comparing two experiments carried out at different times, and in a foreign language, the teacher scaffolds the students' response to her question, by first activating the students' knowledge of the results of the first experiment. She reformulates the questions to help the students focus. The question in lines 8 and 9, for example, *What did the experiment show?*, is too general and generates no response by the students. The teacher then narrows the question by referring to a specific aspect of the experiment (*about water pressure*). She also asks questions for completion (*that water pressure spreads in equal ... ?* or *water pressure increases with the ... ?*), in order to facilitate the students' response with one word. She even accepts the students' contributions, even if they do not happen to be very appropriate (*into all direction in equal distances okay; with the water level with the depths of the water*). At one point, the teacher recognises the students' difficulty in concentrating on the lesson: when they joke about one of the students being unemployed, she takes the topic to the personal non-academic experience of the learners (*did anybody of you oh try to dive already?*). By doing this, the teacher 'builds bridges' not only between the students' experience with the topic at hand and the more academic conceptualisation of it, as argued by Gibbons (2006: 198–9), but also with their own experience outside the classroom (see Figure 3.1).

The students, then, are participating in three different but interrelated registers which scaffold them into the content of the unit and, at the same time, should lead them to work on L2 language skills in different ways. The knowledge moves in a continuum from everyday knowledge outside the classroom (horizontal), via knowledge mediated through the classroom experiment to the vertical or theoretical knowledge of the subject (see Chapter 1 on vertical and horizontal knowledge). The extract also shows instances of negotiation of meaning, the type of modification that takes place during interaction and is claimed to have positive effects on comprehension skills (Long, 1996). One student, for example, uses a confirmation check in English (*try to die?*) reinforced by one in German: *also tauchen* (*so diving*) to make sure he's understood.

99

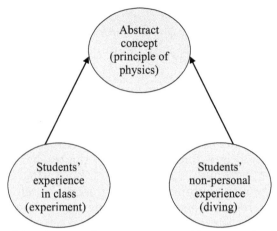

Figure 3.1   Bridging CLIL students' experience with new academic knowledge

Peer scaffolding

Group work activities allow for students' co-construction of knowledge. Extract 3.24 (grade 7, ages 12–13), from a history class following a classroom trip to a theme park built around pre-history, shows the collaborative co-construction of the experience that the children had in the school trip:

Extract 3.24
1   T: All right have you got any questions to ask about the trip?
2   About the pictures?
3   S2: How did you make fire?
4   S1: Eh the teacher put something like ah was eh similar to
5   the – it was called esparto. I don't know how to tell in
6   English. And they put something in inside the esparto
7   and then they blow – no first they made eh some –
8   (S): Sparks.
9   S1: Eh eh eh ((sudden rise at end))
10 (S): Sparks.
11 (S): Sparks.
12 S1: No how do you say *chispas* (Sp. sparks)?
13 SS: Sparks.
14 S1: Sparks start with two stones silex and another stone and
15   they put it into the esparto so then they blow there and the
16   fire appear.

At line 4, S1 can't think of the word for *esparto* in English and tries to explain it in her own words (*something like ... , was similar to the ...*). Interestingly, although studies have shown that CLIL students do not seem to have problems with the mastery of the specific words related to the content under study (Llinares and Whittaker, 2009), this particular student can't remember two keywords for the explanation that she is trying to provide. However, in the student's second unsuccessful attempt to find the right word in English, the other students help her and provide the English term for the Spanish word *chispas* (sparks). This peer scaffolding is not noticed by S1, who explicitly asks, *no how do you say chispas?*

The participation of students in different types of activities provides them with different ways of both using the language and approaching the content. Group work is one of the ways of giving students the opportunity of developing the language and participating in the classroom by taking on roles other than those of respondents to the teacher's questions. In group work, students are not mere 'animators' (Goffman, 1981) of the knowledge they are expected to attain, but they can also become 'authors' of the words being used and 'principals' or generators of the ideas being talked about. Thus, by adopting different roles in classroom interaction, CLIL students will have the opportunity of developing a richer repertoire of language resources in the L2.

3.7 Conclusion

This chapter has analysed different patterns of interaction and their potential for communication and cognitive engagement in CLIL classrooms. We have shown that the IRF pattern has the potential to engage the students cognitively and communicatively, as long as teachers use a wide variety of question types and the role of the participants in the exchange is flexible enough to allow for expanding feedback moves. The examples in the corpus show that this type of feedback move can encourage students to elaborate on their responses, and to produce their own initiating moves in both regulative and instructional registers.

In Chapter 2 we saw the importance of planning for communication systems and interaction formats. In this chapter, at the 'more micro' level of action, we have also shown the importance for CLIL teachers to identify stages in units and lessons and think of different types of scaffolding strategies appropriate for these different stages. We have shown that, in spite of the fact that Coyle's (2007) 'language through learning' is not easily used by the students as they sometimes lack the linguistic resources, certain activities such as project work are more likely to trigger this type of language. Wherever students have difficulties in accessing the language they need to carry out these types of activities, teacher and peer scaffolding can help them find and use these linguistic resources in the L2.

Questions and tasks for reflection and discussion

1. Discuss the advantages and disadvantages of the IRF pattern in the CLIL class in the light of the information presented in this chapter.
2. What kind of activities can you think of that would trigger students' initiations in interactional exchanges? Try to think of different content subjects and their possibilities.
3. Consider the following questions. Identify the type, then decide which ones involve higher cognitive and / or communicative involvement and give reasons why.
    (a) How are places destroyed by natural disasters?
    (b) Do you think there were economic reasons?
    (c) What do you like most about our ancient civilisations, Egypt and Mesopotamia? And why?
    (d) What is the name of this tool here?
4. Using what you read in Section 3.6 of this chapter, identify the stage in the following extract from a CLIL history class. Reflect on the interaction patterns, questions, repair and scaffolding strategies used.

Extract 3.25
1   T: Ah, do you remember, the Middle Ages were, eh, divided
2   into some, well, into some periods. Do you remember the
3   periods of the Middle Ages? ... Yes?
4   S1: Early Middle Ages. High Middle Ages and Late Middle Ages.
5   T: And, why, em, eh, was there a rebirth of cities?
6   S2: In the Late Middle Ages.
7   T: In the Late Middle Ages. Do you remember why?
8   S2: Eh, yes because there was a lot of people in the
9   countryside working and they have no place for everybody
10   so they went to the cities and they went there.
11   T: OK. Very good. So that is the, em, the reason of the rebirth
12   of cities. What about urban life in the Middle Ages and,
13   you present urban life? It is very, different.

References

Brock, C. A. (1986) 'The effects of referential questions on ESL classroom discourse', *TESOL Quarterly*, 20, 13, 47–59.

Christie, F. (2002) *Classroom Discourse Analysis: A Functional Perspective*. London: Continuum.

Coyle, D. (2007) 'Content and language integrated learning: Towards a connected research agenda for CLIL pedagogies', *International Journal of Bilingual Education and Bilingualism*, 10, 5, 543–62.

Coyle, D., Hood, P. and Marsh, D. (2010) *CLIL: Content and Language Integrated Learning*, Cambridge: Cambridge University Press.

Cullen, R. (2002) 'Supportive teacher talk: The importance of the F-move', *ELT Journal*, 56, 2, 117–27.

Cummins, J. (1979) 'Cognitive / academic / language proficiency, linguistic interdependence, the optimum age question and some other matters', *Working Papers on Bilingualism*, 19, 121–9.

Dalton-Puffer, C. (2007) *Discourse in Content and Language Integrated Learning (CLIL) Classrooms*, Amsterdam and Philadelphia: John Benjamins.

Edwards, D. (1987) and Mercer, N. (eds.) *Common Knowledge: The Development of Understanding in the Classroom*, London: Methuen.

Ellis, R. (1985) *Understanding Second Language Acquisition*, Oxford: Oxford University Press.

Foster-Cohen, S. H. (1999) *An Introduction to Child Language Development*, London: Longman.

Geekie, P. and Raban, B. (1994) 'Language learning at home and school', in Gallaway, C. and Richards, B. (eds.) *Input and Interaction in Language Acquisition*, Cambridge: Cambridge University Press, pp. 153–80.

Gibbons, P. (2002) *Scaffolding Language, Scaffolding Learning: Teaching Second Language Learners in the Mainstream Classroom*, Portsmouth, NH: Heinemann.

Gibbons, P. (2006) *Bridging Discourses in the ESL Classroom: Students, Teachers and Researchers*, London: Continuum.

Goffman, E. (1981) *Forms of Talk*, Oxford: Blackwell.

Hall, J. K. (2007) 'Redressing the roles of correction and repair in research on second and foreign language learning', *The Modern Language Journal*, 91, 4, 511–26.

Halliday, M. A. K. (1975) *Learning how to Mean: Explorations in the Development of Language*, London: Edward Arnold.

Halliday, M. A. K. and Matthiessen, C. M. I. M. (2004) *An Introduction to Functional Grammar* (3rd ed.), London: Hodder Arnold.

Hammond, J. and Gibbons, P. (2005) 'Putting scaffolding to work: The contribution of scaffolding in articulating ESL education', *Prospect*, 20, 1, 6–30.

Lemke, J. L. (1990) *Talking Science: Language, Learning, and Values*, Norwood, NJ: Ablex.

Llinares, A. (2005) 'The effect of teacher feedback on EFL learners' functional production in classroom discourse', *Anglogermanica Online: Revista Electrónica Periódica De Filología Alemana e Inglesa*, 3.

Llinares, A. (2007a) 'Young learners' functional use of the L2 in a low-immersion EFL context', *ELT Journal*, **61**, 1, 39–45.

Llinares, A. (2007b) 'Classroom bilingualism at an early age: Towards a more natural EFL context', in Pérez Vidal, C., Juan-Garau, M. and Bel, A. (eds.) *A Portrait of the Young in Multilingual Spain*, Bristol: Multilingual Matters, pp. 185–99.

Llinares, A. and Whittaker, R. (2009) 'Teaching and learning history in secondary CLIL classrooms: From speaking to writing', in Dafouz, E. and Guerinni, M. (eds.) *CLIL Across Educational Levels: Experiences from Primary, Secondary and Tertiary Contexts*, London and Madrid: Richmond / Santillana, pp. 73–89.

Long, M. H. (1996) 'The role of the linguistic environment in second language acquisition', in Ritchie, W. and Bhatia, T. (eds.) *Handbook of Second Language Acquisition*, San Diego: Academic Press, pp. 413–68.

Long, M. H. and Sato, C. J. (1983) 'Classroom foreigner talk discourse: Forms and functions of teachers' questions', in Seliger, H. W. and Long, M. H. (eds.) *Classroom-Oriented Research on Second Language Acquisition*, Rowley, MA: Newbury House, pp. 268–85.

Mehan, H. (1979) *Learning Lessons: Social Organization in the Classroom*, Cambridge, MA, and London: Harvard University Press.

Mortimer, E. F. and Scott, P. (2003) *Meaning Making in Secondary Science Classrooms*, Maidenhead, UK, and Philadelphia, PA: Open University Press.

Nassaji, H. and Wells, G. (2000) 'What's the use of "triadic dialogue"? An investigation of teacher-student interaction', *Applied Linguistics*, **21**, 3, 376–406.

Nikula, T. (2007) 'The IRF pattern and space for interaction: Comparing CLIL and EFL classrooms', in Dalton-Puffer, C. and Smit, U. (eds.) *Empirical Perspectives on CLIL Classroom Discourse – CLIL: Empirische Untersuchungen zum Unterrichtsdiskurs*, Frankfurt: Peter Lang, pp. 179–204.

Romero, J. and Llinares, A. (2001) 'Communicative constraints in EFL preschool settings: A corpus-driven approach', *International Journal of Corpus Linguistics*, **6**, 20, 27–46.

Schleppegrell, M. (2004) *The Language of Schooling: A Functional Linguistics Perspective*, Mahwah, NJ, and London: Lawrence Erlbaum.

Scott, P. and Mortimer, E. (2005) 'Meaning making in school science classrooms: A framework for analysing meaning making interactions', in Boersma, K., Goedhart, M., de Jong, O. and Eijkelhof, H. (eds.) *Research and the Quality of Science Education*, Dordrecht: Springer, pp. 395–406.

Seedhouse, P. (2004) *The interactional architecture of the language classroom: A conversation analysis perspective*, Oxford: Blackwell.

Sharpe, T. (2006) '"Unpacking" scaffolding: Identifying discourse and multimodal strategies that support learning', *Language and Education*, **20**, 3, 211–31.

Sinclair, J. and Coulthard, R. M. (1975) *Towards an Analysis of Discourse: The English used by Teachers and Pupils.* London: Oxford University Press.

Sunderland, J. (2001) *Student Initiation, Teacher Response, Student Follow-up: Towards an Appreciation of Student-Initiated IRFs in the Language Classroom,* Lancaster: Lancaster University, Department of Linguistics and Modern English Language.

van Lier, L. (1988) *The Classroom and the Language Learner,* London: Longman.

Walsh, S. (2011) *Exploring Classroom Discourse: Language in Action.* London: Routledge.

Wells, G. (1993) Reevaluating the IRF sequence: A proposal for the articulation of theories of activity and discourse for the analysis of teaching and learning in the classroom', *Linguistics and Education,* 5, 1, 1–37.

Wells, G. (1999) *Dialogic Inquiry: Towards a Socio-Cultural Practice and Theory of Education,* Cambridge: Cambridge University Press.

Part II
The language of academic subjects in CLIL

4   Genres in CLIL subjects

4.1 Introduction: What do we mean by genre?

Part 1 of this book examined the structure of interaction in the CLIL classroom, the way its organisation, at different levels, allows communication around content to develop, and showed how it can be encouraged to develop further, allowing the talk to achieve a pedagogical purpose. Another focus on the role of language in CLIL can be directed towards the content of the subject, up to now, perhaps surprisingly, less often the focus. In Part 2, then, we will consider different subjects that CLIL students may take, and analyse the language which embodies and creates disciplinary knowledge. In this chapter, we deal with text types, or genres, and how they are structured, while in Chapter 5 we move to the levels of lexis and grammar.

Chapter 1 discussed knowledge as vertical (more academic) or horizontal (more everyday), without describing in detail the language through which these types of knowledge are represented in different subjects. Constructing knowledge in different fields is not achieved in the same way. While in science, for example, phenomena are observed, processes described, properties tested for, and so on, in history the past is investigated by finding and interpreting evidence, with historians building narratives or arguments around it (Coffin, 1997). Students need to understand and participate in the activities which build and extend the store of knowledge that makes up the disciplines they study, activities which to a large extent are carried out through language. While the most obvious difference between disciplines is that of vocabulary – and this is the one usually mentioned in a CLIL syllabus –, research in educational linguistics has also shown a major difference to reside in the functional structuring of discourse.

Discourses in school subjects are structured to do different things, just as they are in everyday life. We don't go about buying a kilo of apples in the same way as we get a dentist's appointment, explain a recipe to a friend, or exchange a bit of gossip. In each of these activities, we don't just use different lexical items, we go through a number of different steps, or *stages*, using language to achieve a goal. One stage might involve greeting, another requesting, another listing items, giving quantities or indicating actions for the hearer to carry out, while others may involve evaluating according to social norms as we do when we gossip. In most cases, the order of the stages is important – if we want the interaction to reach its aim successfully we don't greet the shop assistant after we have bought the products.

A community's knowledge of the normal structure of typical activities carried out through language – that is, knowledge of its everyday genres – can be represented schematically. The generic structure of a shopping episode for example, has the following stages:

Stage 1: greeting
Stage 2: sales request
Stage 3: sales compliance
Stage 4: purchase
Stage 5: price
Stage 6: payment
Stage 7: change
Stage 8: thanks

(adapted from Eggins, 1994: 40)

This is expressed more economically as:

Greeting^Sales Request^Sales Compliance^Purchase^Price^Payment (^Change)^Thanks.

The stages are recognised by their functions, reflected in the names they are given; the circumflex accent means that the stages follow each other in the order shown; parentheses mean the stage is optional. In Box 4.1, this concept of genre is defined and explained:

Box 4.1: Genre

Genre is 'a staged, goal-oriented social process. Social because we participate in genres with other people; goal-oriented because we use genres to get things done; staged because it usually takes us a few steps to reach our goals' (Martin and Rose, 2003: 7–8).

Genre, then, is understood as an activity recognised in a particular society or culture, in which language is involved to a greater or lesser extent. This functional approach to looking at language use in society has been found especially helpful for studying the discourse of specific groups of language users. One such group is the educational community, a community in which knowledge of language is vital for members to succeed. A lot of research has been carried out on the language of school disciplines, in order to give teachers the knowledge which will allow them to 'apprentice' students into a discipline. Knowing the functions of the different texts of a subject, and how they are constructed to fulfil those functions, will give students 'generic competence' (Bhatia, 2004), or the ability to use and produce the genres of school. This is more important than might be thought at first, since a subject and its language are inextricable. As work on school genres proposes, there is: 'an explicit link [...] between the types of learning expected in a subject area and the types of language which embody that learning' (Veel and Coffin, 1996: 194). Language is not simply a means of transport for ideas, carrying the knowledge of a subject, but, in fact, it constructs, structures and even restricts knowledge through discipline-specific texts.

While we may be competent users of the text types of our area, with implicit knowledge of their organisation and characteristics, this does not necessarily allow us to make that knowledge available to our students. The very familiarity of the language we use makes it so transparent that it is difficult to analyse or dissect it. Often we are not readily able to pinpoint what has gone wrong in a student's text – apart from the obvious errors of lexis or grammatical structure. However, if we look at the level of discourse applying a linguistic model, we can reveal, in a simple way, both the structure of the most typical texts, and points where a student's text deviates so far from the norm as to be unsuccessful. In this chapter, then, we analyse the structure of a number of genres from different school subjects. Unlike most L1 subject teachers, many CLIL teachers are aware that an important part of their role is to apprentice students into the language of their subjects. The first level to examine is that of genre.

To investigate the genres of the disciplines, we have turned to research which has come out of large projects on the language of different school subjects carried out in Australia by members of the Sydney school (see Veel, 2006, for a very readable description of the projects). We have also examined a selection of sources used or produced by teachers and students: the syllabus of the subject, textbooks, in-class tasks, and exam questions, both in-class teachers' tests and commercial examinations, specifically the International General Certificate of Secondary Education (IGCSE), which is taken all over the world. While the chapter does not claim in any way to be exhaustive, it aims to give a picture of the main genres in some subjects often taught in CLIL contexts, which may be adapted to other subjects and different contexts. As genres are culturally embedded, differences in genres in different countries are sure to be found. The proposal in this chapter, then, is based on school genres found in English-speaking countries, their reflection in international examinations in English and supported by samples from CLIL classes in non-English-speaking European countries.

Genres in any country are constantly evolving, and in CLIL contexts, which bring cultures into contact, this process is likely to be speeded up. However, the theory on which the analysis is based and the variety of examples, make it easy for teachers to recognise variations as they appear, and include them in their teaching. The examples included here come from subjects often taught in CLIL contexts – science and technology, geography and history. They are taken mainly from lower secondary school classes, grades 7–10, in order to cover a variety of text types which reflect this transitional moment in students' contact with the language of the disciplines (Christie and Derewianka, 2008). At the end of each section devoted to the genres in a subject area, there are tasks from recent IGCSE papers and textbooks preparing students for these examinations and comments on the demands they make on students' generic competence. Making this aspect of the subjects more visible will allow teachers to give their students a principled way to approach the cognitively demanding task of constructing knowledge in the foreign language.

4.2 Genres of science

Introduction to science genres

The different genres through which science is learnt at school reflect the process of building scientific knowledge, presenting this knowledge to students who will later carry the discipline forward. In the genres of school science, then, a pedagogical 'recontextualisation' (Bernstein, 1990) has taken place for the benefit of apprentice scientists. As Veel (1997: 169) explains: 'School science reduces, simplifies, generalises and idealises centuries of scientific activity, in order for students to assimilate important understandings and to move on to "real science", i.e. empirical research and dispute.' This author finds that science at school usually starts with 'fairly open-ended "observations" and "activities"' (1997: 167) and later develops into more formal experiments, the results of which illustrate scientific laws, or accepted knowledge of different types. When studying science, students come into contact with three basic text types: texts which instruct them how to carry out the steps of an experiment or report how one was done – known as *procedures*, texts which organise scientific knowledge – *reports,* and texts which explain scientific processes – *explanations.* We will see a number of these texts, analysed into their functional parts, or stages.

Procedures

The procedure represents a genre found in all cultures, in which an expert introduces a learner into the activities of the community (Martin and Rose, 2008: 182). The procedure may involve face-to-face, spoken instructions, or may be more explicit, highly structured written directions. In the case of school science and technology, the genre of the procedure is found in classes of all levels. However, in different CLIL contexts, not all pupils have hands-on experience of the actual activity, but may observe the teacher carrying it out, or just learn about how the experiment could be done. A written procedure typically includes the following stages:

Aim^Equipment + Materials^Method.

The aim of the experiment is presented first; then, after the symbol ^ indicating the order of the stages in the texts, comes information as to what is required to carry out the experiment, and finally the instructions. Text 4.1 from a textbook (grade 10, ages 15–16) is an example of a procedure:

Text 4.1	
AIM	Comparing the carbon dioxide content of inspired and expired air
EQUIPMENT AND MATERIALS	You can use either lime water or hydrogen carbonate indicator solution for this experiment. Lime water changes from clear to cloudy when carbon dioxide dissolves in it. Hydrogen carbonate indicator solution changes from red to yellow when carbon dioxide dissolves in it.
METHOD	1. Set up the apparatus as in Fig. 6.12. 2. Breathe in and out gently through the rubber tubing. Do not breathe too hard. Keep doing this till the liquid in one of the flasks changes colour.

(Jones and Jones, 2002: 51)

In this table, and whenever we present an example of a genre, the left-hand column shows the generic stages, and on the right the text is reproduced as it appeared in the original, the only difference being the spaces included to distinguish the stages. For this experiment, the main material required is the air the student breathes, which is not mentioned explicitly, but is implicit in the Method stage. In the textbook, a series of questions helping the student to reflect on the results and their possible explanation follows the procedure.

Students who do not follow hands-on, experimental science courses are also apprenticed into the procedure genre, and are asked to reproduce it. The following example is from a test in a CLIL class (grade 10, ages 15–16) which does not have laboratory sessions. The question was: 'Explain how insulin is obtained by genetic engineering'.

Text 4.2	
METHOD	The human gene that codes for the production of insulin is identified. – Special enzymes are used like 'chemical scissors' to cut the insulin-making gene for the rest of DNA. – A circular piece called plasmid is removed from a bacterium. – The human insulin-making gene is put into the plasmid. – The plasmid is put into a bacterium. – The bacterium makes insulin. – The bacteria multiply very rapidly. All the bacteria produced will have the insulin gene
AIM	& will make insulin.

The instruction 'explain how' signals that a procedure genre is expected. The student omits the Aim and the Materials stage, and goes straight into the Method, introducing the materials as he goes. The final sentence, not given visual prominence as a separate stage in the student's text, makes explicit the aim, as expressed in the test question. While all the necessary elements (Aim, Equipment and Materials, Method) are present, some are not very visible. The way the student represents the genre has probably been affected by the task, and, more importantly, by the lack of experience of carrying out this type of activity. Here is an opportunity, then, for a brief intervention by the teacher.

Procedural recounts

In most English-speaking educational contexts, students learn to write up experiments, adapting the procedure genre to the procedural recount. It has the function of recording what was actually done; that is, it is a 'retrospective' genre (Martin and Rose, 2008: 217). It is quite common from the early years, with children as young as 7–8 years writing up and illustrating records of simple experiments. The procedural recount follows the same stages as the procedure, adding the results and a possible reflection on what was found during the activity, as an optional Conclusion stage. The generic structure, then, is:

Purpose^Equipment + Materials^Method^Results^(Conclusion).

In Extract 4.1, produced in a CLIL class (grade 6, ages 11–12) where individual experimental work is not done, the genre is reproduced orally, with considerable support from the teacher.

Extract 4.1	
PURPOSE	T: [...] P, water pressure ... there was another experiment we did! do you remember that one?
MATERIALS	S: Yes we took a bottle ...
METHOD	and we made a ... ahm holes in it T: Mhm S: Yes and *äh* T: Where did we put the holes? ... Where were the holes? S: *ach ja* ... all sides S: on the bottom T: At the bottom of bottle and all around the bottle ... and what did C do? S: She she put water in it
RESULTS	and then the the water ah spread out in all directions ... and equal T: ... in equal? S: Sides (?) T: Distances.
CONCLUSION	... so what does that mean? S: ahm T: For the pressure of water? ... T: Why did the water come out of the holes? S: Because of pressure. T: Because of pressure in water and what does it mean when it's spreads to equal distances? ... S: The water is *(cont.)*

	T:	The water pressure is ...
	S:	is ah ... in a circle.
	T:	How does it act? ... Where ... where do you feel water pressure? ... Is it the same everywhere in water in the bottle? ... No?
	S:	No ... ahm
		...
	T:	If it's not the same how does it dif-fer?
	S:	It is strong!
	T:	Where?
	S	Ahm ... When you ... On the bottom
	T:	at the bottom it's much stronger at the bottom than on top and ... How does it spread I mean the pressure how does the pressure spread in water?
		...
	S:	Through the holes.
	T:	Through the holes which means it spreads into all
	S:	Directions.
	T:	Directions with ...
	S:	Equal ... distance.
	T:	With equal with an equal force, okay?

The Conclusion stage is what the teacher focuses the class on, trying to elicit the properties of liquids: that pressure acts in all directions and pressure increases with depth.

Science reports

The result of experimental procedures is the accumulation of scientific knowledge, which, in school science and technology, has been organised in such a way that pupils can, little by little, learn about the world in a scientific way. The genre which provides them with this information, and which they need to learn to reproduce – at least partially – is the science report. Martin (1993: 187) finds reports to be the most frequent genre in science textbooks, and, in fact, sees these textbooks themselves as a sort of macroreport, making information accessible to pupils in a structured way. Veel (1997: 171) classes the report as the 'documenting' science genre, and recognises two types: *descriptive report* and *taxonomic report*, as do Christie and Deriawanka (2008: 184). A third type found is the *compositional report*. Descriptive reports 'classify a phenomenon and then describe its features'; classifying reports 'sub-classify a number of phenomena with respect to a given set of criteria' and compositional reports 'describe the components of an entity' (Martin and Rose, 2008: 142–3). That is, descriptive reports focus on one entity, classifying reports identify members of a class, while compositional reports describe part–whole relationships. We will see the structure of some reports, including an important stage found in this genre in which the phenomenon is defined.

First, then, a *descriptive report*, which has the generic structure:

Classification^Description (divided into Phases).

The Classification stage involves what Christie and Deriawanka (2008) and Veel (1997) call simply 'general statement', in which the object or phenomenon is introduced and ascribed to a class, using a scientifically accepted term. The classification stage will include some kind of definition, then. Though oral production of definitions by CLIL students seems infrequent (Dalton-Puffer, 2007), students come into contact with the mini-genre of definitions as they read sections of their textbooks or class packs. In this material, students can read canonical definitions, like 'A pathogen is an organism which causes disease' (Jones and Jones, 2002: 135), or definitions with a focus on the technical term, like 'The part of the structure that has a tensile force acting on it is called a TIE and the part that has a compressive force acting on it is called a STRUT' (Cabrales, 2010: 2). Teachers seem to give some importance to them, since they are included in class tests. The following example by a student from a CLIL science class (grade 9, ages 14–15) is a response to the instruction 'Define amnion'.

Text 4.3
Amnion is a bag wich contains the baby and the amniotic liquid, wich protect the baby againts shakes.

While spelling may still be a problem, Text 4.3 shows that this student has internalised the structure of the mini-genre.

The textbook example of a descriptive report, below, reproduced as Text 4.4, is interesting as it comments on the classification usually given to the phenomena described, viruses.

Text 4.4	
CLASSIFICATION	Viruses are very strange organisms. Indeed, some people think they should not be classified as living things at all!
	(cont.)

DESCRIPTION	
PHASE 1	They are not made of cells, but just some protein molecules around some DNA or RNA (Fig 13.2).
PHASE 2	They cannot do any of the things that living things are supposed to do, such as respire or grow.
PHASE 3	They cannot do anything at all until they get inside another living cell- when they begin to reproduce.

(Jones and Jones, 2002: 135)

In the Description stage, the different features of viruses are given in negative terms. In all this report, the student readers are constructed as knowledgeable members of the scientific community, who know the features of living beings.

Students learn the structure of this genre, as we see in the example from another CLIL class test below, for which the question was 'The placenta and its role. Make a drawing to illustrate.'

Text 4.5	
CLASSIFICATION	The placenta is a disc-shaped organ attached to the uterus wall, and joined to the baby by the umbilical cord.
DESCRIPTION	
PHASE 1	In the placenta, oxygen and blood from the mother are exchanged with CO_2 and waste products. This products are carried by the blood, but the bloods don't mix; those substances are exchanged by some little capillars.
PHASE 2	The placenta makes the function of the lungs, the dygestive system and the kidneys.

The student, from a CLIL class (grade 9, ages 14–15), has classified the phenomenon in a correctly structured definition, and included different types of information in the Phases, giving the features.

In a *classifying report* the elements of the second stage of the generic structure differ from those of the descriptive report:

Classification System^Types.

In Text 4.6, from a textbook, the phenomenon of disease has been discussed previously, and the classification system, 'causes of diseases', is announced as the topic of the next section of the report. Stage 2 lists the different types of diseases, depending on their causes.

Text 4.6	
CLASSIFICATION SYSTEM	**There are many causes of diseases** People often think of a disease as being something caused by bacteria or viruses like flu (influenza) or AIDS. While many diseases are caused by microorganisms, there are many other causes of disease. The most important ones are listed below.
TYPES	1. Genetic diseases, caused by **genes**. These include cystic fibrosis, sickle cell anaemia, Down's syndrome and some kinds of diabetes. 2. Infectious diseases caused by other living organisms which are called **pathogens**. These include influenza, AIDS, malaria, cholera, syphilis, gonorrhoea and many others. [. . .]

(Jones and Jones, 2002: 134)

This genre is found in its spoken version, as in Extract 4.2, in which a CLIL class (grade 7, ages 15–16) have been discussing variation in their physical features, and the teacher is explaining sources of the types of variation.

Extract 4.2	
CLASSIFICATION SYSTEM	But there is another type of variation and that is the environmental variation. I mean, that you can, you can have different and different reasons why we can get variations.
TYPES	One is the diet we take, if we eat properly, if we eat a lot of proteins, we can grow more, and if we have an unhealthy diet we *(cont.)*

> (   ). Or else, if we do a lot of exercise like he does, he has developed strong muscles, than the person that doesn't regularly exercise. So, that is environmental, right, that has nothing to do with the genes.

The reasons are signalled clearly in this oral version of the genre: 'One is ... ', 'Or else ... ' and elaborated on.

While students learn the classification systems of their field, and these can form part of exams, this doesn't mean they are asked to reproduce the complete genre in the foreign language. This cognitively demanding task tends to be checked in a schematic form, as shown in Text 4.7 by a CLIL student (grade 7, ages 12–13).

Text 4.7

Moss => non-vascular, non-flowering plant, spores (reproduction)
Fern => vascular, non-flowering, reproduction by spores
Conifer => flowering, vascular, insignificant flower, seeds no protected
Apple tree => flowering, colourfull flower, vascular, seeds protected by a fruit

---

The question which elicited this text asked for the systems involved in the classification of the plants. It simply read 'Classify the following plants: Moss, Fern, Conifer and Apple tree'.

And finally, a *compositional report* has the generic structure:

Classification of Entity^Components.

This was exemplified and analysed in its spoken version in Chapter 1, Extract 1.6, in which the teacher elicits the components of a Romanesque church.

Different types of report, then, represent the basic way science organises information about phenomena, and are visible in our CLIL student data as knowledge structures to be learnt.

Science explanations

While reports describe what things are, scientifically, and how they relate to each other, explanations tell us how and why scientific phenomena occur, dealing with interactions of factors and processes (Schleppegrell,

2004). A number of different classes of explanations have been identified. Veel (1997: 168), for example, recognises six types: sequential, causal, theoretical, factorial, consequential and what he calls 'explorations'. He finds a developmental path which moves from explanations dealing with observable events, to those relating cause and effect and finally to explanations based on scientific theory (Veel, 1997: 175–6). The presentation of explanations in CLIL classes has been found in some research to be rather fragmented (Dalton-Puffer, 2007), whereas other recordings in the corpus show teachers giving fairly elaborated explanations of scientific phenomena. Here, the texts exemplifying some of the genres are taken from written sources. We begin, following the developmental path proposed, with *sequential* and *causal explanations*. The generic structure of both sequential and causal explanations can be expressed as:

Phenomenon^Explanation (in Phases)^(Extension).

The explanation may begin or end with a definition of the phenomenon. Sometimes an Extension phase is included, usually bringing in reference to human activity (Martin and Rose, 2008: 153). Text 4.8 is a sequential explanation from an IGCSE textbook. The definition of the phenomenon of pollination has been given earlier in the section.

Text 4.8	
PHENOMENON	In many flowers, pollination is carried out by insects.
SEQUENTIAL EXPLANATION	
PHASE 1	Small insects, such as beetles and honey bees, come to the flowers, attracted by their colour and strong, sweet scent.
PHASE 2	The bee follows the guide-lines to the nectaries, brushing past the anthers as it goes. Some of the pollen will stick to its body.
PHASE 3	The bee will probably then go to another flower, looking for more nectar.
PHASE 4	Some of the pollen it picked up at the first flower will stick onto the stigma of the second flower when the bee brushes past it. The stigma is sticky, and many pollen grains get stuck on it.

(Jones and Jones, 2002: 83)

In this text, the focus is on the sequence of events, here indicated simply by the order of the clauses, with no explicit time markers. Occasional reference to possible reasons for the actions or events is presented in non-finite clauses: 'attracted by their colour and strong, sweet scent', 'looking for more nectar', and so backgrounded. This makes it quite different from Text 4.9, a *causal explanation*, where, though the events occur chronologically, what stands out for the reader is the series of cause–effect relations.

Text 4.9	
	Sulphur and nitrogen oxides produce acid rain
PHENOMENON	Acid rain damages plants. Although the rain usually does not hurt the leaves directly when it falls onto them, it does affect the way in which plants grow. This is because it affects the soil in which the plants are growing.
CAUSAL EXPLANATION	
PHASE 1	The acid rain water seeps into the soil, and washes out ions such as calcium, magnesium and aluminium.
PHASE 2	The soil becomes short of these ions, so the plant becomes short of nutrients.
PHASE 3	It also makes it more difficult for the plant to absorb other nutrients from the soil.
PHASE 4	So acid rain can kill trees and other plants.

(Jones and Jones, 2002: 173)

Here, cause appears in the lexical verb 'affect', and in the causal conjunctions 'because' and 'so'. Text 4.10, on the other hand, focuses on the consequences of a phenomenon. In this *consequential explanation* we find that an Extension phase is included, closing the text by commenting on the effect of the process on human activity.

Text 4.10	
PHENOMENON	The loss of so many trees can also affect the water cycle. [... definition of water cycle ...] With the trees growing, when the rain falls a lot

(cont.)

	of it is taken up by the trees and taken to their leaves. It then evaporates, and goes back into the atmosphere in the process of transpiration.
EXPLANATION PHASE 1	If the trees have gone, then the rain simply runs off the soil and into rivers. Much less goes back into the air as water vapour.
PHASE 2	The air becomes drier, and less rain falls.
EXTENSION	This can make it much more difficult for people to grow crops and keep livestock.

(Jones and Jones, 2002: 175)

While in the three types of explanations we have seen the phases are related either temporally or causally, in a *factorial explanation*, two or more unrelated reasons are given for a phenomenon. This is shown in Text 4.11 on population growth.

Text 4.11	
PHENOMENON	(There are two main reasons for) this recent growth spurt.
FACTORIAL EXPLANATION	
PHASE 1	The first is the **reduction of disease**. Improvements in water supply, sewage treatment, hygienic food handling and general standards of cleanliness have virtually wiped out many diseases in countries such as the USA and most European countries – for example typhoid and dysentery. Immunisation against diseases such as polio has made these very rare indeed. Smallpox has been totally eradicated. And the discovery of antibiotics has now made it possible to treat most diseases caused by bacteria.
PHASE 2	Secondly, there has been an **increase in food supply**. More and more land has been brought under cultivation. Moreover, agriculture has become more efficient, so that in many parts of the world each hectare of land is now producing more than ever before.

(Jones and Jones, 2002: 168)

The explanations are marked linguistically for the reader to recognise easily: *The first is* ... , and *Secondly* ... . Nested inside the first factor explaining the increase in world population by reduction of disease is another explanation, giving the factors which have led to fewer deaths from previously mortal illnesses, as shown in Text 4.11a:

Text 4.11a	
PHENOMENON FACTORIAL EXPLANATION	The first is **the reduction of disease.**
PHASE 1	Improvements in water supply, sewage treatment, hygienic food handling and general standards of cleanliness have virtually wiped out many diseases in countries such as the USA and most European countries – for example typhoid and dysentery.
PHASE 2	Immunisation against diseases such as polio has made these very rare indeed.
PHASE 3	Smallpox has been totally eradicated.
PHASE 4	And the discovery of antibiotics has now made it possible to treat most diseases caused by bacteria.

(Jones and Jones 2002: 168)

Each factor appears in first position in the sentences making up the Explanation, creating a pattern of listing, which is easy for the reader to recognise. Students are often asked to produce short explanations; in fact, these have been found to be the most frequent genre demanded in writing in science in English L1 contexts (Martin, 1993). It is important then that students are made aware of the structure of the genre and the different types of logical relations in the subtypes.

Tasks requiring scientific genres

The genre of procedure is required in different IGCSE science subjects, both for exams taken in the laboratory, and for students who sit the non-experimental section of the exam. One recent question triggering a procedure was 'Describe how you would carry out a biuret (food) test to show whether protein is present in the "white" of an egg' (IGCSE Biology Paper 5, Oct/Nov 2008), after which the student was instructed to carry out the test in the laboratory. For the non-experimental version, there was a similar question: 'Describe a food test which might show whether there is more protein to be found in the "white" or in the "yolk" of the egg' (IGCSE Biology Paper 6 Oct/Nov 2008). Procedures are also part of the IGCSE exam for design and technology. A recent question asked candidates to design a stand for barbecue implements, and then outline a method used to manufacture a part of the unit.

The report genre is treated differently, however. Even at the level of IGCSE, developed reports are not required, though formal definitions are, according to the explanation of questions on the papers provided in the syllabi for biology and for chemistry (IGCSE Syllabus Biology 2010, IGCSE Syllabus Chemistry 2010). Instead of complete reports, information is usually sought in highly scaffolded texts, as in the example from chemistry below.

Text 4.12

Complete these sentences about the properties of the Group I elements using words from the list.

    acidic – basic – decrease – hard – increase – lithium –
    potassium – soft

The Group I elements are relatively .... metals which .... in reactivity going down the Group. Sodium reacts more violently with water than .... The Group I metals all form .... oxides.

(IGCSE Chemistry Paper 2, Oct/Nov 2008)

Explanations are more prominent in these examinations. Requirements for the different genres we have analysed are commented on in the glossary of terms used in exam questions for chemistry and biology (IGCSE Syllabus Biology, 2010; IGCSE Syllabus Chemistry, 2010). From this it is clear that sequential explanations should be given when the question asks students to 'describe a process'. The other explaining genres also need to be recognised and produced. The syllabus definition says 'explain' is used as a synonym of 'give reasons for' and that the type of reasons will depend on the specific question. For example, a question demanding a sequential explanation was: 'Apart from intercourse, describe two other routes by which HIV can be transmitted from human to human.' A consequential explanation is triggered by: 'Name two other harmful components of cigarette smoke, apart from carbon monoxide. For each, describe an effect it can have on the body of a person who smokes.' And a causal explanation would be the appropriate response to this question: 'Why do farmers need to use fertilisers?' (IGCSE Chemistry Paper 2, 2008). CLIL students, especially when preparing for this type of examination, then, need to recognise and produce these different genres in writing.

4.3 Genres of geography

Introduction

We now turn to the geography genres, many of which are shared with the other sciences, especially since the increasing interest in ecological issues has drawn the different areas closer (Veel, 1998). Geography is chosen as a CLIL subject in a number of countries, and provides a context for student activities which can have either a local or a global perspective.

Research on school geography, again in the framework of the Sydney school's projects, has produced a definition of the geographer's task, and of the role of language in the subject. This definition leads us to the genres which carry out these tasks. Language is used first 'to "observe" the experiential world through the creation of technical vocabulary: a process of dividing up and naming those parts of the world which are significant to geographers' (Wignell et al., 1993: 137). For this, students have to be taken through a process of discovering what aspects of the world are relevant to the discipline, as van Leeuwen and Humphrey (1996) show. Once this is established, geographers 'order the experiential world, through the setting up of field-specific taxonomies' (Wignell et al., 1993: 137). Here we recognise the report genre we saw in science, while the third task, 'to "explain" the experiential world, through the positing of implicational relations among natural or manmade states' (ibid.), will require one of the classes of explanation genres.

Geography reports

Much geographical information is expressed in the form of *descriptive reports*, and they are a frequent genre in the textbooks students read. They show apprentice geographers the phenomena relevant to the field, with its specific terms, and often definitions of terms. They present information about physical features of the environment, or about human groups and their activities in a particular environment (Humphreys, 1996). Their generic structure is:

Identification^Description.

Texts 4.13 and 4.14 represent the two types of descriptive report identified according to topic: physical features of a location and activities of human groups. As often found in the genre, in both examples the Identification stage orients the reader, and indicates the focus of the Description stage, which then presents the expected information.

Text 4.13	
IDENTIFICATION	Chile is a country of enormous contrasts.
DESCRIPTION	It stretches for over 4000 km in length and, at the most, is less than 200 km wide. Among the Andes mountains there are more than 2000 ash and lava volcanoes, of which 500 are active. On 2 May 2008 the Chaiten volcano – which was thought to be dormant – surprised everybody by suddenly erupting for the first time in over 9000 years.

(Cambers and Sibley, 2010: 64)

In Text 4.13, the word *contrasts* in the Identification stage prepares the reader for the focus of the Description, while in Text 4.14, the human activity described is signalled by reference to tourism in the Identification stage:

Text 4.14	
IDENTIFICATION	Montego Bay is an important tourist resort on the north-west coast of the island of Jamaica.
DESCRIPTION	It has a population of about 120 000 people and close by is Jamaica's largest airport, the Sir Donald Sangster International Airport. Flights to and from Montego Bay provide access for increasing numbers of tourists from countries such as the USA, the UK, Germany and Canada.

(Cambers and Sibley, 2010: 190)

The objective of the genre – to organise relevant information – means students are expected to select and classify according to geographical criteria, and use the terms of the discipline to do so.

In geography we find *definitions* are often included in descriptive reports, and textbooks offer good examples which students can learn to reproduce. Texts 4.15 and 4.16 show an expert's definition and a CLIL student's (grade 8, ages 13–14) version from a class test.

Text 4.15

Weather: Short-term day-to-day changes in the atmosphere for a place. Rainfall, temperature, wind direction and strength, air pressure, sunshine, humidity and cloud cover are all studied as 'weather'.
Climate: The average weather conditions over a period of time – at least 30 years. Temperature and rainfall are shown on climate graphs. Climate regions cover large areas.

(Cambers and Sibley, 2010: 86)

In the geography test, the question eliciting the definitions was simply worded: 'What is weather? What is climate?'. Students were able to produce a definition as the answer in Text 4.16 shows.

Text 4.16

Weather refers to the state of the atmosphere in a place at a specific time. Climate refers to the state of the atmosphere in a place during a long period of time.

This academic function is often made explicit, showing the importance teachers give to this mini-genre. 'Choose two of the following features. Define in two lines and draw a sketch of them: underground water, meander, waterfall, delta, estuary, glacier', is from a test for a CLIL class (grade 7, ages 12–13). Text 4.17 contains one student's proposed definitions. They include the basic information, though the criterion for classification is left implicit, perhaps due to a lack of ability to move to the level of generalisation which is needed for a canonical definition in which the term to be defined is assigned to a class: 'A meander is a water formation which appears when ... '.

Text 4.17

Meander: In the middle course of the river, the river take form of S and forms meanders.
Waterfall: In the upper course of the river, the river flows over a cliff. This is a waterfall.

The two student examples in Texts 4.16 and 4.17 illustrate the difference between a taxonomical, 'thing-focused' definition (Text 4.16) and a 'process-focused' definition (Text 4.17), described by Wignall et al. (1993: 151). To solve the lack of classification terms mentioned above, and make the function of defining stand out, students could be shown how to construct the definition in two clauses: 'A meander is when ... '.

Although the construction of taxonomies is a large part of the activity of geography as a science, researchers have found that this is not made explicit to learners, or presented as such diagrammatically (Wignell et al., 1993: 155). This gap, evidently, needs to be filled.

The genre, *taxonomic* or *classifying report*, when found in its complete form, has the same generic structure as that of this type of science report.

Explanations in geography

The explanation genres in geography parallel those of science and technology, and reflect the same relations between the phenomena, though now we are in a different field. *Sequential* and *causal explanations* are frequent genres in geography, expressing how or why something happens. The less demanding sequential explanation is learned early on, and depends on observation of a process. Text 4.18 is an example by a student in a CLIL class (grade 7, ages 12–13). It shows how, while the formal features of the language are still very unstable, the writer is beginning to learn the genre.

Text 4.18	
IDENTIFICATION	The volcanoes are opening or crevices in the earth crust that expulse lava (magma) by he's crater,
TEMPORAL SEQUENCE	the process of this expulse is simple:
PHASE 1	first lava (magma) rise up through the pipe
PHASE 2	and then the volcano expulse by he's crater, the magma is constituyed by hot materials.

In the text, the Identification stage consists of a well-formed definition. The student signals the next stage by naming it 'the process', and divides it into two phases, marking the second step in the sequence by using the phrase from spoken register 'and then'.

Causal explanations are often shown in geography textbooks in diagrammatic form. The result is conceptually clear, but with no text as a model, the students are not provided with the language they need to learn to produce the genre themselves. Given the importance of cause–effect relations in geography, CLIL students should be provided with more support so that they are able to make these relations explicit in the foreign language.

Another type, the *consequential explanation*, focuses more on the effects of natural or human activities. And, finally, geography has its equivalent of the *factorial explanation* in science. Again, a number of different, unrelated factors in combination are used to explain a phenomenon. The generic structure has been given as:

Output^Factors.

The Factors may themselves include explanation or elaboration as in Text 4.19.

Text 4.19	
OUTPUT	**Surviving the desert climate** **The fennec fox**
FACTOR 1	The fennec fox is a mammal and the world's smallest fox.
FACTOR 2 (plus explanation)	It has enormous ears to help radiate heat to help it stay cool.
FACTOR 2	It lives deep in the ground in long, cool burrows
FACTOR 3 (plus elaboration)	and emerges around dusk to hunt when the day is less hot. Most of northern Mali has less than 100mm of rainfall a year – sometimes none. In most places the main source of moisture for animals is dew. The desert is fiercely hot by day but can freeze at night.
Generalisation explaining FACTOR 1	Most animals are small so they can lose heat more easily, as their surface area is large compared with their size.

(Cambers and Sibley, 2010: 95)

Each Factor is followed by explanation or elaboration of why it is involved in the survival of the fox in the inhospitable desert. In the case of the first Factor, the reader has to wait till the end of the text to understand the significance of the size of the fox. Here the writer rounds off the text with a generalisation.

Tasks requiring geography genres

The different genres described in this section are needed if students are to respond to questions on geography, and this applies to the IGCSE papers. To begin with, the exams look for knowledge of technical terms, knowledge which has been found lacking, according to IGCSE examiners' reports. Many answers were described as vague and without enough technical information. This can be understood as showing that students still represent the world in everyday, or horizontal, terms; they are really at the pre-geography stage. The use of the technical terms of the field shows much more than knowledge of vocabulary, and this applies to both first and foreign languages. A science organises the phenomena it studies, and gives them technical names showing where they fit in the field. The set of technical terms created, then, represents more than alternative names: 'It is the resource a discipline uses to name and then order its [...] phenomena in a way distinctive to that field. Through technicality, a discipline establishes the inventory of what it can talk about, and the terms in which it can talk about them' (Wignall et al., 1993: 162). This is what the examiners are looking for in the geographical information students supply.

Related to vocabulary knowledge, definitions are often required, usually in a section of a longer question, with wording like 'What is meant by *fossil fuel*?', for example. Descriptive reports are found in tasks in which students are given some data to study and asked to do tasks like: 'Compare the relief of the three regions in Peru', or 'Describe the differences in fuel use between the three villages', both from the exam preparation section of an IGCSE textbook (Cambers and Sibley, 2010: 175, 159). In fact, the frequency of this type of report led Humphrey (1996) to recognise it as a distinctive genre, that of comparative description. This genre makes demands on a specific area of language, and provides a clear opportunity for planning and cooperation between CLIL and EFL teachers. Work on this area of grammar – comparative forms – could be programmed into the students' English language classes in conjunction with teaching a geography unit.

Different types of explanations are included in the exams, often as part of a series of sub-questions on a topic. A recent question asking for a sequential explanation was 'Give three processes by which the river is likely to carry out erosion [...]. Describe the processes by which a river is likely to transport eroded materials.' (IGCSE Geography Paper 1, Oct/Nov 2008). In another series of questions, students were given pie charts showing the distribution of the use of different types of fuel in three Nepalese villages, and asked for a comparative description, followed by a consequential explanation: 'Suggest how these energy uses might affect: the natural environment; the lives of the people' (Cambers and Sibley, 2010: 159). And a factorial explanation could answer a question like: 'Suggest reasons why the importance of different types of energy varies globally' (IGCSE Geography Paper 1, Oct/Nov 2008). The expression of cause in language is, then, essential, and students need more than visuals if they are to be able to produce these logical relations. Again, CLIL and English language teachers could plan the linguistic support the students will need.

4.4 Genres of history

Introduction

The discipline of history is frequently chosen as a CLIL subject, despite the national, political and cultural sensitivities involved in the choice of content, and the need to ensure that the students will be prepared to take national exams in the subject at the end of secondary schooling. History is a subject in which the role of language is especially present, with so much of its evidence embodied in texts, which are analysed and interpreted by professional historians. School history aims to apprentice students into the methods of comparing and evaluating sources, and to help them learn to become proficient in the language of history. This is very evident in textbooks and in the focus of questions in the different IGCSE history papers, as we will see.

The genres of history in English have had a lot of research devoted to them in the framework of the Australian educational projects (especially by Coffin, e.g. Coffin, 2006a, b; Veel and Coffin, 1996), and this section of the chapter describes a number of important types which embody and create knowledge in the field. The different genres in school history have been found to correspond to distinct conceptions of history and the task of the historian, from the 'grand narrative' with its great historical figures, to views which recognise multiple voices and historical realities. To a certain extent, these genres can be seen to form a developmental path, starting with chronologically structured narration focused on central historical figures, moving on to logically structured explanation of causes and consequences of historical events, and finally, argument or discussion around different interpretations of history (Christie and Derewianka, 2008; Coffin, 2006a; Martin and Rose, 2008; Veel and Coffin, 1996). At the same time, researchers are careful to point out that such a sequence interacts with the different approaches to the study of history, so that quite early in their apprenticeship, pupils can be asked to evaluate sources and motives for different interpretations, and not only to retell an accepted view of events. One frequent genre which gives an accepted view is the period study, the first text type we describe.

Period study

We start with a frequently found history genre which does not take time as its internal structuring device, the *period study*. This is a genre found in textbooks and different CLIL classrooms, in which students show their knowledge of the way things were at a particular time. Its function is to describe the characteristics of a historical period, and so it is set in time, rather than moving through time (Christie and Derewianka, 2008; Veel and Coffin, 1996). At its most simple, the generic structure can be seen as:

Period Identification^Description.

The first stage, however, may not be announced explicitly, but be inferable from previous text. The Description stage may be introduced by a generalisation, framing the detailed information which follows. This can be seen in the textbook extract in Text 4.20 and the CLIL student example in Text 4.21.

Text 4.20	
PERIOD IDENTIFICATION	In the seventeenth century Britain had been torn apart by a violent disagreement about who should rule the country. The winners in this bitter struggle were the landed aristocrats, who owned much of the countryside.
DESCRIPTION	Between 1688 and 1832 these rich landlords controlled parliament. There was not real democracy: all women and most men were barred from voting.
	Aristocrats dominated both the House of Lords and the House of Commons. Elections to the House of Commons were very different from today. There were a very few
	(cont.)

	constituencies, such as Preston and Coventry, where most men were allowed to vote but these were very much the exception. In many more constituencies only a small number of wealthy men could vote: in 1830 there were 77 seats which each had less than a hundred votes. In the Cornish constituency of Helston, for example, only 19 men had the vote. In 1793 it was calculated that about 11,000 men were entitled to elect over half of all Members of Parliament.

(Counsell and Steer, 1993: 80)

The first paragraph of the Description represents a generalisation, while the second gives specific information supporting it. This generic structure also appears in Text 4.21, written by a CLIL student (grade 8, ages 13–14) in answer to a task about life in feudal Europe.

Text 4.21	
PERIOD IDENTIFICATION	In Feudal Europe
DESCRIPTION	
GENERALISATION	there were differents social groups. Were the lord, noblenment and knights, clergymen, peasants, etc.
SPECIFIC INFORMATION	The rural life was very hard, because there was a lot of work, Peasants worked in agriculture, they lived in small wood houses in villages near forest. Forest were very important because there, peasants take wood and food.

While this student's control of grammar and morphology shows considerable variability, the structure and features of the genre are present. The period is identified, and then a number of facts describing it are given. Presentative *there* is used to introduce concepts into the text, generalisations give the activities of the main group, and the past tense is consistently chosen.

As in the reports found in science and geography, the academic function of definition appears in some period studies, as is shown in Texts 4.22 and 4.23.

Text 4.22
In 1750 Britain already possessed some colonies overseas. This was land which had been settled and was governed by British people.

(Counsell and Steer, 1993: 30)

Text 4.23
The King of France ruled over everybody. Louis XVI was called an *absolute monarch*. This meant that his word was law.

(Hetherton, 1992: 11)

Apart from being set in the past, these definitions follow the pattern found in the other subjects analysed.

Recounts in history

One of the aims of the history curriculum is for students to develop an understanding of historical time, not an easy task for them, despite their everyday experience of serial time (Coffin, 2006b), as psychologists have shown (e.g. Carretero et al., 1991). Researchers find developmental stages in the genres of school writing, moving from texts built around the writer's experience, personal recounts, in which events are structured sequentially using markers like 'and then', 'next', to *biographical recounts*, texts recounting the lives of others, a genre included in history textbooks. In these recounts, protagonists are presented in relation to the roles they played in history, excluding personal information not relevant to that role. These third-person recounts are structured by what researchers (e.g. Martin and Rose, 2008: 103) call 'episodic time', in which significant events are selected, and time is segmented into periods.

The different studies agree on the generic stages of the biographical recount, though vary slightly in the terms they choose. We use here the more specific generic structure of Christie and Derewianka (2008: 98):

Person Identification^Episodes (^Evaluation).

The genre is well represented in Text 4.24, from a source book (grades 7/8, ages 12–14):

Text 4.24	
PERSON IDENTIFICATION	**Augustus the first Emperor** **Augustus in power**
EPISODES	Augustus was careful not to call himself King. He knew that the Roman people did not like the idea of a king; it reminded them of the old stories of the early kings of Rome. Augustus tried to show that he respected the Senate. He allowed the senators to carry on discussing laws as they had always done. He or one of his friends was usually chosen to be consul. So he was clever enough to keep the Senate happy. In return the Senate allowed him really to run the government. When some people began to worship him as a god, Augustus did not complain. Sometimes Augustus was nicknamed 'Imperator', which means commander. This is the origin of the title Emperor. Augustus stayed in charge of the army and rewarded soldiers for being loyal.
EVALUATION	During the reign of Augustus there were fewer wars. The Roman Empire was largely at peace. Civil servants were trained to run the provinces in the empire. Money from taxes was spent on strong and glorious buildings throughout the Roman lands. Many new roads were built to link the provinces with each other and with Rome.

(Mantin and Pulley, 1992: 30)

As a biographical recount, Text 4.24 focuses on an individual historical participant, and is set in the period specified in the subtitle, 'Augustus in power'. It develops through episodes relating to how he maintained power, though without giving specific dates, but with time markers like *usually, sometimes,* or the clause beginning *when* ... The Evaluation stage closes the text with a selection of positive results of the period.

The genre most frequently associated with a typical history text is the *historical recount.* The function of the genre is to retell historical events in a sequence. The generic structure:

Background^Record of Events^(Deduction / Evaluation)

is often found, since many recounts close at a more general level, with a deduction (Coffin, 2006a: 64), or with some evaluation of the events. However, studies tend to only include the first two stages in their representation of the generic structure. While historical recounts usually revolve around groups or generic participants, some are more personal, like Text 4.26, which includes named historical figures.

Text 4.26	
BACKGROUND	**Red Cloud's War** In the same year, further west, gold was discovered in the Rocky Mountains. A miner called John Bozeman opened up a trail for gold diggers which ran through the hunting grounds of the Western Sioux.
RECORD OF EVENTS	**Victory for the Teton Sioux** The Sioux, fearing a white invasion and the destruction of the buffalo herds, began attacking travellers on the Bozeman trail. In 1866 Red Cloud received news that the US government was planning to build forts along the trail. Many branches of the Teton Sioux joined together to fight the US army and after a fierce campaign the government tried to make peace with Red Cloud. The only peace term that he would accept was the closure of the Bozeman trail and so in June 1868 the troops were withdrawn and the Bozeman trail was closed.
EVALUATION	Red Cloud had won a great Indian victory. The peace treaty that he signed gave the Sioux a very large reservation area including all their hunting grounds, where no white people would be allowed to settle.

(Edmonds, 1993: 50)

Specific time markers signal key moments in the Background and Events, and the text ends with an evaluation. While the historical actors are groups: *travellers, the Sioux, the US government, the army*, important figures are identified. Time phrases structure the text, chunking it into episodes. Although implicit cause, another feature of the genre, is included – for example, *fearing a white invasion and the destruction of the buffalo herds ...* , – cause is not presented as the focus of the historical recount (Martin and Rose, 2008: 109).

Historical accounts

When cause takes over, structuring the recount, with sequence in time backgrounded, researchers recognise another genre, that of the *historical account*. Its function is 'to account for why events happened in a particular sequence' (Coffin, 2006a: 64), that is, to explain the past (Schleppegrell, 2004). It is made up of the stages:

Background^Account Sequence (^Deduction),

as described by Christie and Derewianka (2008: 101). Text 4.26, a text structured both through cause and effect relations, and by time, exemplifies the genre.

Text 4.26	
BACKGROUND	**Plantation slavery in North America** The first Africans arrived in North America during the early days of the English colonisation, in 1619.
ACCOUNT SEQUENCE	Slavery developed quite slowly in North America, increasing as the growth of the tobacco trade during the 17th century created a demand for workers. By the middle of the 18th century there were over 260,000 African slaves in Virginia alone, most of whom had been transported to, rather than born in, the colony. A few years later the numbers decreased as the tobacco trade reduced, only to increase again with the introduction of cotton as a plantation crop, particularly after the invention of the cotton 'gin' in 1793 by Eli Whitney, an American from Connecticut.

(Field, 1995: 11)

Though the text moves through time, cause is intrinsically involved in the reasons for the temporal changes. Clauses like *as the growth of the tobacco trade during the 17th century created a demand for workers* combine reason with the passing of time. Students also have to recognise that the preposition phrase *with the introduction of cotton as a plantation crop* presents an explanation for a change over time. Typical of the genre is the use of abstractions – *slavery, growth, demand, introduction, invention* – frequently presented as responsible for changes in the Account Sequence stage (Martin and Rose, 2008: 135).

We can see this genre developing in Text 4.27 by a CLIL student (grade 7, ages 12–13), who focuses more on cause and consequence than on temporal sequence in his explanation of the spread of the Black Death.

Text 4.27	
BACKGROUND	Afterwards the plague was brought to Europe by a sailor who came in a ship from Genoa.
ACCOUNT SEQUENCE	The Plague then was carried by rats and was easily expanded through Europe 'thanks' to the very bad health and hygen conditions. It had many consequences in Europe: About 1000000 people died in England. Salarys grew because less people could work.

The Account Sequence moves from cause to consequence, signalled in different ways: in the phrase *'thanks' to ...* , in the noun *consequences* and in the conjunction *because*. The writer introduces abstractions to explain the spread of the disease: *very bad health and hygen conditions*, showing he is beginning to learn the features of the genre (described in detail in Chapter 5).

Historical explanations

A further move away from the history genres organised through time can be seen in the *historical explanation*, in which past events are explained by a number of causes and / or consequences, not presented chronologically but grouped logically, enabling historians to represent a complex view of events. Researchers (e.g. Coffin, 2006a: 75; Christie and Deriwianka, 2008: 126; Martin and Rose, 2008: 117) recognise different types of explanations in history, again paralleling those of science and geography.

A *consequential explanation* is made up of the stages:

Input^Consequences (^Reinforcement of Consequences).

Text 4.28 presents an example, which includes the optional final stage, in which the text moves to a more general level.

Text 4.28	
INPUT	**Social consequences of transport changes** [The needs of industry were the driving force behind] the rapid transport changes,
CONSEQUENCES	but the consequences of the improvements went beyond this. For example, improved road travel led to more newspapers being widely available and to the growth of coaching inns. The railways in particular had many important social consequences. The middle classes and some working-class people used the railways to get away from the towns to the countryside and seaside. It was not only the basic necessities like cheap food which were carried by the railways: newspapers were transported by rail, and music-hall performers and touring theatrical companies were able to travel around the country by train.
DEDUCTION	After the coming of the railways Britain was a more closely knit community in which life moved at a faster pace than had previously been possible.

(Counsell and Steer, 1993: 29)

The text makes very explicit the genre it develops, signalled in the section title, and repeating the noun *consequences* in the text, as well as using the verb phrase *led to*, again indicating consequence. CLIL pupils are also asked to take the step of breaking away from chronological time, as shown by the *factorial explanation* in Text 4.29, written by a pupil (grade 7, ages 12–13). The generic structure is:

Outcome^Factors (^Reinforcement of Factors).

Text 4.29	
OUTCOME	**Why did William win at Hastings?** In October 1066 William of Normandy defeated the English king Harold Godwin, at the battle of Hastings. There were several reasons for Williams victory. William was a great strategist, he had assembled a great army and a great store of weapons before the invasion, he had built a lot of ships to carry his army across the channel he had arranged his army very skillfuly and had a great force of cavalryy, which gave the Normans a lot of attacking power.

FACTORS	Harold also helped William with his victory. He made some mistakes such as he had made his army to walk 190 miles and they where exasted, Harold didn't wait for his army to rest and recover, he just attacked. Harold decided to attack even though hre had lost some of his greatest soldiers in the north.
	    William was also very lucky. The wind had changed at the right moment for William so he could cross the channel very easly. At a key moment in the battle, Harold was killed so his men morale had dropped and some of them fled.
	    William was also a very good leader. He was very brave and at a difficult time in the battle he led his men back up the hill to attack. William also encoureged his men to trick of reatreating to make the English break there possitions and come down the hill where the Normans could sorround them and kill them.

REINFORCEMENT OF FACTORS	While all these causes of William's victory are important and linked together, the most important cause or reason was that Harolds men exahhsted after walking 190 miles to Hastings.

The language of academic subjects in CLIL

In the text, the explanation is made up of a number of unrelated causes, and the historical events are brought in to elaborate on them, rather than appearing in chronological order. To do this, the student writer alternates skilfully between the past and the past perfect, as, for example, in the paragraph explaining the factor of luck. The final stage in this text introduces the writer's evaluation of the different factors involved in the Norman victory, with the student becoming an interpreter of history.

Historical argument and discussion

Many of the sets of questions on a particular topic in the different IGCSE papers include genres which are more complex, both cognitively and linguistically, than the text types just described, and require detailed documented interpretation of historical events, arguing for a thesis or discussing positions towards one. Researchers describe two main genres found in secondary school history which structure quite developed interpretations of the past, and allow the writer either to argue for a specific position or to consider and evaluate a number of possible interpretations of an event, or of the role of a historical figure, and so on. The structure of the first, called *exposition* in genre theory, is described by Christie and Deriwianka (2008: 133) as:

(Background)^Thesis^Argument^Reinforcement of Thesis.

Other researchers either reduce (Martin and Rose, 2008) or expand (Coffin, 2006a) on these stages. The other advanced genre, *discussion*, is structured in a similar way, although it differs in its basic function, which is not to persuade the reader of the thesis, but to consider a number of possible perspectives. This is shown in the names of the stages (Christie and Derewianka, 2008: 133; Coffin, 2006):

(Background)^Issue^Perspectives^Position.

Text 4.30 is an example of the genre of exposition, in which the writer, a student in a CLIL class (grade 7, ages 15–16) takes the role of a contemporary journalist.

Text 4.30	
	Lovely cup of tea
BACKGROUND	Three years have passed since the Boston Massacre. Everyone here, in Boston, knew the intentions of the crowd which jeered at the patrol of British soldiers. They only

(cont.)

	wanted to protest for the abuses coming from Britain, and they received a violent answer from the army.
THESIS	Why is this discontent of the colonists? The killing of the colonist has been the last straw, but before it, there have been some other actions of the British government which have raised this feeling of unhappiness among colonists.
ARGUMENTS	The acts forcing colonists to pay more taxes were one factor. They paid for the army stationed in America when France was been already defeated. This non-sense action means now a waste of £ 1,000,000 every year. In addition, with the Quartering Act, colonists were forced to host British soldiers when they ask for it; 1764 Sugar Act heavily taxed goods as sugar, cutting the profits of making rum; 1765 Stamp Act imposed taxes on any printed paper such as newspapers, legal documents, or even playing cards and the Townshend Acts set out tax glass, lead, paper and tea. Fortunately all this taxes, except the ones on tea, were repealed some years ago.
	Plus taxes, there are strong trade restrictions. Colonists are not allowed to import or export goods except in British ships. Commercial competitiveness is abolished by the prohibition of trade and manufactured their own products.
	Britain has set up some territorial limits for the colonists. This line stops them to cross the Appalachian Mountains, cutting them off from rich fertile land. Many colonists have ignored this statement, crossing into Native American territories.

(cont.)

	'No taxation without representation' is the slogan used by the colonists. They are paying taxes without having a say or being considered in their government. They feel like puppets operated from London.
REINFORCEMENT OF THESIS	These have been the main causes of the colonists´ discontent. They have not been idle and have responded in a very peculiar way. A few weeks ago, a group of colonists disguised themselves as Native Americans, boarded a tea ship in the harbor of this city. They threw the chests of tea overboard, a total of 342 tons of it, in order to protest the British over taxing on tea. The harbor remains closed since that incident. Will be this action the beginning of a rebellion? One thing is for sure, this peculiar event will be remembered forever. Boston, 1773

Historical discussion is considered the most demanding genre, produced towards the end of upper secondary schooling (Christie and Derewianka, 2008). While it is not represented in the corpus in its full form, students clearly are beginning to learn the genre. Text 4.31 shows a student writer (grade 10, ages 15–16) considering different perspectives on the activity of the Europeans in South America.

Text 4.31	
ISSUE	Europeans had a great impact in America.
PERSPECTIVES	In one side, they brought diseases, they killed a lot of them, they kidnapped women, they had the monopoly of commerce with indigenous, they destroyed native traditions and culture and they tried to convert everyone to Catholicism. Although [= Also?], Europeans made a lot of indigenous slaves. In the other hand,
	(cont.)

144

	Europeans brought new irrigation techniques, new ways of agriculture, new products and new ideas.
POSITION	I continue to think that Europeans were a bad thing because the only one beneficiated were them, who got loads of silver and gold, and crops, and slaves. I think they could have been less violent, so everything could be harmless for every body.

The presentation of the Issue is brief but provides a general opening. Readers are prepared for the two types of evidence in the Perspectives stage by the writer's use of different linguistic markers: *in one side*, *although* (probably for *also*, since addition and not contrast follows), *in the other hand*. The writer's Position is clearly signalled by her use of *I think* – the first use, *I continue to think*, seems to make reference to her view of the Issue, which she didn't in fact put in writing – not an uncommon problem in learning to become a mature writer! Here again, the use of the generic stages could serve as a structuring device to discuss students' texts, and help them generate and organise ideas to develop their content.

Tasks requiring history genres

The different history genres often appear in sub-questions on a topic, sequenced in such a way that the developmental stages recognised by researchers are followed. Period studies often form part of the answer to questions on IGCSE history papers, with prompts like 'What were the main features of Russian society before the First World War?' (IGCSE History Paper 1, May/June 2009). According to the Assessment Objectives made public by the board, this type of question would be considered to belong to the first of three levels of difficulty they describe to examiners, the one in which students have to recall facts. Recall of chronologically organised facts is often asked for, in questions like 'What successes did the revolutionaries in Italy have during 1848?' (IGCSE History Paper 1, May/June 2009), which could prompt a short historical recount. And one of the explanation genres would be needed to provide an answer to the IGCSE question: 'Why was Italy not unified in 1848–49?' (IGCSE History Paper 1, May/June 2009). Such explanation is considered to belong to the second level of difficulty, requiring students to both recall facts and provide reasons for the situation they describe.

In preparation for the genres of exposition and discussion, history textbooks include tasks which teach students to consider sources not only for their reliability or bias, but also for their role in a possible argument. In one task, for example, students were given a number of sources on the Peterloo Massacre, and assigned the role of lawyer or journalist. They were first made aware of the different interests and perspectives by the prompt 'What evidence from the sources would you select: a) if you were writing a defence of the soldiers? b) if you were writing in defence of the injured people?' (Counsel and Steer, 1993: 85). They were then asked to take a position on causes of the event, and produce a text defending it: 'Write a script of a radio documentary explaining what you think happened at Peterloo.' Interestingly, the register was specified. Students were given a voice – that of a present-day professional of the media – and a specific mode – the text should be written to be spoken.

Exposition and discussion belong to the highest level in the IGCSE typology of question difficulty, as they include all the different cognitive demands – recall of facts, explanation and analysis – the examiners look for. A question like: '"Napoleon III of France and Cavour played equally important roles in the unification of Italy." How far do you agree with this statement? Explain your answer' (IGCSE History Paper 1, May/June 2009) would only be given top marks if the candidate wrote a discussion, considering and evaluating the issue from different perspectives. Arguing either for or against the statement would receive slightly lower marks, according to the instructions to examiners. Work in preparation for all these question types can be supported by knowledge of the different genres.

4.5 Conclusion

In this chapter we have presented a method for analysing the structure of different types of texts which create meaning in school subjects. It gives teachers a tool they can use to discuss students' texts and explain why some are more successful than others, as well as how they can be improved and why a particular change is, in fact, an improvement. Applications of genre analysis to teaching in content classes in different parts of the world have shown its effective use (see, for example, Martin 2006; Martin and Rose, 2008; Polias and Dare, 2006; Schleppegrell 2006), since understanding the function of a text and of the stages it is made up of allows teachers and students to connect subject knowledge and the use of language. The cognitive functions intrinsic to a subject become visible through a focus on genres and their stages.

We cannot forget, of course, the specificity of CLIL, where some disciplines are learned in a foreign language. Genres are part of culture and so culturally driven. The use of another language in the classroom brings educational cultures into contact, and this adds another dimension to the map of genres. The genres discussed here represent school genres found in English-speaking countries, their reflection in international examinations and in texts recorded or collected in CLIL classes in English. These will overlap to a greater or lesser degree with the set of local genres. And of course, all genres are constantly evolving, with changes in societies. The chapter offers a method which teachers can use and adapt to approach the texts of their subjects.

By making explicit the way language works in the subjects that CLIL students study in English we are helping to expand their generic competence. When CLIL subject teachers, who know the genres of their subjects intuitively, can intervene at key points in their pupils' learning with the linguistic help needed, much time can be saved, frustration avoided and more subject knowledge created. We have indicated some points, revealed by genre analysis, at which intervention by the teacher would be constructive, and teachers will find others.

This way of looking at texts allows teachers to direct their attention to language and content both during the teaching of a topic, as shown in Morton (2010), for example, and when reading and evaluating their students' work. We take up the role of genre in formative assessment in Chapter 9. Chapter 5 continues with the language of the different school subjects, at the level of grammar and lexis.

Questions and tasks for reflection and discussion

1. Do you find similar genres in the material you use for your subject? What genres do you find, and what objectives do they have?
2. Review the questions in tests and exams you have given your students over a period of time. What genres (or perhaps mini-genres) do they trigger? What examples of these genres are there in the material your students study?
3. Look at some of the students' answers to questions. Are any of the problems in them related to the lack of necessary functional stages, or the use of an inappropriate stage?

4. Text 4.32 represents a genre we saw in the area of science. Which genre is it?

<table>
<tr><td colspan="1" align="center">**Text 4.32**</td></tr>
</table>

Text 4.32
SKILLS Giving 4-figure and 6-figure references 1:25 000 and 1:50 000 maps have a grid of numbered squares on them. To see how a 4-figure grid reference is given, look at the grid in Source A and follow these instructions to give the reference for the red shaded square. • 47 is the line left of the square • 16 is the line below the square. Put these two numbers together and you have a 4-figure grid reference: 4716.

(Cambers and Sibley, 2010: 173)

In the box below you are given the stages of the genre. Segment the text and write the segments in the place corresponding to the stage.

AIM	
METHOD	
RESTATEMENT OF AIM	

5. Text 4.33 develops a historical perspective on the country described. What history genre do you see? Name the stages, using the left-hand column.

Text 4.33

	South Africa is changing rapidly. These changes are affecting employment opportunities.
	White minority rule, which began in the 17th century, was overthrown and black majority rule came into being in 1994. Before then white people held all the positions of power and influence – they were the politicians, factory managers, land-owners and farmers. The black majority relied on the white minority for employment, usually in low-paid jobs as farmhands, miners and labourers. Eventually civil riots and international protests and boycotts led to the white minority government relinquishing power, abandoning apartheid, and allowing each person a vote.
	Since the election of a black president in 1994 the employment situation for some black people has improved. However, many people have not yet seen progress.

(Cambers and Sibley, 2010: 122)

6. Text 4.34 describes pre-revolutionary French society. Rather than being developed as a period study, it has the structure of a genre we saw in science. Which genre do you recognise? Name the stages, using the left-hand column.

Text 4.34

	What was an estate? An estate was a very large group or class of people. In France there were three estates. It was difficult for a person to move from one estate to another.

(cont.)

> **The Three Estates**
> The First Estate
> The **clergy** made up the First estate. They
> included archbishops, bishops, abbots, parish
> priests, monks and nuns. [...]
> The Second Estate
> The **nobles** made up the Second Estate. They
> were nobles by birth, and were landowners [...]
> The Third Estate
> This group consisted of **everybody else** in France.
> Some **middle-class** people, such as merchants,
> bankers, and doctors, were quite wealthy but they
> had no chance of power. They had to pay taxes.
> The **peasants** and the town workers paid heavy
> taxes. [...]

(Hetherton 1992: 11)

7. And for a final question look at Text 4.35. This is a typical example
   of explaining 'why something is there' – an important question in
   geography.

Text 4.35
Atoll
These develop around islands. Fringing reefs grow in a circle attached to the land. Sea-level rise or subsidence of the land causes the coral to grow at the height of the rising sea level to reach the light. This eventually forms a ring of coral reefs with a lagoon replacing the island in the centre.

(Cambers and Sibley, 2010: 82)

What genre is it?
It is made up of basically two stages, the second of which has three
parts. Name the stages, and write the corresponding segments of
text in the appropriate part.

Stages	Text segments

Textbooks

Cambers, G. and Sibley, S. (2010) *Cambridge GCSE Geography*, Cambridge: Cambridge University Press.

Counsell, C. and Steer, C. (1993) *Industrial Britain: The Workshop of the World* (6th printing 2009). Cambridge History Programme, Cambridge: Cambridge University Press.

Edmonds, S. (1993) *Native Peoples of North America. Diversity and Development* (11th printing 2007), Cambridge History Programme, Cambridge: Cambridge University Press.

Hetherton, G. (1992) *Revolutionary France. Liberty, Tyranny and Terror* (10th printing 2009), Cambridge History Programme. Cambridge: Cambridge University Press.

Jones, M. and Jones, G. (2002) *Biology*, Cambridge: Cambridge University Press.

Mantin P. and Pulley, R. (1992) *The Roman World. From Republic to Empire*, Cambridge: Cambridge University Press.

References

Bernstein, B. (1990) *The Structure of Pedagogic Discourse*, London: Routledge.

Bhatia, V. (2004) 'Academic literacy in higher education', in Wilkinson, R. (ed.) *Integrating Content and Language: Meeting the Challenge of a Multilingual Higher Education*, Maastricht: Maastricht University, pp. 55–77.

Cabrales, G. (2010) 'Rigid and stable structures. Topic scheme, lesson plan and hands-on activity', handout for a paper presented at the *I Congreso Internacional de Enseñanza Bilingüe en Centros Educativos*, Madrid, June 2010.

Carretero, M., Asensio, M. and Pozo, J. (1991) 'Cognitive development, historical time representation and causal explanations in adolescence', in Carretero, M., Pope, M, Simons, R. and Pozo, J. (eds.) *Learning and Instruction: European Research in an International Context*, Vol. 3, Oxford: Pergamon Press, pp. 27–48.

Christie, F. and Derewianka, B. (2008) *School Discourse: Learning to Write across the Years of Schooling*, London: Continuum.

Coffin, C. (1997) 'Constructing and giving value to the past: An investigation into secondary school history', in Christie, F. and Martin, J. R. (eds.) (1997) *Genre and Institutions: Social Processes in the Workplace and School*, London: Continuum, pp. 196–230.

Coffin, C. (2006a) *Historical Discourse: The Language of Time, Cause and Evaluation*, London: Continuum.

Coffin, C. (2006b) 'Reconstructing "personal time" as "collective time": Learning the discourse of history', in Whittaker, R., O'Donnell, M. and McCabe, A. (eds.) (2006) *Language and Literacy: Functional Approaches*, London: Continuum, pp. 207–32.

Dalton-Puffer, C. (2007) *Discourse in Content and Language Integrated Learning (CLIL) Classrooms*, Amsterdam: John Benjamins.

Eggins, S. (1994) *An Introduction to Systemic Functional Grammar*, London and New York: Continuum.

Hasan, R. and Williams, G. (eds.) (1996) *Literacy in Society*, London: Longman.

Humphrey, S. (1996) *Exploring Literacy in School Geography*, Sydney: Metropolitan East Disadvantaged Schools Program.

International General Certificate of Secondary Education: Biology Paper 6, Oct/Nov 2008; Chemistry Paper 2, 2008; Biology, 2010; Chemistry, 2010; Technology Paper 1, 2008. All available at www.cie.org.uk

Martin, J. R. (1993) 'Life as noun: Arresting the universe in science and humanities', in Halliday, M. A. K. and Martin, J. R. (eds.) *Writing Science: Literacy and Discursive Power*, London: Falmer, pp. 221–67.

Martin J. R. (2006) 'Metadiscourse: Designing interaction in genre-based literacy programmes', in Whittaker, R., O'Donnell, M. and McCabe, A. (eds.) (2006) *Language and Literacy: Functional Approaches*, London: Continuum, pp. 95–122.

Martin, J. R. and Rose, D. (2008) *Genre Relations: Mapping Culture*, London: Equinox.

Morton, T. (2010) 'Using a genre-based approach to integrating content and language in CLIL: The example of secondary history', in Dalton-Puffer, C., Nikula, T. and Smit, U. (2010) *Language Use and Language Learning in CLIL Classrooms*, Amsterdam: John Benjamins, pp. 81–104.

Polias, J. and Dare, B. (2006) 'Towards a pedagogical grammar', in Whittaker, R., O'Donnell, M. and McCabe, A. (eds.) (2006) *Language and Literacy: Functional Approaches*, London: Continuum, pp. 123–43.

Schleppegrell, M.J. (2004) *The Language of Schooling*, Norwood, NJ: Lawrence Erlbaum.

Schleppegrell, M. (2006) 'An integrated language and content approach for history teachers', *Journal of English for Academic Purposes* 5, 254–68.

van Leeuwen, T. and Humphrey, S. (1996) 'On learning to look through a geographer's eyes', in Hasan, R. and Williams, G. (eds.) (1996) *Literacy in Society*, London: Longman, pp. 29–49.

Veel, R. (1997) 'Learning how to mean – scientifically speaking: Apprenticeship into scientific discourse in the secondary school', in Christie, F. and Martin, J. R. (eds.) (1997) *Genre and Institutions: Social Processes in the Workplace and School*, London: Continuum, pp. 161–95.

Veel, R. (2006) 'The Write it Right project – Linguistic modelling of secondary school and the workplace', in Whittaker, R., O'Donnell, M. and McCabe, A. (eds.) (2006) *Language and Literacy: Functional Approaches*, London: Continuum, pp. 66–92.

Veel, R. and Coffin, C. (1996) 'Learning to think like an historian: The language of secondary school history', in Hasan, R. and Williams, G. (eds.) (1996) *Literacy in Society*, London: Longman, pp. 191–231.

Wignell, P., Martin, J. R. and Eggins, S. (1993) 'The discourse of geography: Ordering and explaining the experiential world', in Halliday, M. A. K. and Martin, J. R. (eds.) (1993) *Writing Science: Literacy and Discursive Power*, London: The Falmer Press, pp. 136–55.

5 Grammar and lexis in CLIL subjects

5.1 Introduction

In Chapter 4 we analysed the generic structure of texts, showing how different disciplines carry out activities and structure knowledge in different ways. There we commented briefly on those language features of the texts which are significant as signals of specific genres. Now we examine in detail the vocabulary and grammar used in school texts, and show CLIL teachers how they can help their students become aware of the ways in which language features create meaning in their subjects, and so improve both their comprehension and their spoken and written production.

Learning the grammar and the lexis of a foreign language is often equated with learning that language. In this view, learners need to memorise a store of words, and a set of rules about how to combine those words to make meanings. However, sometimes in foreign language classes it is not always clear to the students what meanings to make, or what to make them for. In content classes taught in a foreign language, the topics to be discussed or written about are clear, as is the purpose for which the language is to be used: to build up the structured knowledge of the content area as specified in the syllabus, and to be able to use this knowledge to reason about the field in ways accepted by the academic community, at the different educational levels. Teachers who offer their subjects in a foreign language face a challenge, since the role of language to construct their disciplines comes suddenly to the fore. That role hasn't changed simply by changing the language, but what usually goes unnoticed when using a shared first language, is inevitably problematised in a second or foreign language.

This chapter aims to show how teachers can think and talk about the language of their subjects from the point of view of its role in understanding and learning the discipline, and as inseparable from its content. The chapter includes examples from content textbooks and from CLIL students' written production, to illustrate the features of language in relation to their functions when English is used in disciplinary learning. It focuses on the language of secondary school disciplines, since it is at this stage in the education system that students start to come into contact with the more demanding features of academic registers. In Chapter 8 we will analyse the students' language from the point of view of development, as they learn to write texts which reflect the language of the disciplines. In this chapter, the examples are taken from history and biology, as disciplines representing the social sciences and 'hard' sciences accessible to all readers.

As explained in Chapter 4, the texts studied and produced in the different disciplines at school have different functions, and are structured in different ways to fulfil those goals. They also require different choices from the grammatical and lexical resources of the language. These choices create the register of the text type or genre. This chapter analyses a number of features which play an important role in the realisation of different types of meaning. Some are important for their role in the expression of content: type of lexis (especially nouns and verbs), prepositional phrases expressing circumstances (time, place, reason etc.), markers of logical relations between clauses (coordinating and subordinating conjunctions). Others are involved in constructing the role the writer or speaker takes on, and that assigned to the reader or hearer (informing, questioning, evaluating, responding). And, finally, others have a function in the organisation of the content in the text (the passive voice and the expansion of nouns with pre- and post-modification). In this chapter, then, we show the role of specific linguistic elements in making the meanings of school texts. We use the framework first presented in the Introduction and Chapter 1 (see Boxes 0.1 and 1.1), now linking the register variables and metafunctions described there with the grammar and lexis which they require. This expanded framework is summarised in Box 5.1.

Box 5.1: Register analysis: The linguistic features studied in the texts		
SITUATIONAL VARIABLE	METAFUNCTION	PART OF THE LINGUISTIC SYSTEM THAT REALISES THAT MEANING
FIELD **Activity, topic**	IDEATIONAL MEANINGS 'Language is used to organise, understand and express our perceptions of the world and of our own consciousness.'	– processes (types of verbs: actions, relations, thinking, perceiving, liking etc.) – participants (nouns in subject and object position etc.) – circumstances – markers of logical relations between clauses (addition, contrast, cause, sequence)

(cont.)

TENOR Relations of power, equality	INTERPERSONAL MEANINGS 'Language is used to enable us to participate in communicative acts with other people, to take on roles and to express and understand feelings, attitude and judgements.'	– clause structure (declarative, imperative, interrogative) – modality (certainty and obligation) – attitude (positive / negative lexis)
MODE Distance between communicators (written / spoken)	TEXTUAL MEANINGS 'Language is used to relate what is said (or written) to the real world and to other linguistic events. This involves the use of language to organise the text itself.'	– devices to move elements, or compress or distribute information – first position versus last position (passive voice) – clauses versus noun phrases etc.

(based on Bloor and Bloor, 1995; Eggins 1994;
Schleppegrell 2004; quotes from Bloor and Bloor, 1995: 9)

This framework is applied to the analysis of a number of extracts from science and history textbooks for secondary school CLIL students, as well as texts written by the students. This type of analysis allows teachers to understand the roles of language in their subjects, and see how, through the subject language, students begin to understand and learn the vertical knowledge of the discipline. In this way, CLIL teachers can anticipate the hidden difficulties that the academic register of a subject presents to students, and prepare the material they plan to use in class, having in mind possible problems of comprehension. As the title of the chapter indicates, difficulties in learning school subjects are not limited to the specific vocabulary of an academic field, but include the grammar in which the content is expressed. To show this, the chapter selects examples which move from simpler to more complex school genres, with their more challenging academic functions, and so more complex language.

5.2 Starting to build the language of school disciplines: The grammar and lexis of procedures and reports

To approach the analysis of the way grammar and lexis make meanings in school subjects, we will start with a text type organised by time, and close to the experience of the students who read it, the *science procedure*. The procedure gives instructions as to how to carry out an observation or experiment, as explained in Chapter 4. The example in Text 5.1 is from a textbook (grade 10, ages 15–16).

Text 5.1
Measuring the rate of transpiration of a potted plant 1. Use two similar well-watered potted plants. Enclose one plant entirely in a polythene bag, including its pot. This is the control. 2. Enclose only the pot of the second plant in a polythene bag. Fix the bag firmly around the stem of the plant, and seal with petroleum jelly. 3. Place both plants on balances, and record their masses. 4. Record the mass of each plant every day, at the same time, for at least a week. 5. Draw a graph of your results.

(Jones and Jones, 2002: 68)

A register analysis allows us to systematise the linguistic features, and explain them in relation to the function of the genre. Following the framework in Box 5.1 we first look at the expression of content, the *field*, and analyse the vocabulary in the text.

(i) Lexis: Nouns

This procedure refers to an activity to be carried out using a series of objects, and so we find a high proportion of concrete, often everyday, nouns, as Table 5.1 (overleaf) shows.

The nouns which can be considered specialised refer to concepts in science, and play a part in inducting the students into the scientific method – for example, that of control and experimental samples.

(ii) Lexis: Verbs

Table 5.2 (overleaf) shows the semantic classes of verbs, or processes, which appear in the text.

All the processes except one are actions to be carried out by the students. The exception, the verb 'to be', expressing a state, appears in the sentence identifying the function of the control sample.

157

Table 5.1   *Everyday and specialised lexis in Text 5.1*

EVERYDAY	plant bag pot stem jelly
SPECIALISED	mass control graph results

Table 5.2   *Process types in Text 5.1*

ACTIONS / MATERIAL PROCESSES	measuring use enclose fix seal place record draw
STATES / RELATIONAL PROCESSES	is

(iii) Expansion of clauses: Circumstances of place, time and manner

In the procedure, different types of circumstantial information are included, making explicit the way to follow the method described.

Table 5.3   *Circumstances in Text 5.1*

PLACE	in a polythene bag around the stem of the plant on balances
TIME	every day, at the same time, for at least a week
MANNER	entirely firmly, with petroleum jelly

Every step in the procedure except the final one, instructing the students to write down the results, carries information about where to put the objects involved, when the actions should be done or how they should be carried out. It is interesting that the most elaborated circumstance is of time, with three different meanings – frequency, location in time and duration –, showing its key role in the experiment.

(iv) Expressing logical relations between clauses

The main structuring device in the procedure – sequence – is marked by numbering the steps to be taken. The purpose of the procedure appears in the title: *Measuring the rate of transpiration* ... Students need to recognise that the *-ing* form of the verb indicates this logical relation.

Moving to the relations between the writer and reader, the *tenor*, the grammar of Text 5.1 shows how the writer takes on a powerful role, that of instructor, by using the imperative to give unmitigated commands to the students. Interestingly, in classes in which this sort of activity takes place face to face, the teachers are often less direct (Dalton-Puffer, 2005). Students, as apprentice scientists, do not normally reproduce this role and write procedures themselves, but this genre is the base for oral inter-action as they carry out the experiment, and for the procedural recount, which they tell or write after having completed the experiment.

To study the way information is organised in a text, the *mode*, one key category to look at is that of nouns. Many of them have different types of modification, as shown in Table 5.4. Building up the nominal group with pre- or post-modification is one of the ways in which writers include information in academic texts.

In the table, the head of the nominal group, that is, the thing which the modifiers classify or describe in some way, is in italics, showing the position of the modifiers more clearly. The modifiers in this pro-cedure specify the class, (e.g. *polythene*), type (e.g. *similar well-watered*

Table 5.4 *Modification of the nominal group in Text 5.1*

PRE-MODIFIED NOUNS	two similar well-watered potted *plants* a polythene *bag* petroleum *jelly*
POST-MODIFIED NOUNS	the *rate* of transpiration of a potted plant the *pot* of the second plant the *stem* of the plant the *mass* of each plant a *graph* of your results

potted) and so on of the object referred to. In this text, there are no nouns with both pre- and post-modification as will be found in the register of other, more complex, text types.

This analysis shows how, for the student reader, the grammar and lexis of the procedure include the familiar – direct commands, sequential organisation and specific, concrete nouns – as well as introducing features of academic language, abstractions and the modification of the nominal group. To help their students learn to understand texts in which this feature becomes more prominent, teachers will find it useful to work on the identification of the head of the nominal group. Students tend to transfer strategies applicable to their first language to the text they are reading in English, and so could, for example, select a premodifier as the head, and misunderstand the phrase, perhaps thinking that *petroleum* is the head of the phrase *petroleum jelly*.

Another basic genre in scientific writing, the *report*, uses grammar and lexis very differently. In a report, writers present accepted knowledge in a field, often in the form of a classification or an analysis by parts or features, as shown in Chapter 4. Text 5.2 is a report which introduces the field of study to secondary school biologists.

Text 5.2
Biology is the study of living things, which are often called **organisms**. Living organisms have several features or **characteristics** which make them different from objects which are not alive.

1. They **reproduce.**
2. They take in nutrients. This is known as feeding or **nutrition.**
3. They **respire** – that is, they release energy from their food, often by combining it with oxygen.
4. They **grow.**
5. They **excrete** – that is, they get rid of waste substances that have been made by chemical reactions, known as metabolic reactions, going on inside them.
6. They **move.**
7. They are **sensitive** – that is, they can sense and respond to changes in their surroundings.
8. They are made of **cells.**

(Jones and Jones, 2002: 1)

Again, using the framework for register analysis in Box 5.1, the field can be described in terms of the vocabulary.

(i) Lexis: Nouns

This text offers the student reader an approach to the discipline by defining the object of study. It starts from everyday, concrete nouns (*things, objects*), so general as to be simply an anchor from which to move to the technical terms of the discipline. In this text, the proportion of nouns which form part of everyday vocabulary is considerably lower than that of those belonging to the specialised lexis of science. This is shown in Table 5.5.

Table 5.5 *Everyday and scientific lexis in Text 5.2*

EVERYDAY (commonsense)	things objects food changes
SCIENTIFIC (uncommonsense)	biology organism features characteristics nutrients nutrition energy oxygen substances reaction cells

The high frequency of scientific words, as compared to everyday vocabulary, shows how the writer leads the reader into the uncommonsense world of biology and its language – that is, from horizontal knowledge to vertical knowledge, as explained in Chapter 1. Given the generalising function of the text, all the nouns are plural or uncountable, unlike those in Text 5.1.

(ii) Lexis: Verbs

The process types in Text 5.2 can be grouped into those expressing actions and those involved in defining and naming, as in Table 5.6.

Clearly, the main focus of Text 5.2 is on what living organisms do, with the actions in the text having those organisms as their subjects. The verbs of defining or describing (relational processes) appear in the introductory sentences, which indicate the function of the text, telling

Table 5.6   *Process types in Text 5.2*

ACTIONS / MATERIAL PROCESSES	reproduce take in respire release combining grow excrete get rid of move respond
STATES / RELATIONAL PROCESSES	is, are make (... different) have
SPEAKING / VERBAL PROCESSES	are called
THINKING / MENTAL PROCESSES	is known as sense

student readers they are learning the language as well as the content of the subject. Those connected with naming (verbal processes) are also related to this function.

The relationship between writer and reader, the tenor, is also made clear in the grammar. As in Text 5.1, the writer is powerful, but, in this text, power is shown in the expression of undisputed knowledge. By using the timeless, simple present tense (*they reproduce*), the writer takes the role of the knower, the informer, who states general truths about the discipline. As part of this role, the writer teaches the reader the terminology of the subject. The text contains a number of signals of this, as Table 5.7 shows.

Table 5.7   *Signals of explanation in Text 5.2*

SIGNALS OF EXPLANATION OF TERMS	feeding *or* nutrition, *that is*, they release energy, *that is*, they get rid of waste substances, reactions, *known as* metabolic reactions, *that is*, they can sense and respond to changes

These linguistic markers alert the reader to points where the writer gives information about the text itself, with an explanation of terms, or proposed synonyms.

As regards the organisation of the information, there is some expansion of nouns with pre- and post-modifiers classifying, specifying or explaining the head of the nominal group.

Table 5.8   *Modification of the nominal group in Text 5.2*

PRE-MODIFIED NOUNS	Living *organisms* metabolic *reactions*
POST-MODIFIED NOUNS	the *study* of living things *objects* which are not alive *changes* in their surroundings
PRE- AND POST-MODIFIED NOUN	waste *substances* that have been made by chemical reactions

Given the introductory nature of the text, rather than including all the descriptive information in the nominal group, some important characteristics are expressed in separate sentences: we are told that some things are *not alive*, and that organisms are *sensitive*. Making such a claim in its own clause, rather than including this information as part of the nominal group, gives it higher information status.

The very simple grammar of Text 5.2 is a vehicle, then, for a basic science register. Students can be made aware of the importance for the subject of generalisation, expressed through plural and uncountable nouns, and of the meaning of 'accepted knowledge' in a discipline, signalled in English by the simple present tense, as well as of the markers which introduce or explain terms in the field.

5.3 Moving towards the abstract language of the disciplines: A historical account by a CLIL student

In the next stage of the study of the grammar and lexis typical of secondary school texts we analyse the language of the genre of explanation. This type of text is more cognitively demanding than the procedure, with its sequential organisation of actions to be carried out by the reader, or the report, which simply states fact. As a corollary, the language of cause and explanation is more complex. This genre is organised by constructing logical relations between events or concepts, and so presents challenges at the level of grammar and lexis. This can be seen in the different ways in which cause can be expressed in academic texts, and in the organisation of information in the nominal group.

The section uses an example written by a secondary school CLIL student in a history class. It represents an intermediate step in the complexity of the grammar of school subjects, allowing the reader to see the differences between the grammar of procedures and reports, on the one hand, and between the grammar of textbook explanation genres on the other. In the analysis, special attention is paid to how the information is organised to make the explanation coherent.

Text 5.3 was written by a student in a grade 10 CLIL class (15–16 years old). The students had been asked to write about World War I, including causes, characteristics, the reason it ended and an evaluation of the Treaty of Versailles. The main aim of the text, then, was to explain the events. The student text is reproduced exactly as the learner wrote it. When discussing examples, the interlanguage errors have been adapted to the standard.

Text 5.3

WWI broke up when Franz Ferdinand was assasinated by a Serbian student in Sarajevo. As there was a great feeling of nationalism in their time and militarism dominated countries, Austria-Hungary declared war on Serbia. The alliances formed in that time made the five main powers in Europe to go war. France, who was allied with Britain, fought against Germany. Germany tried to enter France using the way of Belgium because they thought that nobody will suppose that they wanted to attack France. Britain interfiered in Germany's plans and went to war. On the other hand, Germany had a great naval army who compited with Britain for the sea supremacy. Germany declared that they will sink any boat near his territories. They sank a U.S.A. boat and the U.S.A. president, Woodrow Wilson, decided to war on war just to fight beside the triple alliance against the triple entente.

Meanwhile, the war developed mostly in an stealmate battle. There were two fronts, the eastern and the weastern front. Most of the battles were fought in trenches that were very difficult to pass by. New technical devices, such as tanks, had a lot to do in war. They were introduce in the battle of Somme in 1916. Those metal boxes carry heavy weapons and great protections, and could pass through bared wired without difficulties. Despite this great toughness, tanks were very vulnerable in muddy zones.

(cont.)

> Peace was signed in Versailles the 11th of November 1918 at 11 o'clock. This supposed the end of a terrible war which lasted four years. The treaty was signed by the Britain, France, Italy and the U.S.A.
> I agree with the treaty because it is an anti-war treaty.

As in earlier sections of this chapter, the text will be discussed first from the point of view of the representation of the content (the field), then from that of the writer–reader relationship it builds up (the tenor), and, finally that of the organisation of the information or content (the mode). The analysis shows differences between the two disciplines, history and science, in the way each represents its field.

(i) Lexis: Nouns

As in science, there is an important distinction in the type of vocabulary used in class as pupils go up from primary to secondary school. Text 5.3 shows command of the vocabulary of the topic, using a good proportion of words from a formal register. The student develops his topic using two types of nouns: some more abstract and others which are concrete, as shown in Table 5.9.

Table 5.9   *Concrete and abstract nouns in Text 5.3*

CONCRETE (commonsense)	army boat trenches tanks weapons
ABSTRACT (uncommonsense)	nationalism militarism alliances supremacy treaty

The proportion of more abstract nouns immediately characterises the text as not belonging to everyday language. The more concrete nouns are mainly from the semantic field of warfare. The writer frequently generalises, as expected, using plurals. He also displays his knowledge using proper nouns, referring to the historical figures, outstanding individuals who played important roles in the events, and to the countries and cities involved, as shown in Table 5.10.

Table 5.10 *Proper nouns in Text 5.3*

HISTORICAL ACTORS	Franz Ferdinand Woodrow Wilson
COUNTRIES (PRESENTED AS HISTORICAL ACTORS TOO)	France Germany Britain U.S.A. Italy
CITIES (AS LOCATIONS)	Sarajevo Versailles

The countries are nearly always presented as historical actors rather than locations for the events, since they are subjects of a number of verbs expressing actions of humans. The cities, on the other hand, appear as locations in prepositional phrases of place.

(ii) Lexis: Verbs

In Text 5.3, which is longer and more complex functionally than the science procedure and report, a greater variety of classes of verbs is required. First, it describes a series of events using action verbs like those in Table 5.11.

Table 5.11 *Process types in Text 5.3: Material processes*

ACTIONS / MATERIAL PROCESSES	WWI *broke out* when Ferdinand *was assassinated* France *fought* against Germany They [Germany] *sank* a U.S.A. boat The treaty *was signed* by Britain ...

The writer also gives background information, characteristics of the war or its actors expressed in verbs representing states of being or having, as in Table 5.12.

Table 5.12 *Process types in Text 5.3: Relational processes*

STATES / RELATIONAL PROCESSES	Germany *had* a great naval army tanks *were* very vulnerable trenches ... *were* very difficult to move along it *is* an anti-war treaty This *meant* the end of a terrible war

The last example is slightly different, since it interprets an event for the reader described previously in the text, the signing of the treaty, explaining its significance.

Another semantic set of verbs in the text expresses thought and feeling. The writer uses these mental processes to introduce explanations of events, in which the different historical actors are presented as thinking and taking decisions, as shown in Table 5.13.

Table 5.13   *Process types in Text 5.3: Mental processes*

THINKING AND FEELING / MENTAL PROCESSES	they [Germany] *thought* that ... nobody will *suppose* that ... they *wanted* to attack France Woodrow Wilson *decided* to go to war

The set of verbs of speech, verbal processes, is also represented in this text, since relations between countries and an important part of the activity of war itself can be enacted verbally. There is only one example of the set, *declare*, but it is used in two different ways, as the examples in Table 5.14 show:

Table 5.14   *Process types in Text 5.3: Verbal processes*

SPEAKING / VERBAL PROCESSES	Austria-Hungary *declared* war on Serbia Germany *declared* that they will sink any boat near his territories.

In the first sentence, *declare* means to formally announce the start of hostilities. In the second, it introduces indirect speech, representing what Germany said, which, in fact, is a threat.

Another type of verb simply indicates the existence of a participant or a concrete or abstract entity. In Text 5.3, we find *there* used to bring new information into the text.

Table 5.15   *Process types in Text 5.3: Existential processes*

EXISTENCE / EXISTENTIAL PROCESSES	*there was* a great feeling of nationalism in their time *There were* two fronts

The variety of meanings in the verbs, or process types, in this history text reflects the wider range of types of experience covered, in comparison to the short science texts analysed earlier.

(iii) Expansion of clauses: Place, time, manner

As is usual in history, the writer introduces quite a lot of key information into his text by expanding the clauses with circumstances, realised in prepositional phrases. The examples appear in Table 5.16.

Table 5.16   *Circumstances in Text 5.3*

PLACE / TIME	They [tanks] were introduced *in the battle of Somme // in 1916.*
PLACE / TIME	Peace was signed *in Versailles // the 11th of November 1918 at 11 o'clock.*
PLACE	tanks were very vulnerable *in muddy zones.*
PLACE / MANNER	[tanks] could pass *through bared wired // without difficulties.*

With relation to the Treaty of Versailles, marking its importance, the writer gives an unusually exact time circumstance.

(iv) Expressing logical relations

The writer of Text 5.3 was asked to explain why the war happened and how it developed. That means he had to write a historical account, a text giving information related to the causes and consequences of a series of events located in time. To do this, he linked the clauses he constructed using markers of the logical relations between them. In the text we find examples of markers of time and cause / purpose, mainly in finite subordinate clauses, as shown in Table 5.17.

Table 5.17   *Markers of cause, purpose and time in Text 5.3*

CAUSE	*As* there was a great feeling of nationalism *because* they thought that *because* it is an anti-war treaty
PURPOSE	just *to* fight beside the triple alliance
TIME	*when* Franz Ferdinand was assassinated

Some clauses in the text are linked by the conjunction *and*, an additive marker which often includes temporal or causal meanings, as Table 5.18 shows:

Table 5.18   And *marking addition and consequence in Text 5.3*

ADDITION	Those metal boxes carried heavy weapons and great protections, *and* could pass through bared wired without difficulties.
ADDITION / CONSEQUENCE	They sank a U.S.A. boat *and* the U.S.A. president, Woodrow Wilson, decided to go to war

In some cases, the clause introduced by *and* simply adds more information, at the same level of importance as that in the first clause. In others, it signals both addition and consequence. In the second example, *and* can be interpreted by the reader as *and so*. In general, the grammatical structures, with subordination and coordination of clauses, used here to express logical relations, are more characteristic of spoken language (as Chapter 8 discusses), and not very often found in the more abstract language of school disciplines.

Turning now to the relations between writer and reader, the tenor, as we saw in Chapter 4, there are a number of roles that writers of history texts may take on. They may be simple recorders of past events, they may be interpreters, proposing explanations for events, establishing cause–consequence relations among events, or they may take the role of judge, evaluating the past and its actors. The grammar of Text 5.3 shows the principal role of the writer to be that of recorder and interpreter. This role is expressed mainly in the verb forms and clause linkers. The writer uses the declarative (or statement) form, in the past tense, to present the record of events and background information, indicating there can be no doubt about them.

Table 5.19   *Use of the past tense in Text 5.3*

PAST DECLARATIVE FORMS	France, who *was allied* with Britain, *fought* against Germany. They *sank* a U.S.A. boat.

Besides this, he uses a number of resources to indicate the logical relations of cause and consequence between events, given the principal function of the text, as we saw in Tables 5.17 and 5.18. Both these features show that the interpretation presented is not open to question. The content, consisting of facts and events of the past with their explanations, is presented as accepted knowledge. There is no use of conditionals of the type *If Germany had not attacked ... , if the USA had not entered the war ...* , nor of **modality** markers like *the reason might be, the French could have ...* , to open up the text to the possibility for alternative interpretations. Thus, the reader is positioned to accept the writer's presentation of events.

The student writer does not argue for his interpretation, or judge the historical actors. However, there is some indication of his attitude to the events in the use of evaluative adjectives like *great* (though this seems to refer mainly to size), and *terrible*, and in the final sentence in the text, where he firmly states his position and justifies it.

Text 5.3 is also interesting from the point of view of information management, the mode. Its length and its more complex functions, in comparison to Texts 5.1 and 5.2, demand the use of linguistic devices to present information to the reader coherently. The writer uses the nominal group to carry a lot of the content, and the passive to move elements to first or final position in order to help the reader follow the topic, or to recognise important new information placed at the end of a sentence.

(i) Expansion of nouns

In this text, the writer has rarely used a single noun with its determiner. As just mentioned, there are a number of long noun phrases, a resource also found in the science texts. In the examples in Table 5.20, the nouns which function as the head of the phrase are in italics, showing how the phrases are expanded with information included before and after the noun.

Table 5.20 *Modification of the nominal group in Text 5.3*

PRE-MODIFIED NOUNS	Those metal *boxes* the sea *supremacy* a stalemate *battle* heavy *weapons* and great *protections* this great *toughness* an anti-war *treaty*
POST-MODIFIED NOUNS	The *alliances* formed at that time *France*, who was allied with Britain, *trenches* that were very difficult to go along
PRE- AND POST-MODIFIED NOUNS	a great *feeling* of nationalism the five main *powers* in Europe a great naval *army* which competed with Britain for the sea supremacy New technical *devices*, such as tanks a terrible *war* which lasted four years

Pre-modifiers classify or describe their nouns, as in *sea supremacy* or *heavy weapons*. The post-modifiers are of different classes: prepositional phrases (e.g. *feeling of nationalism*) and finite clauses (e.g. *war which lasted four year*). Including a lot of information in the noun phrase in this way is characteristic of academic language, especially of written texts.

(ii) The passive

The passive is usually chosen in English to place certain information at the beginning of a clause or at the end of a clause or sentence. It can also be used to control the amount of information the writer decides to include, in particular the identity of the agent who carried out the action. The student writer seems to be aware of this, and in Text 5.3, there are a number of examples of the passive, as shown in Table 5.21.

Table 5.21   *Use of the passive in Text 5.3*

PASSIVE WITHOUT AGENT	I Most of the battles *were fought* in trenches II They [tanks] *were introduced* in the battle of Somme III Peace *was signed* in Versailles the 11th of November 1918 at 11 o'clock
PASSIVE WITH AGENT SPECIFIED	IV The treaty *was signed* by the Britain, France, Italy and the U.S.A. V Franz Ferdinand *was assassinated* by a Serbian student in Sarajevo

Here the examples have been numbered to make them easier to identify in the analysis. In Example (i) the passive is functional for two reasons. On the one hand, readers know who was fighting, so this information, which would be in first, or subject, position in the active voice, can be excluded. On the other, the topic of this paragraph is the war, how it develops, and its characteristics. By using the passive voice, reference to the war, in its battles, can take first position, as the subject of the verb, signalling topic continuity in the paragraph.

Example (ii) has a similar explanation. In this part of the paragraph the writer develops the topic of characteristics of the war with relation to new technology, and the passive again allows topic continuity by placing reference to the tanks in subject position. The reader is left to assume that both sides used tanks from this moment on, information that would have to be made explicit in the active voice.

Example (iii) leaves the important information as to who signed the peace treaty for its own separate sentence – Example (iv) in Table 5.21 – and

171

places the important temporal data at the end of the sentence, where it can have full focus.

In example (iv), the passive allows the signatories to be placed in final position, with focus as the new or important information. Writers distribute information into sentences on the basis of its importance, and readers use this convention in their interpretation. By allocating two separate sentences to the treaty, first giving the dates, and later identifying the agents of the agreement, the writer is signalling information status: there are two equally important things to say about the treaty, when it was signed, and who it was signed by.

Finally, example (v) uses the passive in order to place the important figure of Franz Ferdinand at the beginning of the clause explaining the outbreak of the war, and at the same time include the identity of the assassin in the sentence.

Both the use of noun phrase modification to include information in the text and of the passive to move elements to different positions are necessary to produce coherent text. This student writer, then, is beginning to control a number of linguistic conventions of the written register for the genre. However, CLIL students will find in a typical explanation in their textbook more challenges related to the expression of scientific activities or historical events in ways which make the actual events difficult to recover as they read the text. Teachers, who are used to reading in their field, are normally unaware of the complexity of its language, and of the processes needed to reconstruct the event described. The next section is devoted to uncovering them.

5.4 Distancing the grammar from the event: Challenges for CLIL students in the language of textbooks

This section continues studying mode, the way in which language 'is used to organize itself' (Bloor and Bloor, 1995: 9), showing that secondary school textbooks use different linguistic strategies for information management from those found in the previous section. These language choices often pose problems for inexperienced readers.

Mode in life sciences

To do this, we return to an example of a factorial explanation from a biology textbook, discussed in Chapter 4, and repeated here as Text 5.4. This is a paragraph written for students aged 15–16, both native and non-native speakers of English, and it represents the typical language of school subjects at secondary level. The topic is population growth.

Text 5.4
There are two main reasons for this recent growth spurt.
The first is the **reduction of disease**. Improvements in water supply, sewage treatment, hygienic food handling and general standards of cleanliness have virtually wiped out many diseases in countries such as the USA and most European countries – for example typhoid and dysentery. Immunisation against diseases such as polio has made these very rare indeed. Smallpox has been totally eradicated. And the discovery of antibiotics has now made it possible to treat most diseases caused by bacteria.

(Jones and Jones, 2002: 168)

The text is explaining a series of events carried out by humans, but rather than specifying who these people were and the actions they did, the writer presents this information using a number of abstractions, in fairly complex nominal groups. The grammar, then, has been distanced from the events it represents (Martin, 1993). While experienced readers have no difficulties with this type of text, many studies have shown the need to work with students as they read, helping them to recover the events, the people involved in them and the logical relations between them. These studies have shown remarkable improvement in students' reading comprehension when the abstract, nominalised language of this type of text is made more accessible (see Acevedo, 2010; Martin 2006; Martin and Rose, 2005). The analyses in this section indicate how teachers can prepare to do this.

The main grammatical transformation in Text 5.4, and the one most frequent in academic register, is nominalisation, discussed briefly in Chapter 1. There are a number of instances in the second paragraph. In its first sentence we find: *The first is the reduction of disease.* The nominal group, *the reduction of disease*, expresses an event, but the writer has not chosen to use a word from the typical category for actions, a verb, *reduce*, but has used the nominalised form *reduction*. Had this event been expressed using the verb, the writer would have had choices like those shown in Text 5.4a, in which the right-hand column shows the expanded versions.

Text 5.4a	
ORIGINAL TEXT	REFORMULATION INTO CLAUSES
There are two main reasons for this recent growth spurt.	[i] Firstly, we have reduced disease
The first is the reduction of disease	[ii] Firstly, disease has been reduced

173

Choice (i) adds information, the agent, thus changing the focus of the sentence, while (ii) makes *disease* the subject of the sentence, and thus the topic. Also, placing *disease* at the beginning of the sentence, just after *growth spurt*, would probably puzzle the reader for a moment: *There are two main reasons for this recent growth spurt. Firstly, disease ...* In the chosen version, by using *the first (reason)* as subject and topic, and later equating it with the *reduction of disease* the writer presents the information in a more effective order, helping the reader to follow the explanation.

As most writers know, the order of information is crucial to the construction of coherent text, and, in English, where there are restrictions on the order of constituents within a sentence, grammatical transformations of different types are needed to move concepts around. The use of the passive is one which immediately springs to mind, especially as it is a feature of scientific language, but there are many more. The example in Text 5.4a is of nominalisation. Nouns are mobile elements in a sentence, since they can be subjects or objects, or part of prepositional phrases, and so can be placed in different positions in the clause.

Nouns are also flexible, as they can be modified in a number of ways. This happens in the next sentence in Text 5.4, in which the actions which led to the reduction of disease are also nominalised, and have pre- and post-modification of different classes: *Improvements in water supply, sewage treatment, hygienic food handling and general standards of cleanliness.* The actions can be recovered by expressing them in the form of clauses, as in Text 5.4b:

Text 5.4b	
ORIGINAL TEXT	REFORMULATION INTO CLAUSES
improvements in water supply	water supply has been improved
sewage treatment	sewage is now treated
hygienic food handling	food is handled hygienically
General standards of cleanliness	generally we do everything more cleanly

This type of reformulation of nominal groups has been shown to be necessary to help secondary school readers really understand what is going on in a text (see chapters in Fang and Schleppegrell, 2008, for examples from different school subjects). When they read nominal groups with pre-modification, it is often not clear to students which word is the head of the group, the *thing* which is being talked about, especially as they may meet more than one noun as they read, with the first functioning as a classifier, as in *water supply, sewage treatment* and *food handling*. For scientists, though, expressing these processes in abstract nominal form is functional, since it plays a part in building up the technical meanings of their specialised field, as discussed in Chapter 4.

These examples show the typical use of nominalisations of processes, but other categories are often interchanged in secondary school texts. The introductory sentence in Text 5.4, *There are two main reasons for this recent growth spurt*, includes a number of examples of these transformations, probably chosen for both textual and technical reasons. First, looking at the textual reasons, the writer has started the text by using 'presentative' *there*, a signal of new information. The alternative, eliminating the *There* structure, would produce something like Text 5.4c.

Text 5.4c	
ORIGINAL TEXT	REFORMULATION INTO CLAUSES
There are two main *reasons* for this recent growth spurt	We can explain this recent growth spurt in two main ways

By using the noun *reason*, which can be counted (*two*) and qualified (*main*), rather than the verb *explain*, the writer is able to signal the two-part structure of the factorial explanation, which has the function of giving a number of unrelated reasons for a phenomenon (see Chapter 4). This makes the sequential marker at the beginning of the paragraph which gives the reasons very effective in anticipating the content to the reader.

The technical reasons are related to the scientific content of the paragraph, which is expressed in *this recent growth spurt*. Here the writer has chosen a nominalised process, *growth*, and an adverbial meaning (fast) expressed as a noun, *spurt*, with the process (*growth*) pre-modifying and so classifying the *spurt*. The actual process the writer is referring to is shown as Text 5.4d.

Text 5.4d	
ORIGINAL TEXT	REFORMULATION INTO CLAUSES
[... reasons for] this recent growth *spurt*	[... explain why] the population has recently grown very fast

This noun, *spurt*, expresses briefly, or encapsulates, a concept in the field of demography, a type of growth, which could contrast with slower, sustained increases. Interestingly, this nominalised form does not make explicit who or what has grown.

The phenomenon of the use of one grammatical category in place of another, such as nominalising processes, has been termed 'grammatical metaphor' by Halliday (e.g. Halliday and Matthiessen, 2004), in his studies of the differences between spoken and written language. The concept was introduced in Chapter 1, and now this section focuses on it and its role in more detail. Box 5.2 summarises and exemplifies the concept, and shows the processes of recovering meanings from this type of scientific language.

Box 5.2: Grammatical metaphor
Grammatical metaphor is a phenomenon typically found in academic written language, in which a word from one grammatical category is replaced by one from a different category. The lexical root word is usually the same, or, if not, carries similar meaning. To reveal the participants, processes, logical relations and so on, and so improve understanding, we can 'unpack' these metaphors.

Reduction of disease explains population growth

GRAMMATICAL METAPHORS	UNPACKING INTO CLAUSES
Logical relation in the verb 'explain'	*Because of* the reduction of disease, the population has grown The population has grown *because* disease has been reduced.
Process as participant 'Reduction of disease'	Disease has been reduced Scientists have eradicated some diseases
Process as participant 'population growth'	The population has grown There are more people

The example in the box shows another transformation frequent in academic language, the logical relation of cause expressed by a verb: *explain*.

Mode in social science

The social sciences, too, use this method to move elements to different positions in the clause, and so organise information into a logical presentation for the reader, or to include in a noun phrase a lot of information used by the discipline in a technical sense. This extract from a CLIL textbook on the same history topic as that of the student text in Section 5.2 contains a number of examples. The text has been reduced considerably to allow the reader to compare the language used in the two types of writing. The grammatical metaphors and causal expressions to be analysed are marked in italics.

Text 5.5
The First World War On 28 July Austria-Hungary declared war on Serbia. By 4 August Germany and Austria-Hungary (the Central Powers) were at war with Russia, France and Britain (the Allies). Generals in all countries were desperate to mobilise their troops; that is, to get them moving towards the frontier with the enemy. *Rapid mobilisation reduced the time available for discussion and negotiation to virtually nothing.* [...] Once the fighting *had led to* stalemate, the leaders had no idea how to end the war without losing face ... [...] The U-boat campaign *helped to bring* America into the war on the side of Britain and France. By 1917 U-boats were trying to sink any ship that might be trading with Britain. This involved attacks on American ships. The American government *responded by* declaring war on Germany in April 1917. The power and wealth of the USA greatly strengthened the position of the Allies.

(McAleavy, 2002: 8–9)

We start with the last sentence in the first paragraph, which includes three nominalisations.

Text 5.5a	
GRAMMATICAL METAPHOR	UNPACKING INTO CLAUSES
Rapid mobilisation reduced the time available for	i The governments in the countries mobilised their soldiers very rapidly, and so they didn't leave any time.
discussion and *negotiation* to virtually nothing.	ii So the governments couldn't discuss their disagreements and negotiate solutions.

The writer uses the nominalised form of the verb *to mobilise* – *mobilisation* – to summarise the main point of the previous sentence – getting armies together and near the enemy – and to include in the noun phrase the pre-modifier *rapid*, which is very important to the writer's point. As a nominal group, the phrase *rapid mobilisation* can be placed in first position in the sentence, as subject of the verb *reduced*, with its object *the time available*. In this way *rapid mobilisation* is presented as the reason for the lack of time. This is made explicit in the reformulation in Text 5.5a, Example (i).

The second, the coordinated nominalisations *discussion and negotiation* used in the original text indicate what governments might have done if there had been more time at the outbreak of the war. When those two nominalisations are expressed as verbs, in full clauses, as in (ii), their subject, *governments*, and direct objects, *disagreements* and *solutions*, appear. The nominalised forms chosen by the writer of Text 5.5 leave readers to infer what is made explicit in the reformulation.

In the sentence presented in Text 5.5a, then, a lot of information has been compressed by the use of nominalisation. CLIL teachers can help their students recover the information by talk around the text, with reformulation into clauses like those in the right-hand column of Text 5.5a, as a base for questioning the students. This way of engaging the students with the content has been found to lead to deeper understanding, and one which can provoke a more critical view of the event. In the case of Text 5.5a, the more explicit version would suggest to the students that all the countries were responsible for going to war. The use of nominalisation produces the abstract registers of history, in which the human actors in the events are frequently absent, and cause–effect relations are not made explicit (Coffin, 2006). If we want students to understand what they are reading, this is an area in which talk around the text is known to be very beneficial.

Turning to the important function of explaining in historical accounts, another feature of the grammar of the language of history appears in Text 5.4. While the student's Text 5.3 made cause explicit by using a number of subordinate clauses of cause, in the textbook segment in Text 5.4, there is no use of *because* to introduce explanations. Instead, cause and consequence are expressed using lexical verbs. Examples are shown in Text 5.5b.

Although the logical relation of cause can be recovered, it is not totally transparent, as we see when comparing the two versions above. The lexicalised, clause-internal expressions of cause in the original are more difficult to recognise than when the meaning is expressed in two clauses joined by a conjunction. Here we see a feature of the language of history, and of written academic language in general. In more advanced texts, information which at earlier stages of schooling would be expressed in a number of clauses becomes 'packed' into one clause,

Text 5.5b	
GRAMMATICAL METAPHOR	UNPACKING INTO CLAUSES
Once the fighting *had led to* stalemate	There was stalemate *because* the two sides fought but neither managed to beat the other.
The U-boat campaign *helped to bring* America into the war on the side of Britain and France.	America came into the war *partly because* the Germans started the U-boat campaign.
The American government *responded* [to the attack] by declaring war on Germany	The American government declared war on Germany *because* their boats had been attacked

and the logical relations are expressed in different ways, using nouns, verbs and prepositional phrases. These frequently include nominalisations, as we saw.

The process, obviously, is not carried out by writers consciously – what writers seem to do is use the technical concepts of their area in a compact and effective order, following the register conventions of their subjects. How these have evolved over time has been the object of a lot of research (e.g. Bazerman, 1988; Halliday and Martin, 1993), but what interests us here is how CLIL students understand and learn to produce this type of language. While the central concept, nominalisation, is a feature of the first languages of many of our students, this does not necessarily make all the meanings packed into the nominal group in academic texts easy to unravel when they are reading, nor does it allow them to structure their own texts taking advantage of this possibility. It is important that CLIL teachers, and indeed all secondary school teachers, know how the language of their subjects makes its meanings conventionally, as argued by Christie and Derewianka:

Control over grammatical metaphor is central to success in secondary schooling. It is intimately involved in the building up of technicality – the specialized knowledge of the different disciplines. It enables the development of argumentation, providing resources for the accumulation, compacting, foregrounding and backgrounding of information and evidence so that the argument can move forward. It is not simply a matter of style – an 'optional extra' to render a text more 'sophisticated'. Rather it is fundamental to the very nature of educational processes in the higher levels of schooling – the construal of experience into specialised domains and the reasoning about experience in abstract, logically developed terms.

(Christie and Derewianka, 2008: 25)

By using the more abstract nominalised grammar of the advanced history genres, then, the textbook writer leaves the reader to interpret the cause – effect relationship. For inexperienced readers, or CLIL learners working with texts in a foreign language, this reconstruction, mapping the language of the text onto real-world events, needs to be supported, or scaffolded, until students are mature enough to reconstruct them without help. At the same time, it is important for students to be working with the register in which the discipline they are studying is built up – simplified texts are not the solution at this stage. The reformulated, clause-based register is appropriate for the spoken language used to talk round the topic, as it chunks the information into segments which are easier to process in real time, but not for the written mode. Later, in Chapter 8, analysis of the typical distribution of information in oral register using examples of spoken dialogue from CLIL classes will show development on a cline, or continuum, from spoken to written academic register in different subjects.

5.5 Conclusion

This chapter has analysed a number of texts from the point of view of their vocabulary and grammar, showing how their meanings are built up by different choices from the grammatical and lexical possibilities of the language, and how these choices are appropriate for the different functions of texts in different subjects. CLIL teachers need to know how their subjects are constructed in language if they are to help their students understand their textbooks and use language to explore topics both orally and in writing, in order to learn the content of the subject. The aim, then, is both to improve CLIL students' comprehension of academic texts by translating the discourse of the disciplines into commonsense language that students will understand, and to help them produce academic texts themselves by learning how to rework their language into the uncommonsense discourse of disciplinary knowledge.

How, then, do we propose CLIL teachers should go about this? We are obviously not suggesting that content teachers should teach grammar and lexis in the way they learned the foreign language (we are assuming that a large number will be non-native teachers). But we do propose teachers gain an awareness (Carter, 1990) of the way the language of their subject is structured for use, and apply that knowledge at particular moments during their teaching, moments that they identify as having potential for their students' language development for the task and topic. Bringing the students' attention to features of the lexis and grammar which are functional in the texts they read, discuss or write, forms part of the process of learning the content, and is inseparable from it. If teachers have some knowledge of the language of their subject and the way it makes meanings, they are in a position to anticipate difficulties, or solve them when they arise. Both reading comprehension and writing of texts in different disciplines have been shown to improve substantially in a short time when teachers are given basic linguistic tools and shown how to question for understanding and to model for writing.

Questions and tasks for reflection and discussion

1. This chapter has shown some of the difficulties that the language of school disciplines can present to CLIL students. Think about the advantages and disadvantages of using simplified texts, and fill in the table:

ADVANTAGES	DISADVANTAGES

2. Text 5.6 is from a geography book for CLIL students. A number of nominal groups in it have been marked showing their pre- and post-modifiers, by using square brackets. Prepare a series of questions to help the students recognise the nouns which are the heads of each group, the 'thing' the writer is talking about. For example, for the first group, you could ask: 'What two things do we protect if we are interested in conservation of the planet?' This will also help the students to notice that (i) is a coordinated noun phrase.

Text 5.6
Conservation, sustainability and management
Conservation involves protecting [i][natural resources as well as the biodiversity of plant and animals in their habitats]. Today there are [ii][many global conservation movements such as Greenpeace and the WWF].

Sustainability involves fulfilling [iii][the requirements of the present generation] without reducing [iv][the ability of future generations to do the same]. To be sustainable [v][the Earth's resources] must be used at [vi][a rate that allows for replenishment].

Management involves putting into action [vii][policies to conserve resources for the future]. Conferences take place at international level to agree on environmental policies but this is difficult as each country has its own agenda for economic development. Politicians are often interested in [viii][the short-term future of their own country] rather than [ix][the long-term future of the planet]. |

(Cambers and Sibley, 2010: 165)

3. The paragraph in Text 5.7 is from a textbook chapter on the political system in 18th-century Britain. The first sentence, marked in bold, is difficult because it has a lot of information packed into it, mainly in the nominal groups, enclosed in square brackets. Using the information in the whole paragraph, prepare a question sequence to help the students recover the people and the actions they carried out, and so understand the sentence better.

Text 5.7
[Moves to reform parliament] were delayed by [a series of wars and rebellions]. Britain was at war with her American colonies from 1775 to 1783 and with revolutionary France from 1793 to 1815. In 1798 a group of Irish people staged an armed rebellion against British rule. These rebels and revolutionaries argued for more democratic government. The British government became very defensive and suspicious of any suggestions of change in the way parliament was elected.

(Counsell and Steer, 1993: 82)

4. Text 5.8, on the change of energy sources over time, is from the same textbook for students studying history in English. Identify all the cause–effect relations you can find in the text, and transfer this

information to a table. Then find where you have used inference to recognise the logical relation, and where there are clear linguistic markers in the text. To do this, it is a good idea to write clauses linked with *because* or *and so*. Finally, prepare a question sequence to direct students to these half-hidden meanings.

Text 5.8
Using fossil fuels
People's use of energy resources has changed over time. Up to the 18th century wood-burning provided most of the world's energy. With the Industrial Revolution affecting western Europe and the USA in the 19th century, coal became the most used energy source. The 20th century saw the rise of transport and industry, which required large amounts of fuel, usually oil. In the 21st century oil is the most sought-after source. Because only a few countries have oil supplies, and so dictate who gets it at what price, many countries are searching for oil reserves of their own or looking at alternative ways of meeting their energy demand.

(Cambers and Sibley, 2010: 140)

5. Choose an extract from a textbook which could be used for a CLIL subject. Analyse it using the framework explained in this chapter (field, tenor, mode). Write brief notes on how you would help your students access the meanings in the text.

References

Acevedo, C. (2010) 'Will the implementation of Reading to Learn in Stockholm schools accelerate literacy learning for disadvantaged students and close the achievement gap?' A report on school-based action research, Stockholm, Sweden: Multilingual Research Institute.

Bazerman, C. (1988) *Shaping Written Knowledge. The Genre and Activity of the Experimental Article in Science.* Madison: WI: University of Wisconsin Press.

Bloor, T. and Bloor, M. (1995) *The Functional Analysis of English. A Hallidayan Approach*, London: Hodder Arnold.

Carter, R. (ed.) (1990) *Knowledge of Language and the Curriculum*, London: Hodder and Stoughton.

Christie, F. and Deriwianka, B. (2008) *School Discourse: Learning to Write across the Years of Schooling*, London: Continuum.

Coffin, C. (2006) *Historical Discourse: The Language of Time, Cause and Evaluation*, London: Continuum.

Dalton-Puffer, C. (2005) 'Negotiating interpersonal meanings in naturalistic classroom discourse: Directives in content-and-language-integrated classrooms', *Journal of Pragmatics* 37, 1275–93.

Eggins, S. (1994) *An Introduction to Systemic Functional Linguistics*, London: Pinter.

Fang, Z. and Schleppegrell, M. (2008) *Reading in Secondary Content Areas: A Language-based Pedagogy* (Michigan Teacher Training Series), Ann Arbor, MI: University of Michigan.

Halliday, M. A. K. and Martin J. R. (1993) *Writing Science: Literacy and Discursive Power*, London: Falmer Press.

Halliday, M. A. K. and Matthiessen, C. M. I. M. (2004) *An Introduction to Functional Grammar* (3rd ed.), London: Hodder Arnold.

Jones, G. and Jones, M. (2002) *Biology. International Edition for IGCSE and O Level*. Cambridge: Cambridge University Press.

Martin, J. R. (1993) 'Life as a noun: Arresting the universe in science and the humanities', in Halliday, M. A. K. and Martin, J. R. (1993) *Writing Science: Literacy and Discursive Power*, London: Falmer Press, pp. 221–67.

Martin, J. R. (2006) 'Metadiscourse: Designing interaction in genre-based literacy programmes', in Whittaker, R., O'Donnell, M. and McCabe, A. (eds.) *Language and Literacy: Functional Approaches*, London: Continuum, pp. 95–122.

Martin, J. R. and Rose, D. (2005) 'Designing Literacy Pedagogy: Scaffolding asymmetries', in Webster, J., Matthiessen, C. and Hasan, R. (eds.) *Continuing Discourse on Language*, London: Continuum, pp. 251–80.

McAleavy, T. (2002) *IGCSE Twentieth Century History. International Relations since 1919*, Cambridge: Cambridge University Press.

Schleppegrell, M. (2004) *The Language of Schooling. A Functional Linguistics Perspective*, Mahwah, NJ: Erlbaum.

Part III

Students' language development and assessment in CLIL

6 Focusing on students' language: Integrating form and meaning

6.1 Introduction

This chapter addresses the important challenge of finding a way to focus on students' language in CLIL classrooms. Drawing on studies with a 'focus-on-form' approach, we consider language in a broad sense, that is, language forms as conveying meanings and functions, which are necessary for students' successful development of specific academic genres and registers.

The term Content and Language Integrated Learning means that there should be an integrated focus on learning both content and second / foreign languages. One of the main differences between CLIL and other similar educational practices such as content-based language teaching is that CLIL is content-driven, meaning that content is the main course objective (Coyle et al., 2010). In fact, in European countries like Spain, Austria or Finland, most (if not all) of the CLIL teaching, at least at the secondary school level, is done by content specialists and the main role of the foreign / second language is that of a vehicle for learning content and is to be learnt incidentally. Canadian immersion programmes are also content-driven (see the Introduction on similarities and differences between immersion and CLIL programmes). However, researchers such as Lyster (2007: 6) have pointed out the need to recognise the importance of language in these programmes: 'second language learning and academic achievement are inextricably linked and thus share equal status in terms of educational objectives'. Previous experience in bilingual instructional contexts, such as those of Canada where some features of the second language were not acquired by mere exposure, suggests the need to focus on language form. Lyster insists on the learners' focusing on, 'on the one hand, the content to which they usually attend in classroom discourse and, on the other, target language features that are not otherwise attended to' (2007: 4).

Throughout this book we highlight the importance of integrating content and language in CLIL, in terms of both research and educational practice. This chapter will provide specific examples of how students' language can be addressed in a way which does not separate the language used from the content it expresses. In the first part, we will look at instances of CLIL teachers' focus on language, following the relation between the linguistic features selected and the contextual variable of field, in the realisation of the ideational function (the use of language to represent content, as explained in Chapter 1). Chapter 7, in turn, will address CLIL students' management of interpersonal meaning (tenor), Chapter 8 will mainly focus on textual meanings and the development of students' language from the spoken into the written mode. In this chapter, the contextual variables of field and tenor will also be revisited in terms of the role they play in academic written texts.

The present chapter also suggests activities appropriate for raising CLIL students' language awareness, depending on the degree of immersion in the L2. In the final part of the chapter, we argue for the importance of CLIL teachers providing feedback which raises awareness of formal features that play a part in creating the register of the genres through which the content is expressed. While in Chapters 4 and 5 we saw a detailed account of different school genres and the lexico-grammatical features that characterise them, our main concern in this chapter is the importance of 'upgrading' CLIL students' language production in those genres and registers.

6.2 Focus on form / focus on meaning in CLIL

The tension between focus on form and focus on meaning can be said to have existed since the origins of Applied Linguistics as an independent field in the 1940s. Since then, Applied Linguistics researchers have explored a number of different approaches to teaching foreign languages which were clearly linked to linguistic theories that gave more prominence to either linguistic forms or to meaning. For example, the Audiolingual method in the 1940s focused on drilling linguistic patterns, and, based on behaviourist theory, was linked to Structuralism, a linguistic theory that was interested in the formal aspects of language. In response to Chomskian linguistics, which was also interested in children's ability to form grammatically correct sentences, Hymes's (1972) concept of 'communicative competence' changed the type of pedagogy used in foreign language teaching which became more meaning-focused and included the contexts where people communicate (*notions*) and uses of language in those contexts (*functions*) (Van Ek and Alexander, 1975; Wilkins, 1976). More recently, an approach called 'focus on form' has become more prevalent (Doughty and Williams, 1998; Lyster, 2007). In this approach, teachers draw learners' attention to language forms while retaining a communicative approach. This contrasts with 'focus on forms', which involves teachers identifying specific language items or points for teaching, rather than dealing with language problems incidentally as they come up. Recent research on second language acquisition reveals the importance of focusing on form for students' language development in content classes (Doughty and Williams, 1998; Lyster, 2007 etc.). This chapter addresses the positive aspects of teachers' use of a focus on form approach in the CLIL classroom. However, we widen the scope and extend the focus to those meanings and functions that are necessary to understand and deliver academic content successfully.

CLIL practitioners generally agree that the focus on communication is essential for their students' success. However, the question regarding the relevance or priority that is given to form, meaning or function needs to be related to two main factors:

- the specific characteristics of the programme
- the role of the second / foreign language

Some CLIL programmes include specific language objectives within the curriculum of content subjects, and courses are shared between language teachers and content teachers. In these cases, it is necessary to make sure that content and language are not taught separately (following a 'focus on forms' approach). In order for a programme to be defined as CLIL, students need to learn content through language and language through content rather than learn the language separately from the content. As Coyle et al. (2010: 33) put it: 'Students have to be able to use the vehicular language to learn content *other* than grammatical form otherwise this would not be CLIL.' However, in most CLIL courses, usually run by content teachers only, the foreign / second language is only used as a vehicle for learning content with the assumption that this will lead the student to learn the language naturally and incidentally. Canadian immersion programmes have also been an example of this second type of programme. Results of the research carried out in those programmes showed that the students became quite fluent in the L2 but did not achieve a level of grammatical accuracy comparable to that of native speakers of the same age. The question of whether CLIL students should aim for accuracy levels similar to those of native speakers leads us to the second factor proposed here: the role of the second language.

The role of the second / foreign language in content-based instruction or bilingual programmes also varies across different contexts. There are contexts like those in Canada, for example, where the students' second language is an official language and, thus, knowledge of this language is crucial for success and integration in society. In contrast, in CLIL contexts in Europe the language of instruction is a foreign language, mainly English, rarely used outside the CLIL classroom. Needless to say, there are contexts somewhere in between, such as Sweden, for example, in which English is a foreign language but is more present in students' life (through the media and other activities) than in other countries where the use of the target language is limited to the classroom. What seems clear is that the expectations regarding CLIL students' competence and performance of language forms are different across contexts.

We would like to argue, then, in line with other researchers such as Coyle et al. (2010) or van Lier (1996) that, in CLIL, the language priority does not need to be specifically form but language in a broader sense (form+meaning+function). In the following sections in this chapter, we will address issues related to language forms in relation to the meanings, functions, registers and genres that they realise.

6.3 A focus on CLIL students' lexico-grammar in the representation of content

Researchers such as Schleppegrell (2004) recognise that there isn't a need to separate meaning from form but rather language should be looked at as a whole. She states that this holistic view of language can be applied at the same time as content is introduced: 'Informed by a theory of language that is discourse and meaning-based, a focus on language can be brought to learning even as new content is introduced' (2004: 159). As we have shown throughout this book, we align ourselves with systemic functional linguistics, which claims it is impossible to separate form and function. In this section we focus on students' language use in their representation of content.

The ideational function: Using language to represent content

As argued in Chapters 4 and 5, CLIL teachers need to be aware of the characteristic features of different genres and registers in order to be able to identify those lexico-grammatical features that need attention, not simply because they are not accurate or grammatically correct, but mainly because they are necessary for the realisation of ideational meanings. According to Perrett (2000: 97), one of the drawbacks of SLA research on negotiation of meaning is that these studies have not taken into account the contextual features of different situations of use.

Choosing the appropriate lexis: Creating field

The field of discourse is related to what the language is about (see Chapter 1, Box 1.1). In order to demonstrate what they have learned, students need to make the appropriate vocabulary choices. One specific feature of learning a second language in CLIL contexts is that the vocabulary needed to represent content in the instructional register (see Chapter 1) is often technical and abstract, in contrast with the type of vocabulary necessary to communicate in foreign language classes. In CLIL classes, teachers are aware of the importance of eliciting the right technical word from the students, especially when it is particularly relevant for the topic under study, as shown in Extract 6.1 from a history class (grade 9, ages 14–15):

Extract 6.1
1 T: ... Ok, so ah ... what can you say about mercantilism,
2 remember, which was spreading around Europe for
3 different circumstances and how did it affect? Come on.
4 Go on. Yes, P, go on.
5 S1: Eh ... with the mercantilism, the ... (   ) and also
6 the ... the ... philosophy changed according with the main
7 activities ... there were also eh ... (   ) easier because
8 the ... (   ) have been explored and ... also increase the
9 commercial ... the commercial ...
10 T: Ok. Good, ok. So, what do we have about the immediate
11 effects? So there are lots of things happening around ok?
12 So, in the everyday life how did it affect? Yes, M?
13 S2: Everyday life.
14 T: Sorry?
15 S2: Everyday life.
16 T: Ok. So, whatever you wanted to say, then
17 S2: Eh with the mercantilism the ... the countries start to
18 export more than import and ... to become self-sufficient,
19 not to depend on other countries and ... depending on
20 themselves.
21 T: Right. Ok, so the main word for them was profit. Correct?
22 The keyword: profit. So they needed to make profit at all
23 costs ok?

In this extract, S1 is clearly looking for specific nouns, as his pauses after the definite articles reveal (lines 5–8). The teacher asks for the effects of mercantilism and, even though she provides positive feedback, she is not totally satisfied with the answer, as her question in her next turn reveals: *So, in the everyday life how did it affect?* (line 12). The teacher's feedback to S2's response is also positive or, at least, indicates acknowledgement: *Right*, but she then focuses clearly on the technical word that she expected the students to provide: *profit*. CLIL teachers' focus on technical lexis is likely to have a positive effect on students' development of the specific vocabulary related to the topic. In contrast to the belief that learners acquire most of their vocabulary incidentally, Hulstijn (2003) reports that retention is higher when students are exposed to intentional teaching of specific L2 vocabulary.

Intentional spontaneous teaching of vocabulary does occur in CLIL classes, as Extract 6.2 illustrates, but focus on form does not usually happen, with priority mainly given to the meaning of key concepts for the understanding of important subject content, as illustrated in the following extract from a biology class (grade 7, ages 12–13):

Extract 6.2
1   T: Can anybody tell me what to be harmful means?
2   S: That damage
3   T: It damages yeah produces damage. Ok? How do you say
4   harmful in Spanish?

In this extract, the teacher does not explicitly correct the grammatical error in the student's turn; on the contrary, she is happy to hear that the student understands the meaning of *harmful* and simply recasts the students' utterance and provides positive feedback (*it damages yeah*).

Another area related to lexis which is necessary for the representation of content in CLIL is that of process types used to portray reality. As we saw in Chapter 5, Halliday and Matthiessen (2004) distinguish six types of processes: material, behavioural, mental, verbal, relational and existential. A number of researchers have looked at the role of different process types in the construction of different types of texts from a pedagogical perspective (for example Christie, 2002; Martin and Rothery, 1986). In Whittaker and Llinares's (2009) analysis of the types of processes used by teachers and students in secondary CLIL social science classrooms, it was found that both students and teachers used a higher percentage of material or action processes in geography, as the topic focused on events and why they happened. On the other hand, the percentage in history was higher for relational processes or processes of being. This was especially the case in the students' written compositions, where, without the presence of the interlocutor, the student writers included more description than in their spoken performance when responding to the same prompt. In class discussions, students preferred to use material processes even in response to a prompt that required historical description. In Extract 6.3, from a history class on feudal Europe (grade 8, ages 13–14), the students and teacher were participating in an end-of-topic class discussion. In this particular episode they were responding to the question in a prompt: *What was life like in rural areas?*, so they were working with the genre identified by Christie and Derewianka (2008) as period study (see Chapter 4 for a detailed account of this genre).

Extract 6.3
1   S1: Serfs ... without pay, remuneration, they don't pay them and
2   the free peasants they ... they give them money.
3   T: OK. And ... em ... about serfs, (   ) they were similar to
4   something. I hope you remember.
5   S1: The slaves.
6   T: To slaves.
7   S1: Were property of someone.

S1 uses two material processes to describe serfs and free peasants. He struggles with the description by beginning a sentence with *serfs* as a subject (line 1) and then moving it to the direct object position following the material process *pay* (*they don't pay them*). He goes through exactly the same process when describing *free peasants*, in this case using another material process (*give*). The teacher responds by also topicalising *serfs* (*And ... em ... about serfs*), in line 3, but then she uses a relational process to trigger a description (*they were similar to something*). S1 provides the word elicited: *The slaves* (line 5), and continues in his next turn with the use of a relational process (*were* again) to proceed with the description of slaves. Thus, the CLIL teacher's implicit focus on the appropriate process might have led S1 to stop using material processes and use a relational process, to meet the requirements of the task in a better way. As pointed out above, Whittaker and Llinares (2009) found the CLIL students in their data to use more relational processes in writing than when they discussed the same prompt orally in class. The more frequent use of relational processes might be partly related to the teacher's role in scaffolding the students with relational processes when performing historical descriptions in end-of-topic discussions previous to their written compositions, which followed the same prompt. The result of this analysis shows the importance of CLIL teachers' scaffolding the appropriate lexis required by the register in classroom interaction in order for the students to be able to use it successfully later in individual tasks, such as writing. We have called this 'register scaffolding at the microlevel'. The role of register scaffolding at the macrolevel, in the transition from spoken mode to written mode, will be described in Chapter 8.

Expressing logical relationships in the expression of content

As indicated above, the ideational metafunction refers to those aspects of the language involved in the representation of the world. We have already discussed the lexical resources used to represent experience (experiential). In this section we will focus on the connections between the meanings of clauses (logical). Some of the logical meanings that contribute to the presentation of reality (field) are addition, time, cause / consequence and comparison. Our corpus shows that neither CLIL teachers trained as language teachers nor those trained as content teachers focus on students' difficulties in establishing logical relations in a text, as Extract 6.4 from a CLIL history class on feudal Europe shows (grade 8, ages 13–14):

Extract 6.4
1	T:	That is true. Very good. More things about about
2		marriage. Who knows something about marriage?
3	S1:	That eh the girl of the lord had to dowry, they dowry her to
4		a nobleman and they pay him ... eh ... for marry with her.
5	T:	Mm. Yes. They give a dowry. More things about this?
6		About, em, about children.

In this extract the student does not use the right conjunction to express purpose (cause) in this context (*in order to*). The teacher's feedback to *they pay him ... eh ... for marry with her*, which is final in the student's turn, is positive *Mm, yes*. The teacher recasts the use of *dowry* by providing the correct use of this word as a noun (line 5), as it is incorrectly used by the student as a verb. However, the teacher in this extract does not pay attention to the incorrect expression of the logical relation.

In their analysis of clause complexes (i.e. sentences containing more than one clause) in CLIL classrooms, Whittaker and Llinares (2009) found that CLIL students used more coordination than subordination to join their clauses. This is common in spoken discourse in general, where a few frequently occurring conjunctions are used to realise a variety of logical connections, and even more in informal spoken interactions, where the same conjunction is often used to express different logical meanings (Schleppegrell, 2004). Together with addition, time sequence is frequently introduced by *and* (Halliday, 2004) but contrastive meanings can also be expressed, as illustrated in Extract 6.5, which shows the use of *and* in a CLIL student's report on the development of a new economy in feudal Europe (grade 8, ages 13–14).

Extract 6.5
1 S1: they had the agriculture (   ) *and* they develop a new
2   economy, *and* the salary grows for the people *because* in ...
3   they were eh ... less people, the salary grows for the
4   people who work.

In this extract, the first *and* could be interpreted as having a contrastive meaning while the second *and* seems to introduce a consequence of the new economy. The fact that other conjunctions are not used creates ambiguity and a lack of clarity in the transmission of ideas. In their comparison of CLIL students with their L1 counterparts studying the same topics and responding to the same prompt, Llinares and Whittaker (2010) found similar patterns in their frequent use of additive clause complexes, mainly introduced by the conjunction *and*. Students' awareness of these different meanings introduced by *and* would not only improve their production in the L2 but would also aid their comprehension of lectures or any other spoken texts that they might encounter on the subject and topic under study. CLIL students (and also students studying content in the L1) should be introduced, then, to different ways of presenting logical connections in their texts, especially when they move into the written mode (see Chapter 8 on this issue). This involves a wider variety of conjunctions used for more specific meanings, for instance, including conjuncts such as *however, furthermore* or *nevertheless* to express contrast or others such as *for instance* to express exemplification, a type of addition. In Schleppegrell's words (2004: 57): 'This means that the students need to learn alternative strategies in school-based texts for realising the logical relationships that they use common conjunctions for informal speech.'

One interesting difference between CLIL students' expression of logical relations and that of their L1 counterparts, also reported in Llinares and Whittaker (2010), is that many CLIL students seem to have difficulties in expressing circumstances through prepositional phrases, with the exception of those of time and place. These students usually express cause through clauses whereas L1 students more often use phrases for this logical relation in academic contexts. The following extract from Llinares and Whittaker (2010) shows the response to the same question on the Black Death by a student studying this topic in the L1 (Spanish) and by a CLIL student (grade 8, ages 13–14):

Extract 6.6
1 T (L1): *¿Por qué creéis que se propagó tan rápidamente la Peste* 2   *Negra? A ver*, J. 3   (Sp. Why do you think the Black Death spread so 4   rapidly. Let's see, J.) 5 S (L1): *Por el hacinamiento.* 6   (Sp. Due to overcrowding.) 1 S (CLIL): Because the people are not clean.

The student from the L1 context answers the question with a prepositional phrase including an abstract noun (*Por el hacinamiento*), whereas the CLIL student uses a clause and everyday lexis (*Because the people are not clean*). As several studies on the language of history have shown (i.e. Martin, 1993; Veel and Coffin, 1996), in this discipline, reasoning takes place within and not between clauses, in other words, content is more often displayed through phrases than clauses, which indicates that the L1 student's answer represents academic language while the CLIL student's does not. This might also have an effect on the teacher's assessment of this student's response, as in academic registers logical connections are often also made through nouns and verbs (Halliday and Hasan, 1976), as we will discuss in Chapter 8. This aspect of academic language, which seems to be more integrated into the language of secondary school students in the L1, should lead CLIL teachers and material designers to reflect on the need for a focus on phrases and nominalisations, not as independent grammatical elements to be acquired by the students, but as part of the linguistic requirements of academic language, also in the spoken mode.

In this section, then, we have identified linguistic features related to the representation of content (ideational function), focusing on the language used for representing experience (experiential function) and the importance for the CLIL teacher to help students notice process types other than material or action (which are the most common in students' productions). For this, CLIL teachers should identify the type of lexis which is necessary for the specific genre (see Chapter 4) and integrate it into classroom interactions, even creating activities to develop students' awareness, as we will illustrate in the next section. We have also analysed the role of logical connectors in the representation of content (logical function) and have referred to the importance of encouraging the students to use a wider range of conjunctions and move beyond the clause into more academic ways of connecting ideas by using phrases, verbs and nouns.

6.4 The role of language-focused tasks and activities

Although most CLIL programmes in Europe focus primarily on content, as we have shown throughout this book, it is necessary for CLIL teachers to be aware of the language students require to express that content and to participate in classroom interaction. Some researchers from Canadian immersion contexts have argued that students in these programmes should be exposed to tasks that encourage them to notice and use difficult grammatical forms (Lyster, 2007; Swain, 1998). Stern (1992), for example, refers to the integration of language and content in content-based teaching by combining two types of instruction: analytic (which focuses on pronunciation, grammar, functions etc.) and experiential (which focuses on content, fluency, the use of purposeful tasks etc.). Again, he recommends a stronger emphasis on analytic instruction in those educational contexts.

In our view, it is necessary to distinguish between CLIL contexts with different amounts of exposure to the target language (i.e. high-immersion and low-immersion contexts), in order to decide on the best type of instruction. In her analysis of the effect of different types of activities on very young learners' extended production in the L2 in high-immersion CLIL contexts, Llinares (2007b) found that, in these contexts, where young children were taught in English for most of the school day, Stern's experiential type of instruction was enough to trigger a wider variety of language functions. Thus, for example, show-and-tell sessions were found to encourage the students' use of the L2 to convey a personal function, identified as the most frequent type of communicative function in preschool children's language (Beveridge and Brierley, 1982). This is illustrated in Extract 6.7 (kindergarten, ages 5–6), in which a student (S1) is showing and talking about his cards:

Extract 6.7
1   S1: If you get a magic more, if you are more stronger ehh you
2   can win
3   T: But how do you get stronger?
4   S1: With this card.
5   T: Oh, I see. If you get these cards, that makes you stronger.
6   S1: Yeah.
7   T: Yeah? And the more of these cards you get, then the bigger
8   the chance you have of winning. Is that correct?
9   S1: Yes.
10   T: Ok. Good. Thank you.
11   S1: This was a goody. This was a baddy. This was a goody. All
12   these cards are baddies.

In his first turn, S1 uses a complex sentence containing a conditional subordinate clause. He makes a grammatical error which is corrected by the teacher through a recast (correct reformulation of the student's sentence). We don't know whether this correction will turn into **uptake** as the student's following turns are reduced responses to the teacher's questions. In fact, Lyster and Mori (2006) argue that recasts are not very effective in content classes in which the students are not trained to focus on form. What is interesting in this example is that even after the teacher has signalled the end of the conversation, the student intervenes again, expressing his personal view on the characters that appeared on the cards. This suggests that the task itself seems to be triggering the students' participation in the foreign language.

However, in low-immersion CLIL contexts (where the students are exposed to the L2 for one or two hours a day), Llinares (2007a) argues that there might be a stronger need for more analytic types of instruction, as far as language functions are concerned. In her study, the students' variety of language functions could only be extended with concrete activities designed to trigger specific functions, for example, asking the students to choose their favourite character in a story and justify why they have chosen that character. If we follow Lyster's (2007) distinction between proactive and reactive approaches in form-focused instruction, this would correspond to the first type (see Box 6.1).

Box 6.1: Proactive and reactive approaches (Lyster, 2007)	
Proactive	Instructional interventions designed to promote noticing and awareness, as well as opportunities for practice
Reactive	Attempts to draw the learners' attention to language features in unplanned ways

In most CLIL contexts the space for a focus on specific language aspects (grammatical elements, specific phonemes, communicative functions etc.) is more restricted to a reactive type of instruction. The following extract (grade 8, ages 13–14) shows an example of this type of approach with a focus on pronunciation:

Extract 6.8
1   T: Ok, very good. Ok. So we have mentioned one keyword, 2   which is ... ? If we say housing, what is the keyword 3   [you've mentioned? They live in ... ? 4   S1:   Villages. Villages (non-standard pronunciation) 5   T: Villages. Villages or ... ? 6   S2:   Villages (standard pronunciation) 7   T: Villages, villages (standard pronunciation) rather than 8   villages (non-standard pronunciation) and ... ?

In this extract the teacher focuses on the standard pronunciation of *villages* triggered by one of the student's correction of her peer's pronunciation. In this class, where the teacher often focuses on formal linguistic features, mainly at the word level, the students also participated occasionally with corrections, probably as a signal of deeper awareness of language accuracy in the content class. Interestingly, in their comparative analysis of CLIL teachers of social science (geography and history), Whittaker and Llinares (2009) found that there were differences in the way these CLIL teachers focused on language that were related to their background. One of the teachers was a content specialist and her classes focused exclusively on content, whereas the other teacher (a participant in Extract 6.8), with a background as both content and EFL teacher, included language while working on content.

As we argue throughout this book, proactive approaches would need to be planned as part of specific genres and registers. Regarding activities in textbook materials, we suggest that some activities could easily integrate a focus on formal features that pushes the students to use specific forms while focusing explicitly on meaning and content. For example, the following text illustrates the first part of an activity presented in a unit of a CLIL textbook on geography and history for Year 1 junior secondary school students in Spain (12–13-year-olds) (Essential Geography and History 1, 2008):

Text 6.1

Copy the following passage, circle the correct words:

The Earth spins in a/an clockwise / anticlockwise direction. It completes a rotation every 48 / 24 hours. The Earth / Sun moves round the Earth / Sun in an elliptical orbit. The angle at which the Sun's rays reach each hemisphere changes during the year ...

One possible adaptation of this exercise that would lead the students to focus on form might be to present the students with blanks and ask them to fill these in with an appropriate verb, which would address content knowledge but would also force the students to be aware of subject–verb agreement (see Text 6.1.a). Another possible adaptation could be to ask the students to circle the appropriate preposition (see Text 6.1b):

Text 6.1a

Copy the following passage, filling in with an appropriate verb:

The Earth _____ in an anticlockwise direction. It _____ a rotation every 24 hours. The Earth _____ round the Sun in an elliptical orbit. The angle at which the Sun's rays _____ each hemisphere _____ during the year ...

Text 6.1b

Copy the following passage, circling the correct preposition:

The Earth spins under / in an anticlockwise direction. It completes a rotation every 24 hours. The Earth moves towards / round the Sun in / in front of an elliptical orbit. The angle at / under which the Sun's rays reach each hemisphere changes on / during the year.

In both adaptations of the activity, there is a clear integrative focus on language (in this case, specifically on form) and content. The grammatical elements practised do not exclude a clear focus on content. In a geography class on the rotation of the Earth the students are expected to learn the verbs (material / action processes) which are necessary to explain the rotation of the Earth. By performing this task, at the same time, the students are forced to notice the morphological feature of verb agreement (Text 6.1a). Similarly, the use of an appropriate preposition is necessarily linked to the specific content under study. The knowledge of the type of movement that the Earth performs in relation to the Sun is inextricably related to the knowledge of the preposition (*round*).

In sum, although CLIL teachers are usually expected to focus on content while their language colleagues are expected to address those formal features of the language that might be necessary for the students to work on specific subject genres or registers, planned activities designed to focus on language while working on content could be very useful. Recurrent practice of one specific morphological feature in one exercise or activity is likely to make the students notice it while working on content. This is supported by Schmidt's (1990, 2001) noticing hypothesis, which claims that certain language features will not enter the students' second language systems unless they notice them. In fact, a recent study carried out by Vázquez (2010), on the development of CLIL students' subject pronoun and article use, concluded that the teachers' way of formulating questions could play a role in the students' progressively more correct use of the pronoun in classroom interactions. In her comparison of two CLIL groups following the same syllabus and responding to the same prompt, she found that the students' responses to questions that included the pronoun, as in Extract 6.9a, did not show instances of subject dropping, whereas more general questions or prompts of the type illustrated in Extract 6.9b were sometimes followed by answers in which the students didn't include the pronoun (subject dropping), probably due to transfer from their L1, Spanish:

Extract 6.9a
1   T: What was *feudal Europe* like? What was *it* like?

Extract 6.9b
1   T: Tell me about feudal Europe.

The students responding to questions of the type in Extract 6.9a, which includes the pronoun, only had to pick up the pronoun from the question and use it in their answers. Interestingly, the teacher who formulated questions including pronoun prompts was a CLIL history teacher with long experience as an ELT teacher, which might explain a more careful formulation of the question. This teacher's reformulation of the question probably had the aim of facilitating the students' comprehension but this, incidentally, seemed to have a positive effect on the decrease of subject dropping. It seems important to identify those grammatical features that would benefit from a specific focus in classroom interaction. Following Lyster's (1998, 2007) concept of proactive approaches, CLIL teachers should be made aware of the potential of question reformulations, not only to facilitate students' comprehension, but also to ensure that certain forms are more salient in their discourse by increasing their frequency in their oral input. The next section introduces the role of reactive approaches to second language learning in content classes, mainly the role of corrective or pedagogic feedback in classroom interaction.

6.5 The role of corrective feedback in CLIL: Focus on content / focus on language

Chapter 3 introduced the concept of feedback in CLIL, distinguishing between interactional and pedagogic feedback (Llinares, 2005). Interactional feedback has no evaluative purpose and takes place in everyday conversations outside the classroom. Pedagogic or corrective feedback has an evaluative function. Chapter 3 addressed the positive effect of interactional feedback on CLIL students' language and content engagement. In this chapter, we focus on the role of CLIL teachers' use of pedagogic or corrective feedback, in other words, the type of feedback aiming at evaluating and correcting their students' performance.

Within form-focused reactive approaches to second language acquisition in content classes (see Box 6.1), Lyster highlights the importance of getting students to focus on language in content classes by means of instructional practices such as corrective feedback. Lyster and Ranta (1997) developed a taxonomy that describes the types of corrective feedback that teachers can give on students' errors. By observing interactions in a number of French immersion classrooms, they identified six main types of feedback: explicit correction, recasts, clarification requests, metalinguistic feedback, elicitation and repetition (see Box 6.2). In the following sections examples of these types of feedback will be provided from CLIL classroom interactions. These categories allow for a focus on language features such as pronunciation and grammar. However, in line with our theoretical approach in this book (SFL), we will also interpret these corrective strategies not only from a focus-on-form perspective but also from the perspective of how forms are used to convey specific meanings and functions, drawing on studies such as Mohan and Beckett's (2003) functional analysis of recasts.

Box 6.2: Types of corrective feedback (Lyster and Ranta, 1997: 203)	
Clarification request	Indication that an utterance has not been heard or understood, sometimes with the purpose of drawing attention to non-target forms
Explicit correction	Provision of the correct form, indicating that something was incorrect
Recast	Implicit correction of an utterance by means of reformulation
Elicitation	Direct elicitation of the correct form using techniques such as asking for completion
Repetition	Repetition of the error with rising intonation
Metalinguistic feedback	Reference to the well-formedness or correctness of the student's utterance without providing the correct form

Clarification requests and explicit correction

Clarification requests indicate to students that either the utterance / word was not heard or understood or that it is incorrect and the students' self-correction is expected. In CLIL classes, teachers' clarification requests might be perceived by the students either as an interactional strategy (other-initiated repair), signalling that the teacher has not heard or understood, or as corrective feedback. This strategy, then, might not have an uptake effect if the student does not notice the error. The following extract from a secondary school CLIL class on geography (also analysed in Chapter 2, Extract 2.8) provides an example of a clarification request strategy used by the teacher which has a positive effect on the student's response (grade 9, ages 14–15):

Extract 6.10
1   T: A. OK, so why did you choose that? Why is that the main 2   factor of development? 3   S1:   I think the wealth is the most important because if you 4   don't have ... 5   T: Wealth or health? 6   S1:   Health. 7   T: Health? Yes –

In this extract, the teacher makes a clarification request including an 'or choice' question (line 5), a typical input modification strategy in talk addressed to non-native speakers (Long, 1981). This 'or choice' question helps the student notice the problem and conclude that the right word should be the alternative one provided by the teacher. This type of clarification request, focusing on the students' production of the right word to express the right meaning is more frequent in our CLIL corpus than those addressing grammatical accuracy.

It is interesting to notice that the student's incorrect use of the article to introduce generic reference (*I think the wealth*) is either not noticed or not addressed by the teacher. In her longitudinal analysis of article transfer errors in CLIL students' oral language performance, Vázquez (2010) concluded that errors in article use did not necessarily decrease with the general improvement in proficiency levels. Regardless of whether these students' errors are due to L1 transfer or to lack of attention to accuracy when trying to achieve a communicative aim, we believe this area would benefit from specific instructional focus. In our view, this would need two consecutive types of intervention by CLIL teachers and curriculum / material designers: (a) the teaching of article use should be integrated within a more general focus on the linguistic features which are necessary to organise the content and create cohesive texts (e.g. the passive voice or the expansion of nouns with pre- and post-modifiers, as seen in Chapter 5); and (b) a focus on the textual function of language (see Chapter 8 on the development of this function) should be integrated within the teaching of specific content. This methodological approach could be followed by content and language experts and curriculum designers, who could work together on contextualising specific language features, as these cannot be addressed separately from the function and meaning they have in a specific context.

Interestingly, one aspect of L2 accuracy that CLIL teachers occasionally address is the correct pronunciation of key lexical elements. In the following extract from a technology lesson (grade 7, ages 12–13), the teacher begins his second turn with a clarification request with the purpose of signalling that the keyword (*designing*) is not pronounced correctly by the student.

Extract 6.11

1	T:	The first one, not the third one. And P, don't you know ( )
2		Ok, P, can you go on with the third?
3	S1:	(reading very softly) The first topic was designing.
4		(non-standard pronunciation)
5	T:	Please, the first topic was?
6	S2:	Designing (standard pronunciation).
7	T:	Could you say that word again please?
8	S3:	Designing (standard pronunciation).
9	T:	Could you say this word again P? I've told you several
10		times, "design design design" (standard pronunciation)
11		maybe I'm not English and I have an accent, but (I don't)
12		say (non-standard pronunciation) I've said that a hundred
13		times. And you can't say that because you have never heard
14		that. Design (standard pronunciation) please.

Going back to Extract 6.10, the teacher signalled the corrective function of her clarification request by using an 'or choice' question that included the expected lexical element. In this extract, however, the corrective purpose of the clarification is marked by the use of *please* (line 5). This clarification request is responded to by two other students (S2 and S3), who pronounce the word correctly. However, the teacher explicitly refers to the correct pronunciation by engaging in metalinguistic talk about the impossibility for this pronunciation error to be related to wrong input, as this is supposed to be a high frequency word (*I've said that a hundred times*) and the teacher is aware of his correct pronunciation in this case, even though he acknowledges *I have an accent*.

In contrast to clarification requests, explicit correction does not give the student the opportunity to carry out self-repair (Lyster and Mori, 2006). However, both clarification requests and explicit correction tend to be used by CLIL teachers with the purpose of focusing on key vocabulary. This is illustrated in the following extract from a secondary school biology class (grade 10, ages 15–16):

		Extract 6.12
1	T:	... Can you give me an example of a mutant? ... What is
2		a mutant?
3	S:	In plants when you –
4	T:	In plants? ... Do you have any mutant plants at home?
5	S:	No.
6	T:	A mutant. It sounds like ... something that happens in
7		films.
8	S2:	The Doberman.
9	T:	But ... actually it doesn't. It happens in nature. Hm?
10	S2:	And the Doberman?
11	T:	The Doberman. Is that a mutant? The Doberman?
12	S:	( )
13	T:	It looks it looks weird yes but it's not a mutant actually ...
14		the Doberman=
15	S:	It's a mixture.
16	T:	The breed. It's a mixture yes ... of what.
17	S2:	Of races of dogs ... of dogs races
18	T:	Different uh breeds you say *razas* (Sp. breeds) breeds ...
19		of of dogs. Yeah they've been mixing different dogs
20		throughout time, throughout time

In this extract, the teacher makes a clarification request with a corrective function addressing content: *In plants?* (line 4). The interpretation of this clarification request as corrective feedback is reinforced by the teacher referring to the student's personal experience with *mutant plants* (*Do you have any mutant plants at home?*). Towards the end of this extract (line 18), the teacher explicitly corrects the word *races* (*breeds you say*). However, she does not check the students' uptake and continues clarifying the concept of mutant.

Extract 6.13 from another biology lesson (grade 7, ages 12–13) could also be considered an example of explicit correction, as the teacher refers to the preference for using one term instead of another:

	Extract 6.13
1	S: (provoke) illness
2	T: Produce produce ((writing on board)) illnesses or let's call it
3	disease.
	(cont.)

4		disease is a bit more ... strong than illness.
5	S:	Like pneumonia.
6	T:	Like pneumonia for instance we're going to talk about many
7		diseases. Write down some of them. Pneumonia is caused by a
8		type of bacteria. Let me see what shall I write down there then

However, this example shows a different approach to correction by the same teacher. In this extract, the teacher suggests a more academic and precise term for the students' management of the topic (*disease* instead of *illness*) and tries to explain the appropriateness of one term over the other. She even approves of the student's choice of *illness* but provides a better term, *let's call it disease*. The teacher refers to *disease* as being stronger, probably meaning more appropriate for the register (more formal). In this case, it is not a question of 'right' or 'wrong' in terms of formal accuracy, it is a question of using the appropriate register. CLIL teachers' professional development should include activities that enhance their awareness of the importance of the registers of their subject and their ability to offer alternative lexis and grammar for the register required. In this way, they will be able to notice and provide feedback on their students' production when it is not appropriate for the register.

Recasts

Recasts involve teachers' implicit correction of the student's utterances by reformulating all or part of the utterance, in the hope that the student notices the error without interrupting the flow of communication. Lyster and Ranta (1997) found recasts to be the most frequent type of corrective feedback used by the teachers in the classes they observed in Canadian immersion contexts (in fact, more than half of the total feedback provided in those classes). In Extract 6.14 (grade 7, ages 12–13), from a CLIL class on history, the teacher's recast is successfully followed by uptake, as the student picks up the correct pronunciation of the word *Venus*, after her teacher's recast.

Extract 6.14	
1	S: The most famous early image of a human a woman
2	called Venus (non-standard pronunciation) of Willendorf
3	T: Venus (standard pronunciation).
4	S: Venus (standard pronunciation) of Willendorf
	(cont.)

5	that was find was found in ninety eighty
6	by archaeologist ((writes on board)) Josef Szombathy.
7	T: Where is Willendorf?
8	S: Willendorf is in Austria.
9	T: In Austria that's right so it's German.

This extract is another illustration of how teachers focus on students' errors with key content words. However, the grammatical error made by the student in line 5 by using an inappropriate relative pronoun (*that* instead of *which*) for a non-defining relative clause is not recast by the teacher, who proceeds to ask a question on the content (*Where is Willendorf?*). The teacher is, then, missing an opportunity here for reformulating the student's error while still focusing on content.

In their study, Lyster and Ranta (1997) also found that student uptake was least likely to occur after recasts. This can be observed in the following extract from a history class on feudal Europe:

	Extract 6.15
1	T: OK. And ... em ... about serfs, ( ) they were similar to
2	something. I hope you remember
3	S: The slaves.
4	T: To slaves.
5	S: Were property of someone.

S's second turn (in line 5) does not reflect uptake of the teacher's recast (*To slaves*). On the contrary, he seems to focus on the meaning of the term and provides a reformulation for *slaves*, which was not triggered by the teacher. CLIL students' perceptions of their role, regarding their use of the L2, seem to give priority to the use of appropriate lexis and to showing knowledge of the meaning of key content words, in line with the content-focused communicative orientation of these classrooms. In fact, in Llinares and Whittaker's (2009) study of CLIL students' language performance in history classes, lexis was an area that was generally mastered, as shown in both the students' spoken and written discourse.

Recasts made on key lexis may also remain unnoticed by the students, as shown in the following extract from a history class (grade 9, ages 14–15):

Extract 6.16
1	T: What was the name of this?
2	S: Aisles? (non-standard pronunciation)
3	T: That's right, the aisles (standard pronunciation) here.
4	And what cardinal point is this part? The apse?
5	This, what's this, the cardinal point for this?
6	S: The east?
7	T: This is the east. And what's this?
8	S: The West

Here, the teacher recasts the error in the student's pronunciation (line 3) but in the rest of her turn she does not provide a signal to the student that there is something wrong with the pronunciation of the word *aisles*. On the contrary, the teacher provides positive feedback on the student's choice of the right word, regardless of the pronunciation, and proceeds with the description of a Romanesque church.

An alternative approach to the analysis of recasts is the notion of **functional recast** adopted by Mohan and Beckett (2003), who analyse sequences that do not involve the correction of grammatical errors. They pay attention to those teachers' recasts aiming at suggesting less congruent (less expected) linguistic devices to convey specific meanings, as well as more compact statements (see Chapter 5 on the role of grammatical metaphor). In other words, they analysed those types of recasts that addressed the students' language as appropriate for the specific academic context. This can be seen in the following extract from a CLIL history class on the topic of feudal Europe (grade 8, ages 13–14):

Extract 6.17
1	S1: Eh, yes because there was a lot of people in the countryside
2	working and they have no place for everybody so they
3	went to the cities and they went there.
4	T: ... so that is the, em, the reason of the rebirth of cities.

In this extract, the teacher uses two instances of grammatical metaphor. She uses a noun that represents a cause–effect relationship (*reason*) instead of a conjunction (*because, so* etc.) and another noun to express action (*rebirth*) instead of an action verb. The non-congruent and compact way in which the teacher expresses the content contrasts with the language used by the student. The student uses the conjunction *because* to express cause, and verbs (*working, went*) to express actions. Her long and repetitive explanation contrasts with the compactness of the teacher's phrase (*the reason of the rebirth of cities*). These difficulties should be addressed by teachers and we suggest that one way of doing this would be through the use of functional recasts. As Mohan and Beckett (2003) argue, more research is needed on the role of grammatical metaphor in second language learning, but it is clear that students in general have difficulties with the grammatical and lexical compactness required in academic discourse, and this is even more true when the medium of instruction is a foreign language.

Elicitation, repetition and metalinguistic feedback

Other types of corrective feedback with less presence in our CLIL corpus are elicitation, repetition and metalinguistic feedback. Elicitation is defined by Lyster and Ranta (1997) as the technique used by the teacher in order to get the students to produce the correct form either by asking them to complete the teacher's utterance through questions to elicit correct forms, or by asking the students to reformulate their utterances. In the CLIL classes observed, this technique is mostly used to elicit content and is sometimes interpreted by the students as a clarification request, as Extract 6.18 illustrates (grade 10, ages 15–16):

Extract 6.18
1   T: Ok, France wanted to take Alsace Lorraine. It was because
2   of France, not really because of any other country?
3   S: And Russia
4   T: Ok, and?
5   S: And Russia, because they wanted to have access to the
6   Mediterranean and they take Austria

In this extract, even though the teacher signals with *Ok* an acceptance of the student's response, the student still interprets *and?* (line 4) as a misunderstanding by the teacher and, thus, repeats his answer in the following turn (line 5). Throughout the corpus, the students' use of the L1 also triggered the teachers' elicitation of specific words or utterances in the L2 (*How do you say it in English? In English, please* etc.). Again, this type of feedback was mainly used to address key vocabulary. Interestingly, elicitation was also used to obtain more academic vocabulary as illustrated in Extract 6.19, from a geography class (grade 7, ages 12–13):

Extract 6.19

1	T: OK. So, let's use a, a, another word for, a lot of water
2	together? A lot of water together in English.
3	S1: Precipitations.
4	T: Another one. OK?
5	S1: Inundation.
6	T: Inundation. Probably.
7	Who can give me the right word for inundation? Mmm, A?
8	S2: Floods.
9	T: Floods. Right. Very good. OK.

In this extract the teacher focuses on register by asking for *another word for a lot of water together* (lines 1–2), which a student had just used in a previous response. The students come up with register-appropriate words, *precipitations* and *inundation*, which are only partially accepted by the teacher (*Another one, probably*) as she is looking for the key term used in the topic (*flood*). The teacher here is probably trying to make sure her students don't rely on cognates, and to get them to learn this word and its pronunciation, difficult because of the irregular correspondence between sound and spelling.

Although in some bilingual contexts teacher repetitions may have the role of drawing attention to non-target forms, in the CLIL classes analysed they are mainly used for negotiation of meaning or focusing on content, as illustrated in Extract 6.20, from a session on medieval art (grade 9, ages 14–15), where the teacher is asking the students to describe a portrait:

Extract 6.20

1	T: ... what is the other thing he's doing?
2	S: Escape from his mother
3	T: Escape? Haha, sometimes, but I don't think so, now look at
4	the hand, look at the baby's hand, look at his hand, now,
5	does the hand remind you of something?

In this example, the teacher repeats the word *escape*, using rising into-nation (line 3). She uses laughter and even adds explicit correction (*I don't think so*) to ensure that the student does not understand her repetition as negotiation of meaning. However, the teacher does not give the student the opportunity to generate his own response, which would have forced him to look for a better word to describe the action carried out by the baby and, thus, improve his oral description of the picture.

Metalinguistic feedback contains information related to the correct-ness of the student's utterance, without explicit correction. The use of metalinguistic feedback is not very frequent in CLIL classrooms. The examples that we have found focus again on lexical elements, as in the following extract from a CLIL history class (grade 8, ages 13–14), an extension of Extract 6.8:

Extract 6.21
1	T:	Ok, very good. Ok. So we have mentioned one keyword,
2		which is ... ? If we say housing, what is the keyword [you've
3		mentioned]? They live in ... ?
4	S1:	Villages. Villages (non-standard pronunciation)
5	T:	Villages. Villages or ... ?
6	S2:	Villages (standard pronunciation).
7	T:	Villages, villages (standard pronunciation) rather than
8		villages (non-standard pronunciation) The first letter is 's'
9	S:	Surrounding.
10	T:	And the last one is a 'd', all right?
11	S:	( )
12	T:	Sheds all right? Sheds. Shed, remember?

In this example, we find a variety of corrective feedback strategies leading to the students' production of the word *sheds*. First, the teacher is trying to get the students to produce the word by means of a number of elicita-tions (*They live in ... ?, Villages or ... ?*), then she recasts the pronuncia-tion of *village* (line 4), next she uses explicit correction (*villages rather than villages*) and, finally, she ends up using metalinguistic feedback (*The first letter is 's' ... and the last one is a 'd'*).

Corrective feedback in student–student interactions

Studies on corrective feedback have mainly taken their data from whole-class interactions as these tend to occupy a greater portion of the classroom time (Lyster, 2007), and also due to the interest in observing the effect of teachers' corrective feedback on students' uptake. However, as an alternative to whole-class IRF interactional patterns, group work has been claimed to be effective for language development. Advantages of group work include more opportunities to talk, more chances for message redundancy, more referential questions to clarify meaning etc. (Gibbons, 2002). In group work, Swain's (2006) concept of 'languaging' takes place ('the use of language to mediate higher mental cognitive and affective processes'), as group work not only offers opportunities for students to engage in meaningful communication and, thus, practise the L2 in different ways, but also offers opportunities for the students themselves to provide corrective feedback and carry out metalinguistic exchanges. Extract 6.22, from a pair-work activity between two students discussing the topic of the American Civil War (grade 7, ages 12–13), is an example of a student's explicit correction of his peer's lexical item, providing a more appropriate word, which is taken up by S2:

Extract 6.22
1   S1: Okay ... so what was the reason why northern union won
2   S2: They had more people and more everything
3   S1: ((laughing)) more everything
4   S2: They had more ...
5   S1: More guns.
6   S2: They had more trains they had more factories they had more
7   fields they had more production they had more people.
8   S1: Population.
9   S2: Or population ... they even had (   )

In this student–student interaction on subject content, S1 seems to be adopting the role of the teacher. He begins an IRF exchange (see Chapter 3, Box 3.1, on the IRF pattern) by formulating a display question related to the topic (line 1) and provides negative feedback on his peer's response by repeating, with laughter, S2's phrase *more everything* (line 3). He even finishes his peer's turn by providing a word that he thinks S2 is searching for, as signalled by his pause after *they had more* (line 4). Finally, in line 8, he recasts the term used by his peer by using a more abstract word (*population*), which is then picked up by S2 (line 9). The pause that follows this student's repetition of the keyword could be interpreted as a signal of the student's noticing (Schmidt, 1990), and not merely repeating, that *population* is a better choice.

Group-work activities in CLIL classes do not usually create opportunities for students to correct each other on language-related aspects. However, by creating, for example, group-work interactions where one student adopts the role of the teacher, there might be more opportunities for students to give each other feedback and reflect upon language issues which still arise incidentally but are motivated by the characteristics of the task.

To summarise this section, in the CLIL corpus, most of the examples of teachers' use of corrective feedback tend to focus on lexical errors, which are both language- and content-integrated errors, as well as on pronunciation errors, mainly of the keywords related to the topic under study. These observations are in line with the results obtained by Dalton-Puffer (2007) in her analysis of error types in Austrian CLIL contexts. In her data, grammar errors were less frequently corrected / repaired by the teacher and discourse errors were only corrected in 1.2 per cent of the cases. Our proposal in this chapter is that CLIL teachers' pedagogic or corrective feedback should focus on formal features integrated within the study of content.

6.6 Conclusion

In this chapter we have illustrated the advantages of the focus-on-form approach in CLIL classrooms. We follow the idea developed by many researchers (see Lyster, 2007, for example) that some formal language features should be attended to explicitly or implicitly (through proactive or reactive approaches), and cannot be left to be acquired by the students incidentally. Our proposal, however, extends the traditional focus-on-form approach in SLA research to a focus on language functions in academic registers and genres. We argue that some lexico-grammatical features are more relevant than others to the production of the genres and registers required in particular disciplines.

We have also discussed the importance of the degree of students' immersion in the target language. In low-immersion contexts it is probably more necessary to plan some communicative tasks and activities which trigger specific language features (analytic and proactive approach), forcing students to use them, whereas high-immersion contexts might allow for more experiential types of learning where a focus on language would arise from any task designed to guarantee interaction, within a more reactive approach. However, even in such high-immersion contexts certain grammatical features might remain unnoticed. For this purpose, target-language-oriented activities should be included in textbook materials and planned by the teachers in order to make sure that the students work on these linguistic forms, integrated within the content under study.

Even though we agree with authors like Lyster (2007) that the potential of CLIL or immersion classrooms for language learning has probably not been sufficiently exploited and that language-learning opportunities can be missed when relying on incidental language learning, in this chapter we argue that a focus on form in CLIL classrooms should be specifically linked and integrated with focus on content / meaning. With this, we do not mean that formal language errors should not be addressed, but that teachers should also focus on functional language errors. This approach encourages the integration of language and content, something which is widely proclaimed in CLIL but rarely achieved. Specific language focus should then be integrated in genres and registers as lexico-grammar cannot be independent from meaning. We suggest that CLIL teachers work collaboratively with their students in the functional relation between form and meaning / language and content.

Questions and tasks for reflection and discussion

1. How could a CLIL teacher intervene to make this student's spoken text on the Modern Age more academic? Use the ideas in Section 6.3.

Extract 6.23
1 S: When mercantilism appears, the countries try to make them-
2   selves self-sufficient to export more things than they import ...
3   So they have a (   ) to spend it on services and ... what they
4   like ((laughs)) *No te rías* (Sp. Don't laugh). But with when the
5   capitalism arrives after the mercantilism eh ... there is an infla-
6   tion because the price is rise very much and the people can't ...
7   Can't buy things and cannot ... Do not have resources

2. Identify the different meanings of *and* in the following text produced by a CLIL student responding to the prompt *What can be done to mitigate the consequences of a natural disaster?*

Text 6.2
The people go to help *and* build their house *and* start other time all his life ... *and* some people pay to them *and* other are no paying, they help because they want to.

3. Identify the types of corrective feedback in the following exchanges. Decide if they are effective or not. Which of these types focus on form only (grammar, pronunciation) and which focus on form in relation to the function they perform in specific genres and registers, adapting the utterance to the register of the school subject?

Extract 6.24
1   S: She makes a special box to make the neck
2   T: Neck ... ?
3   S: Neck.
4   T: Necklace, ok?
5   S: Because more people lived there
6   T: Because of population growth, that's right.
7   S: Yes, population growth.
8   S: Some peasants (non-standard pronunciation) were slaves
9   T: Sorry?
10   S: Some peasants (standard pronunciation) ... were slaves

References

Beveridge, M. and Brierley, C. (1982) 'Classroom constructs: An interpretative approach to young children's language', in Beveridge, M. (ed.), *Children Thinking Through Language*, London: Edward Arnold, pp. 156–95.

Christie, F. (2002) *Classroom Discourse Analysis: A Functional Perspective*, London: Continuum.

Christie, F. and Derewianka, B. (2008) *School Discourse: Learning to Write Across the Years of Schooling*, London: Continuum.

Coyle, D., Hood, P. and Marsh, D. (2010) *CLIL: Content and Language Integrated Learning.* Cambridge: Cambridge University Press.

Dalton-Puffer, C. (2007) *Discourse in Content and Language Integrated Learning (CLIL) Classrooms.* Amsterdam and Philadelphia, PA: John Benjamins.

Doughty, C. and Williams, J. (1998) *Focus on Form in Classroom Second Language Acquisition*, Cambridge: Cambridge University Press.

Gibbons, P. (2002) *Scaffolding Language, Scaffolding Learning: Teaching Second Language Learners in the Mainstream Classroom*, Portsmouth, NH: Heinemann.

Halliday, M. A. K. and Matthiessen, C. M. I. M. (2004) *An Introduction to Functional Grammar* (3rd ed.), London: Hodder Arnold.

Halliday, M. A. K. and Hasan, R. (1976) *Cohesion in English.* London: Longman.

Hulstijn, J. H. (2003). *Incidental and Intentional Learning.* London: Blackwell.

Hymes, D. (1972) 'On communicative competence', in Pride, J. B. and Holmes, J. (eds.) *Sociolinguistics*, Harmondsworth, Middlesex: Penguin Education, pp. 269–93.

Llinares, A. (2005) 'The effect of teacher feedback on EFL learners' functional production in classroom discourse', *Anglogermanica Online: Revista Electrónica Periódica De Filología Alemana e Inglesa*, 3.

Llinares, A. (2007a) 'Young learners' functional use of the L2 in a low-immersion EFL context', *ELT Journal*, 61, 1, 39–45.

Llinares, A. (2007b) 'Classroom bilingualism at an early age: Towards a more natural EFL context', in Pérez Vidal, C., Juan-Garau, M. and Bel, A. (eds.) *A Portrait of the Young in Multilingual Spain*, Bristol: Multilingual Matters, pp. 185–99.

Llinares, A. and Whittaker, R. (2009) 'Teaching and learning history in secondary CLIL classrooms: From speaking to writing', in Dafouz, E., and Guerinni, M. (eds.), *CLIL Across Educational Levels: Experiences from Primary, Secondary and Tertiary Contexts*, London and Madrid: Richmond / Santillana, pp. 73–89.

Llinares, A. and Whittaker, R. (2010) 'Writing and speaking in the history class: A comparative analysis of CLIL and first language contexts', in Dalton-Puffer, C., Nikula, T. and Smit, U. (eds.) *Language Use and Language Learning in CLIL Classrooms*, Amsterdam: John Benjamins, pp. 125–43.

Long, M. H. (1981) 'Questions in foreigner talk discourse', *Language Learning*, 31, 1, 135–57.

Lyster, R. (1998) 'Immersion pedagogy and implications for language teaching', in Cenoz, J. and Genesee, F. (eds.) *Beyond Bilingualism: Multilingualism and Multilingual Education*, Clevedon, UK: Multilingual Matters, pp. 64–95.

Lyster, R. (2007) *Learning and Teaching Languages through Content: A Counterbalanced Approach*, Amsterdam and Philadelphia, PA: John Benjamins.

Lyster, R. and Mori, H. (2006) 'Interactional feedback and instructional counterbalance', *Studies in Second Language Acquisition*, 28, 321–41.

Lyster, R. and Ranta, L. (1997) 'Corrective feedback and learner uptake', *Studies in Second Language Acquisition*, 19, 37–66.

Martin, J. R. and Rothery, J. (1986) 'What a functional approach to the writing task can show teachers about "good writing"', in Couture, B. (ed.), *Functional Approaches to Writing: Research Perspectives*, Norwood, NJ: Ablex, pp. 241–65.

Martin, J. R. (1993) 'Life as noun: Arresting the universe in science and humanities', in Halliday, M. A. K. and Martin, J. R. (eds.) *Writing Science: Literacy and Discursive Power*, London: Falmer, pp. 221–67.

Mohan, B. and Beckett, G. H. (2003) 'A functional approach to research on content-based language learning: Recasts in causal explanations', *The Modern Language Journal*, 87, 3, 421–32.

Perrett, G. (2000) 'Researching second and foreign language development', in Unsworth, L. (ed.) *Researching Language in Schools and Communities*, London: Cassell, pp. 87–110.

Schleppegrell, M. (2004) *The Language of Schooling: A Functional Linguistics Perspective*, Mahwah, NJ; London: Lawrence Erlbaum.

Schmidt, R. W. (1990) 'The role of consciousness in second language learning', *Applied Linguistics*, **11**, 2, 129–58.

Schmidt, R. (2001) 'Attention', in Robinson, P. J. (ed.) *Cognition and Second Language Instruction*, Cambridge: Cambridge University Press, pp. 3–32.

Stern, H. H. (1992) *Issues and Options in Language Teaching*, Oxford: Oxford University Press.

Swain, M. (1998) 'Focus on form through conscious reflection', in Doughty, C. and Williams, J. (eds.) *Focus on Form in Classroom Second Language Acquisition*, Cambridge: Cambridge University Press, pp. 64–81.

Swain, M. (2006) 'Languaging, agency and collaboration in advanced language proficiency', in Byrnes, H. (ed.) *Advanced Language Learning: The Contribution of Halliday and Vygotsky*, London: Continuum, pp. 95–108.

Van Ek, J. A. and Alexander, L. G. (1975) *Threshold Level English*, Oxford: Pergamon Press.

van Lier, L. (1996) *Interaction in the Language Curriculum: Awareness, Autonomy, and Authenticity*, London: Longman.

Various authors. (2008) *Essential Geography and History*, Madrid: Richmond Publishing-Santillana.

Vázquez, A. (2010) 'A study of linguistic transfer in the oral discourse of learners of English as a foreign language in the framework of content and language integrated learning (CLIL) in the autonomous community of Madrid. Unpublished Master's dissertation, Madrid: Universidad Autónoma de Madrid.

Veel, R. and Coffin, C. (1996) 'Learning to think like an historian: The language of secondary school history', in Hasan, R. and Williams, G. (eds.), *Literacy in Society*, Harlow, Essex: Addison Wesley Longman, pp. 191–231.

Whittaker, R. and Llinares, A. (2009) 'CLIL in social science classrooms: Analysis of spoken and written productions', in Ruiz de Zarobe, Y. and Jiménez Catalán, R. M. (eds.) *Content and Language Integrated Learning: Evidence from Research in Europe*. Bristol: Multilingual Matters, pp. 215–34.

Wilkins, D. (1976) *Notional Syllabuses*, Oxford: Oxford University Press.

7 Students' academic and interpersonal language in CLIL

7.1 Introduction

The aim of this chapter is to establish a link between CLIL students' academic and interpersonal language development. While Chapters 4, 5 and 6 focused on the role of academic language, this chapter turns to the role of language in realising interpersonal relationships and expressing attitude towards content in the CLIL class.

The distinction between academic and social language has always been an important area of research on language learning in immersion contexts. With his reference to BICS (Basic Interpersonal Communication Skills) and CALP (Cognitive Academic Language Proficiency), Cummins (1979) highlighted the necessity of distinguishing the two functions of language. BICS refers to the everyday language needed to interact socially, whereas CALP is the type of language which is essential for students to succeed in school. Cummins's distinction between BICS and CALP had its roots in the move of immigrant students from language education programmes to mainstream classes. Educators and educational policy makers held the assumption that 'surface' knowledge of the target language (BICS) was the only requisite for learners to be successful in the different subjects taught in that language. This led decision makers in US bilingual programmes to send immigrant learners with a good level in BICS to mainstream classes (Cummins, 1984) with the subsequent risk of academic failure. The distinction between BICS and CALP, then, took on importance for educators when they tried to explain why these students with good interpersonal language skills (BICS) were not successful academically (CALP) when they were moved into mainstream classes. In fact, according to Cummins, it takes students about two years of exposure to the target language to acquire conversational fluency and much more (about five years) to catch up with native speakers in the control of academic features of the target language.

A different scenario is found in CLIL classrooms. In most CLIL contexts in Europe, Latin America and much of Asia, students are only exposed to the foreign language in the classroom, that is, in an academic context. As CLIL students do not usually have many opportunities for exposure to the target language outside the classroom, this means that there are also limited opportunities for them to use the foreign language for social purposes and thus to develop their BICS. In addition to the concern about the acquisition of academic language skills, some educators and researchers in these contexts are worried that the students' development in the target language is bound to be limited to CALP (Dalton-Puffer, 2005). In fact, in her comparison between CLIL and non-CLIL students, Várkuti (2010) states that for BICS purposes non-CLIL students were as good as the CLIL students. Therefore, CLIL contexts do not seem to represent learning environments where BICS is acquired more or less automatically.

In this book we give importance to the 'language of schooling' but we also believe it is necessary to explore the potential of the CLIL class to provide the learners with opportunities to use the target language for communicative purposes other than those necessary to work on specific school genres and to operate in the classroom. Given the lack of possibilities for CLIL students to develop BICS in the foreign language outside the classroom, teachers should make sure that basic interpersonal communicative skills are put into practice in the CLIL class. In EFL classes, everyday communication is often the main focus of activity, whereas in content classes, carried out in the L1, everyday communication is expected to help the students participate in the tasks and activities related to those disciplines. In CLIL, the function of everyday language is similar to that of content classes in the L1 but, additionally, CLIL students are expected to be able to transfer the use of the foreign language for social purposes to other communicative situations outside the classroom.

7.2 The interpersonal function of language

As described in the Introduction, in systemic functional linguistic theory, language is seen to convey three main metafunctions: ideational, interpersonal and textual (Halliday and Matthiessen, 2004). Here we focus on the interpersonal function, which refers to the use of language to construct interpersonal relationships. This includes the use of language to carry out social communicative functions (requests, offers, complaints etc.) but also the language used to understand and express attitudes towards the academic content.

In the classroom context, the interpersonal function is not only part of the regulative register (see Chapter 1), where it plays a role in the organisation of classroom work and role assignment in the class, but it is also part of the academic content being taught and learned (instructional register). The students are expected to express an attitude to what they are writing / talking about, both from the point of view of their own personal experience or reality and by interpreting and evaluating subject content (Thompson and Hunston, 2000). Students' control of the language of argumentation, for instance, is necessary if they are to move beyond the mere presentation of facts in a certain discipline (Dalton-Puffer, 2007). This is very relevant in content teaching in the L1 and is especially necessary when content is taught in / through a foreign language: learning argumentation is important for understanding content more deeply and, at the same time, for allowing students to use and learn the foreign language for a wider range of communicative purposes.

SFL studies on the role of language at different educational levels show that knowing how to use the language for interpersonal purposes also plays an important role in school success (e.g. Christie, 2002; Coffin, 1997; Schleppegrell, 2004). According to these studies, many students, both native and non-native speakers of the target language, need support in their use of interpersonal resources (for example, modality). For this reason, the development of the interpersonal function constitutes one of the key elements in the evaluation of English as a second language (Polias, 2003).

One of the benefits of CLIL is said to be the fact that it provides a more authentic context for language learning and, as a consequence, more opportunities for developing communicative competence in the target language. However, research carried out in two different contexts, Austria and Finland, has come up with different findings in this respect. As we saw in Chapter 1, Dalton-Puffer's (2005) analysis of directives in Austrian CLIL classrooms shows that CLIL students in fact do not seem to have more opportunities than EFL learners to experiment with directives. In Dalton-Puffer's words, 'In this sense, Cook's statement that "the opportunities for language socialization are very limited in the foreign language classroom" (Cook, 2001: 84) also holds for CLIL classrooms, despite their reputation for being somehow "more real and authentic" communicative environments than are classical foreign language lessons' (Dalton-Puffer, 2005: 1290).

On the other hand, Nikula's comparison of CLIL and EFL patterns of Initiation–Response–Feedback (IRF) shows that CLIL students in her context have more opportunities for initiating interactions and practising argumentation: 'CLIL lessons thus seem to provide students more opportunities than EFL lessons to practice argumentation: to back up statements with reasons and justifications whereas knowledge of English in EFL lessons seems to be constructed as a collection of facts that need to be memorized but that do not need to be explained or discussed' (Nikula, 2007: 195).

It seems, then, that the dynamics and methodology of the CLIL class vary across contexts and this seems to have an impact on the extent to which students can use more or less interpersonal language. It could also be argued that some interpersonal language functions are easier to develop in the CLIL classroom than others. For example, the language needed for argumentation is more likely to be used and practised than the students' use of directives, precisely due to certain constraints related to the role of participants in the classroom context.

Our view of the role of interpersonal language in the CLIL class is inspired by Schleppegrell's (2004) distinction between the interpersonal features that are typical of informal conversation and those that are characteristic of formal academic discourse in specific school genres. We have referred to these two as language for socialising and language for school genres. To these we add two other functions of interpersonal language: language for operating in the classroom and language for expressing personal experience. The first is related to Coyle's (2007) function of language *for* learning, which she defines as the language needed to operate in an educational context in a foreign language, regardless of the specific discipline. We suggest, then, that interpersonal language in the CLIL classroom has four main purposes (see Figure 7.1): language used for socialising, for sharing personal experiences, for operating in the classroom context (language for learning) and for operating in specific school genres:

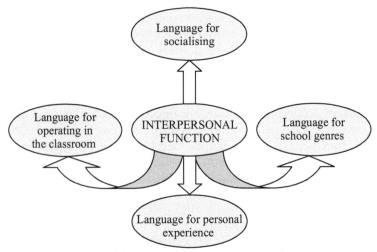

Figure 7.1 Interpersonal language functions in CLIL classes

As we show in this figure, CLIL teachers need to be aware of the importance of students evaluating the content that they are learning and the specific language needed for that (interpersonal language for school genres). CLIL students also need to be allowed to integrate their personal experience with the specific subject content that they are studying (interpersonal language for personal experience). At the same time, students need to be able to participate in classroom activity in a foreign language (interpersonal language for operating in the classroom), regardless of the subject or content that they are learning. Finally, the CLIL class also has the potential for providing opportunities to use the language for social purposes which may arise in everyday situations (interpersonal language for socialising). This is especially important in CLIL contexts in which the language of instruction is only used in the classroom. In the following sections we will discuss each of these aspects in turn.

7.3 Interpersonal features of language in CLIL: The language of evaluation and appraisal in school genres

Formal academic discourse in certain genres contains some form of evaluation (see Chapters 4 and 5 on the role of evaluation in specific genres). However, some content subjects are more likely to include evaluation and opinion than others. For instance, evaluating whether natural disasters are the product of human behaviour in the environment or not, or whether the Treaty of Versailles was fair for the Germans are aspects of the content that are usually integrated as part of curricula. Studies of history genres have given rise to interesting analyses on evaluation in learners' discourse (Coffin, 2006a; Derewianka, 2007). Evaluative language is referred to as **Appraisal** in SFL and this model is described in Box 7.1:

Box 7.1: Appraisal

Appraisal, in Systemic Functional Theory, refers to the way language is used to evaluate, to adopt stances and to manage interpersonal relationships (Martin and Rose, 2003; Martin and White, 2005).

> Appraisal is concerned with evaluation: the kinds of attitudes that are negotiated in a text, the strength of the feelings involved and the ways in which values are sourced. and readers aligned.

(Martin and Rose, 2003: 22)

According to Martin and White (2005), this system of meanings encompasses three main domains: Attitude, Graduation and Engagement.

- *Attitude* reflects the ways we express emotions, how we evaluate things and the judgement of behaviours:
  Examples: *I was <u>torn to pieces</u>*
  A <u>frivolous</u> question
  this is a <u>mean</u> administration

(cont.)

- *Graduation* allows us to adjust our opinions or emotions:
  Examples: *very miserable*

- *Engagement* has to do with allowing alternative points
  of view:
  Examples: *There must have been someone out there who is still
  alive*

(Examples from Martin and Rose, 2003,
and Martin and White, 2005)

Appraisal in CLIL students' spoken and written discourse

Schleppegrell (2004) identifies the use of evaluative language as one of the challenges of academic writing, and shows how this develops in students' writing. In CLIL, the resources that students use to express evaluation of the content they are writing and talking about tend to be reduced to a limited number of lexical and grammatical devices. The examples in Extract 7.1 have been taken from the same students' written and spoken responses to one of the questions in a prompt designed to elicit secondary school students' spoken and written production on the topic, 'The Modern State: Strong and Weak Monarchs' (grade 9, ages 14–15). The question asked: 'Do you think Philip II was a good or a bad monarch? Give reasons.' To answer this question, the students were expected to produce a short text in the exposition, or argument, genre (see Chapter 4 on history genres). To do this, they needed to use the linguistic resources of appraisal to evaluate Philip II's reign, and base their explanation on this evaluation. The following extract shows the same students' responses to the question in the written and spoken registers:

Extract 7.1	
S2 (WRITING): I think he was a good king because he achieved lots of things but he had bad luck with meteorology and Elisabeth.	S2 (SPEAKING): ... so ... Philip the second was a good king but he had very ba- very bad luck and ... in the ... battle with the English people, eh his Armada was defeated by storms and metereology so he was ... he was very unlucky. *(cont.)*

S3 (WRITING): I think he did good and bad things like developing the country, but I think he killed a lot of people without reason and he tried to control people's mind by banning foreign books people wanted to study.	S3 (SPEAKING): Well, I think he was ... eh ... good in certain things, and bad. For example, in trying to control people minds, that was a bit crazy because you can't control everybody.
S4 (WRITING): I think he was a bad monarch because he followed ~~the~~ Machiavelli's ideas of being hypocrit, false, and he didn't respect the laws of, for example, Aragón. He invented that Antonio Pérez was practising heterodox religion to could captured him.	S4 (SPEAKING): in the middle because he was a bad following the Machiavelic ideas of being hypocrite, false, that he can lie when he only wants to ... to the ... to rise the empire and then a good because he have a very great empire and he made ... many wars and in ... some points he was good because he ... he wants to increase and to make huge the empire, but he didn't follow the laws and the ... and the ... *fueros* (Sp. charters).

In both speaking and writing, the CLIL students' interpersonal resources in evaluating the content are limited to the use of *I think*, the use of the pre-modifiers *very*, *lots of / a lot of* and the adjectives *good* and *bad*. Other resources for expressing appraisal, such as placing interpersonal elements at the beginning of clauses (interpersonal themes), to prepare the reader or listener for a certain attitude towards the content, are rarely found in the corpus. One exception was the following student's use of this device in a written text: *Unfortunately, for him, his empire suffered two bankruptcies.* Most appraisal devices are linked to the expression of attitude (*good, bad, hypocrite, false, great, achieved, unlucky, huge*) and the use of pre-modifiers to show graduation (*lots of / a lot of, very, a bit*). The use of *in some points* in S4's spoken text is interesting as it goes against the general tendency for students to use intensification rather than attenuation in their arguments. As far as engagement is concerned, the students mostly relied on *I think*, presumably as a means of avoiding bare assertions. There is only one case, S1's writing sample, where other voices are recognised: *Some say that he was a bad monarch and others he was good.* All in all, there seems to be little difference between the students' spoken and written registers as far as appraisal is concerned, with the exception of S3, who interacts directly with her interlocutor in her spoken performance, using a generic *you* and the modal *can't*: *you can't control everybody*.

These few samples of secondary school students' talk, although limited to one specific school genre, offer some insight into the importance for students of meeting the interpersonal (as well as ideational and textual) requirements of different genres and approaches to school subjects. CLIL teachers at the secondary level need to be aware of these needs. This is clearly a difficult area: even L1 students are not found to develop arguments until the later stages of secondary education (Christie and Deriwianka, 2008). Learning specific subject content not only involves learning the vocabulary and the grammar necessary to present facts but also, when necessary, learning how to evaluate these facts in the L2. An evaluative approach to content also has positive effects on the students' communicative competence through broadening the scope of language functions needed. This is also likely to have a positive effect on language form and complexity.

The use of modality

One of the key areas of grammar used to express interpersonal meanings is modality (resources of language for expressing possibility, ability, probability etc.). In Schleppegrell's words, 'In school-based texts, attitudinal meanings emerge in modality ... ' (2004: 63). According to this author, modality is a suitable resource for expressing interpersonal meanings, presenting the speaker's / writer's evaluation but still maintaining an academic register. In their analysis of secondary school students' performance in a social science CLIL classroom, Whittaker and Llinares (2009) found a very limited set of resources in the area of modality. As they put it, 'This distance from academic register is also shown in these students' use of modality, a resource without which academic communication remains at a very rudimentary level' (2009: 231). This study found that the students' repertoire was made up basically of multifunctional *can*, used to express ability, probability and permission. Some of the prompts used to elicit the spoken and written data in the UAM-CLIL corpus (see the Introduction) demanded modals of ability and permission, as in 'What were the obligations and rights of the peasants in the feudal system?', but this did not succeed in getting the students to use them. Dalton Puffer (2007) explains the lack of hypothesising and, thus, scarce use of modals in Austrian CLIL students' oral discourse as related to gaps in their L2 general competence. In addition to using a limited set of resources, the students in Whittaker and Llinares's study frequently used modality inappropriately (both formally and functionally). In the following example from a geography class the student uses *can* to express obligation: *And to not contaminate the atmosphere, we can no make factories.* Here, perhaps, support from EFL colleagues could be brought in, in helping CLIL students prepare certain topics.

The communicative situation seems to affect the use of modality by students. Our CLIL corpus shows that students used more modals of obligation / permission in one-to-one interviews than in whole-class discussions. This suggests that different educational contexts affect the students' degree of involvement and, in consequence, their linguistic performance. In the UAM-CLIL corpus, the interview format seemed to encourage the students to use more interpersonal language features than the whole-class discussion. However, one cannot ignore the fact that students, in general, are expected to display their knowledge in the context of the whole classroom and the interview format does not represent a common classroom practice.

We believe, then, that it is necessary to raise CLIL students' awareness of the functions of modals. The following example from a secondary school student's written text (grade 7, ages 12–13) shows the overuse of the modal *can* to express different meanings:

Extract 7.2
The consequences can[1] be that: the houses could[2] float and the people could[3] die. We can[4] cut less trees but that means produce less wood. I can't[5] do anything ... but, well I could[6] think it and teach my sons and maybe they can[7] say something, but is no probably.

Can or the past form *could* expresses probability in instances 1, 2 and 3, and ability in 4, 5, 6 and 7. CLIL curricula usually expect the students to move beyond the presentation of facts. Modality is one necessary resource for CLIL students to accomplish this successfully.

7.4 Interpersonal features of language in CLIL: The language for operating in the classroom

In this section we will discuss the language for operating in the classroom, that is, the type of language that learners need so that they can participate in learning activities regardless of the language of instruction and independently of what the particular subject is (Coyle's language *for* learning). This function could be related to Christie's concept of *curriculum macrogenre*. The term macrogenre was proposed by Martin (1994) as a larger unit created by a text that incorporates several elemental genres. To take an example from CLIL materials, in a grade 2 primary school textbook on science, 'wind' is defined as 'air moving'. The definition is then followed by explanations of why and how the air moves. Drawing on Martin's concept of macrogenres, Christie (2002) proposed the concept of *curriculum macrogenre*, referring to instances of classroom activity across a sequence of lessons. Students and teachers need certain language resources for operating in different types of classroom activity, independently of the subject, the language of instruction and the educational level. This language is partly related to Coyle's (2007) concept of 'language *for* learning', that is, the language that learners need to operate in the class in a foreign language. An example of this is students' dialogic performance in group work.

CLIL students need to develop discourse strategies that allow them to operate successfully in a foreign language in the classroom. These involve learning and using not only genre-specific language features, as shown above, but also other features related to different types of classroom activity common to different subjects. For example, if students are expected to give a chronological recount of a school experience, they need to be trained in using appropriate time discourse markers in their presentation (see Coffin, 2006b). Teachers' and students' awareness of those discourse features needed for carrying out specific tasks across subjects is necessary in both L1 and L2 content classes. However, this often causes difficulties if the content is taught in a foreign language. In Extract 7.3 the students are discussing the history topic of medieval times in groups before sharing the discussion in the whole class (grade 8, ages 13–14):

Extract 7.3
1   S1: ... Okay ... Society was based on an extent of (   ) and
2   allegations ... the Economy was based on agriculture ... *Vale*
3   (Sp. OK), okay ... okay ... so, what definition shall we
4   write? ... ((reads again from her notes, the same but faster))
5   S2: So we put that *¿no?* (Sp. Shall we?)
6   S1: Right, to the second question ... right, the second question.
7   *Espera* (Sp. Wait).
8   S2: Okay ((Reads second question aloud)) what was ...
9   What was life like for peasants.
10   Describe their rights and obligations ... Eh ... .

With this task the students are given the opportunity of participating in the regulative register. The language for organisational purposes used in this extract demands the use of specific discourse markers. The students use a variety of them (*okay, so, right*) with the function of focusing or marking topic initiation. In addition, one of the students uses the Spanish discourse marker *¿no?* with the function of sympathetic circularity. Romero (2001) describes this function as that with which speakers try to keep the attention and understanding of their message by showing an intellectual collaboration with the audience. In Llinares and Romero's (2008) analysis of discourse markers in teacher talk, they found that the use of *¿no?* was prevalent among non-native CLIL teachers, rather than the use of question tags. There is evidence, then, that there is a need for both CLIL learners and their teachers to expand the range of discourse markers they use for interpersonal purposes.

7.5 Interpersonal features of language in CLIL: The language of socialising

Classrooms tend to offer little opportunity for experiencing informal socialising. This is true not only of foreign language classes (Cook, 2001) but also of CLIL classes. According to Dalton-Puffer (2009), we need to recognise that CLIL classrooms are a type of educational context and that they cannot be expected to prepare learners for other external situational contexts. Hence, expectations about CLIL classes preparing learners for all-purpose foreign language uses needs to be revisited and revised. However, we believe that, in certain curriculum macrogenres, there is potential for developing basic interpersonal communicative skills (BICS).

Socialising in group work

A lot of group-work activities in some CLIL contexts tend to be carried out in the L1. This is the case in the Austrian context (Dalton-Puffer, 2007). However, in other contexts, such as Finland (Dalton-Puffer and Nikula, 2006), students usually conduct group-work activities in the target language. This difference seems to be related to the role of English in different cultures. What is interesting is that whenever group work happens in the target language, a range of opportunities for the development of pragmatic competence arises. These opportunities hardly ever appear in teacher-fronted content classes, whether in the L1 or the L2. In the following example from a CLIL geography class (grade 7, ages 12–13), students are preparing for their participation in a whole-class discussion on natural disasters. The focus of the discussion is on whether natural disasters can be prevented or not.

Extract 7.4
1   S1: We can help a natu- a natural disaster never occurs.
2   S3: True.
3   S1: We can send water.
4   S4: And money, money for we help ... Earthquakes another
5   disaster happens.
6   S1: No because we have to put why.
7   S3: ((Writing)) Natural disasters-
8   S4: Are occurred.
9   S3: ((Writing down the answers.)) Put happen, better happen
10   S4: When the tectonics plates-
11   S1: Move.
12   S4: Yes. And that, and that is earthquakes.
13   S3: ((Writing.)) And that ... is earthquakes.
14   [...]
15   S4: OK. We can help a lot if a natural disaster ever occurs. It
16   is true because we have aeroplanes and a lot of transport.
17   [...]
18   S1: We can send things that people need every day, for
19   example paper.
20   S4: They need it everyday?
21   S3: Things that they need. ((Laughter.))
22   S4: That is a silly thing.
23   S1: No, I think.
24   S4: What do you, what do you need first, the food or the
25   paper for cleaning your bottom?
26   S3: Paper but food, food the first, first the food.
27   S4: I say the first. Who say the second?
28   S1: Eh I say the second.
29   S4: You say the second. You N? Five, three

This extract represents a very rich example of learners participating not only in the instructional register but also in the regulative register, which is almost always controlled by the teacher (see Chapter 1 on the differences between instructional and regulative registers). An example of this can be found at line 6, where S1 says *we have to put why.*

Another example is found in the last three turns of the extract, where the students are deciding who says what in the whole-class discussion that will follow their group work. Throughout the extract students express a wide range of functions, such as agreement (*true, yes*), disagreement (*No, I think; that is a silly thing*), directives (*put happen*), referential questions (*Who say the second?*) and even rhetorical questions such as: *They need it every day?* or *What do you need first, the food or the paper for cleaning your bottom?* They also use personal pronouns that represent the here and now (*I, you* and *we*) to address the different members in the group. This wide range of functions in such a short interaction is rarely found in teacher-fronted classroom discourse, where the students' functions are usually limited to responding to the teachers' questions.

Such a variety of functions being produced in situations that encourage learners' participation has also been found in young EFL learner classes. In her analysis of young EFL learners' realisation of communicative functions, Llinares (2006, 2007a, 2007b) found that learners exposed to a lower quantity of input outperformed other learners in high-immersion contexts in the amount and functional variety of the language produced, given specific tasks designed to encourage learners' participation in self-initiated interactions. In CLIL, certain activities such as group work should be more frequent if opportunities are to be created for more social aspects of the language to be practised in the CLIL classroom.

Role plays: Integrating content appraisal and language for social purposes

Role plays are considered useful for developing communicative competence in foreign language learning. This has been shown to be the case in CLIL, too. A study by Gassner and Maillat (2006) compared the impact of role plays on the students' production in the L2 with the effect of the same activity in the L1. They found that this activity increased student production in the L2. They explained this phenomenon as a 'mask effect' produced by the fact that the students felt safe when playing a role that could not be confused with their real identities.

Doing a role play certainly generated quite a lot of language in Extract 7.5, which shows two CLIL secondary school students acting out a dialogue between a Spanish coloniser and a Native American after the exploration of America (grade 9, ages 14–15):

Extract 7.5
1 S1: Ok. We brought ... a new religion that I think is better
2 because your religion eh ... have a lot of rites that you
3 need to kill people to ... and sacrifices for eh and this
4 religion eh ... eh tells about good to make good things
5 and ... and love and ...
6 S2: I don't think so because eh all the people eh have to
7 believe in something and we don't need to believe in the
8 same eh ... what you say about the rites ... not all the
9 religions have those rites and ... most of them are ... are
10 not ... very frequent. I I think everybody have ... must
11 have their own opinion and beliefs. You don't need to
12 impose us your religion.
13 S1: But the polytheistic religion make ah a lot of people death
14 and ah ... the Catholicism is is ... you can believe also in
15 that and is not doesn't cause any problem.
16 S2: Well, the catholic religion create the Inquisition that
17 kill a lot of people and ... yo- your religion also kill
18 many people.

This extract again shows the role of interpersonal language, with the expression of positive and negative attitude (*better, good things, impose, problem*) and graduation (*a lot of rites, all the people, not all the religions, most of them, very frequent, any problem*). In contrast with the earlier example in Extract 7.1, taken from students' compositions and their spoken performance in an interview, this extract shows more features of personal involvement. This is shown in the here-and-now personal pronouns *I, you* and *we*, the use of modals of obligation *you don't need to impose*, and even resources such as the manipulation of sentence elements to make the direct object an emphatic point of departure of the sentence as in: *what you say about the rites, not all the religions have those rites*, including attenuated disagreement (*not all*). All in all, the students produce an informal register that, although not totally appropriate for academic purposes, allows them to practise the target language for social / non-academic purposes that might be useful in the future outside the classroom.

7.6 Interpersonal features of language in CLIL: Students' personal experiences

We now turn to the fourth and final feature of our model for the interpretation of interpersonal language in CLIL. The importance of the personal function in children's language, including in the classroom context, has been shown in a number of studies. This function can be described as the language used to give information about one's own world. Cazden (1988) considers the personal function as one of three main functions in the language of the classroom. In their analysis of young EFL learners' communicative functions in classroom settings, Llinares and Romero (2007) also conclude that it is the most frequent function, provided that the task allows for certain communicative freedom and that the teacher scaffolds and encourages the learners' own contributions.

Expanding the range of communicative functions

The use of the students' personal experience in CLIL classes plays an important role in these students' development of communicative functions in the L2. The example below comes from the UAMLESC (UAM Learner English Spoken Corpus) and is taken from a bilingual school. In this particular science session, the children and teacher were discussing the state of the plants in the classroom. The extract shows a five-year-old CLIL learner's sharing of his own experience with death:

Extract 7.6
1   T: Look, this plant has died. We haven't watered it properly.
2   S1: Miss, L. You know what? My grandmother is dead.
3   T: Your grandmother is dead? Oh, that's sad. Was she very
4   old when she died?
5   S1: Yeah.
6   T: Yeah ... because, you know, people when they are very
7   very old, we have to die, we all die when we are old.
8   S1: He had nearly ... in Spanish *cien* (Sp. A hundred.).
9   T: Wow. She lived very old, didn't she? She was lucky to live
10   so old.
11   S2: Why he was lucky to be old?

In this interaction S1 leaves his classroom role aside and takes the initiative, interrupting the teacher's agenda. The teacher supports and encourages the learner in telling her and his classmates about his grandmother's death. This has interesting implications in terms of other learners' participations, as can be seen in another student's initiation of an exchange with a question: *Why he was lucky to be old?* In all types of classroom contexts most questions are asked by the teacher and they tend to be display questions (Long and Sato, 1983), that is, questions whose answers are already known by the speaker (see Chapter 3). The question asked by S2 is a referential question (he does not know the answer) and the extract, in general, reflects a type of interaction that could also be expected to take place in natural contexts, outside the classroom, in the L1. The idea of CLIL as creating 'conditions for naturalistic language learning' (Dalton-Puffer and Smit, 2007: 8) can acquire validity if the learners' own world is included and encouraged as a legitimate and valued source of topics.

Of course, this proposal must be considered in the light of the effects of age or educational level on the role of personalisation. It could be argued that the students' use of language to refer to their own personal world is more straightforward at lower levels but becomes more challenging in higher grades because the curricular content becomes more abstract and therefore cannot always be related to subjective / extramural experience in such direct ways. It may be seen as acceptable for a five-year-old to mention his grandmother's death when talk turns to a dead plant in a biology class, because language socialisation (no matter whether the L1 or the L2) has not progressed at that age to the point where speakers are expected to distinguish between speech events. However, it might be considered inappropriate for a secondary school child to do the same in the middle of a content lesson. They may also be less likely to do so given the fact that teenagers are not usually as spontaneous as young children.

The space for the students' personal experience in the content class is not necessarily dependent on the students' own initiatives. CLIL teachers need to be aware of those aspects of topics that can be connected with students' lives and use these to encourage more participation at suitable points. One such example comes from a secondary school biology class in English. The topic of the lesson was bacteria. It was a teacher-fronted introductory lesson where the teacher explained and asked display questions mainly following an IRF format (see Chapter 3). Some of these questions were intended to elicit students' knowledge of the topic from their own personal experience (grade 7, ages 12–13):

Extract 7.7
1   T: Can you think of the name of the yoghourt that you
2   normally eat at home that has a funny name in Latin?
3   S: L-Casei Immunitas.
4   T: Good! Lactobacillus Casei Immunitas is a type of bacteria.

In this classroom, the teacher made constant links with students' experiences. In fact, the only questions asked by learners themselves in this class referred to social experiences linked to the topic of bacteria. For example, at one point, the teacher refers to a type of bacterium that causes salmonella and she mentions an artificial egg substitute in order to avoid this disease. She uses the Spanish word *huevina* (egg powder). A student asks: *Do you use huevinas for fried eggs?* So, whether triggered by the students' own initiative or encouraged by the teachers, the reference to the CLIL students' personal experience seems to encourage their use of language functions (such as questioning), which do not frequently happen in the students' output in the instructional register.

Expanding the students' turns in interaction

Another positive effect of integrating the students' personal experience in CLIL classes is on the length of the students' turns. Extract 7.8 is taken from the UAM-CLIL corpus, which contains spoken and written data from secondary school students studying geography and history in English. The extract is part of an interview with a 13-year-old student on the topic of 'Feudal Europe', a topic that had been studied in class, following the same points covered earlier in an end-of-topic class discussion and a written composition:

Extract 7.8
1 INT: OK. Good. Now, can you remember why there was a
2   rebirth in the cities? Why did people move from the
3   countryside to the cities?
4 S: Eh because the, the country developed fast or-. I don't
5   remember that very well.
6 INT: Mm. The country developed fast and?
7 S: And eh, I don't remember.
8 INT: You can't remember why so many people moved to
9   the cities? No? OK. Uh, now, can you compare life
10   in the cities in the Middle Ages with your present
11   life now?
12 S: Eh, it had changed a lot, a lot, mmm because before,
13   eh mmm, everybody was, very bad, they lived very
14   bad, except kings and knights, and now everybody
15   almost have the same rights, I think. And now we have
16   more medicines and, less disease ... and we can save
17   more lives.

This example reveals that the student's first two turns are much shorter than the third one (16 and 6 words in the first two turns, 50 in the third one). An interesting aspect related to the idea of content and language integration is that the student does not seem to remember much about the content as shown in her two first responses. However, when she is asked to relate the content learned with her personal world she does actually show some knowledge: she refers to the differences between social classes in the Middle Ages and the reference to diseases.

Expanding the students' linguistic resources in the foreign language

In Extract 7.8, the student's third turn (lines 12–17) shows a richer type of language than the other turns and this language is related to her personal experience. She uses modality, expressed both through modal verbs and other lexical verbs (*can save, I think*), different types of circumstances (*now, except kings and knights*), as well as comparative expressions.

The two examples below, which belong to a primary school CLIL lesson on materials (grade 4, ages 9–10), are presented together to show the contrast between the resources used when a student simply answers display questions based on facts and when personal experience is brought into the exchange in the classroom:

Extract 7.9a
1   T: Ok and now ... and now ... flowers. What are they
2   made of?
3   S1: They are made of wood.
4   T: Wood? Do you agree with him? Give him a clue. Tell, tell
5   him the name of the animal that produce this material.
6   Who knows the animal? ((Many learners raise their
7   hands)) OK, let's listen. You say it: one, two, three.
8   SS: ((All of the them answering at once, as requested by the
9   teacher)) Caterpillar.
10   S1: ¿*Eh*? (Sp. What?)
11   S: Caterpillar.
12   T: OK. Can you tell me the name of the material?
13   S1: Leather
14   T: Leather? ... Do you agree with him?
15   S: No
16   T: No
17   S2: How do you say *seda* (Sp. silk)?
(*cont.*)

236

18	T:	How do you say *seda* (Sp. silk)? ... A
19	S3:	Silk
20	T:	Silk ...

Extract 7.9b

1	T:	Well, OK. Let's check the answers of the exercise on
2		page five.
3	S4:	P, can I ... ?
4	T:	Yes.
5	S4:	On Sunday I go to a
6	T:	I went to ... ?
7	S4:	I go to a
8	T:	I went.
9	S4:	I went to a ... How do you say *exposición*
10		(Sp. exhibition)?
11	T:	Exposition, exhibition.
12	S4:	Exhibition and I find and I found a ... a ... person that that
13		that is making with two, ... with two ... *dos palos*
14		(Sp. two sticks)
15	T:	With two sticks.
16	S4:	With two sticks.
17	T:	She was making what? Or he was making, that person
18		was making ...
19	S4:	She was making the glass with a protect glass, is make
20		glass with with the fire and ...
21	T:	OK, with heat and ... ?
22	S4:	She makes a special box to make the neck ...
23	T:	Necklace? And where, where, where was that, here in T?
24	S4:	In M.
25	T:	In M. ((Now addressing all the students)). Maybe we can
26		talk to R, go and see it because that experience is
27		interesting.
28	S5:	I see it in S.
29	T:	You saw it in S?

Extract 7.9a shows a typical classroom interaction where the teacher initiates, the students respond and the teacher provides feedback. In Extract 7.9b, in S4's performance, Coyle's four Cs (content, communication, cognition and culture) are activated. Using an initiating turn, which interrupts the interaction pattern led by the teacher (line 3), this student is 'communicating' a personal experience in the L2, she's

learning the 'content' from a different perspective, she's referring to a 'cultural' event in the town where she lives and she is also 'cognitively' engaged. Her performance is a clear example of what Cummins calls 'active student learning' as opposed to 'passive reception of knowledge' (Cummins, 2005: 108) and it clearly motivates other classmates to share similar experiences as well, as seen in S5's participation (line 23) where she claims to have seen that type of exhibition somewhere else.

When we look at these students' performance in the L2, S4's production is much richer than that of the other three. She uses longer sentences (including subordinate clauses, such as *she makes a special box to make the neck* (line 22)), she also activates new vocabulary (*sticks, exhibition*) that comes up in her recount of events. These words were obviously not part of the lesson plan designed by the teacher and constitute a clear example of what Coyle calls 'language *through* learning' (Coyle, 2007). The student also makes mistakes that she sometimes self-corrects as in *and I find and I found a ...* (line 12). Following Swain (1996), it is only by producing longer pieces of text that students can test their hypotheses about the foreign language, and so learn more. Although unplanned by the teacher, this example shows a social constructivist approach to learning that focuses on a type of interaction led by the student herself. This type of interaction helps her to develop her own individual thinking, starting from a personal / well-known experience.

7.7 Conclusion

Can interpersonal features of language be taught? Research on interlanguage pragmatics has shown that students can benefit from the direct teaching of pragmatic features (Rose and Kasper, 2001). In this chapter we have shown that certain types of tasks (group work, role plays etc.) may promote the use of interpersonal functions of the language.

The integration of interpersonal and academic features in CLIL is not only important for the improvement of target language skills but also for adopting a wider perspective in learning the content. CLIL teacher-training methodology, then, should go beyond adapting learners' materials and training teachers in their foreign language competence. Traditional content classes, as well as traditional foreign language classes, constitute a very structured context that may limit the learners' opportunities to approach the content in more personal and varied ways. As content and the language used to represent it are inextricable, different approaches to content are necessary both for widening the range of perspectives in learning the content (incorporating students' experience, getting the students to

238

evaluate the content etc.), as well as for using the target language in various ways (widening the range of communicative functions etc.)

In second language immersion contexts such as Canada students have more opportunities for learning BICS (Basic Interpersonal Communicative Skills) outside the classroom. Parents and educators involved in immersion education were worried about the children's academic achievement and assumed that L2 competence would be completely achieved by virtue of the naturalistic learning situation. However, this turned out not to be the case and French immersion students were found lacking in productive language skills even though the L2 is present in the out-of-school environment. The situation for CLIL in foreign language contexts such as Europe, South America or Asia is even more challenging in this respect, as there is usually no other context for using and learning the foreign language for socialising apart from the classroom, where academic content (and thus academic language) is a priority.

The CLIL class, then, needs to give space to both academic and social language practices. The understandable worry in CLIL research circles about the few opportunities for learners to develop interpersonal features in the foreign language might be mitigated if CLIL teachers are trained in the use of a wide range of tasks and activities that go beyond teacher-fronted classes where teachers ask and students respond (see Chapter 2 on the importance of dialogic teaching). This would also mean training the students to take on a different role in the classroom, a more active one that involves leading some of the activities, even deciding on them at some points, and initiating interactions. In this way the pro-CLIL argument of 'naturalness' in learning would acquire a double dimension: the target language is learned naturally, regardless of the type of methodology used, just because it is not the direct learning objective, but it is also learned 'naturally' in the sense of approaching the ways languages are used and learned in non-instructional contexts. It is this second understanding of 'naturalness' that requires methodological changes.

Questions and tasks for reflection and discussion

1. The CLIL learner can be said to perform three main roles. In your own CLIL context, which role(s) would you highlight as most important? Give reasons.
   - an apprentice historian / mathematician etc. in the L2
   - a classroom participant in the L2
   - a social participant in the L2

2. Identify different functions of the interpersonal language in Extract 7.10 where CLIL students (grade 8, ages 13–14) are discussing the topic of feudalism in groups, in preparation for a whole-class discussion. Describe the language used to convey those functions:

Extract 7.10
1 S1: Okay, first question, give a short definition of
2   feudalism.
3 S2: Eh ... well, it's a society, they live on agriculture, in
4   which land is power, and it was a political arrest
5   because of convenient pattern.
6 S1: It's also developing during the ninth, tenth eleventh
7   and twelfth century and
8 S2: and if it's an exchange of duty, communication
9   following some rules.
10 S3: It's also ((reading)) the social, economic and political
11   system that developed in Western Europe during the
12   ninth, tenth and eleventh century.
13 S2: Yeah but we know that it is also the relationship
14   between the vassal and the lord.
15 S1: where they all got something from each other ... yes
16 S2: The short definition ... eh. eh. It's the social, economic
17   and political system that developed in western Europe.
18 S1: Yes but we first have to say in what consists?

3. What are the advantages and disadvantages of CLIL and FL classrooms as contexts for the development of the four functions of interpersonal language proposed in this chapter?
4. Think of a specific topic in the CLIL subject you teach (or will teach). Using this topic, how would you create opportunities for the use of the four functions of interpersonal language as described in this chapter? Think about the types of activities you would use.

References

Cazden, C. (1988) *Classroom Discourse: The Language of Teaching and Learning*, Portsmouth, NH: Heinemann.

Christie, F. (2002) *Classroom Discourse Analysis*, London: Continuum.

Christie, F. and Deriwianka, B. (2008) *School Discourse: Learning to Write Across the Years of Schooling*, London: Continuum.

Coffin, C. (1997) 'Constructing and giving value to the past: An investigation into secondary school history', in Christie, F. and Martin, J. R. (eds.) *Genre and Institutions. Social Processes in the Workplace and School*, London: Cassell, pp. 196–230.

Coffin, C. (2006a) *Historical Discourse: The language of Time, Cause and Evaluation*, London: Continuum.

Coffin, C. (2006b) 'Reconstruing "personal time" as "collective time": Learning the discourse of history', in Whittaker, R., O'Donnell, M. and McCabe, A. (eds) *Language and Literacy: Functional Approaches*, London: Continuum, pp. 15–45.

Cook, H.M. (2001) 'Why can't learners of JFL distinguish polite from impolite speech styles?', in Rose, K. and Kasper, G. (eds.) *Pragmatics in Language Teaching*, Cambridge: Cambridge University Press, pp. 80–102.

Coyle, D. (2007) 'Content and Language Integrated Learning: Towards a connected research agenda for CLIL pedagogies, *International Journal of Bilingual Education and Bilingualism*, 10, 5: 543–62.

Cummins, J. (1979) 'Cognitive / academic language proficiency, linguistic interdependence, the optimum age question and some other matters', *Working Papers on Bilingualism*, 19, 121–29.

Cummins, J. (1984) *Bilingualism and Special Education: Issues in Assessment and Pedagogy*, Clevedon, UK: Multilingual Matters.

Cummins, J. (2005) 'Using information technology to create a zone of proximal development for academic language learning: A critical perspective on trends and possibilities', in Davison, C. (ed) *Information Technology and Innovation in Language Education*, Hong Kong: Hong Kong University Press, pp. 105–26.

Dalton-Puffer, C. (2005) 'Negotiating interpersonal meanings in naturalistic classroom discourse: Directives in Content and Language Integrated Classrooms', *Journal of Pragmatics*, 37: 1275–93.

Dalton-Puffer, C. (2007) *Discourse in Content and Language Integrated Learning Classrooms*, Amsterdam: John Benjamins.

Dalton-Puffer, C. (2009) 'Communicative competence and the CLIL lesson', in Ruíz de Zarobe, Y. and Jiménez Catalán, R. (eds) *Content and Language Integrated Learning*, Bristol: Multilingual Matters, pp. 197–214.

Dalton-Puffer, C. and Nikula, T. (2006) 'Pragmatics of content-based instruction: Teacher and student directives in Finnish and Austrian classrooms', *Applied Linguistics* 27, 241–67.

Dalton-Puffer. C. and Smit, U. (2007) 'Introduction', in Dalton-Puffer, C. and Smit, U. (eds) *Empirical Perspectives on CLIL Classroom Discourse*. Frankfurt: Peter Lang, pp. 7–24.

Derewianka, B. (2007) 'Using Appraisal Theory to track interpersonal development in adolescent student writing', in McCabe, A., O'Donnell, M. and Whittaker, R. (eds) *Advances in Language and Education*, London: Continuum, pp. 166–84.

Gassner, D. and Maillat, D. (2006) 'Spoken competence in CLIL: A pragmatic take on recent Swiss data', *VIEWS* 13, Special CLIL Issue, 15–22.

Halliday, M. A. K. and Matthiessen, C. M. I. M. (2004) *An Introduction to Functional Grammar* (3rd ed.), London: Hodder Arnold.

Llinares, A. (2006) 'A pragmatic analysis of children's interlanguage in EFL preschool contexts', *Intercultural Pragmatics*, **3**, 2, 171–93.

Llinares, A. (2007a) 'Young learners' functional use of the L2 in a low-immersion EFL context', *ELT Journal*, **61**, 39–45.

Llinares, A. (2007b) 'Classroom bilingualism at an early age: Towards a more natural EFL context', in Pérez Vidal, C., Juan-Garau, M. and Bel, A. (eds) *A Portrait of the Young in Multilingual Spain*, Bristol: Multilingual Matters.

Llinares, A. and Romero, J. (2007) 'Getting personal: Native speaker and EFL pre-school children's use of the personal function', *International Journal of Applied Linguistics*, **17**, 2: 198–213.

Llinares, A. and Romero, J. (2008) 'Discourse markers and the pragmatics of teachers in a CLIL corpus', in Romero, J. (ed.) *Pragmatics and Corpus Linguistics*, Berlin: Mouton de Gruyter, pp. 191–204.

Long, M. and Sato, C. (1983) 'Classroom foreigner talk discourse: Forms and functions of teachers' questions', in Seliger, H. and Long, M. (eds) *Classroom Oriented Research in Second Language Acquisition*. Rowley MA: Newbury House, pp. 268–86.

Martin, J. (1994) 'Macrogenres: The ecology of the page', *Network*, **21**, 21–52.

Martin, J. and Rose, D. (2003) *Working with Discourse. Meaning beyond the clause*, London and New York: Continuum.

Martin, J.R. and White, P.R.R. (2005) The Language of Evaluation, Appraisal in English, London: Palgrave Macmillan.

Nikula, T. (2007) 'The IRF pattern and space for interaction: Comparing CLIL and EFL classrooms', in Dalton-Puffer, C. and Smit, U. (eds.) *Empirical Perspectives on CLIL Classroom Discourse*, Frankfurt: Peter Lang, pp. 179–204.

Polias, J. (2003) *ESL Scope and Scales*, Adelaide, South Australia: DECS Publishing.

Romero, J. (2001) 'A mathematical model for the analysis of variation in discourse', *Journal of Linguistics* 37, 527–50.

Rose, K. and Kasper, G. (2001) *Pragmatics in Language Teaching*, Cambridge: Cambridge University Press.

Schleppegrell, M. (2004) *The Language of Schooling*, Mahwah, NJ: Lawrence Erlbaum.

Swain, M. (1996) 'Three functions of output in second language learning', in Cook, G. and Seidlhofer, B. (eds.) *Principle and Practice in Applied Linguistics*. Oxford: Oxford University Press, pp. 125–44.

Thompson, G. and Hunston, S. (2000) 'Evaluation: An introduction', in Hunston, S. and Thompson, G. (eds.) *Evaluation in Text. Authorial Stance and the Construction of Discourse*, Oxford: Oxford University Press, pp. 1–27.

Várkuti, A. (2010) 'Linguistic benefits of the CLIL approach: Measuring linguistic competences', *International CLIL Research Journal*, vol. **1**, 3.
Whittaker, R. and Llinares, A. (2009) 'CLIL in social science classrooms: Analysis of spoken and written productions', in Ruiz de Zarobe, Y. and Jiménez Catalán, R. M. (eds.) *Content and Language Integrated Learning*, London: Multilingual Matters, pp. 215–34.

8 Developing CLIL students' writing: From oracy to literacy

8.1 Introduction

The role of writing as part of learning in CLIL contexts is, at present, largely unrecognised, with much more interest being shown in the development of oracy, being able to talk about subject content. Teaching and learning in the classroom are mainly carried out through talk, though support from other modes is brought in as the teacher turns to the use of board or screen, or students consult textbooks and other print materials. Support from the written mode is especially important, since it provides the students with both information and models of subject-specific language as they read. While the process of understanding text written in a foreign language demands considerable effort, that of writing a text in a foreign language requires much more. Writing involves decision making at different levels, from what is the purpose of writing – the genre – to what is the right word or structure for the meaning we want to make – that is, choices at the level of register. It also allows reflection, since it leaves a permanent trace for the writer to examine. The inclusion of writing tasks in CLIL classes can be seen as a way of enhancing the learning process. This is because the activity of creating written text in the foreign language is an exercise which has value for a number of reasons.

Writing is not only useful to show what has been learned, but the process of writing leads to discovery and knowledge creation, as all writers know. Writing about content is, on the one hand, a way for students to find out what they know and don't know about what they have studied. It is also a way to develop and expand language resources in the foreign language. This has been shown in detailed studies of L2 writers during the actual process of writing a text. Researchers have analysed the points at which these students struggle with the foreign language, looking for lexical items, a grammatical structure or a reformulation which will really express the writer's ideas (e.g. Manchón et al., 2009; Roca et al., 2006). Their results have convinced them of the role of writing in learning a foreign language. Psychologists have found, too, that the effort involved in expressing meaning in a foreign language leads to deeper processing of content (Heine, 2010). This means writing is also especially effective for the learning of content when this takes place in a foreign language.

Writing about subject content requires different choices from the linguistic system from those used for spoken classroom interaction. Even in L1, many students need help to learn the written registers of their subjects when they move into the disciplines at secondary school, and this is even more true for students studying in a foreign language. To support CLIL students in the transition from the spoken to the written mode in school subjects, there are different types of *register scaffolding* which can have beneficial effects on students' performance. On the one hand, there is planned register scaffolding at the macrolevel, or task scaffolding (Llinares and Whittaker, 2009), in which the activities are sequenced, so that students first work in the spoken mode, building up knowledge of a topic area – that is, building a stable knowledge base from which to move into the more difficult written mode (Bereiter and Scardamalia, 1988). This is the format in which many of the examples of CLIL student writing in this chapter have been produced, with class discussion of the topic followed a few days later by the composition task. Besides this type of planned scaffolding, teachers can use spontaneous register scaffolding, at the microlevel, as exemplified in Chapter 6, reformulating the students' spoken production to make it represent knowledge in more effective and academically acceptable ways.

This chapter, then, continues with the perspective of the learners, and the roles they need to take on in language as they become apprenticed into their subjects. It exemplifies the continuum of register features found in CLIL classrooms, from more informal to more academic, showing how the type of activity and the roles of the speakers, and that of language in that activity, influence the language produced. The chapter aims to help teachers work with their students to develop their ability to write the language of the school disciplines, that is, to develop subject literacies.

The chapter begins with the different functions, and so different features, of spoken language in the classroom. This leads us to the functions of written language, and to the roles CLIL students have to play as writers in a particular subject. By learning the literacy of a subject, students enter its community – they know how to 'behave', as it were, in writing. The chapter shows stages in the development of their writing, as they learn to represent the role of member of a subject community.

8.2 How speaking is different from writing

Observation of language in use in the classroom shows different points on a cline from typically spoken to typically written genres (Martin, 1992). The function of language in an activity type determines its register features (as shown in Box 1.1). Hands-on activities in which students use language to get things done during group work, for example, require different choices in the grammar and lexis from those of formal teaching moments. These moments need the language of knowledge-showing, when teachers present or elicit information, or knowledge-creating, when interpretations are proposed and defended, based on facts which have been learned (Bazerman, 1988). This means that even when content is the focus of the interaction, different moments in class will produce different types of language, and these will differ, again, from those of written texts on the same topic. The first example is of spoken interaction.

Extract 8.1, an extract from a CLIL technology class (grade 7, ages 12–13), shows language being used to get something done.

Extract 8.1
1 T: Glue it, here. Just put this there, tie it tight, not just stick it
2   to the wood but (   ) it. Let's see. That's it, and
3   the other, C.
4 S: This is in here.
5 T: That's it, then it's (   ) And then you can
6   ( )
7 S: Yeah.
8 T: You give it back. You ( ) it again.

The transcript gives us some clues as to what is going on in the classroom, but key information is in the context – we would need to be in the room to interpret a lot of the language. Spoken language, then, is context dependent. The participants who are present know perfectly well what *it* refers to in the first clause of the teacher's first turn, *Glue it, here,* and where exactly *here* is. They can identify, too, in his next clause, *Just put this there,* the referent of *this* and where *there* is. They also know that the next three *its* (*tie it tight, not just stick it to the wood but ( ) it*) are co-referential with *this,* but that the *it* in *That's it* refers to the outcome of the whole activity the teacher has directed and now evaluates. The students are clearly interpreting all these referring expressions without any problem, as we see in the response to the teacher's indication *and the other,* to which a student answers: *This is in here.* In the 51 separate words of this extract, only eight are lexical items with dictionary definitions. Of these, we find one noun (*wood*), one adverb (*tight*), and six action verbs: *glue, put, tie, stick, see, give back* (*give back* would be considered one item). We now compare this segment of spoken interaction with an extract from a handout for the same class, here working on the centre of gravity (abbreviated to CG) of objects.

Text 8.1
• Tilt the shape and the limit angle beyond which the vertical from the CG moves outside of the base area, which is the limit beyond which the figure would topple over • Find out whether the given limit angle corresponds to the actual limit angle in the true object

The appearance of Text 8.1 shows that this is a much denser text, though it is the same length. It is 50 words long, but the words are now distributed in two sentences, rather than in a number of turns. The sentences are still activity focused, as shown by the imperatives at the beginning of each: *tilt, find out*. However, of the 50 separate words, this time 22 correspond to lexical items (here *find out* counts as one item in a dictionary). Of the 31 words in the first sentence, 30 build up the nominal group indicating to the students what exactly they have to tilt: *the shape and the limit angle beyond which the vertical from the CG moves outside of the base area, which is the limit beyond which the figure would topple over*. In the second sentence, again, nominal groups take up the majority of the words: *the given limit angle* and *the actual limit angle in the true object*. The written instruction has to be explicit, and this means using much more language than in the face-to-face interaction, in which *this, it, the other, here, there*, were enough for efficient communication. This explicitness is key to understanding the difference between spoken and written language, and students should be made aware of that difference, so that they are able to produce effective written texts.

Extract 8.1 and Text 8.1 represent language which the same young people produced (the dialogue in class) or consumed (the class handout), during the same school year. Both texts have the function of getting something done in the subject of technology, as we see from the vocabulary, especially the types of verbs. In both, the communication takes place between teacher and students, an unequal relationship which is very noticeable in the imperatives. The differences between the examples, then, are the result of the mode, the channel of communication. Differences are also a result of different intended uses. The class pack that Text 8.1 comes from allows students to be independent of the teacher's physical presence as it contains information about the subject, including specific facts about materials used in class, and generalised concepts or theories related to the applications of materials. Written text, then, has different uses from spoken language, and this is why it has the features it does.

What we have observed in the use of spoken and written language in one class can be related to the development of writing over time, which makes even clearer the fact that writing is not just speech presented in visual form, but has quite different functions. The history of writing shows how it evolved as a result of changes in the way of life of early societies, changes which created the need for permanent records of communication, which were not necessary for the previous small mobile hunting groups (see, for example, Halliday, 1989: 45). So writing was not, and is not, just a different way of expressing the same things, but has different functions and, to serve these uses, languages combine their resources differently. This is found in all literate cultures, and so pervasively that even very young users of a language can recognise a variety of registers, as has been demonstrated experimentally with children (Littlefair, 1991). The practice of writing, too, has produced profound changes in literate societies (Ong, 1982), changes which have spread as education became available to wider and wider segments of the population.

One of the results of schooling is the extension of pupils' repertoire of registers, allowing them to function linguistically in more, and more sophisticated, contexts, and giving them 'linguistic capital', as Bourdieu (1991) has argued. Being able to write in a foreign language will clearly increase our students' value in the linguistic marketplace, and an understanding of the features of written language of their subjects should form part of the knowledge CLIL teachers bring to the classroom. Analysis of examples showing the use of more spoken or more written-like language in CLIL classes in a number of subjects will reveal points at which teachers can identify specific features of the written language of their subjects and so help students produce that language.

8.3 The spoken mode in the CLIL classroom

Different pedagogical objectives, with the varied activities they require, involve different types of language use, as has been shown throughout this book. In Extract 8.1 above, where students were being helped to carry out an activity with the teacher, very few lexical words gave clues as to what was going on. And being activity-based, these words were mainly verbs. In this section, we analyse a number of extracts, to see how the activity type, and the roles played by the participants in it, influence the language used. The analysis reveals intermediate stages on the cline between the lexically light example of Extract 8.1 and the lexically dense written segment in Text 8.1, showing the functional reasons for such differences.

The following extract, Extract 8.2, shows another stage of an activity in class. In it, three students discuss the results of a task they have just finished in a physics class, in which they had to count the number of waves produced by a large spring after they had pressed it against the floor.

Extract 8.2	
1	S1: When we have the waves like this, I go – you just counted
2	that there's one, two, three.
3	S2: No I don' count it like that.
4	S1: What countin' look like?
5	S2: I counted (lot like this).
6	S3: Look P.
7	S1: Well then how did C get three then?
8	S3: Here's
9	S2: I dunno.
10	S3: One, here's two, an here's a half.
11	S2: I counted like this one two three.
12	S1: There weren't that many there weren't that man.

In this extract, there is no teacher giving instructions, and the three participants have an equal right to intervene, though S1 dominates, as she challenges the results of counting the waves. The discussion revolves around the activity, with the verb *count* repeated five times, and *go* and *get* used as synonyms. Numbers appear frequently, and the preposition *like* is repeated as the girls demonstrate how they got to the number of waves they saw. There are different pronouns: *we, I, you*, and proper names to address, or to refer to, the members of the group who are talking. In the entire discussion, which has 69 words, including two proper names, only one common noun is used: *waves*. This makes it similar to Extract 8.1, and very different from the written Text 8.1, and those analysed in Chapters 4 and 5. Studies of the difference between spoken and written language have shown that dependence on verbs in the case of speaking, or nouns for writing, is key to the way language in the two modes is built up (Halliday, 1989).

Spoken language, with fewer demands in the area of lexis, is still complex, as Halliday described (1989: 63): 'the complexity of written language is lexical, while that of spoken language is grammatical'.

Extract 8.3, from a maths class (grade 5, ages 10–11), gives us an impression of this grammatical complexity in the teacher's language. She is helping the students find which two consecutive numbers produce the figure she has given them when multiplied. The teacher is interested in students developing a sensitivity to mathematical methods.

Extract 8.3
1   T: I probably would have realised
2   that they would be too big
3   because that's nearly forty.
4   OK?
5   So, I'm going to give you another one of those
6   to do now,
7   but try 'n' use all the clues
8   that you've got.

The extract is presented with each new clause on a different line. These make up three independent 'sentences'. The segment shows typical features of spoken language, in the way clauses are linked, and the verbal group developed. This segment of 40 words is made up of seven clauses, joined by structural markers *that, because*, in Sentence 1, and logical markers *so, but* in Sentence 3. The verbal groups are expanded in Sentence 1: *would have realised, would be*, where the teacher talks around mathematical processes of deduction and then in Sentence 3: *'m going to give, to do, try and use, 've got* where she gets the students to do the same task themselves. There is only one noun in the entire extract: *clues*.

The difficulty for the students here is mainly related to the academic function of hypothesising, as the teacher thinks aloud. This function is particularly important during secondary schooling, and students need to be exposed to it, but it doesn't seem to happen a lot in CLIL classes, as Dalton-Puffer (2007) found. In the spoken mode, forms which express hypothesis or deduction, like *would, would have*, are usually rather indistinct, given the lack of stress on auxiliaries and modal verbs in English. Knowledge of these forms, with their meanings and functions, could be reinforced when students are given written maths problems, with the teacher discussing the text to help them understand what they are being asked. In fact, studies of students' ability in maths in their L1 have found that much of the difficulty resides in the wording of the problem (OECD, 2010). The function of hypothesising is, of course, needed in most, if not all, subjects at secondary level.

The spoken activity transcribed in Extract 8.4 has a different aim, and so here the students (grade 10, ages 15–16) are exposed to a different type of language.

Extract 8.4
1 T: If a light ray hits the mirror
2   something's going to happen with that light ray
3   and it's it's going to be reflected
4   and the way it's er being reflected
5   is like this er
6   and to find the actual direction
7   first of all I'm going to draw another line
8   and that's this line perpendicular to the
9   surface of the mirror at the place
10   that light ray hits the mirror

Here we have another monologue by the teacher, a formal teaching moment, as she demonstrates properties of reflection. To show its grammatical structure, again, the extract is presented on different lines, with each line having a verb, showing the number of clauses through which the teacher has constructed this part of her explanation, which is made up of 67 words. There are nine clauses. In this extract, the verbs are related to what the light does: *hit, reflect*, and what the teacher does to demonstrate the behaviour of light: *find, draw*. In contrast to Extract 8.2, there is only one first person pronoun, used as the teacher comments on her diagram, but no *we* or *you* to build interaction. The other pronouns are third person – *it, this* or *that* – focusing on the topic, the line and its position. And, unlike the technology teacher in the hands-on activity in Text 8.1, this teacher who is explaining properties as she draws on the whiteboard uses very explicit language with full noun phrases: *a light ray, the mirror*, and especially: *this line perpendicular to the surface of the mirror at the place that light ray hits the mirror*. The students are all watching her as she draws the line, but, nevertheless, she verbalises very explicitly the position of the line, which is the point she is demonstrating to the class. The nominal group, made up of 18 words, is presented as Extract 8.4a in order to show how the phrases which modify it are structured. The head noun, *line*, is followed by a series of reduced relative clauses (the elided relative pronouns are included in square brackets) and prepositional phrases.

Extract 8.4a
1 T: This line
2 [which is] perpendicular to the surface
3 of the mirror
4 at the place
5 [where] that light ray hits the mirror

There are nine content words in this clause, all in the nominal group, whereas in the other eight clauses in the extract, the teacher has used only one or sometimes two lexical items. That is, in the earlier part of the explanation she distributed the lexical items among the different clauses, but at the end she concentrates them in this final, long nominal group. This build-up of information signals the importance of this part of the explanation. It also supports the learners by giving them elaborated input, providing scaffolding for tasks in the written mode.

The spoken Extract 8.4 illustrates the way different uses of language in the classroom require changes in the distribution of the lexical, or content, words in relation to the number of grammar, or function, words, since this distinction plays an important role in presenting and receiving information in spoken and in written modes. Function words in English form systems, the members of which belong to closed sets. For example, one set is that of the English determiners, which includes definite and indefinite articles (*the, a, an, some*), another is that of prepositions (*in, at, like* ...). Other sets are made up of the different pronouns, and so on. Table 8.1 shows the words in Extract 8.4 grouped according to the class they belong to: grammar words or lexical words.

Table 8.1	
GRAMMAR / FUNCTION WORDS	LEXICAL / CONTENT WORDS
If a the	light ray hits mirror
something's going to with that	happen light ray
and it's it's going to be	reflected
and the way it's er being	reflected
is like this	
and to the	find actual direction
first of all I'm going to another	draw line
and that's	
this to the of the at the that the	line perpendicular surface mirror place light ray hits mirror

Presenting the two types of words in columns shows the distribution of the two classes: there are 49 grammar words (including six abbreviated forms of the verb *to be*) in the extract, to a total of 23 lexical words, of which only 14 are different. The extract, then, is lexically light up to the key final sentence.

In more informationally rich spoken language, there will be a higher density of lexical words, as in written texts, especially those found in school subjects. This means, of course, that their comprehension requires more effort, and more vocabulary knowledge. An everyday activity like listening to the news takes real concentration, even in our native language, if we want to take in more than just the topics mentioned. This is because the news presenter is reading a written text, packed with information, and so lexically dense, with a lower frequency of function words showing the relations between the different content words. When we hear a lexical word we need to access its meaning and hold it in memory, and use the function words to build up the meaning of the segment. Grammar words are normally rapidly processed by the brain. When we read, we have the support of the written text to help us hold the words and the concepts they activate available as we work out the meaning the text is building up. When we listen, what we miss is lost and cannot be recovered. The higher demands produced by the density of lexical items in written language are offset by the permanence of the text, and the possibility for re-reading. In any case, reading or listening to lexically dense texts in a foreign language is extremely challenging, and students generally benefit from scaffolding in the form of talk around the text.

A spoken text with the function of explaining in a discipline may include a greater variety of lexis, without representing the register of the school subject. This is what happens in Extract 8.5, previously analysed in Chapter 6 for a different purpose. In this dialogue, S1 takes on the job of asking the display question, encouraging S2 to explain the reasons for the Union winning the American Civil War.

Extract 8.5
1   S1: Okay ... so what was the reason why northern union
2   won?
3   S2: They had more people and more everything
4   S1: ((laughing)) More everything
5   S2: They had more ...
6   S1: More guns.

(cont.)

7	S2:	They had more trains, they had more factories, they had
8		more fields, they had more production, they had more people.
9	S1:	Population.
10	S2:	Or population ... they even had ( )

S2 starts off answering in a rather vague way: *they had more people and more everything.* When S1 indicates he requires more specific information, S2 complies, bringing in the facts to answer the question using a variety of lexis. However he seems to resist the register of history, in which we would expect a generalisation like *resources* followed by exemplification; that is, using a nominal group with post modification. Instead, S2 plays with the repetition of the one structure he produces *they had more ...* , varying the lexical item five times. He makes creative use, then, of the structure of everyday talk (Carter, 2004), introducing one lexical item per clause.

Possibly, the unequal roles assigned to the two classmates, with S1 given the more powerful role, have led S2 to collaborate only partially, maintaining the grammar of everyday communication while giving the explanation S1 has asked for. This could be a type of 'register resistance' between classmates, with S2's unwillingness to use academic register when talking to a peer showing sensitivity to the meaning and power of register. It could, on the other hand, simply reflect lack of control of the abstract language of school history. This example contrasts with responses to teacher-led elicitation in which students are beginning to produce the register of history. Answers like *the filth of the cities promoted the expansion of it,* or *the agriculture was first ... the base of the economy* (from grade 8, ages 13–14) show students bringing more lexis into their turns, using the nouns typical of the field.

The different extracts have shown the way the spoken language of teaching and learning incorporates features of the written language of the disciplines as the activities in the classroom become more dependent on language itself. By studying a discipline in a foreign language, students are learning to enter its academic community. In participating in the classroom activities, they are taking steps towards becoming full members of the community, but to do this, control of the written mode of the subject is also necessary. The next section turns to the academic roles secondary school students must learn to develop in their writing, in order to present themselves as knowledgeable, authoritative members of the community. If we claim, as we do in this book, that work on language must start from an analysis of what we need to *do* with it, we must make explicit why certain features are functional, and so required for a particular role. The next section exemplifies this for two subjects, biology and history.

8.4 Developing language functions in writing

Overview: The roles

A very clear framework to understand secondary school students' writing has been developed by Mary Schleppegrell (2004), based on systemic functional linguistics and using her years of experience working with students learning subjects in English as a first and second language, and with teachers. Her summaries of the actions pupils must learn to carry out in language at school, and the linguistic features that allow them to do this for the areas of school science and history, are reproduced (slightly adapted) in Boxes 8.1 and 8.2. The summaries bring together the SFL descriptions of school genres we saw in Chapter 4, and the register features presented in Chapter 5. They allow us to discuss examples from texts produced by CLIL students, showing different stages of development in a number of key features of written language, again differentiating the language of science from that of the humanities. We begin with the roles of students in science. In Box 8.1, the left-hand column contains the roles students have to learn to represent in language; on the right are the linguistic features which enable them to do this. Readers will recognise that the roles correspond to the ideational, interpersonal and textual functions of language, with their clusters of choices from the linguistic system.

Box 8.1: Science	
Student role	**Grammatical features**
Display knowledge –by classifying things, explaining processes, building theories	Processes: material for action + relational for descriptions and definitions Technical terms; modified nominal groups Logical relations: implicit cause
Be authoritative	Present scientific knowledge as fact; include probability impersonally
Structure texts – for science genres – for information distribution	Grammatical metaphor to structure information in clause

(slightly adapted from Schleppegrell, 2004: 118)

First, then, students must present themselves as knowers, displaying knowledge of their field in the different science genres. To do this, they must make appropriate choices of process types (discussed in Chapter 5), selecting material processes for actions, and relational for descriptions of properties, or defining terms. They need to use the technical language of their subject, developed in taxonomies as discussed in Chapter 4, and structured in nominal groups with pre- and post-modification. To be authoritative, they should make impersonal statements of fact on scientific topics, rather than appearing themselves in the text as the source of knowledge, by using *I think*, for example. When qualifying statements with information about their probability, this should also be presented impersonally: *it is likely that* ... , *this could be explained by* ... . Their written texts need to be carefully structured, in two ways: structured in the stages which realise the genre involved, and structured at sentence level for the presentation of information to the reader. This requires the use of grammatical metaphor, to move elements to different positions in the sentence.

Turning to history, the roles and grammatical features for the subject appear in Box 8.2.

Box 8.2: History	
Student role	**Grammatical features**
Display knowledge – by presenting and interpreting past events	Processes: action + relational for background; verbal + mental to construct points of view
	From individual to abstract / institutional participants Logical relations: time + cause
Be authoritative – recording, interpreting, judging	Implicit modality Evaluative lexis Point of view
Structure texts – for history genres – for information distribution	Grammatical metaphor to structure information in clause, time / cause prepositional phrases; internal conjunction, lexicalised cause

(slightly adapted from Schleppegrell, 2004: 128)

As historians, the students' activities are related to showing they are knowledgeable and can write on historical events, and that they are able to explain and interpret history. Here, as well as providing representations of the past in descriptions of states and events, using the appropriate process types, students have to be able to recognise that such reconstruction is the result of the activity of historians, by using verbal and mental processes. These processes also form part of the content they display, since this includes the motives of historical actors involved. This means the language should include expressions indicating whose point of view is being presented. In the more advanced genres, students should present as historical actors collectives or institutions rather than individuals. As the student historians write on the past, they will show their position of authority as knowers, by evaluating the events or judging the participants, through lexical choices. Rather than appearing in their texts explicitly, probabilities or hypotheses should be couched in impersonal terms, as in science. Again, the students should control the generic structure of the text types they have to write. They need to express time and cause inside the clause, using prepositional phrases, or lexical items, rather than in *because* or *so* clauses. To do this, and to move the information to different positions in the sentence to make texts coherent for readers, students need to learn to use grammatical metaphor.

In the extracts which follow, we show how CLIL students represent the different roles described, and also suggest ways in which CLIL teachers may intervene to develop their learners' resources for performing these roles.

Displaying knowledge in writing (field)

Learning a discipline means developing knowledge of the concepts and, at the same time, of the terminology of its field, and so gradually advancing in the expression of the content in the subject area. As we saw in Schleppegrell's table of tasks for apprentice scientists in Box 8.1, as well as in Chapter 5, key features are technical terms and expanded nominal groups. The technical terms of the subjects are recognised as forming part of subject knowledge, and play a role in CLIL classes, and in the written material read or produced by students. However, researchers have found a difference between science and humanities subjects in the treatment of terminology: 'For many students, abstraction probably forms more of a problem than technicality, since science teachers do teach the concepts and terms that make up scientific discourse whereas [...] history teachers do not focus explicitly on nominalization ... ' (Martin, 1993: 213). Extract 8.6 shows a CLIL teacher making her class aware that the language of science is part of the subject. The lexical item *name* appears five times, and *word* once, in this 52-word-long extract, showing the teacher's purpose.

Extract 8.6	
1	T: ... science- scientific names well bacteria also have scientific
2	names ok? each bacteria each species of bacteria has a scientific
3	name and that's one lacto bacillus casei immunitas ... but
4	we can leave it in the two first words lactobacillus casei ...
5	ok? so those would be the two names (but they're?) scientific
6	name

Knowledge of terminology is assessed in examinations, another mark of importance which students are very sensitive to, and we have evidence that these CLIL students are learning to do this in writing. Chapter 4 included examples of the subgenre of definitions by science students. Text 8.2 shows an answer from an exam question set for a CLIL science class (grade 10, ages 15–16): 'Differentiate homologies from analogies. Which prove evolution? Why?'

Text 8.2
• Homologies: bones and structure show that that animal, compared with their ancestors, has evolved. • Analogies: they show that different animals (for example, an insect and a mammal) did evolve from different animals but with the same features like wings or fins, because they live in the same site. *Examples:* Homologies: Bats and humans have the same structure and bones even though they do not look the same. Bats have adapted to fly because of the membrane between their fingers. Humans do not have any membrane so they can take things. Analogies: Dolphins and fish evolve from different species and they share the same form of their fins because they need to be well adapted to swim.

Here, the student has made an attempt to generalise in her definitions, and shows she understands the importance of relating scientific concepts to specific examples. While there are many features of spoken language, like the use of *because* and *so* clauses, she is beginning to be 'literate' in science.

In history, a focus on the lexis of important concepts appears at times in the corpus, as in Extract 8.7 from a CLIL history class (grade 9, ages 14–15), in which the teacher checks the meaning of a key item of vocabulary.

Extract 8.7
1	S: Eh ... th-the mercantilism was influenced by the king, th-
2	because they want to have more capital.
3	T: What do you mean by capital?
4	S: The money.
5	T: Mmm. Exactly.

An interesting moment in which language comes to the fore is transcribed in Extract 8.8 (grade 8, ages 13–14) when the CLIL history teacher provides an important correction of the student's offer of information, making explicit the academic function of generalising in history, and the use of abstractions, rather than concrete, everyday terms. The class was giving reasons for the spread of the Plague.

Extract 8.8
1	S1: The people are not clean ... are not clean people ...
2	T: K, we are not speaking about individuals, if they were
3	clean or dirty. We are speaking as a group of people if
4	they had good conditions.

While what the student says is correct in terms of content, this is not the way historians represent history. The teacher makes this very clear: history is not about a number of individuals, but generalises about social groups. It is here, according to Martin (1993: 213), that a large part of the difficulty of secondary school history lies: in the conceptual step from individual to abstract or institutional participants. This is a step that not all history teachers may be aware of. In this example the teacher has seen the problem, and provides functional register scaffolding for her students which they can later use in their writing.

The students seem to have internalised the need to display knowledge of the language of their subject, as shown in the way they sometimes spontaneously offer definitions or explanations when they write, as in Texts 8.3 to 8.5. Interestingly, they show they know a variety of linguistic markers indicating the function of definition (marked in bold in the texts).

Text 8.3
Also kings controlled economy, and there was capitalism, **that is**, to have money.

Text 8.4
Mercantilism regulated economic activity. It was lead by protectantism, **which consisted in** buying and selling within your own country.

Text 8.5
All the battles were hard and continuous, and all of them ended in a stalemate, standstill, or deadlock, **this meant** neither the troops of each country could move forwards or backwards.

The last of the three segments, in which a student (grade 10, ages 15–16) uses three synonyms to refer to the type of warfare: *a stalemate, standstill, or deadlock*, is a good example of overlexicalisation, showing the importance the teacher must have given to academic language in the work on the topic.

Another difference between the content of science and the humanities, noted by Christie and Derewianka (2008: 116), is reflected in process types. In terms of the ideational metafunction, history represents what participants think and say, and so constructs the point of view of its actors using verbal and mental processes, while this is not found in school science. CLIL students of history seem to have difficulties with this area of meaning, and their attempts to display this area of knowledge are often less successful than others. Extract 8.9 (grade 10, ages 15–16) from an interview in which the researcher asked the student to explain how World War I started, pinpoints the problem.

Extract 8.9	
1	T: ... and then they begin to be stronger, and then for exam-
2	ple, em, some countries were ... and that make the less
3	powerful ones think that ok, they are powerful, they
4	can ... they can attack my country, and I'm not ... I'm not
5	ok with that. And ... and then for example, well, they were
6	very angry, and just a little thing more could, eh, could
7	break out a war, and that little thing was the, well, little,
8	was the assassination of Franz Ferdinand ...

The student presents her explanation as motivated by personal relationships among individuals, rather than the reactions of international powers, by using everyday terms and representing the thoughts of the powers in colloquial terms. That this is not the effect of the informal interview situation in which she is involved when she produced Extract 8.9 is clear from the text on the same topic by the same student written a few days later, Text 8.6.

Text 8.6

After 4 years of fighting, **everybody was fed up** of it and **they just wanted** it to finish as soon as possible, the problem was that it was difficult to make a fair peace treaty.

Her explanation for the signing of the Treaty of Versailles is couched in the same informal language (marked in bold in the text) she used in the interview, and represents the signatories as a group of friends having problems with their relationship.

A step towards the written language of history to present the thoughts and feelings of nations is shown in the paragraph making up Text 8.7, written by another student in the same class.

Text 8.7

There were before this assasination **conflicts** between countries and the main ones were that Germany started to build a large navy and so **Britain feared** because that navy supposed a powerful army that could killed a lot of people. Also Germany had Alsace-Lorraine took from France, and **France was worried** about that and also **wanted** Alsace Lorraine back. **Germany wanted** also colonies, because it had very few and so this also meant **a fearness of the French and British** because **they wanted** to be the one, ones with control.

While the student has organised the content of her text mainly by linking clauses together, her lexical choices are more formal, and she creates some nominal groups to express the mental processes: *conflicts between countries; a fearness of the French and British.*

A further stage in the expression of the feeling of a historical actor is seen in Text 8.8 in which the writer combines the use of pre- and post-modified nominal groups with the expression of cause using nouns or a verb.

Text 8.8

... [the mos important **cause**] was [the anxiety of Germany to build up a great Empire and control all Europe with his army and navy]. [Another important **cause**] was [[the differences of costums, languages and traditions in the Balkans] that **led to** [many crisis that raised temperature in Europe]].

The nominal groups have been enclosed in square brackets, showing how the two sentences are, in fact, made up exclusively of examples of this structure, linked by the verb *to be*, a choice often found in textbooks. The phrases expressing cause are in bold. They are similar to examples in history textbooks.

In this section, we have seen points at which the language in the subjects has been supported by the teachers, as they check academic terms, and raise students' awareness by means of register scaffolding. The students' written texts, however, could be improved if this type of support for the specific features required by the field of study were integrated into the classes. A focus on the kinds of meanings their different subjects build, and the ways the language allows them to do this would allow students to display their knowledge of the field more effectively.

Being authoritative (tenor)

As they learn the language of their disciplines, students should also learn to represent the voice of authority in their subjects. To do this, in the case of school science, in which students are learning accepted knowledge built up over time by experts, there should be no overt attitude expressed towards that knowledge, since fact is presented as external to the scientist. The example in Extract 8.10 is interesting in this respect.

Extract 8.10

1	T: So, listen, this is the way it is. I'll write something on the
2	board for you, OK?
3	OK, proteins are over. Have you studied at all?
4	S: (Yes)
5	T: OK, listen, you all know this? You know this, don't you?
6	OK, now OK, a compound A, that's going to turn into

(cont.)

7		a compound B, ok? Chemical reaction, catalysed by an
8		enzyme one, right? Enzyme one, OK? Enzymes are
9		proteins, are they not? Yes. So, there must be one gene,
10		gene one, that codes for this enzyme one. Do you agree?
11	SS:	Yes.
12	T:	Yes. Now, OK, now. Compound B turns into compound
13		C. This chemical reaction must be catalysed by enzyme
14		two, which in turn would be coded for by gene two. Do
15		you agree? Yeah? Well that's the way it is.

In her explanation, the teacher marks the status of scientific knowledge both at the beginning of the extract: *So, listen, this is the way it is*, and retrospectively, at the end: *Well that's the way it is*. While she appeals to the students to corroborate her explanation at different points, she usually answers for them. Science at this level, then, is about the way things are. Though taxonomies of science have been created by scientists, they are represented as 'natural kinds'. When some evaluation is introduced, the source is science itself. This appears in the responses to the teacher's question about bacteria in Extract 8.11.

Extract 8.11	
1	T: ... Is it something good or something bad?
2	SS: Bad.
3	S: (Or good) it depends the-
4	T: Something that happens ( )
5	S: They are toxic they are (toxic substance)
6	T: (Put that one down?) They can produce toxic substances
7	substances and therefore contaminate foods ok and then if
8	you eat those contaminated foods what are you gonna get
9	disease OK

The evaluation required is not a personal one, but related to scientific processes – the production of toxic substances leading to disease – and classification.

In writing, we find CLIL students presenting knowledge in this scientifically impersonal way. In Text 8.9, the student from a CLIL biology class (grade 10, ages 15–16) answers the command: 'Indicate two applications of genetic engineering to agriculture'.

Text 8.9
Transgenic plants: plants that have 'foreign genes'. They are useful because they can be disease-resistant, or have bigger fruits or develop more rapidly.

The effects of genetic modification are evaluated from an agricultural perspective in which qualities like disease resistance, or more productivity and faster growth are appreciated. There is no mention of negative effects from the point of view of society. Had the question been posed in the subject of ecology, or in geography, the answer would have probably included a more social evaluation of the effects on the system.

History, on the other hand, is value laden, and making judgements is part of the role of the historian, who has not only to record facts, but also to interpret and evaluate them, and their actors. To respond to the indication 'Be authoritative' in history, then, is more complex, involving as it does taking a stance based on historical knowledge. At the same time, the historian should show awareness that history itself is constructed by the historian (Christie and Derewianka, 2008: 117), and so should leave space for alternative interpretations. Most examples from the corpus show students to be at an early stage of development of this role, suggesting that this area of interpersonal meaning presents more difficulties than the ideational.

Research into this linguistic area of evaluation, or appraisal (see Chapter 7), has produced a detailed taxonomy of resources (Martin and White, 2005). The use of these resources has been traced in the writing of L1 pupils as they move up through the different levels of schooling (Christie and Derewianka, 2008; Coffin, 2006). Here, a brief look at the types found in CLIL classes will help teachers to be aware of the type of needs students have in their expression of tenor in their writing.

Evaluation may be presented from the point of view of the field of history, as in Texts 8.10 and 8.11.

Text 8.10
Mercantilism was very important and affected many things.

Text 8.11
This **amazing fact was really relevant** to history ...

In these extracts a number of features combine to create an impression of immaturity, rather than the authority of the historian. Both examples assess importance as measured by an external norm, that of the field, as in science. However, both present the evaluation in the predicate, rather than in a nominalisation; this is the way very young writers use adjectives (Perera, 1984). Both use intensifiers – *very* and *really* – which are typical of speech. Besides, in Text 8.11 the pre-modifier *amazing* represents a choice found in texts by immature writers (Christie and Derewianka, 2008). In Text 8.10, while the writer justifies her evaluation, this is done in very vague language *affected many things*, again a feature of speech (Carter and McCarthy, 2006).

Evaluation can also be presented from the point of view of the historical actor, as in the example in Text 8.12.

Text 8.12
Unfortunately, for him, his empire **suffered** two bankroupts

While this student has used an adverb, *unfortunately*, a feature of more advanced writing (Christie, 2010), the evaluation is seen more as a personal problem than one related to a state.

Another type of evaluation appears in Text 8.13:

Text 8.13
It was a **horrible** war, lots of people died and a lot of land was destroyed.

Here, the grounds for the judgement come from an ethical stance. Again, though, the lexical choice, *horrible*, while understandable, is not normally part of academic register. As justification for his evaluation, the writer adds two more clauses, also in the register of everyday language. No attempt at grammatical metaphor through the use of nominals, in phrases like *with a high number of deaths and terrible destruction*, is made. Here, then, though the students are beginning to take on the authoritative role in the subject, their register choices could be improved by systematically being exposed to and analysing the language of evaluation.

Finally, the role of the historian as interpreter involves recognition of other perspectives. This leads to an important task, the task of evaluating sources, and so acknowledging that there can be many points of view, and interests in foregrounding one or another. An example from the written corpus, by a CLIL student (grade 10, age 15–16), shows that this awareness raising seems to have been successful.

Text 8.14
First World War broke out by a lot of reason that we don't know and other ones that we know. In the first case we had the confrontation of Serbia and Austria, Serbia want the independence so they killed the Archduke Franz Ferdinand. Also the allyes that Serbia had (triple Entente) and the allies the Austrians had (Triple Alliance) were confronted and World War starts.

In his rather bald opening statement, the writer of Text 8.14 recognises the difficult role of the historian, with historical events attributable to multiple, or even unknown, causes. History textbooks provide sources for students to analyse, in which the conflicting interests and different values of historical participants are distinguishable. The CLIL corpus of recordings and written texts includes examples from spoken and written activities which help the students develop an awareness of perspective. The last part of the section on tenor contrasts a written and a spoken example, in order to show the different ways the students represent evaluation of history in their linguistic choices.

Extract 8.12 and Text 8.15 were produced in response to the same prompt, asking students to evaluate the impact of the European conquest of South America. The two texts represent different modes. Extract 8.12 is a segment from the transcription of a role play between two CLIL students (grade 9, ages 14–15). They had been asked to take the roles of a Spanish conqueror, played by S1 – a boy – and a representative of the indigenous population of South America, played by S2 – a girl – and consider the good and bad aspects of Spanish colonisation. The students are in the middle of the debate; *different opinions* refer to a previous lack of agreement on their views about their religions.

	Extract 8.12
1	S1: Ok. There are different opinions so I will try to ... to
2	convince you in another way ... by commerce. Eh ... we
3	take eh gold and silver from America, and we change
4	with European countries, but also the benefits were for
5	the American colonies and in American colonies you live
6	there so I think that you also empower a little bit your
7	economy and ... and you have new materials and
8	new things
	(cont.)

9	S2:	I think that ... you did a good ... job, but I think there
10		are other ways to do it, not ... maybe not killing people
11		because they don't think what you think or ... raping
12		women ... I think there are other ways to do ...
13	S1:	That's true, rape women is is not good but eh we ... we try
14		to do a new human ... a mestizo ((S2 and the researcher
15		laugh)) between a native American and a Spanish so ... but
16		I think that ... our troops were not good but ah ... we try
17		to ... to make eh ... positive things in order to ... in order
18		to improve your ... your standard of living but we ... if we
19		did negative things we are sorry but ... I think that we gave
20		you a ... great possibility to ... to empower yourself, yeah.

The presentation of the content shows that the speakers are equals, and the knowledge they are exchanging is not accepted truth, but a point of view. Because of this, they negotiate. S1 says *I will try to ... to convince you*, and both speakers show themselves as responsible for their evaluation, using *I think* rather than bald statements. At the same time, both evaluate, using *good, positive, great, negative*, showing they have the power to do so. In fact, the conqueror apologises for the wrong that was done to the indigenous population, but justifies the motives (!).

Text 8.15, written in class by S2 a few days after participating in the debate transcribed as Extract 8.12, offers a more complex developmental scene.

Text 8.15
Europeans had **a great impact** in America. <u>In one side</u>, they **brought diseases**, they **killed a lot** of them, they **kidnapped women**, they **had the monopoly** of commerce with indigenous, they **destroyed native traditions and culture** and they tried to **convert everyone to Catholicism**. <u>Although</u>, Europeans **made a lot of indigenous slaves.** <u>In the</u> <u>other hand</u>, Europeans brought **new irrigation techniques, new ways of agriculture, new products and new ideas.** <u>I continue to think</u> that Europeans were **a bad thing** because the **only one beneficiated were them,** who got loads of silver and gold, and crops, and slaves. <u>I think</u> they could have been **less violent**, so everything could be **harmless** for every body.

In the text, the phrases including evaluation are in bold; underlining is used for logical markers and overt signals of the writer's opinion. The writer presents her evaluation in a more impersonal way in the first part of the paragraph, by the selection of facts, though she reverts to a more speech-like register when she recognises to herself and her readers that she is now introducing evaluation explicitly, and from a personal point of view: *I continue to think ...* . There is a marked contrast between the successful written register based on the nominal group in the first two-thirds of the paragraph, and the spoken features in the language used when the writer presents herself in her text and so speaks, as it were, with her own voice.

Structuring texts (mode)

When they write, students need to learn to structure their texts according to the requirements of the genres of the subject, and the needs of the reader. Good writers calculate the reader's state of knowledge at any point in the text to decide how to organise the information they want to transmit. They place information which links up with concepts presented previously towards the beginning of the sentence, and lead the reader to new information, introduced later, towards the end (as shown by linguists like Firbas, 1992, or Fries, 1994, for example). As discussed in Chapter 5, in English the use of grammatical metaphor allows the writer to move information to different positions in the sentence, and produce more effective texts. Learning to take on the role of expert writer in a discipline involves becoming aware of the reader, and being able to use grammatical metaphor to pack information into the nominal groups. Writers must also know when and how to use the passive to place the nominal groups in the best position from the point of view of the information the reader has and is receiving. The rest of this section presents examples of different stages in the development of information management in writing.

Starting with apprentice writers in a science subject, comparison of Texts 8.16 and 8.17, from a class test (grade 10, ages 15–16), reveals degrees of control of grammatical metaphor. The pupils were asked to 'Explain how the fossil record supports evolution'. In this prompt, the teacher is, in fact, exposing her students to a grammatical metaphor typical of the field, *fossil record*. This noun phrase summarises a process in the real world which involves scientists studying fossils, and using them as evidence – a record – to support the theory of evolution.

Text 8.16
The fossil record, or Paleonthology supports evolution because we can observe in fossil reccords things that are in common with another organism, so you can see that probably that individual has evolved from the one shown in the fossil reccord.

The writer of this text has clearly understood the grammatical metaphor in the prompt. She can also display knowledge of the topic. However, she also 'unpacks' the metaphor, making explicit the activities of scientists: *we can observe in fossil records ... , so you can see that probably ...* . To do this, she brings the observers, the scientists, into the text. When doing this, she is not consistent in her choice of pronouns, alternating between *we* and *you* in clause-initial position as subjects of the verbs of perception *observe* and *see*. She structures her answer in a number of clauses, with the explanations signalled by *because* and *so*, features of spoken language, as has been shown. Also, she explains the evidence for evolution in everyday language: *things that are in common.* All these choices produce the unstable focus on the topic which makes the text less successful than another student's answer to the same test, reproduced as Text 8.17.

Text 8.17
Some fossil record shows skeletons of animals with the same bones and structure but with some changes. For example, the ancestors of the horse were smaller and with fingers. Nowadays, the horse has only one nail and larger body.

In this text, the writer represents the *fossil record* as responsible for revealing the original structures, as in the prompt. This allows her to focus the reader on the topic in a more effective way, placing in first position and in final position in each sentence concepts related through exemplification and contrast. The presentation in Text 8.17a shows this.

Text 8.17a		
Marker	Beginning of sentence	End of sentence
	Some fossil record	skeletons of animals with the same bones and structure but with some changes
For example, Nowadays,	the ancestors of the horse the horse	smaller and with fingers only one nail and larger body

The way writers control the position of information in a sentence is a convention of the register of academic writing which seems to develop little by little through exposure to such texts. Research on the phenomenon in

L1 texts by young adolescents finds these writers beginning to use grammatical metaphor to focus on phenomena, rather than on the actors doing an experiment or observing the world (Christie and Derewianka, 2008: 156). At that age, L1 students also use abstraction. The CLIL student who wrote Text 8.16 seems to be struggling with a lack of lexis, turning to the vague word *things*, post-modified by a relative clause: *that are in common with another organism*. Highly compacted phrases including abstractions, like *adaptive divergence*, used by the teacher in her corrections of some of the answers, were not found in her students' speech or writing. This is an area in which teachers could scaffold their students' learning, both before writing, orally in class talk on the topic, as explained in Chapter 7, or after writing, by sharing with the class a number of students' texts, and commenting together on reasons for success, or ways to improve them.

To learn to write like historians (Veel and Coffin, 1996), students also need to develop control of grammatical metaphor to structure information inside the clause, as well as to produce other features which allow them to present information in logically ordered, dense texts. We find in the writing of younger CLIL secondary school students many features of orality (Llinares and Whittaker, 2009). Text 8.18 from an in-class writing task (grade 8, ages 13–14), shows a simple historical account, explaining causes for an event, developed by chaining clauses together, as in spontaneous speech.

Text 8.18

The black death transpasit because of the rats, **because** they may be go to the food **and** they infected **and** later the humane eat **and** they die **and** may be because of the dogs too **because** the rats go with the dogs **and** they infected **and** then the human touch the dog **and** they then die, **and** because of the black death most of the people die.

The student has written a sentence made up of 11 short clauses, linked by the coordinating and subordinating conjunctions: *and* and *because* (in bold in the extract), and using *then* as the only sequence marker. However, the older student (grade 10, ages 15–16) who wrote Text 8.19 is beginning to experiment with register, opening his text with an attempt at a grammatical metaphor.

Text 8.19

It's broke out was due to the differences between countries and the final event which caused it was caused by the murdering of the archiduque of Austria by a Servian of the black hand.

The writer creates a nominal group, *its outbreak* (written by the student as *It's broke out*), which he can then place in first position as subject of *was*. His control of the language is quite variable, but he uses several nominal groups with post-modification in this first sentence in the text (*the differences between countries, event which caused it, murdering of the archduke of Austria, a Serbian of the black hand*).

Other linguistic features which apprentice historians need to develop are related to the expression of time and cause. In order to be able to organise an argument, students need to break away from the clause, because the grammar of the clause restricts the position of conjunctions like *when* or *because*, used to signal logical relations. If, instead of writing clauses, writers use clause-internal markers, like temporal or causal prepositional phrases, or choose lexical items expressing these concepts, they can move pieces of information to different positions in their sentences. In Text 8.20 a CLIL student (grade 10, ages 15–16) is beginning to do this, as the words and phrases in bold in the text show.

Text 8.20
The First World War broke out **due to** several long term **causes** and immediate facts. I think **the mos important cause** was the anxiety of Germany to build up a great Empire and control all Europe with his army and navy.
Another important cause was the differences of costums, languages and traditions in the Balkans that **led to** many crisis that raised temperature in Europe.

This writer builds his short paragraphs around nominal groups including pre- and post-modification, with causality appearing as a noun, *cause*, as a preposition phrase *due to*, and as a verbal group, *led to*. This allows him to contrast the underlying reasons for the outbreak of war with the event which triggered it. By expressing the concepts as nouns, he can include in the pre-modification slot the contrasting terms: *long-term* causes and *immediate* facts. This type of expansion of nominal resources is found to develop in L1 students through adolescence (Christie and Derewianka, 2008: 126). Given its importance for writing in the disciplines, CLIL teachers could intervene to speed up the development of the use of strategies like these, which allow the creation of nominal groups and their movement.

Structuring text also includes something as simple as telling the reader who or what the writer is referring to at any moment. Text 8.21 shows the first sentence of a text (grade 7, ages 12–13), in which there is no attempt to make the composition context independent.

Text 8.21

They start in **that places** because the population grow.

The reader needs to be able to refer to the teacher's prompt for the composition task in order to find the referents and so interpret the pronoun *they* and the demonstrative *that*. This written text is not context independent, then. Other writers were more successful. Text 8.22 is the first paragraph of a composition by a boy in a class one year older.

Text 8.22

Many people lived in rural places. **These people** worked the lands. **They** lived in small houses in villages near to forests. **These people** were called peasants ...

This writer presents the participants, a collective, to the reader in a full nominal group *Many people*, and indicates he is referring to the same group in the second and third sentences using the demonstrative *these people*, and then the pronoun *They*. To avoid ambiguity, he later reintroduces the full form, *These people*. This aspect of textual meaning in CLIL students' spoken and written texts has been studied, and some development found in the management of reference over the four years of compulsory secondary schooling (Whittaker et al., 2011).

Other indications of more mature writing also reflect awareness of the needs of the reader. Text 8.23 shows a student indicating change of topic at different points in his composition.

Text 8.23

[...]
Talking about his personality we can say that he was a very rencorous man.
[...]
Talking about mercantilism, we have to say that it was the first idea of capitalism.

Finally, closing a text at a more general level is not easy to achieve when writing in a foreign language. The paragraph in Text 8.24 concludes a short composition (grade 8, ages 13–14).

Text 8.24
It had many consequences in Europe. About 1000000 people died in England. Salarys grew because less people could work People tried to improve health. Aristocrazy lost power. Europe became ready to start the reinassance. **So it** was very devastating.

The writer starts by signalling the method of development of the paragraph, a consequential explanation, and goes on to specify the consequences announced. Finally, *so*, a consequence marker, announces the conclusion, and the last sentence moves to a more general level, in which *it* refers to the content of the whole paragraph, allowing the writer to close the topic with an evaluation of the whole set of consequences.

These texts show how some CLIL students are becoming writers in their fields, beginning to show some reader awareness, and to experiment with grammatical metaphor in their management of information. If subject teachers are aware of the language features which allow writers to make their texts more coherent and readable – that is, to express the subject content clearly in the written mode – they can offer linguistic support to their students which is integrated into their work on that content.

8.5 Conclusion

This chapter has presented an approach to the development of students' writing in CLIL classes, using as a framework the requirements of subject literacy found in studies of writing in schools in the mother tongue. The chapter took the perspective of the transition from spoken to written language in the CLIL classroom. It first showed how different types of spoken interaction in the classroom make demands on different areas of the linguistic system. This is because when carrying out some activities, speakers require a limited variety of lexical words – mainly verbs or nouns – while for other purposes their language needs to be much more lexically rich and explicit.

We then described the roles CLIL student writers have to learn to take on by means of language in order to participate in different subjects. For this, the language the students use as apprentice scientists and historians was analysed following the areas of meaning which realise each of the three metafunctions, according to the systemic functional model. To this end, we examined a number of features of the language of the disciplines in the writing of CLIL students. First, we looked at how students display field knowledge. Here, the technical terms of science were shown to form an important part of the teaching of the area. This contrasts with a difficulty of the language of history, that of abstraction and generalisation, which is not often recognised as a problem. As regards the students' attempts to represent the thoughts and reactions of historical actors, these seemed to be less successful. In their representation of tenor in writing, where students need to show authority, there were different degrees of development, corresponding to the varying demands of the subject areas. Science, being more factual, seemed easier for students, while controlling the expression and degree of evaluation required for history presents problems for immature writers. And in the analysis of how the students deal with the challenges of information management in the written mode, the students' development of grammatical metaphor was shown. Examples illustrated, above all, those transformations which nominalise processes. These frequently create the abstractions which form part of taxonomies and allow knowledge creation in secondary school subjects. This area showed considerable variablity and greater or lesser success in information management to produce coherent written texts.

We feel that writing has an important role to play in CLIL classes, both for the development of the students' language, and for the learning of content. Indeed, we have argued that language and content are inseparable. The school is a community in which written communication is highly valued. As sociocultural theory explains, it is participation in communities by using language that leads to development in that language. Thus, by being given opportunities to interact in the written mode, new members entering the community will be expected to develop these skills. Here, the role of the teachers, with their knowledge of the language of their subjects, and their ability to use this knowledge to raise students' awareness of the resources specific to written communication is paramount. Different training programmes have shown that content teachers can acquire the skills which enable them to help their students write effectively, and that this does not necessarily take a lot of time. For example, Acevedo's (2010) recent work on literacy in Swedish showed immigrant pupils in schools in the Stockholm area making very significant improvement in reading and writing when their content teachers followed an in-service course on subject literacy. Schleppegrell et al. (2004) too, describe how content teachers who were not language specialists, working with students learning history in English as L2, started to apply the notions discussed in this chapter to their teaching, after participating in summer training sessions, and were extremely satisfied with the way their students responded. Readers will find that work on areas such as information management, evaluation or the expression of cause as they co-construct texts with their students is a way towards language development as they focus on building knowledge in their subject areas.

Questions and tasks for reflection and discussion

1. Extract 8.13 is from a CLIL history class (grade 7, ages 12–13). What is the teacher doing in her reformulations of the students' answers? The students' language changed by the teacher is marked in bold to guide you.

	Extract 8.13
1	T: Loud. Loud and clear. The ancient religions?
2	S1: **The people**, eh, believe that the gods, have shape of
3	humans and now is not eh, very clear.
4	T: OK. Yeah. OK. Correct. So the, the idea, the beliefs
5	have changed, ( ) accepted religious, beliefs. Yes?
6	S2: Eh, mm, before, em, they, wear, with, different clothes.
7	T: They wear ...
8	S2: **They** wear with different clothes than, today.
9	T: OK. So clothes have changed as well. OK.

2. Text 8.25 was written by a boy in a CLIL class (grade 10, ages 15–16). The students had been asked to define the terms: *Use and Disuse*, and *Inheritance of acquired traits*. How could grammatical metaphor be used to make the student's answer more academic?

Text 8.25
*Use and Disuse: Lamarck said that if any animal use an organ very much, the organ will develop, streght and enlarge, but if the animal not use that organ it deteriorates and finally disapears. *Inheritance of the acquired traits: Individuals that have changes in their physic, they will pass these acquired changes to their offspring.

3. Compare the paragraphs in Texts 8.26 and 8.27, written by CLIL students (grade 10, ages 15–16), using the features for the roles of writers in science and history in Boxes 8.1 and 8.2.

Text 8.26	
A B C somatic egg cell cell	A mammal can be cloned by this process: If we want to clone individual A, we need two more individuals. You first take the nucleus from the somatic cell of A. Then, you extract the nucleus of the egg cell in B and you introduce the nucleus of the somatic cell in it. Finally, you introduce the cell in the 'C' and it will be a clone of A.

Text 8.27
The War was cruel and lot of soldiers died, due to the new and more advanced weponery in the two bands. As time passed more people died, and at the end both bands decided to sign a treaty of peace, because the war was unsustainable. This treaty was called the Treaty of Versailles, the territories were redrawn, and Prussia lost most of their conquered territories.

4. Text 8.28 is a short text from a mid-semester test taken by a CLIL biology class (grade 10, ages 15–16). The question it responds to asked the students about Darwin and his theory of evolution. As a historical view on science, the text contains linguistic features from both disciplines analysed in this chapter. Look back to Boxes 8.1 and 8.2, and comment on how this student writer plays the roles of scientist or historian.

   - How does he display knowledge? Look at process types and technical terms.
   - How is he authoritative? Look at how he presents the information as fact, or possibility.
   - How does he structure his text? Look at the nominal groups, the expression of cause and the use of the passive.

Text 8.28
Charles Darwin was an English Naturalist who wrote 'On the Origin of the species' in 1859. Evolution occurred thanks to 'Natural selection', the survival of the fittest. Darwin saw that species had large amounts of offspring and had to struggle for life, there was a shortage of food, there were not enough resources for all of them, they had to avoid diseases and *(cont.)*

predators ... Species with features which helped them to survive in a certain environment were more likely to survive than those without them, so they were more likely to breed. There was a higher percentage of 'superior* species' breeding, their genes passed from one generation to an other, so finally some difference was apreciated between an old form of an species and a new form of it. It had evolved.

*corrected by the teacher to 'better fit'

5. Think about the role of writing in your subject, or a subject you are interested in. After reading this chapter, what difficulties specifically related to expressing the content in writing do you anticipate for student writers? As in the previous question, you can look at the way knowledge is displayed, how writers show authority or are tentative about a topic, and the structure of the genres. Can you suggest any areas of language the CLIL teacher could prepare to be ready to help them?

References

Acevedo, C. (2010) 'Will the implementation of Reading to Learn in Stockholm schools accelerate literacy learning for disadvantaged students and close the achievement gap?', a report on school-based Action Research. Multilingual Research Institute, Stockholm Education Administration. Available at: www.pedagogstockholm.se

Bazerman, C. (1988) *Shaping Written Knowledge*, Madison, WI: The University of Wisconsin Press.

Bereiter, C. and Scardamalia, M. (1987) *The Psychology of Written Composition*, Hillsdale, NJ: Lawrence Erlbaum.

Bourdieu, P. (1991) *Language and Symbolic Power*, Cambridge: Polity Press.

Carter, R. (2004) *Language and Creativity. The Art of Common Talk*, London: Routledge.

Carter, R. and McCarthy, M. (2006) *Cambridge Grammar of English*, Cambridge: Cambridge University Press.

Christie, F. (2010) 'The ontogenesis of writing in childhood and adolescence', in Wyse, D., Andrews, R. and Hoffman, J. (eds.) *The Routledge International Handbook of Language, Literacy and Language Teaching*, Oxford: Routledge, pp. 146–58.

Christie, F. and Derewianka, B. (2008) *School Discourse: Learning to Write Across the Years of Schooling*, London: Continuum.

Coffin, C. (2006) *Historical Discourse: The Language of Time, Cause and Evaluation*, London: Continuum.

Dalton-Puffer, C. (2007) *Discourse in Content and Language Integrated Learning (CLIL) Classrooms*, Amsterdam: John Benjamin.

Firbas, J. (1992) *Functional Sentence Perspective in Written and Spoken English*, Cambridge: Cambridge University Press.

Fries, P. (1994) 'On theme, rheme and discourse goals', in Coulthard, M. (ed.) *Advances in Written Text Analysis*, London: Routledge, pp. 229–49.

Halliday, M. A. K. (1989) *Spoken and Written Language*, Oxford: Oxford University Press.

Heine, L. (2010) *Problem Solving in a Foreign Language: A Study in Content and Language Integrated Learning (Sola studies on second language acquisition)*, Berlin: de Gruyter Mouton.

Littlefair, A. (1991) *Reading all Types of Writing: The importance of Genre and Register for Reading Development*, Milton Keynes: Open University Press.

Llinares, A. and Whittaker, R. (2009) 'Teaching and learning history in secondary CLIL classrooms: From speaking to writing', in Dafouz, E. and Guerrini, M. (eds.) *CLIL Across Educational Levels*, Madrid: Santillana / Richmond, pp. 73–87.

Manchón, R., Roca de Larios, J. and Murphy, L. (2009) 'The temporal dimension and problem-solving nature of foreign language composing processes: Implications for theory', in Manchón, R. (ed.) *Writing in Foreign Language Contexts: Learning, Teaching and Research*, Bristol, UK: Multilingual Matters, pp. 102–29.

Martin, J. R. (1992) *English Text. System and Structure*, Amsterdam: Benjamins.

Martin, J. R. (1993) 'Technicality and abstraction: Language for the creation of specialized texts', in Halliday, M. A. K. and Martin, J. R. *Writing Science: Literacy and Discursive Power*, London: Falmer Press, pp. 203–20.

Martin, J. R. and White, P. R. P. (2005) *The Language of Evaluation: Appraisal in English*, New York: Palgrave Macmillan.

OECD (2010) *PISA 2009 Results: What Students Know and Can Do – Student Performance in Reading, Mathematics and Science* (Volume I). Available at: http://dx.doi.org/10.1787/9789264091450-en

Ong, W. J. (1982) *Orality and Literacy: The Technologizing of the Word*, London: Methuen.

Perera, K. (1984) *Children's Writing and Reading*, Oxford: Basil Blackwell.

Roca de Larios, J., Manchón, R. M. and Murphy, L. (2006) 'Generating text in native and foreign language writing: A temporal analysis of problem-solving formulation processes', *The Modern Language Journal*, 2006, **90** (1), 100–114.

Schleppegrell, M. J. (2004) *The Language of Schooling*, Norwood, NJ: Lawrence Erlbaum.

Schleppegrell, M., Achugar, M. and Oteíza, T. (2004) 'The grammar of history: enhancing content-based instruction through a functional focus on language', *TESOL Quarterly* **38**, 1, 67–93.

Veel, R. and Coffin, C. (1996) 'Learning to think like an historian: The language of secondary school history', in Hasan, R. and Williams, G. (eds.) *Literacy in Society*. London: Longman, pp. 191–231.

Whittaker, R., Llinares, A. and McCabe, A. (2011) 'Written discourse development in CLIL at secondary school', in Lyster, R. and Ballinger, S. (eds.) (2011) *Content-Based Language Teaching: Convergent Concerns Across Divergent Contexts*. Special issue of *Language Teaching Research*, pp. 343–62.

9 The role of language in assessment in CLIL

9.1 Introduction

In this final chapter we come full circle by taking up again the main issues we have looked at in previous chapters, but this time from the perspective of assessment. Thus, we will see that classroom interaction appears again, as do the ideas of genre and register. In many ways, this last chapter could be the first, because, as we shall argue, assessment is so fundamental to the success of CLIL that it needs to be considered and planned for in detail before any teaching takes place. In this sense, assessment is not something that comes after instruction, but is an indispensable part *of* instruction. It is by thinking about assessment that we really start to sharpen up our ideas of what CLIL is about, and the role of language within it. Indeed, whenever groups of CLIL practitioners get together, assessment emerges as one of the issues that most concerns them, and many questions can arise about the role of language in assessment in CLIL. These include questions about the relative balance of content and language in CLIL assessment, or even whether language should be assessed at all. And, if language is to be assessed, what aspects of language, and how they can be integrated with content. Other questions concern the role of the L1 in assessment, such as whether students' use of the mother tongue as a communication strategy should have an effect on their grades (Hönig, 2010).

This chapter aims to address CLIL teachers' concerns by establishing some general principles about the role of language in assessment in CLIL. We introduce some concepts and tools which should be of practical use in planning for, and using, more reliable and robust forms of assessment which integrate content-learning objectives with language. However, at the outset, it is important to be clear about the scope of the chapter, in terms of which aspects of assessment we will be focusing on. Byrnes (2008: 38–9) provides a useful distinction between three levels at which content in L2 programmes can be assessed:

- Classroom-based content assessment which links to pedagogy in specific classrooms and curricula.

This is what we discuss below as 'formative' assessment, that is, assessment carried out by teachers to support learners in achieving learning outcomes.

- Programme or curriculum-based content assessment where content is defined broadly and abstractly, and results of assessment important to a diverse range of stakeholders.

This is generally **summative** assessment, largely consisting of exams and tests taken at the end of courses of study, and the information used to make decisions, for example, about progression through the curriculum.

- Content assessment for a professional community in which content knowledge is assessed for purposes of certification for membership of professional communities such as business, law, health professions.

Much attention in assessment circles, particularly in language education, has been paid to the second and third levels, those of more 'summative' types of assessment. This is not surprising because, as Broadfoot and Black (2004) point out, we live in an 'assessment society', wedded to a 'belief in the power of numbers, grades, targets and league tables to deliver quality and accountability, equality and defensibility' (p. 19). CLIL as a publicly accountable educational enterprise is no exception to this. If CLIL programmes do not deliver results in terms of content learning and language development, then the whole enterprise will be called into question.

However, in the past 15–20 years, in the wider field of education, there has been a powerful trend in the other direction, that is, towards Byrnes's first level, in which assessment practices are linked to specific classrooms and curricula. This is the movement towards formative assessment, sometimes known as 'assessment for learning'. According to Popham,

> Formative assessment is a planned process in which assessment-elicited evidence of students' status is used by teachers to adjust their ongoing instructional procedures or by students to adjust their current learning tactics.

(Popham, 2008: 6)

Formative assessment is thus an ongoing process carried out during instruction, which can feed back into instruction, as opposed to summative assessment, which is the judgement of learning outcomes at the end of units or programmes. In 1998, Black and Wiliam published a highly influential research review which reported substantial learning gains for students when teachers had used formative assessment. Since then, there has been enormous interest in this type of assessment in the educational community, with many publications (e.g. Gardner 2006; Harlen 2007; Marzano 2010; Popham 2008) and initiatives such as the

UK's Assessment Reform Group's principles for assessment for learning (2002).

However, this growth in interest in formative, or classroom, assessment has not necessarily been reflected within second and foreign language education, where, as Rea-Dickens (2008: 266) points out, 'classroom language assessment research is still in its infancy'. CLIL, because of its Janus-like nature, looking in two directions, towards the general concerns of educational assessment and the more particular concerns of the assessment of foreign language proficiency, can help bridge this gap. In the field of assessment, CLIL should not stand outside the debates around more innovative forms that have been developing within mainstream education in the last decade or so. The field of assessment can become another way in which CLIL can be a powerful catalyst for educational innovation, by linking the general move within educational assessment towards formative, classroom-based assessment to the particular needs and concerns of CLIL.

In this chapter we will argue that a key to ensuring CLIL students meet content- and language-learning goals is the principled and planned use of formative, or ongoing, classroom assessment. As research has shown, the overuse of testing can be harmful for students' motivation for learning, and can reduce the amount of useful formative assessment that takes place (Harlen, 2005; Harlen and Crick, 2003). This reduction in time for formative assessment can also be related to 'washback' – that is, the often negative effects on instruction of tests – in that teachers 'teach to the test' rather than focusing on supporting their learners in meeting learning objectives.

Another aspect of this problem is the type of test used. Rea-Dickens warns that 'traditional and psychometric approaches are incompatible with the values underlying particular pedagogies and curricula' (2008: 267), and when L2 learners are not shown in a good light by such methods, the result is 'a continued decoupling of content and language' (Byrnes, 2008: 40). In this chapter we propose moving in the opposite direction, 'recoupling' content and language by the use of planned and principled formative assessment, or assessment *for* and *as* learning. However, our focus on formative assessment does not mean that we ignore the assessment of 'final' learning outcomes (i.e. summative assessment), but rather that we can't have one without the other. We will try to show that the rigorous planning and use of robust instruments for formative assessment in CLIL can also lead to much more soundly based summative assessment. This is especially important in some CLIL contexts in which students are entered for international examinations such as the Cambridge IGCSE (International General Certificate of Secondary Education, see Chapter 4).

9.2 Language and assessment in CLIL

In CLIL, the primary focus of assessment is on content (Coyle et al., 2010). Teachers are concerned with students' demonstration of skills and understanding in relation to key aspects of curricular knowledge. In this sense, assessment in CLIL may have more in common with the model of curriculum planning in non-language subjects than with the way assessment has often been considered in second and foreign language teaching. As Cumming (2009) argues, the 'conventional' model of assessment is one in which learners are evaluated on the extent to which they have achieved learning outcomes as a result of participating in the curricular activities. However, as he puts it, second and foreign language education 'has often stood apart from this paradigm because schooling is not the sole (or necessarily the most effective) basis by which people develop language proficiency. People may develop language proficiency independent of schooling through interactions at home or in local subcommunities or while traveling' (2009: 91).

He goes on to argue that this can lead to a situation in which 'evaluation assumes roles beyond the conventional function of determining students' achievements directly from an educational program' (ibid.). These include the gatekeeping roles of the second and third levels identified by Byrnes above, namely those of screening candidates for admission to academic programmes or employment. This means that we need to be very careful in CLIL about the role of language in assessing our students' learning achievements, or indeed the role of subject learning in their language achievements. As CLIL takes place in the context of schooling, it may not be appropriate to use language-testing materials not based on the actual curriculum content studied. This danger is that, by doing so, we may be in fact assessing a non-academic competency, that is, one that has been gained outside the context of schooling and / or the specific CLIL programme or course. As Marzano (2010: 17) points out, 'Mixing non-academic competencies with academic competencies contaminates the meaning of a grade.'

There are other important ways in which conventional language assessment may not meet the needs of CLIL. As we have emphasised throughout this book, the language used in learning academic content needs to be distinguished from the language used in carrying out everyday tasks (Byrnes, 2008). This relates to Cummins's well-known distinction between BICS and CALP, which we discussed in Chapter 7. It is important to avoid the situation in which CLIL students are assessed on language skills which have nothing to do with the ways in which they have been using language in the learning of curricular content. However, these differences relate not only to language tests which have a communicative orientation, that is, based on the transaction of life's tasks, as Byrnes puts it. We should also be very careful about more conventional grammar-oriented assessment, in which language is not integrated with content, but is 'mainly talked about in terms of formal grammar and grammar in terms of errors' (Low, 2010: 254). Thus, neither those assessment activities which focus on the performance of everyday communicative tasks, nor those which test the control of formal grammar isolated from academic context will meet the needs for principled assessment practices in CLIL.

Of course, all CLIL students, in order to demonstrate content understanding and skills, need to use language, along with other modes, to a greater or lesser extent. This means that using grammar and vocabulary effectively is deeply implicated in the quality of their performance. The problem is that, if the language which is needed to perform assessment tasks effectively is not brought out into the open, it can remain as an 'invisible' component of assessment. Students may get higher marks than their content understanding merits because of language proficiency gained outside the programme, or judgements of 'poor' language use may disguise the fact that students are actually showing understanding of content. Wherever language is an invisible component of performance, as in many educational contexts, this can lead to gross unfairness in assessment practices. This can happen, for example, when English language learners who are 'mainstreamed' have to do high-stakes assessments designed for native speakers. As McNamara and Roever (2006: 241) point out, these standardised assessments 'are not equally appropriate for ESL learners and measure their content knowledge imprecisely'. Indeed, this situation is not limited to ESL situations. It is also a danger in CLIL, as described in the Austrian context by Hönig (2010), where she claims that language ability plays a largely invisible role in the awarding of grades for oral assessments of content knowledge.

Two important principles emerge from what we have argued above. Starting with the point just discussed, the first principle is that the language needed for the competent performance of content learning or assessment tasks should not be an invisible component of these tasks. The language CLIL learners need to use must be brought into the open as an explicit component of the tasks they do. Related to this is the second principle that any language-related assessment in CLIL should be directly linked to the achievement of content-based learning objectives. Language assessment in CLIL should not assume roles beyond determining students' achievements directly from the educational programme. Where external language performance standards such as the 'can-do statements' in the Common European Framework of Reference are used, these should be explicitly linked to content-learning objectives. Once language has been brought out into the open in this way, and clearly linked to content knowledge and skills objectives, CLIL teachers will be in a stronger position to provide the support their learners need to use this language appropriately and accurately as part of learning activities. The main way in which they ensure that their teaching is constantly adjusted to meet the learners' needs in attaining both content and language objectives is by the use of formative assessment, or assessment *for* learning.

9.3 The case for formative classroom assessment in CLIL

In this section we present a detailed argument for the importance of formative assessment in CLIL. We highlight three key characteristics of formative assessment and apply them to CLIL, and then go on to describe two of its main uses and their importance for CLIL. Popham's definition of formative assessment in Section 9.1 is useful for our first purpose as it highlights three important characteristics: it is planned, since teachers need to identify what they will assess and how they will collect evidence about learners' current knowledge states; it is reactive because teachers will need to adjust their tactics in the light of the information they gain; and it is reciprocal as both teacher and learners may adjust their tactics based on information from the formative assessment process. Each of these characteristics, while important in all educational contexts, has particular implications for assessment in CLIL.

To take the first characteristic, formative assessment is *planned* in that educators need to identify the building blocks necessary to achieve learning objectives, and to sequence these in terms of the learning progression their students must go through (Heritage, 2008; Marzano, 2010: 10–11). In this sense it is also an example of 'backward design' (Wiggins and McTighe, 2005), in which we first establish where we want our students to end up, and then work backwards to trace how they will get there. This involves not only putting these building blocks in place, but also identifying some ways in which information can be gathered about how well the students are getting on with them. In CLIL, this means that teachers will need not only descriptions of the concepts, knowledge and skills to be learned, but also clear statements about language linked to these (Coyle et al., 2010). To do this, as we saw in Chapters 4 and 5, CLIL educators will need awareness of the genres and registers with which the content in their subject is built, and the grammar and vocabulary through which these genres and registers are realised. This language can then be built up during the teaching of the unit, reinforced through instructional feedback, and its role recognised in any summative assessment. CLIL teachers' planning for formative assessment will also involve thinking of some ways in which they can gain information about their learners' abilities to use this language, for example by unobtrusive observation during learning activities (see Marzano, 2010: 24–25, for advice on this).

Turning to the second characteristic, formative assessment is *reactive* in that teachers need to constantly update their instructional procedures in the light of information they gather about their students' current understandings of the topic. As the Assessment Reform Group's principles put it:

> Much of what teachers and learners do in classrooms can be described as assessment. That is, tasks and questions prompt learners to demonstrate their knowledge, understanding and skills. What learners say and do is then observed and interpreted, and judgements are made about how learning can be improved. These assessment processes are an essential part of everyday classroom practice and involve both teachers and learners in reflection, dialogue and decision making.

(Assessment Reform Group, 2002: 2)

In CLIL, these judgements about how learning can be improved are likely to be language related, at least some of the time. However, it is important that the main focus of these instructional adjustments should be on aspects of language important for the learning outcomes in the particular topic being studied. In this sense, such language-based adjustments would be truly formative in that their intention is to support the learner in meeting the pre-specified content learning goals. This depends crucially on the first stage of backward design having been carried out: that is, the planning of a learning progression with the linguistic elements integrated into this progression. If this has been done, the teacher can know at any time to what extent the students are capable of making the word–meaning relationships necessary for understanding the content. For example, if students are having problems with the language of cause / consequence, more attention will need to be paid to this area during classroom instruction (preferably in collaboration with the foreign language teacher).

The third aspect of Popham's definition of formative assessment as *reciprocal* highlights the fact that it is not only the teacher who may need to adjust her tactics. CLIL students can use feedback from formative assessment to adjust their own learning tactics where they are being found to be less effective than desired. For example, they could consider whether learning material by heart for oral presentations is a good tactic. Or they may decide that using a format for planning, or a checklist for revising, will help them produce better writing. These learner adjustments to tactics can take place inside the classroom or may be introduced in work done outside the classroom such as homework or projects. In this way, formative assessment can be used as a pedagogical strategy to encourage learner autonomy, something that is linked to the development of L2 competence (Benson, 2011).

Having considered the important characteristics of formative assessment, we can move on to thinking about what it is used for. Marzano (2010) distinguishes two main uses of formative assessment – scoring systems and instructional feedback – which involve collecting and providing different types of information. The first use involves *recording scores*, for example by using a scale, and using this information to track students' progress over a whole course or teaching unit. Summative scores can then be derived from these formative scores to give information about overall attainment of the learning goals. The second main use of formative assessment is to give *instructional feedback*. This is information that is not recorded, but is given to students to help them improve their performance, often during the moment-by-moment interaction in the classroom.

Both uses of formative assessment have important implications for CLIL. We need to develop scoring systems which can provide us with reliable and consistent information about our students' performances during a course and their achievements at the end. These systems need to reflect both the content-related knowledge and skills that the students need to learn, and the L2 registers and genres required to express this knowledge and use the skills. Turning to instructional feedback, we can link this with the kinds of dialogic interaction and scaffolding in L2 that we described in Chapters 2 and 3. By adding these dimensions of L2 language use (register, genre and classroom interaction), we can make both types of formative assessment reflect the unique nature of CLIL. In the following two sections of this chapter, we explore each of these dimensions of formative assessment in CLIL. We begin by examining the first broad use of formative assessment: the use of scales for scoring achievement. We introduce a content–language integrated assessment scale for CLIL, based on Marzano's (2010) new assessment scale, but adapted to CLIL by the addition of a language component.

9.4 A content–language integrated scale for formative assessment in CLIL

One problem in assessing learning in any educational context is that of consistency. Teachers and educational systems use a wide range of numerical and letter-based scoring and grading schemes to report information about their students' attainment, thus making it difficult to compare between different classes or programmes. Often, these scores are not based on discrete-item tests, but are based on more subjective criteria, for example in the grading of more holistic tasks, such as essay writing. Even when the same grading system is used, there can be wide inconsistencies in the scores and grades awarded by different teachers. This difficulty is compounded by the dual focus of CLIL. Language may be playing a more or less visible role in the scores and grades awarded (Hönig, 2010). CLIL brings into even sharper focus the need to 'speak the same language' when scoring students' achievements. We need a robust and reliable scoring system which will be a fair reflection of our learners' progress with regard to learning goals, and, when necessary, the role of language in meeting or not meeting these goals.

In this section, we propose a scale for content–language integrated assessment based on the new assessment scale introduced by Marzano. Table 9.1 shows the generic form of the scale (Marzano, 2010: 45).

Marzano argues that traditional scales such as giving marks out of 100 are rather unwieldy instruments for reflecting students' achievement of learning goals. Apart from the inconsistency in their application, they do not reflect the different levels of complexity at which students can respond to assessment tasks. Scores are simply added up according to how many questions students got right, or subjective judgements are given of written work on less discrete tests. The new assessment scale proposed by Marzano is designed to reflect differing levels of complexity in achieving learning goals. This is based on the idea that the same assessment task can be carried out by using more or less sophisticated thinking skills. The scale consists of five values, which go in descending order from four to zero (see Table 9.1).

Table 9.1 *Generic form of Marzano's new assessment scale (Marzano, 2010)*

Score 4.0	More complex content
Score 3.0	Target learning goal
Score 2.0	Simpler content
Score 1.0	With help, partial success at score 2.0 content and score 3.0 content
Score 0.0	Even with help, no success

To achieve the highest score (4.0), learners will have to use higher-order thinking skills such as suggesting new solutions to problems or

providing their own interpretations. At score 3.0, they will satisfacto-
rily meet the target learning goals. At level 2.0, learners will produce
simpler responses, such as recall of facts. Score 1.0 allows for the possibility of learners achieving partial success with assistance.

For CLIL, this scale can be the basis for a principled approach to
assessment that begins with the 'two Cs' of content and cognition (the
C of culture can also be included where aspects of intercultural competence are highlighted for assessment). Content (knowledge and skills)
targets are established at various levels of achievement, with rising levels
of achievement requiring more sophisticated thinking processes. These
thinking processes can also be linked to a scale or taxonomy, such as
that of Anderson and Krathwohl (2001), as suggested by Coyle et al.
(2010: 30), or by Marzano and Kendall's (2007) taxonomy of educational objectives. In order to illustrate the scale in action, it will be
useful to go through a worked example. For this, we shall use an assessment task from a CLIL history unit on Oliver Cromwell and the English
Civil War. Table 9.2 shows how the scale could be used to set assessment targets for this topic.

Table 9.2   *Assessment scale for history topic (adapted from
Marzano, 2010)*

	CONTENT
4.0	Students will be able to argue that Cromwell was either a hero or a villain, taking into account different points of view. They will also compare Cromwell's actions in parliament with an event from the 20th century.
3.0	Students will be able to describe the events leading up to the English Civil War, explain their significance and how they contributed to the war breaking out.
2.0	Students will be able to identify key events in Cromwell's political career, particularly those leading up to the Civil War. They should produce a simple statement as to his historical importance.
1.0	Students, perhaps with help, will achieve some of the goals at scores 2.0 and 3.0.
0	Even with help, no success.

In the table, the score of 3.0 represents achievement of the target learning goal. This would be the relevant standard for the topic, what the
local history curriculum expects students to know and be able to do

in relation to the content. Thus, if a student is able to describe the events leading up to the English Civil War, explain their significance and show how they contributed to the war breaking out, without any serious errors or omissions, s/he will score 3.0 on the scale. A score of 2.0 represents successful performance with less complex content. In terms of Marzano and Kendall's (2007) taxonomy, this may be at the level of factual recall. So, in this case, a student may be able to remember basic and important facts about Cromwell and make a simple statement about his importance as a historical figure, but may not be able to produce an adequate explanation of how these events contributed to the outbreak of the Civil War. A score of 4.0 represents achievement beyond the target learning goal. For example, the student may draw implications or make comparisons beyond what was taught in class, or show more sophisticated understanding of the content. In our example, the student may be able to use the kind of appraisal resources that were discussed in Chapter 7 to successfully balance different points of view, produce his/her own argument or draw comparisons with another historical period or event. The ways in which students may do this need to be considered carefully by the teacher, so that attaining a 4.0 score requires deeper understanding of a topic or more sophisticated skill performance, not going off the topic in possibly irrelevant ways.

The scale has several advantages over other scoring systems. It is positive and fair, in that it gives students credit for what they *can* do, whether that capability is at a simpler level than the target, meets it or goes beyond it. It requires educators to use backward design, in that they must establish the building blocks and work out the steps that need to be carried out in order to reach the learning goals. As we discuss below, this becomes an even more powerful tool for CLIL, in that statements about language have to be worked out for each of the levels of attainment, thus linking the subject-specific registers and genres to the levels of cognitive complexity inherent in the content. As Marzano's scale has not been designed for this purpose, we can use other frameworks to integrate language objectives. However, even before we add the language component, as we will do below, the scale can be a powerful ally for CLIL educators. It is a flexible instrument, in that it can be used at a simpler level, with the five whole-point scores, or at a more complex level with one-half or one-third divisions between scores, for example, with students getting a score of 3.5 for fully meeting the learning goals but showing that they are beginning to work with ideas and show skills at the higher level.

It is a key principle of formative assessment that learners know what they will be assessed on and how they will be assessed at the outset of any learning unit. As the Assessment Reform Group's principles put it,

'Planning should include strategies to ensure that learners understand the goals they are pursuing and the criteria that will be applied in assessing their work' (2002). In order for learners to understand these goals, there must be a shared language. Marzano (2010) advocates working with students to translate the learning targets into 'student-friendly' language. He gives the example of a scale for the biology topic of heritable and nonheritable traits. At level 4.0, the learning goal is expressed like this:

> Students will be able to discuss how heritable traits and nonheritable traits affect one another.

(Marzano, 2010: 45)

However, the student-friendly version goes like this:

> We should be able to talk about how the traits we inherit and the traits we develop on our own are related to one another. For example, a person born in a family that has always lived near the equator might have darker skin and enjoy warm-weather hobbies such as swimming or scuba diving, but someone born in a family that has always lived in a cold climate might have fair skin and enjoy cold-weather hobbies such as skiing or ice skating.

(Marzano, 2010: 46)

In terms of language, the student-friendly version is much richer, and already previews some of the key vocabulary, or language of learning (Coyle et al., 2010) for the topic, such as 'trait', 'inherit', 'dark' and 'fair skin', as well as a host of more 'everyday' language which will be necessary to discuss aspects of the topic. Such a discussion of learning targets makes as clear as possible what students will be assessed on, and how, without pre-empting the actual tasks they will do to demonstrate their knowledge and skills. Marzano recommends that the whole class participate in rewriting the content at each score value (2010: 46). Apart from being entirely justified in terms of assessment for learning, this is also an extremely valuable language exercise in itself. It is an example of how an approach which uses backward design as a part of assessment for learning, and involves students in sharing understanding of learning goals and assessment criteria, can be a powerful force for the meaningful integration of content and language.

The scale as proposed by Marzano is designed for content assessment across the wide range of subjects in the school curriculum and the different grade levels. However, on its own it does not address the special characteristics of CLIL as an educational approach with a dual focus on content and language. It can be used effectively for assessment in

291

modern foreign language instruction, as Marzano shows in an example from the teaching of French (2010: 49). But, as we have seen, combining assessment criteria from non-language subjects and second / foreign language instruction does not capture the essential characteristics of CLIL. For this, we need a principled approach which links statements about language to the content and to the cognitive operations used in dealing with the content.

In assessment in CLIL, language is always present in that it is an essential ingredient for the achievement of the specified learning goal. This has important consequences for formative assessment. For many CLIL students, not achieving an expected score may be due to limitations or gaps in linguistic knowledge. A student may get a score of 2.0 on some skill or topic, but not attain 3.0 because of a problem with some aspect of the language necessary for the cognitive operations required to meet the learning goal at score level 3.0. For example, the student may have problems with the language of cause and effect necessary for constructing an adequate explanation (Llinares and Morton, 2010). The important point here is that, in order to give this student constructive feedback about what s/he needs to do in terms of the CLIL language to meet the learning goal at level 3.0, we need to have already established, and shared with the class, just what language is needed to do the task. If we don't, we will end up with the situation described by Mohan et al. (2010: 230–31) where teachers decide that one piece of writing is better than another in meeting a learning goal without really being able to specify why, and thus being unable to pass on useful information to their students.

For this reason, it is crucial that backward design in CLIL includes clear statements about the kinds of language required for the achievement of learning goals at the different levels of complexity. One very useful instrument for doing this is the ESL Scope and Scales (Polias, 2003), an assessment tool developed in Australia which provides a detailed description of language development in the context of schooling not only for learners of English as a second language but for those who speak English as their primary language. This tool is very compatible with the approach to language taken in this book, as it is based on the systemic functional model of language. Thus, the 'Scope', which outlines the model of language underpinning this tool, uses the concepts of genre and register (field, tenor and mode) to identify language-learning outcomes compatible with subject matter content at all the grades in the curriculum, from early years to upper secondary. Table 9.3 shows some of the genre and register features highlighted as learning objectives at scale 10 (of 14). These objectives would be suitable for students grade 9 (ages 14–15).

Table 9.3 *Excerpt from Scope and Scales level 10 (Polias, 2003: 66–9)*

Genre	Register

Constructs longer, increasingly complex examples of the factual genres, analysing and combining information from more than one source and using a range of cohesive language elements:
 	
• Constructs longer oral and written arguments in which the argument is sustained and concluded
 	
• Constructs longer oral and written recounts:
  • writes a biographical recount, accompanied with a timeline graph or chart listing major achievements
 	
  • writes and draws explanations which are principally sequential but also include causal meanings
	Field
	Begins to make more delicate choices of vocabulary: verbs expressing action processes; noun groups expressing the participants; phrases expressing the manner of an action.
	
	Tenor
	Uses a range of simple forms of language expressing modality (i.e. degrees of certainty or obligation) with a greater degree of accuracy.
	
	Mode
	Begins to foreground causal elements in explanations and discussions: 'Because of more rainfall, floods ... '

Language-learning objectives from the Scope and Scales tool can be linked to the content (knowledge and skills) objectives for particular topics, by adding another column to the content scale. Thus, we have a content–language integrated scale which includes the language statements based on genre and register analysis for the learning goals at each level. For example, in Table 9.4 we show how the two-column scale could be used for the history content we discussed earlier.

This example incorporates a genre approach to language in the teaching of history, as we discussed in Chapter 4, and includes some descriptors taken from the Scope and Scales tool. As this is a topic from the higher levels of secondary history, students should be familiar with the recording genres used to provide simple recounts of historical events, and the explaining genres to construct factorial or consequential explanations. The arguing genres, in which they put forward and contrast different perspectives, may just be coming within their reach,

Table 9.4 *Example of assessment scale, with language component added*

	CONTENT	LANGUAGE (GENRE AND REGISTER)
4.0	Students will be able to argue that Cromwell was either a hero or a villain, taking into account different points of view. They will also compare Cromwell's actions in parliament with any event from the 20th century.	Arguing genre (discussion): Background, the issue at stake, different perspectives; own point of view. Text organised according to arguments (not time or causal factors). Uses language for comparing and contrasting points of view.
3.0	Students will be able to describe the events leading up to the English Civil War, explain their significance and how they contributed to the war breaking out.	Factorial explanation: answer organised according to reasons or factors, not timeline. Uses causal language (nouns, verbs, phrases and clauses that express causality). Uses simple language forms to express degree of certainty (*The war was probably caused by ...*) Uses evaluative language to highlight importance / significance.
2.0	Students will be able to identify key events in Cromwell's political career, particularly those leading up to the Civil War. They should produce a simple statement as to his historical importance.	Biographical / historical recount: uses appropriate vocabulary to describe participants; uses a range of action verbs in the past tense; uses simple evaluative vocabulary.
1.0	With help, students may produce elements of a simple recount of Cromwell's career and mention one or two isolated events connected with the Civil War.	May use some genre and register features of levels 2.0 and 3.0 with partial success. *(cont.)*

Table 9.4 *(cont.)*

0	Even with help, students are unable to provide even a simple recount of Cromwell's career or identify any events leading to the Civil War.	

and for this reason could be set at level 4.0, as providing evidence of going beyond the strictly required knowledge. As each genre itself is constructed using a set of identifiable lexical and grammatical features, it then becomes possible to write clear statements about what language is needed for successful demonstration of understanding or skill at each score point. For example, at score point 3.0 in our history assessment about Cromwell, students would need to organise their answer according to reasons or factors, and not time. They would need to use a range of lexical and grammatical resources to express cause, and evaluative language to highlight the importance or significance of certain events. In identifying content goals at different levels of cognitive complexity, it will also be possible to match them with language performance at different levels from the Scope and Scales instrument. Thus, the language requirements to attain a score of 2.0 could use descriptors from a lower scale, such as scale 8. This would reflect the reality that many CLIL learners, even though they are studying content at the same level, may be at quite different stages in their L2 development.

In using the content–language integrated scale, no separate score need be given for language. Students can be given the appropriate score on the scale according to their achievement of the content-related learning goals. Of course, language will contribute to their achievement or otherwise of these goals. A student may not use appropriate vocabulary to describe the events leading up to the Civil War, or may not use causal language effectively enough to attain score point 3.0. A student's very effective use of the arguing genre (for example with a clearly stated thesis and supporting arguments) may contribute strongly to the achievement of a score of 4.0. Another student may not achieve a 3.0, perhaps getting a 2.5, if he or she is able to recall all the basic information, but there are some language problems with the level 3.0 content (e.g. problems in organisation, or use of causal expressions).

But whatever role language plays in the attainment or otherwise of learning goals, it need not be assessed separately from content. There is no requirement for a mark for 'language' alongside the content-based score. In many CLIL contexts, it may be preferred to keep language as an issue for purely formative assessment. Information about language performance gained from assessment activities can be incorporated into the kinds of instructional adjustments which are an essential part of formative assessment. Language would then be seen as an enabler, something that is an indispensable component in the achievement of learning goals, but not targeted for separate assessment. This would help to preserve one of the main benefits of CLIL, the motivating effect for students in knowing that they will not be punished for incidental language errors that do not interfere with their expression of the content-relevant knowledge or their performance of skills. And when teachers do want to insist on formal accuracy, there will be much more credibility if it can be shown that this is necessary for understanding and talking about the content. For example, in the context of using L2 Italian and Romansh in the teaching of primary maths, Serra (2007: 585) makes this distinction:

> (...) from the very beginning the grammatical opposition between singular and plural forms proved relevant to both teaching / learning maths and L2, while gender was not.
>
> (Serra, 2007: 585)

This example points to another way in which the language statements in the scale can be strengthened. It is easy to imagine that, in Serra's example, the importance of the distinction between singular and plural became apparent through experience. It may emerge in the first teaching of a CLIL unit that an unexpected aspect of language turns out to be crucial for the achievement of learning goals. Students may have unexpected difficulties with specific vocabulary, or features of a genre they are expected to use without having being taught about these features. Rather than lamenting this situation as a disaster, we can seize upon it as a way of strengthening the descriptions of learning goals at the different score points. If this is done during the teaching of a unit, it is a clear example of one of the key features of formative assessment discussed above, that of teachers adjusting their instructional procedures in response to the evidence revealed by the assessment activity. In doing this, they can be supported by the foreign language teacher, and the language points identified can be incorporated into planning for future teaching of the unit.

Another advantage of using the content–language integrated scale as a part of Wiggins and McTighe's backward design process is that it can be used for the generation of assessment tasks. Rather than setting exam questions, for example, and then working out a scale for marking students' answers, we work backwards from the content and language statements at each score level and design assessment tasks through which the students would be able to demonstrate their achievement of the learning goals. In our example about Cromwell and the English Civil War, the task could look something like this:

Answer all three questions:

1) What were the main events in Cromwell's political and military career? Say in one sentence why he is important in British history.
2) What were the main causes of the English Civil war? How was Cromwell involved in these events?
3) Was Cromwell a hero or a villain? Give both points of view and decide which you agree with. To help you decide, compare the events Cromwell was involved in with any events you know about from the 20th century. What can we learn from these comparisons?

We can see that question (1) relates to the 2.0 score point in that it requires the recall of factual information. The addition of a statement about Cromwell's importance is motivated by the fact that an evaluation is part of the biographical recount genre. In this context, it is a reasonable expectation. Question (2) is designed to elicit content at score point 3.0. At this higher secondary level in history, students are required to show understanding of the causes and consequences of events, not just factual information. Question (3) is aimed at score point 4.0 content, which stretches students to go beyond required content to demonstrate more sophisticated levels of understanding. Again, we can see the influence of both the explaining and arguing genres in the construction of questions two and three. The IGCSE examiners recognise similar distinctions, as we saw in Chapter 4.

The Cromwell example is rather complex in that it incorporates learning goals at various levels of complexity alongside a genre-based approach to constructing the relevant statements about language. However, the scale can be used to differentiate student performance without the need to design separate tasks for the differing complexity of learning goals. In the example below from secondary CLIL biology, analysed in Chapter 5, students were given the following task in an assessment:

Give an account of Darwin's journey on *The Beagle* and explain his theory of evolution

The task for the teacher in assessing students' performance of this task is to establish criteria to distinguish between levels of achievement in carrying out the task. Otherwise, the assessment will be impressionistic and will not generate information with which to provide students with constructive feedback. An example of a content–language integrated scale is given for this assessment in Table 9.5.

Table 9.5 *Content–language scale for secondary biology assessment task*

	CONTENT	LANGUAGE
4.0	Students will be able to provide accurate and detailed information about the journey of *The Beagle*, and an accurate summary of Darwin's theory, including some technical information. Explanation of the theory is linked to what Darwin observed on his voyage.	Well-organised and integrated use of description and explanation genres to show links between Darwin's observations and theory.
3.0	Students will be able to provide accurate information about the journey of *The Beagle*, and a reasonably detailed explanation of his theory.	Ideas are clearly expressed using appropriate vocabulary (*struggle, offspring, survival of the fittest*). Some evidence of language of explanation.
2.0	Students will be able to provide some basic facts about Darwin's life and show a basic understanding of the main points of his theory.	Students use simple sentences to describe Darwin's voyage and basic ideas in his theory. They use some topic-related vocabulary. Ideas may be expressed in isolated points or sentences, with no logical links between them.
1.0	With help, partial success at score 2.0 content and 3.0 content	
0	Even with help, no success	

In this example, the main emphasis is on factual information, with the increase in level relating to the richness of description of Darwin's voyage, and the ability to give an accurate explanation of his theory. Students scoring at level 4.0 will be able to make clearer links between what Darwin observed on his voyage and his theory. The main genre involved in this task is that of explanation. That is, a phenomenon is identified, and the process by which it comes about is described. In this case, the phenomenon is natural selection, and this is linked to Darwin's voyage on *The Beagle*. The aspects of language which are involved in successful completion of this assessment at the different levels of attainment relate to the ways in which ideas are linked together in building the explanation, and the appropriate and rich use of specific vocabulary. Descriptors for these can be readily found in the Scope and Scales tool at the relevant levels.

In both examples, the focus has been on formative assessment. We have seen how the use of content–language integrated backward design in the form of assessment scales can be used to generate information that can be fed back to CLIL students during the teaching of a unit. However, it is important to remember that in CLIL, as in any other learning context, we will also be responsible for summative assessment in the form of the final grade students receive at the end of a unit, term or academic year. The mistake to avoid here is to award students a grade based on one final assessment such as an end of unit / term / year exam. As Marzano (2010: 27) warns, 'A summative score should not be derived from a single final assessment.' He advocates that scores for formative assessments should be kept and used to contribute to the final, summative score. This helps teachers and learners keep track of learning. However, it is not advisable to compute an average of all the student's formative scores. As Marzano points out (p.28), this would break all the principles of formative assessment. A student's summative score should be based on his or her progression in tackling similar content and tasks. Students try the same kind of thing, and get better at it with the help of feedback. It is not the working out of an average based on the performance of tasks aimed at different learning goals, but on progression through a set of tasks aimed at one learning goal, or closely related set of goals.

9.5 Instructional feedback as formative assessment in CLIL

In the previous section we explored the use of formative assessment as a way of tracking CLIL students' progress by giving formative scores based on a content–language integrated scale. In this section, we shift our attention to the other important use of formative assessment identified by Marzano (2010), that of instructional feedback. The focus shifts from the kind of backward design that can largely take place before we enter the classroom, to what happens in moment-by-moment interaction in the classroom. This relates to Lyster's (2007) distinction between proactive and reactive approaches to language form in content-based classrooms (see Chapter 6). In this sense, formative assessment is clearly classroom assessment (Popham, 2008; Rea-Dickens, 2008). As such, it 'typically involves a great deal of interaction between teacher and students' (Marzano, 2010: 32). As we saw in the Assessment Reform Group's principles for assessment for learning, it is the kind of assessment that goes on all the time in classrooms. As one Spanish CLIL science teacher put it when asked how often and how she got information about how the students were doing:

> Oh all the time, feedback feedback feedback. All the time. Asking them to see how much they have understood. What scaffolding they have constructed so far. You see I try to ask them to to find out how much they are learning all the time. Just by asking them orally you see what I mean.
>
> (Interview with teacher, authors' data)

As it is described by this teacher, instructional feedback can be seen as fairly spontaneous adjustments carried out by the teacher in the light of the students' demonstrations of their current understanding or levels of skill in relation to a learning goal (see Chapter 3 on interactional scaffolding). It can be a form of what Sharpe (2006) describes as 'contingent scaffolding', that is, support provided on the spur of the moment to help students complete learning tasks and / or express their understandings of content.

However, instructional feedback becomes a much more powerful instrument for CLIL if the backward design work has been carried out. If CLIL teachers have clear statements about the genres and registers and associated language through which the content is expressed, then their feedback can be directed to precisely those features. Attention can be directed towards precisely those register features through which the relevant content knowledge is shaped. Mohan and Beckett (2003) and Mohan et al. (2010) show how teachers can use 'functional recasts' (see Chapter 6) in which they respond to students' utterances by showing them how they can express their ideas in more appropriate 'causal' language. Gibbons (2003, 2006) discusses a 'mode continuum' which shows how teachers can help move their students' output from more spontaneous spoken forms to language with more 'written' features which more appropriately expresses the academic content.

Instructional feedback in the classroom moves assessment towards what has been described as 'dynamic assessment'. Dynamic assessment has roots in Vygotsky's (1978) theory of cognitive development through social mediation, especially his concept of the **zone of proximal development** (ZPD). The ZPD describes not just the learner's current state of development of cognitive functions, but also the extent of development that may be reached through appropriate support in the form of mediation. Dynamic assessment, in the spirit of Vygotsky's work, is a form of intervention in which the teacher actively works with the learner to move forward through the ZPD. The objective, then, is not to use assessment to show what learners do not know, but to probe where they are and to provide the kind of mediation that will help them to move on. In this sense, it can be seen as a shift from assessment *for* learning to assessment *as* teaching / learning (see Leung, 2007).

Dynamic assessment is only beginning to be explored in language teaching (Lantolf and Poehner, 2008; Leung, 2007), but it opens up exciting possibilities for CLIL. If, as we have suggested above, language can have an enabling function in CLIL, rather than being something that is separately assessed as a learning goal, then dynamic assessment, as an interventionist strategy, is entirely appropriate. In using dynamic assessment we would need to shift the focus from teacher intervention as feedback – that is, providing information about performance in relation to a goal – to that of mediation – that is, providing means by which learners can move towards more advanced levels of development. In her work with ESL learners learning academic content in mainstream classes, Gibbons (2003, 2006) uses the idea of mediation. She describes the teacher's role as being that of a mediator on two fronts – between the students' current understandings of the content and the understandings required by the curriculum, and between the students' current capacities in using language to express the content and the more 'written' registers through which this content is expected to be expressed. In CLIL, we also see the teacher as having this mediating role, by providing the learners with the linguistic resources they need to meet the content-related learning goals. As we have argued here, however, such instructional feedback, or dynamic assessment through mediation, can only happen effectively if teachers are working with clear statements about what has to be learned, and the role of language in learning it.

To illustrate the range of interactive skills used by CLIL teachers in providing instructional feedback, it will be useful to provide some examples of mediation of both content and language. The first example comes from a secondary CLIL history lesson from the same class which was working on the topic of Cromwell and the English Civil War in the previous section. This example shows how, in probing students' knowledge and providing feedback, the teacher engages in a form of dynamic assessment which pushes the learners towards the more sophisticated learning goals identified at score point 4.0. The class has been discussing the idea that Cromwell was the most powerful soldier of his time.

Extract 9.1
1   T: What do we call a soldier who leads a coup d'état?
2   S1:   Rebels.
3   T: ((writing 'coup d'état' on board)) This is a French word.
4   When someone finishes with the power, the political power,
5   with the system, the political system. Pardon?
6   S1:   Rebels.
7   T: Pardon?
8   S1:   Rebels.
9   T: Erm no it's another word which has got more important
10   connotations than rebel. It's not only a rebel. Someone
11   who may cause a war.
12   We've got some examples in contemporary history.
13   S1:   Dictator.
14   T: Dictator, that's right. A dictator, okay?
15   Okay, I wrote it here, but it's just a break, okay?
16   Just to see the similarities between a twentieth century
17   dictator and a soldier in the seventeenth century who leads
18   a coup d'état. Okay?
19   But remember that these comparisons are sometimes very
20   dangerous in history.

At line 1, the teacher probes the students' current state of knowledge by asking them to come up with a word for a soldier who leads a coup d'état. In rejecting *rebel* (line 9), she is giving immediate feedback. But she doesn't just reject the word, but points out why it is not adequate (lines 9–11). A word with wider or more significant connotations is needed. At line 12, she shifts the focus of attention to contemporary history. This is very likely to have helped another student to come up with *dictator* and she accepts this term (lines 13–14). However, she quickly draws her students' attention to the fact that although she wrote this word on the board, *it's just a break* (line 15). She then goes on to highlight an aspect of being a historian, the fact that it can be dangerous to make these kinds of comparisons (lines 19–20). By doing this she is going beyond the transmission of historical facts and the making of historical comparisons to position her students in the role of historians. Historians have to be careful about the comparisons they make. In this classroom, these 'breaks' were the teacher's way of signalling to the students that she was going beyond the strictly expected learning goals for any particular curricular content. In terms of the assessment scale, this would be level 4.0 content, and in having these breaks, she was pushing the class to achieve at this level by reflection on their role as apprentice historians.

This example of instructional feedback has elements of dynamic assessment, or assessment as teaching. She is not just probing what the students know, but is using classroom interaction to mediate between their current levels of understanding and those which are appropriate for history as a practice. It is not just getting facts right or wrong, but adopting appropriate habits of mind, such as comparing historical epochs, but exercising caution when one does so. Dynamic assessment, as classroom interaction, consists of keeping track of where students are in relation to the key learning goals, but pushing them within their ZPDs to achieve more advanced goals. And it is not just the student engaged in interaction with the teacher who can benefit. As Marzano puts it, 'assessments used for instructional feedback are scaffolds that gradually increase the knowledge level of the class as a whole' (2010: 32). In CLIL, language is deeply involved in this process. In this example it revolves around the meanings of important terms such as *coup d'état*, *rebel* or *dictator*. But at other times the meaning–wording relations essential to constructing the content could revolve around grammar, or academic language functions such as explanations or definitions (Dalton-Puffer, 2007).

The second example of classroom interaction as instructional feedback comes from a CLIL physics lesson (grade 10, ages 15–16). The topic of the lesson is the use of the lens formula to calculate the position of images when light is refracted through a lens. The specific objective in this lesson is to show how this position can be calculated using a drawing. The teacher first demonstrates by doing a drawing on the board, and then asks the class to do a similar drawing:

Extract 9.2
1   T: Erm, I want you to do er two things in your own drawing, 2   and use 2 or 3 minutes with that. <div align="right">(*cont.*)</div>

3	First, calculate with the lens formula what the image
4	distance would be and check that in your drawing, does
5	that match?
6	Erm, I also want you to have a look at the size of the candle
7	and compare that with the size of the image. Yeah?
8	A few minutes. ((walks around class))
9	T: ((to individual student)) Are you managing okay?
10	S: *Het klopt niet.* (Dutch: It's not right.) I did something wrong.
11	T: Did you do anything wrong?
12	S: In your drawing it seems to be ...
13	T: Yeah, but yours is better.
14	S: Okay so this one ...
15	T: This is just a sketch.
16	S: So this one has to be smaller okay.
17	T: If you have a look at my drawing you think that that looks fine,
18	the lines are straight, but although they're just a little bit
19	out of place, the differences can be very big.
20	So for you it's important that you have sharp pencils
21	and you use a set square.
22	S: *Helemaal geen toch, kan je dit toch niet tellen,* English.
23	(Dutch: None at all, right, you can't count this, can you?)
24	T: It should be okay. Erm, I saw several outcomes.
25	Most of the outcomes were the same.
26	The image distance is 5.3 centimetres.
27	And most yeah, ladies, can I go on? Yeah you're right.
28	L commented a little bit and he's right,
29	but I'm going to do it a little bit differently. 7 point zero, is
30	over here and 3 point zero is over there, so I have 5.3 over
31	here yeah?
32	Erm if you made your drawing very precise,
33	then you will find that this distance is 5.3 centimetres erm,
34	and some of you said, what did I do wrong
35	because it if you've done it right, you will find that the
36	image the image which is formed over here, which is a little
37	bit smaller than the object size, erm, in my drawing it looks
38	like it's more or less the same or even an image which is a
39	little bit bigger.
40	That's because I drew all the lines just ya, well, without a
41	set square without a sharp pencil,
42	so this is not that it's not a proper drawing,
43	it's not a proper construction, it's just a sketch.

At lines 1–7 we can see how the teacher sets up a task and builds clear expectations about the learning goals: they need to use the lens formula to calculate the image distance and check it with their drawing, and they have to compare the sizes of the candle and the image. The teacher has already done a drawing as a sketch but throughout the extract we can see an expectation that the students better her performance. By getting them to do this task, she can see where they are, not just in applying the appropriate content knowledge, but also in using the appropriate tools (*set square, sharp pencil*). It can be seen as an example of dynamic assessment, as its function is not just to give the students feedback about what they might have got wrong, but also to provide appropriate mediation to improve their performance. This mediation can be in the form of encouragement (*Yeah, but yours is better* – line 13), suggestions as to proper tools and procedures (lines 20–21), or comparisons between one's own performance and that of others in the classroom, including the teacher (lines 37–43).

In CLIL terms, it is clear that the mediation here is focused on content, not language. And indeed, in terms of mode, language is not the main means used to complete this task. Drawing and mathematical symbols are much more important. However, this does not take away from the crucial role that language is playing here in knowledge construction, assessment of performance and giving feedback. Even though the task itself depends on other modes for its completion, it is through language that the following is done:

a. The criteria for adequate performance of the task are established (lines 1–7).
b. Information is gathered about the students' current state as regards completing the task (line 8 onwards).
c. Encouragement is given (line 13).
d. Information is given about the extent to which the performance was adequate (both for individuals and the whole class) (lines 27–28).
e. Information is given about how performance could be improved by using appropriate tools (lines 20–21).

And we can see that the teacher has to use quite specific language in providing instructional feedback. She needs to describe the lines in the drawing, for example whether they are straight or *out of place* (line 19). She needs to talk about relative size and precision, and the tools used for achieving this (sharp pencils, set square) (lines 37–43). She is quite subtly bringing out the distinction between a sketch and a more precise drawing, and implicitly, the purposes to which either can be put.

In this example, then, we can see the crucial role that language plays in the giving (and getting) of instructional feedback as formative or dynamic assessment. In CLIL, the focus need not always be on assessing the students' language output, but on gaining a greater awareness and control of how to use language in classroom assessment for the good of learners. This means that giving this kind of content-focused instructional feedback as part of classroom formative assessment is a crucial language skill for CLIL teachers. As it is highly intensive in terms of interaction, it can place a strain on some CLIL teachers' language skills. Teachers themselves can be aware of this, as one teacher of design technology explains:

> When they are starting building whatever, making whatever they have to make in the workshop, they don't know how to get started with the thing. They don't know where to start from. So I should help every team work more particularly. I may tell you this is where I find myself not so prepared to teach in English. When you're in the classroom I manage with the language I have to use very very well. But here I find that if I don't find a certain word that's – I don't know – because it's quite particular specific language you have to use. 'You have to put this thing into this hole and drill this' or whatever. And I don't find myself comfortable in the workshop speaking in English.
>
> (Teacher interview, authors' data)

In fact, data in the corpus of this teacher's interactions with students in the workshop show that he was well able to use English to give this type of instructional feedback. This suggests that professional development for CLIL teachers should help them become more aware of how language can be used for formative assessment in different interactional formats (see Chapter 2). They could thus gain a more realistic understanding of what they are already doing well, and where they could improve.

9.6 Widening the range of assessment methods in CLIL

In the two previous sections we looked at two functions of formative assessment in CLIL: the use of a scale to provide formative (and eventually summative) scores, and the giving of instructional feedback as a kind of dynamic assessment. In this section, we shift the focus from the functions of assessment to the different methods for eliciting students' performance. Our argument here is that, in CLIL, we need to follow good educational practice by using a wide range of assessment methods. There are several reasons for doing this which are particularly important in CLIL. On the one hand, we need to maintain credibility by using the kinds of assessment methods which are accepted within the subjects we teach. On the other hand, we need to make sure that our assessment methods are fair to students who are not only learning the subject, but also learning the language through which it is taught. In this section we argue that it is possible to use assessment techniques which do not compromise the content-related learning goals, but which at the same time do not add unnecessary 'invisible' language elements that may contaminate the fairness of the assessment.

It is important to note here that the content–language integrated scale that we introduce in this chapter is neutral as to the technique used for eliciting the knowledge and skills to be assessed. Scales can be constructed for any type of activity, including essays, oral presentations, labelling, drawing and physical performance in subjects such as music, dance, drama and physical education. All of these have their place in CLIL, as CLIL experiences cover a wide range of subjects in the curriculum. The important thing is for CLIL teachers to be clear-headed about the role of language in any assessment activity and its possible effects on students' performance. This will entail careful choice of assessment tasks, and the necessity to choose from a broader range of task types.

The argument that we should broaden the range of assessment techniques when our students are language learners is not a new one. In an influential paper, Short (1993) proposed using a range of alternative assessment measures in integrated language and content instruction. As she argued, the introduction of alternative assessment methods is already entirely justified as part of general educational reform in which assessment is more clearly linked to classroom practices. These include such methods as performance-based tests, portfolios, journals, projects and observation checklists. However, as Short points out, even the entirely justified use of these alternative assessment procedures can cause problems when the students are English language learners. As she puts it, 'Complications arise first because teachers must determine whether the language or the content is being assessed in these alternative measures. Then teachers must distinguish between the language and content knowledge of the students and decide if one is interfering with the demonstration of the other' (Short, 1993: 633).

Widening the range of assessment procedures will allow language learners to show their content knowledge and skills in different ways. If CLIL teachers have at their disposal a broad repertoire of assessment techniques, they will be better placed to avoid those in which language issues may unnecessarily interfere with students' demonstrations of content knowledge and skills. They can choose assessment methods in which they are more able to control the ways in which students use language in carrying them out. One way of doing this is to vary the modes in which students present information, for example by using tables, diagrams and other graphic organisers. Language will then not be the only means of demonstrating knowledge or skill, and its role in any assessment task can be more clearly specified. Reliance on one type of assessment, such as essays, while already questionable from a content-learning perspective, will be doubly so from a CLIL perspective as it may place linguistic barriers on students' demonstration of learning.

Not only can we expand the range of assessment techniques we use, but we can also more precisely define just what aspects of content we are assessing. Doing so will allow us to find a better match between aspects of content or language to be assessed and the means of doing so. With this purpose in mind, Short introduces a matrix in which different areas (problem solving, content-area skills, concept comprehension, language use, communication skills, individual behaviour, group behaviour and attitude) can be measured using a range of alternative assessment techniques (skill checklists and reading / writing inventories, anecdotal records and teacher observations, student self-evaluations, portfolios, performance-based tasks, essay writing, oral reports and interviews). Unlike the content–language scale we propose in this chapter, one of the aims of the matrix is to allow teachers to focus on either content or language, according to their needs. In any case, the choice of areas to be assessed would be a matter for CLIL educators in any specific local context to decide. The main point, and this is driven home by Short in her argument and her practical examples, is the need to use a range of alternative methods to give students a fair chance of demonstrating their knowledge and skills.

To give a flavour of the approach taken by Short, here is an example of matching the learning objective of concept comprehension with the assessment technique of a performance-based task:

Concept comprehension: Performance

Objective: To measure student ability to distinguish between regular and irregular polygons

In a geometry class, the teacher distributes paper, scissors, yarn, and several geoboards. Because the teacher wants to minimize the language barrier that might interfere with the students' performance, the teacher provides written and oral instructions for each task. Beginning with the paper and scissors, students are instructed to cut out geometric shapes, such as an isosceles triangle, an irregular pentagon, and a circle. Next, they are told to create a square, a rectangle, and an irregular six-sided figure with their geoboards and yarn. Scanning the room, the teacher can quickly assess the students' comprehension of these polygons.

(Short 1993: 646)

Note here that the teacher has taken the conscious decision to provide both written and oral instructions for each task, so as to minimise the risk of language problems interfering with performance. However, it need not be the case that all assessment methods used in CLIL need to minimise language use. It may well be that students have been well prepared for a certain way of using language, for example by receiving instruction about and practising a genre that is important in their subject. In these cases, the assessment could be designed to allow students to show off this knowledge and skill. The important thing to note is that, whatever the role of language in any assessment method we use, we need to be clear-headed and explicit about it. It should not be an invisible trap that makes the assessment unfair, by not allowing CLIL learners to demonstrate their skills and understanding. This involves CLIL educators increasing the range of assessment procedures they use, and at the same time gaining a clear understanding of the role of language in each, so that they can choose the most suitable methods for the aspects of content learning they want to measure.

9.7 Conclusion

In this chapter, we have considered the 'what', the 'why' and the 'how' of assessment in CLIL, with a particular focus on the role of language. In terms of the 'what' we strongly agree with other writers that the focus of assessment should primarily be on content. However, throughout this book we have shown that language has an enabling role in constructing content knowledge, and in this chapter we have highlighted the importance of taking this into account when considering assessment. We have suggested that, in formative assessment, CLIL teachers could focus on this enabling role of language, so that language would not explicitly be assessed for summative purposes. This would mean that CLIL students would receive only one grade, which would reflect their level of achievement of content-related learning objectives. However, if it is decided that language should be more formally assessed, we agree with Short that it is better to focus on a single objective, whether content or language, than to give separate grades for content and language (1993: 634). As for the 'why', we have indicated two main purposes of assessment: the provision of formative (which can lead to summative) scores by use of a content–language integrated scale, and the giving of instructional feedback, which can be respecified as mediation during dynamic assessment. In discussing the 'how' of assessment, we highlighted the necessity of broadening the range of assessment techniques used, in order to maintain credibility within the different subject areas taught through CLIL and to be fair to CLIL students as language learners.

We began this chapter by mentioning the idea that we live in an 'assessment society'. This can have a negative effect if assessment means the application of high-stakes tests which have been developed outside the local CLIL context. However, throughout this chapter, we hope to have shown that assessment, when seen as formative classroom assessment *for* learning or even *as* teaching, can be an incredibly powerful tool in the hands of CLIL educators. As with any tool, we need to become experts in its use through practice. This means that the skills of backward design, particularly those of writing clear statements about language to go alongside content-learning goals, the skills of providing content–language integrated feedback and mediation and the skills of selecting and designing appropriate CLIL-friendly assessment methods need to be painstakingly gained by CLIL educators through professional development and classroom teaching experience.

Questions and tasks for reflection and discussion

1. Look at the six assessment activities from Marzano (2010: 24) in the box below. As you can see, a range of different assessment techniques is used. However, the activities were designed for non-CLIL classrooms, so it is probable that the teacher didn't need to think so carefully about the language component of each one. Now:

   (a) Identify the assessment techniques used (you don't need to be too specific, just a general description of the type).
   (b) Identify how the students would use language in performing the activity (reading, writing, listening, speaking).
   (c) Identify some of the language needed to do the activity and consider any difficulties CLIL students might have.
   (d) Discuss ways in which, if necessary, you could modulate the language component of the task, or even change the task, to make it more suitable for a specific group of CLIL learners.

ASSESSMENT ACTIVITIES

   (a) Mathematics: To assess the students' ability to make reasonable estimations of weight, students are given four objects each. They must consider the weight of each object and write down estimations they consider to be reasonable using the units of measure studied in

class. They must also write brief justifications for their answers. At
the end of class, the students turn in their assessments.

(b) Science: To assess the students' understanding of the systems of
the human body, the teacher provides them with a blank outline
of a human body. He asks them to graphically locate the heart,
the lungs, the liver, and the stomach. They are also asked to write
down the system associated with each organ and provide brief
explanations of that system's major purpose.

(c) Social studies: To assess the students' knowledge of United States
geography, the teacher provides a blank map of the country.
Students must write in the names of as many states as they can in
the time allotted.

(d) Physical education: To assess the students' ability to hit a golf ball,
the teacher asks each student to demonstrate a golf swing using a
driver. After hitting the ball, each student is asked to evaluate his
or her own swing and name one thing he or she could have done to
make it better. After analyzing the swing, the student is asked to
demonstrate again, this time thinking in advance about what he or
she needs to improve on.

(e) Art: To assess the students' ability to draw using perspective,
the teacher presents them with three-dimensional objects such
as cylinders, prisms and cubes. They are asked to choose one
object and use the relevant elements of perspective to draw it as
realistically as possible within the allotted time.

(f) Technology: To assess the students' ability to use PowerPoint, the
teacher assigns students the task of creating a brief PowerPoint
presentation designed to teach their classmates about one of their
hobbies. Students begin the task in class and are asked to finish
the projects at home in preparation for in-class presentations the
next day.

(Marzano, 2010: 24)

2. Look at the three students' responses to the assessment task we discussed in Section 9.4 of this chapter. Here is the task question again:
'Give an account of Darwin's journey on *The Beagle* and explain his
theory of evolution.' Using the assessment scale for this task which
we gave on page 298, assign each text a grade. If you are working in
a group, discuss your grades and the reasons for your decisions. Be
sure to refer in detail to the students' texts.

Student Text A

Darwin was a naturalist. He wrote "The Origin of Species". He started discovering his theory in the HMS Beagle. The statements of his theory were:

- Organisms produce a large number of offspring and there is always a naturally occuring variation among this offspring.
- Not all of them can survive. There is a struggle for life. They have to compete for food, space and adapt to avoid predators and diseases. Only the fittest will survive. Survival of the fittest.
- The fittest is selected by nature. Natural selection.

If a individual has traits that help it to survive in a certain environment, then it will breed and pass on its genes to its offspring. On the other hand, individuals without useful traits are less likely to survive and to breed. Natural selection chooses the fittest. Therefore, the next generation will have a larger proportion of these better adapted individuals and so on.

Student Text B

Charles Darwin was an English naturalist. He emerged on a trip in HSM Beagle for 5 years around the world. He was fascinated with vegetation and animals that he had seen during that trip. When he came back, he developed his theory of evolution and published his book, which had great success.

STATEMENTS OF HIS THEORY

- Individuals produce a large number of offspring, which are going to inherit the same characteristics as its parents.
- Individuals are not the same. There's a struggle for life. They compete for food, space, mate, ... and they adapt to avoid predators, diseases. The fittest ones are going to survive.
- The survival of the fittest occurs by natural selection.

Student Text C

Charles Darwin was an English naturalist who wrote "On the Origin of the Species" in 1859. Evolution occured thanks to "Natural Selection", the survival of the fittest. Darwin saw that species had

(cont.)

large ammounts of offspring and had to struggle for life, there was a shortage of food, there were not enough resources for ~~everyon~~ all of them, they had to avoid diseases and predators ... Species with features which helped them to survive in a certain environment were more likely to breed. There was a higher percentage of superior species breeding, their genes passed from one generation to an other, so finally some difference was appreciated between an old form of a species and a new form of it. It had evolved.

3. In Extract 9.3, a design technology teacher is talking to a small group of students (grade 7, ages 12–13) who are beginning work on the task of making a wooden toy. Can you identify any features of instructional feedback or dynamic assessment in the teacher's talk?

Extract 9.3	
1	T: You are working very well you know.
2	They ((group at another table)) aren't doing any previous
3	drawing. You are doing very well. What's your drawing?
4	Is this one the toy you wanna do?
5	You start, saw it, and then you do another one just like
6	this one. And then in the meantime you can saw the arms
7	and the legs.
8	SS: Okay.

References

Anderson, L. W. and Krathwohl, D. R. (eds.) (2001) *A Taxonomy for Learning, Teaching, and Assessing: A Revision of Bloom's Taxonomy of Educational Objectives*, New York: Longman.

Assessment Reform Group. (2002) *Assessment for Learning: 10 Principles*, Cambridge: University of Cambridge School of Education.

Benson, P. (2011) *Teaching and Researching Autonomy in Language Learning* (2nd ed.), Harlow, UK: Longman.

Black, P. and Wiliam, D. (1998) 'Inside the black box: Raising standards through classroom assessment', *The Phi Delta Kappan*, 80, 2, 139–44, 146–8.

Broadfoot, P. and Black, P. (2004) 'Redefining assessment? The first ten years of assessment in education', *Assessment in Education: Principles, Policy & Practice*, 11, 1, 7–26.

Byrnes, H. (2008) 'Assessing content and language', in Hornberger, N. H. (ed.) *Encyclopedia of language and education*, Boston, MA: Springer, pp. 2182–97.

Coyle, D., Hood, P. and Marsh, D. (2010) *CLIL: Content and Language Integrated Learning*, Cambridge: Cambridge University Press.

Cumming, A. (2009) 'Language assessment in education: Tests, curricula, and teaching', in Spolsky, B. (ed.) *Language policy and assessment, Annual Review of Applied Linguistics*, **29**, 90–100.

Cummins, J. (1979) 'Cognitive / academic language proficiency, linguistic interdependence, the optimum age question and some other matters', *Working Papers on Bilingualism*, **19**, 121–9.

Dalton-Puffer, C. (2007) *Discourse in Content and Language Integrated Learning (CLIL) Classrooms*, Amsterdam and Philadelphia, PA: John Benjamins.

Gardner, J. (2006) *Assessment and Learning*, Thousand Oaks, CA: Sage Publications.

Gibbons, P. (2003) 'Mediating language learning: Teacher interactions with ESL students in a content-based classroom', *TESOL Quarterly*, **37**, 2, 247–73.

Gibbons, P. (2006) *Bridging Discourses in the ESL Classroom: Students, Teachers and Researchers*. London: Continuum.

Harlen, W. (2005) 'Teachers' summative practices and assessment for learning: Tensions and synergies', *Curriculum Journal*, **16**, 2, 207–23.

Harlen, W. (2007) *Assessment of Learning*, London: SAGE.

Harlen, W. and Crick, R. D. (2003) 'Testing and motivation for learning', *Assessment in Education: Principles, Policy & Practice*, **10**, 2, 169–207.

Heritage, M. (2008) *Learning Progressions: Supporting Instruction and Formative Assessment*, Washington, DC: Council of Chief State School Officers. Retrieved 3 April 2011 from www.k12.wa.us/assessment/ClassroomAssessmentIntegration/pubdocs/FASTLearningProgressions.pdf

Hönig, I. (2010) *Assessment in CLIL: Theoretical and empirical research*. Saarbrücken, Germany: VDM Verlag Dr. Müller.

Lantolf, J. P. and Poehner, M. E. (2008) 'Dynamic assessment', in Hornberger, N. H. (ed.) *Encyclopedia of language and education*, New York: Springer, pp. 2406–17.

Leung, C. (2007) 'Dynamic assessment: Assessment *for* and *as* teaching?' *Language Assessment Quarterly*, **4**, 3, 257–78.

Llinares, A. and Morton, T. (2010) 'Historical explanations as situated practice in content and language integrated learning', *Classroom Discourse*, **1**, 1, 46–65.

Low, M. (2010) 'Teachers and texts: Judging what English language learners know from what they say', in Paran, A. and Sercu, L. (eds.) *Testing the Untestable in Language Education*, Bristol: Multilingual Matters, pp. 241–55.

Marzano, R. J. (2010) *Formative assessment & standards-based grading*. Bloomington, IN: Solution Tree.

Marzano, R. J. and Kendall, J. S. (2007) *The new taxonomy of educational objectives* (2nd ed.), Thousand Oaks, CA: Corwin Press.

McNamara, T. F. and Roever, C. (2006) *Language Testing: The Social Dimension*, Malden, MA: Blackwell.

Mohan, B. and Beckett, G. H. (2003) 'A functional approach to research on content-based language learning: Recasts in causal explanations', *The Modern Language Journal*, 87, 3, 421–32.

Mohan, B., Leung, C. and Slater, T. (2010) 'Assessing language and content: A functional perspective, in Paran, A. and Sercu, L. (ed.) *Testing the Untestable in Language Education*, Bristol: Multilingual Matters, pp. 217–40.

Polias, J. (2003) *ESL Scope and Scales*, Adelaide, South Australia: DECS Publishing.

Popham, W. J. (2008) *Transformative assessment*, Alexandria, VA: Association for Supervision and Curriculum Development.

Rea-Dickins, P. (2008) 'Classroom-based language assessment', in Hornberger, N. H. (ed.) *Encyclopedia of language and education*, New York: Springer, pp. 2391–405.

Serra, C. (2007) 'Assessing CLIL at primary school: A longitudinal study', *International Journal of Bilingual Education and Bilingualism*, 10, 5, 582–602.

Sharpe, T. (2006) '"Unpacking" scaffolding: Identifying discourse and multi-modal strategies that support learning', *Language and Education*, 20, 3, 211–31.

Short, D. (1993) 'Assessing integrated language and content instruction', *TESOL Quarterly*, 27, 4, 627–56.

Vygotsky, L. S. (1978) *Mind in society: The development of higher psychological processes*, Cambridge, MA, and London: Harvard University Press.

Wiggins, G. P. and McTighe, J. (2005) *Understanding by Design* (2nd ed.), Alexandria, VA: Association for Supervision and Curriculum Development.

Appendix: Answer key to tasks

Chapter 1

Task 1

The box contains some examples of features of the regulative register. There may be more, but this is a representative sample.

Action in regulative register	Example
Stopping an activity	*Can we just stop here for a minute* (line 1)
Getting attention	*Okay listen* (line 2)
Requesting actions	*Can you put your pencils down* (line 2)
Announcing upcoming instruction	*What I want you to do next* (line 3)
Telling students what they are going to do	*You are going to choose another pair, at the most two other pairs. And you're going to ask them about their answers. Etc.* (lines 4–14)
Checking understanding	*Ok?* (lines 10, 13 and 14) *Right?* (line 11)
Organising the physical space of the classroom	*So for instance this group over here, this pair over there* (line 7).
Summarising and recapping instructions given so far	*So just compare your answers and three no more groups ok? Right?* (line 10)

Task 3

Extract 1.13 is laid out in the table with the regulative register in the left-hand column and the instructional register in the right-hand column. The extract shows how the two registers can be interwoven in classroom interaction. The teacher seems to be addressing student K (but of course what she says may well be intended for the whole class). The main activity going on is her explanation about the behaviour of light rays, but this is interrupted twice by stretches of the regulative register. In the first, the teacher is directing K's attention away from another problem, presumably towards the explanation she is now giving. In the second segment of regulative register, the teacher acknowledges difficulty in keeping attention due to weather conditions outside (very hot? snowing?), and makes a plea for more time to give her explanation. There is also a warning, that if the students don't stop talking, they will have to put up with more explanation. The extract shows the subtle ways in which teachers can shift in and out of the two registers, and highlights some of the L2 interactive skills that CLIL teachers need to have.

Regulative register	Instructional register
	K diverging lines don't intersect in infinity, just parallel lines, but, this situation ...
K, K leave that problem for now, you can return to the problem later on erm,	
	I still can use this situation in with this lense for something else, because imagine, imagine that someone is sitting over here looking with an eye and the eye is, through a nerve, connected to the brain, ((laughter)) yeah these light rays ((laughter))
it's hard to keep up the attention (yeah it's the weather outside) erm I think I need I need five more minutes please be concentrated for five more minutes and then you can go to work by yourselves erm, but if you keep talking, if you keep talking then I need more than five minutes.	
	The light rays hit the eye, an eye connected to the brain, well, brains can think, and a brain well, it's a little bit stupid because this brain doesn't know that this light ray is refracted over here. A brain always thinks that light rays just travel in a straight line, so his brain thinks that this light ray comes from this direction

Chapter 2

Task 1

In Extract 2.10, the interaction moves from an interactive / dialogic communicative system (lines 1–29) to a non-interactive / authoritative one (lines 30–49). From lines 1–29, the teacher is exploring the class's ideas about whether bacteria are helpful or harmful. The interaction is dialogic because the students are able to express what they think, and this is encouraged by the teacher (at lines 1–2, 8, 10, 13, 15, 17, 19, 22). However, in engaging in this dialogue, the teacher hears that at least some students think bread is made with bacteria. In order to correct this misconception, she changes the communicative approach to a non-interactive / authoritative one (only she speaks, and the information is not the students' ideas, but scientific, or *vertical* knowledge). In fact, the teacher even signals that she is doing this by saying, *I'm telling you that right now*, at line 32.

Task 2

Recall that Haneda and Wells gave the following three reasons for using dialogic teaching for learners using an additional language to study school subjects: they receive comprehensible input and can produce comprehensible output; they can learn appropriate social and communicative strategies for expressing content and participating in the classroom community; and they come into contact with different perspectives on topics. The students who speak in Extract 2.11 are getting the opportunity to produce comprehensible output in quite extended contributions. At times their lexical and grammatical resources are limited, but they are able to use them to present a range of causes and consequences of the Plague. In putting these resources to use, they are also practising strategies for appropriately expressing content and participating in the community. Here, they are chaining together a succession of ideas elicited by a prompt from the teacher. As for the third reason, the students are being exposed to a range of different ideas about the topic, and sometimes the same ideas expressed in different ways. For example, at lines 13–14, S4 says that people who caught the plague, *were, eh, let alone for not to, eh, contage, the eh, the disease*. At lines 27–30, S3 expresses a similar idea in a different, and improved, manner: *And if you were infected by the Black Death, the people of the, of your family let you apart, to die, because if not you passed the Black Death to another member of the family.* Here, *let* is substituted for the more appropriate *left*, and S4's borrowing from Spanish *contage* becomes *passed to*. This is also an example, then, of S4 receiving comprehensible input, and of

S3 producing comprehensible output. These opportunities would argu-ably not appear in a class where there was no dialogic teaching.

Chapter 3

Task 3

Consider the following questions:

- Identify the type:

  (a) How are places destroyed by natural disasters? *Display question for explanation*
  (b) Do you think there were economic reasons? *Display question for facts / referential question for opinion*
  (c) What do you like most about our ancient civilisations, Egypt and Mesopotamia? *Referential question for opinion* And why? *Metacognitive question*
  (d) What is the name of this tool here? *Display question for facts*

- and decide which ones involve higher cognitive and / or communica-tive involvement and give reasons why:

Display questions for facts, as in example (d), usually trigger short answers. The answer expected in example (d) is a single lexical item.

   On the other hand, questions for explanation as in (a) require longer and more elaborated responses by the learner. Questions for opinion followed by a metacognitive question are expected to involve higher cognitive and communicative involvement. Questions (b) or (c) could be followed by short responses but the metacognitive question follow-ing in (c) would prompt a more complex / elaborate response. Question (b) could be identified as both display question for facts and / or referen-tial question for opinion. In fact, the teacher might be asking a question for fact: 'Were there economic reasons? And if so, which were they?', but the way the question is formulated could make the students feel they are not just displaying facts and their opinion is important. This again should trigger more cognitive and communicative involvement.

Task 4

Stage:	End-of-topic discussion
Questions:	Display question for facts (formulated as a refer-ential question): *Do you remember the periods of the Middle Ages?*, followed by a display question for reason: *Why was there a rebirth of cities?*,

and finally a referential question, *What about urban life in the Middle Ages and, your present urban life?* So, the questions are sequenced in degree of complexity.

Scaffolding: The teacher reformulates the questions to make sure they are understood. In line 2, in the first sentence, she focuses on the keyword at the end of the sentence: ... *some periods*, and then she formulates a question about the periods.

Repair: In turn 6 (lines 8–10), the student does not respond to the teacher's question correctly. However, instead of evaluating the student's response negatively, the teacher acknowledges the response and persists in asking for the reason: *Do you remember why?*

She uses a functional recast by reformulating the student's response in a more academic way (see Chapter 6), *So that is the, em, the reason of the rebirth of cities.*

Interaction patterns: IRF pattern with expanding feedback by the teacher in line 7.

Chapter 4

Task 4

Text 4.32 is a procedure. The stages are given below.

Text 4.32	
	SKILLS
AIM	Giving 4-figure and 6-figure references
METHOD	1:25 000 and 1:50 000 maps have a grid of numbered squares on them. To see how a 4-figure grid reference is given,
	look at the grid in Source A and follow these instructions to give the reference for the red shaded square.
	• 47 is the line left of the square. • 16 is the line below the square.
	Put these two numbers together
RESTATEMENT OF AIM	and you have a 4-figure grid reference: 4716.

Task 5

Text 4.33 is basically a historical recount, and could be analysed as you
see below.

Text 4.33	
ORIENTATION	South Africa is changing rapidly. These changes are affecting employment opportunities.
RECORD OF EVENTS	White minority rule, which began in the 17th century, was overthrown and black majority rule came into being in 1994. Before then white people held all the positions of power and influence – they were the politicians, factory managers, landowners and farmers. The black majority relied on the white minority for employment, usually in low-paid jobs as farmhands, miners and labourers. Eventually civil riots and international protests and boycotts led to the white minority government relinquishing power, abandoning apartheid, and allowing each person a vote.
REORIENTATION	Since the election of a black president in 1994 the employment situation for some black people has improved. However, many people have not yet seen progress.

The Orientation focuses the reader on the purpose of the Recount, and
gives the context for the series of Events, sequenced in time. Finally, the
Reorientation comments on the significance of the Recount, here pointing out the limits of the changes described in the Events.

Task 6

Text 4.34 is organised in the same way as a classifying report, starting
off with a definition.

Text 4.34	
DEFINITION	What was an estate? An estate was a very large group or class of people. In France there were three estates. It was difficult for a person to move from one estate to another.
CLASSIFICATION	**The Three Estates** The First Estate The **clergy** made up the First estate. They included archbishops, bishops, abbots, parish priests, monks and nuns. [...]
	The Second Estate The **nobles** made up the Second Estate. They were nobles by birth, and were landowners [...]
	The Third Estate This group consisted of **everybody else** in France. Some **middle-class** people, such as merchants, bankers, and doctors, were quite wealthy but they had no chance of power. They had to pay taxes.
	The **peasants** and the town workers paid heavy taxes. [...]

Task 7

Text 4.35 is a sequential explanation.

Text 4.35	
IDENTIFICATION	**Atoll** These develop around islands.
IMPLICATIONAL SEQUENCE PHASE 1	Fringing reefs grow in a circle attached to the land.
PHASE 2	Sea-level rise or subsidence of the land causes the coral to grow at the height of the rising sea level to reach the light.
PHASE 3	This eventually forms a ring of coral reefs with a lagoon replacing the island in the centre.

Chapter 5

Task 2

Questions like the following could be included in the class discussion around this text:

• What two things do we protect if we are interested in conservation of the planet? What are the two types of biodiversity?
• What are Greenpeace and the WWF (World Wide Fund for Nature) examples of? Where do these movements operate? What is the purpose of the movements?
• What sort of things would you include in *the requirements of the present generation*?
• What does *the same* refer to?
• Where do the resources come from?
• How fast can we use the resources? What must we do when we use some resources?
• When we manage resources, what guides our actions? What are the objectives of the policies we design?
• What is the writer contrasting in these two phrases?

Task 3

The first sentence in the paragraph generalises from the facts which are given later. Some questions to help the students recognise this could be:

• What wars are mentioned in the paragraph? Who fought whom, and when?
• These conflicts shared similar aims – what were they?
• What sort of changes would those aims involve?
• What was the purpose of the rebellion by the Irish in 1798?
• Which institution would be affected if the government was made more democratic? And in what way?
• Which part of the first sentence makes this explicit?
• What was the reaction of the British government to the conflicts?
• What did the government do as a result of that reaction?
• Which part of the first sentence makes this explicit?

Chapter 6

Task 1

A reformulation could include more relational processes (verbs of being), turn clauses into phrases and use nominalisations. For example, *With the arrival* of mercantilism, there was an attempt by the different countries to increase exportation and decrease their imports for the purpose of self-sufficiency. But with the arrival of capitalism, after mercantilism, inflation appeared due to rises in prices. This had an impact on people's economies.

Task 2

In the first case, there is a relation of purpose: People build their house (of those affected by the disaster) in order to help them. The second *and* introduces consequence and time: After this help / and because of this they can start a new life. The third *and* indicates the addition of another clause. Finally, the fourth *and* expresses contrast: *While some people pay ... , others don't ... .*

Task 3

1. S: She makes a special box to make the neck
   T: Neck ... ? *Elicitation* (focusing on vocabulary)
   S: Neck
   T: Necklace, ok? *Explicit correction* (focusing on vocabulary)
2. S: Because more people lived there
   T: Because of population growth, that's right *Functional recast* (using a prepositional phrase *because of population growth* instead of a clause *because more people lived there*)
   S: Yes, population growth
3. S: Some peasants were slaves (non-standard pronunciation)
   T: Sorry? *Clarification request* (focusing on pronunciation)
   S: Some peasants ... were slaves (standard pronunciation)

Chapter 7

Task 2

1 S1: *Okay, first question*, give a short definition of feudalism.
2 S2: Eh ... well, it's a society, they live on agriculture, in which
3   land is power, and it was a political arrest because of
4   convenient pattern.
5 S1: It's also developing during the ninth, tenth eleventh and
6   twelfth century and
7 S2: and if it's an exchange of duty, communication following
8   some rules.
9 S3: It's also ((reading)) the social, economic and political
10   system that developed in western Europe during the ninth,
11   tenth and eleventh century

12 S2: *Yeah but we know* that it is also the relationship between
13   the vassal and the lord
14 S1: Where they all got something from each other ... yes
15 S2: *The short definition* ... eh.eh. It's the social, economic and
16   political system that developed in western Europe
17 S1: *Yes but we* first *have to say* in what consists?

There are examples of interpersonal features mainly <u>for operating in the classroom</u>, especially in group work: *Okay, first question, give a short definition of feudalism* (line 1). *Okay* is used to mark topic initiation and focus on the first question, characteristic of the regulative register. Topic initiation is also used in line 15 (*The short definition* ...). Another example of the regulative register is, *Yes, but we first have to say in what consists* (line 12), with the use of the modal of obligation: *have to.*

The use of *yeah yes but* (lines 12 and 17) to express disagreement and the use of personal pronouns (*we* in lines 12 and 17) are characteristic of the language for <u>socialising in a group-work activity</u>.

Appearance of mental and verbal processes (*know* in line 12 and *say* in line 17), which are not common in students' language in the instructional register (compared to other processes like material or relational), but are used for operating in the classroom and socialising in group work.

Chapter 8

Task 1

While the two students both include humans in their answers, the teacher's reformulations eliminate them. S1 includes the generalised group *the people*, and answers using two clauses, *the people believe that ... and now is ...* . The teacher reformulates this using an abstraction as subject *the beliefs* and one clause *the beliefs have changed*. The same happens with S2's answer: in the reformulation, humans are no longer the subject of the verb. This move towards the disappearance of humans as agents is typical of the discourse of history.

Task 2

In the first definition, the student writer represents what is a process in reality as a process in language, using a high density of verbs: *use, develop, strengthen, enlarge, not use, deteriorates,* and *disappears.* Grammatical metaphor would allow compacting and organisation of the answer, as in, for example: *the frequent use of an organ leads to its development in size and strength, while the consequence of disuse is deterioration and final disappearance of the organ.* In the second definition, the student includes more information in the nominal groups by using modifiers.

Task 3

The **science text** is a procedure, organised sequentially, and signalled by the markers: *first, then, finally.* The **history text** is a historical account, organised chronologically: *as time passed, at the end,* and by cause–effect: *due to* (prepositional phrase), *because* (subordinating conjunction introducing a clause).

In the **science text** the writer is authoritative by stating the method using the timeless simple present, and including a final strong prediction: *it will be.*

In the **history text** the writer is authoritative in presenting the events as fact using simple past tense, and evaluating the war as *cruel; unsustainable.*

The **science text** mainly uses material (action) processes, while in the **history text** relational processes are used to introduce the writer's evaluation. Here, material processes are used for the actions and a mental process appears, attributed to the historical actors, *both bands decided ... .*

In the **science text** technical terms are used: *the nucleus, the somatic cell,* while in **history** we find some institutional participants *both bands, Prussia.*

Task 4

- As well as material and relational processes for action and description, some mental processes typical of history appear – *saw, was appreciated.* Technical terms of science like *species, offspring, predators* and *genes* are used.
- The writer states the theory as accepted fact, though uses the past tense rather than the timeless present which is usually found in science, probably due to the historical focus of the question. The writer's role as 'knower' is also shown in the use of modal verbs – *had to struggle, had to avoid* –, as he goes further than simply stating that the animals, birds or insects etc. struggled, or avoided being eaten, and gives an interpretation of the reason for these actions. He also evaluates the probability of certain events: *were more likely to survive, were more likely to breed.*

• As regards the structure of the information in the text, this writer builds quite long nominal groups to carry a lot of the information: *Natural selection, the survival of the fittest* (using apposition), *large amounts of offspring, a shortage of food, species with features which helped them to survive in a certain environment* (postmodification using prepositional phrases and a relative clause) etc. There are a number of signals of cause and consequence in the paragraph: logical markers of addition (*and*) and consequence (*so*) between clauses, and clause-internal signals: a prepositional phrase (*thanks to*) and a verb (*helped to*). The choice of the passive in: *some difference was appreciated between an old form of an species and a new form of it* allows the writer to summarise the previous text in the general word *difference*, as subject, and leave the postmodifying prepositional phrase to the end of the clause where it links with the final sentence which underlines the answer to the question: *It had evolved.*

Chapter 9

Task 1

(a) Mathematics: The assessment technique is a mixture of hands-on (the students touch and feel the objects) with a practical task (estimating the weight). It also involves writing. They would use language orally to make their estimations as they handle the objects, and they would use written language for their justifications. Depending on their level, and whether they were used to speaking the L2 together in group activity, CLIL students might have problems with using the L2 to make guesses orally (or be unwilling to do so), and therefore resort to L1. They may be more comfortable doing the written task in the L2. It may be useful to give them some phrases they could use for making estimations of weight (these could be used in both the oral and written phases of the assessment, with appropriate adaptation for register).

(b) Science: This again is a mixture of techniques, involving the use of graphics (drawing) and writing. The language mode used in this activity is mostly writing. Writing down the system is relatively straightforward (if they know it), but the second section of the written part involves the use of a specific genre: an explanation. This might cause difficulty for CLIL students if they are not aware of the structure, purpose and language features of this genre. Depending on level and learning aims, it may be feasible to omit the explanation task. If it is used, a template for reminding them of the relevant explanation genre could be given (only if this genre has been taught previously).

(c) Social studies: The assessment technique is map completion. The language used in this task is quite simple, as students only have to write the names of states. Depending on level, CLIL students might have difficulty with remembering the names or the spelling (they would have greater difficulties if the activity involved filling in the names of foreign countries in a foreign language). The task instructions indicate that a time limit be given. It would be possible to adjust the difficulty of this task by giving the students more or less time to do it.

(d) Physical education: This is a clear example of a performance task. In terms of language, students could do this task in either speaking or writing. In either mode, it may be quite challenging for CLIL students to use their L2 to evaluate a golf swing, and there are particular grammatical difficulties in talking or writing about what could have happened. Bearing this in mind, it might be helpful to allow the students to write their evaluations first, and then possibly use what they have written to give an oral evaluation. They could also be given some help with the grammar with the use of sentence frames, such as *I could have ...* or *One thing I can do to improve my swing is ...* .

(e) Art: This is another performance activity, as students have to do a drawing within an allotted time. In terms of language, there is no real role of the linguistic mode in the assessment task itself, though, in a CLIL setting, the L2 will be used in the setting up of the task, explanation of its purpose, reminders of key ideas about perspective and so on. If it was thought desirable from the point of view of learning / teaching the subject, the teacher could introduce a language element. For example, the students could write brief justifications of the elements of perspective they used in their drawings and / or assess their peers' drawings according to a set of criteria.

(f) Technology: This is quite a complex task which involves collecting information, writing, using ICT and public speaking. Language is important throughout this assessment task. Students need to produce descriptions and / or explanations of their hobbies, and incorporate these with other modes such as sounds or images in a PowerPoint presentation. They need to use oral communication skills in giving their presentations. CLIL students may have difficulties and need language support at any of these stages. They will need to find the appropriate vocabulary for describing their hobbies, and 'package' the information in an appropriate genre, such as a report. They may also need help with public speaking skills, so some techniques, as well as useful phrases for beginning, moving between slides and ending presentations, could be introduced.

Task 2

Each of the three student texts has different strengths and weaknesses, and arguably none of them fulfils the criteria to reach a score of 4. It has to be kept in mind that these are short exam answers, and that students would likely need to produce a longer piece of writing to fully meet these criteria. The scores suggested here are fairly tentative suggestions. More information would be needed about the teachers' goals and the students' characteristics to give an accurate assessment. Some discussion among teachers would also be very useful. Text A is arguably the strongest. Although the writer doesn't link the voyage of *The Beagle* with Darwin's theory, the explanation of the theory is clear and well organised, with appropriate use of logical connectors (*on the other hand, therefore*) and an effective use of topic-relevant vocabulary, particularly collocation (*produce ... offspring; naturally occurring variation; struggle for life; compete for food; avoid predators; fittest will survive; useful traits*). A possible score could be 3.5, with the mark being pushed up by effective use of language.

Text B has more to say about the voyage of *The Beagle*, but Darwin's *being fascinated with vegetation and animals* does not meet the rubric's criterion for linking what Darwin actually observed to his theory. The explanation of the theory is sketchy and not always accurate. The sentences in the explanation of the theory are quite simple, but there is some use of appropriate topic-related vocabulary. Possible score 2.5.

Text C is rather interesting as it embeds the explanation of Darwin's theory with what he observed on his voyage, without even mentioning the voyage of *The Beagle*. It can't meet all the criteria to get a score of 4 then, even if the explanation of the theory is linked to what he saw on the voyage. In terms of coherence, the text jumps rather abruptly from who Darwin was and what he wrote (a biographical recount) to the explanation of the theory itself. It would lose some marks here for organisation. The explanation itself is fairly accurate, and uses some logical connectors. It also uses some appropriate topic-related vocabulary, such as *offspring, species, predators, genes*. However, the expression of the key ideas is a bit vague (*so finally some difference was appreciated*). Possible score: 3 (see Chapter 8 for a more detailed analysis of this text).

Appendix

Task 3

The teacher gives the group positive feedback on the way they are going about doing the task. He highlights the fact that they have done a drawing before starting to saw the wood (unlike another group who we can infer went straight on to the sawing stage). He uses the interaction with the students to collect information about their intentions (lines 3 and 4), something which is indispensible in order to offer mediation. He not only positively assesses how they are doing the task, but gives them some advice on how they can proceed, that is, by being economical with time by sawing the arms and legs while presumably another activity is going on (*in the meantime you can saw the arms and legs*). If this were an assessment activity, the teacher's intervention could thus be seen as dynamic assessment, as he not only gives the students feedback on their performance so far, but provides mediation in the form of guidelines for successful completion of the task.

Glossary

The following terms are used throughout this book. Many of the terms are more fully explained in the main text, but are included here as a ready reference guide.

Additional language: Any language that a learner adds to the language(s) that s/he already has competence in.

Appraisal theory: A theory within **systemic functional linguistics** which describes the systems used for expressing evaluative meanings in English. It comprises three main resources for evaluation: attitude, graduation and engagement.

Assessment for learning: Any assessment that is carried out for the main purpose of supporting students' learning. It is informal, and carried out by teachers as part of the normal classroom activity. See also **formative assessment**.

Backward design: A three-stage process of curriculum design which begins by identifying learning outcomes, then determining assessment procedures by which learners can show evidence of reaching them, and finally planning the instructional activities learners will do. The concept is introduced and explained in Wiggins and McTighe (2005).

BICS (Basic Interpersonal Communicative Skills): Cognitively undemanding everyday language skills needed to participate in local social interactions (Cummins, 1979).

Bilingual education: This refers to programmes in which academic content is taught in a language which is not the student's home language.

CALP (Cognitive Academic Language Proficiency): This refers to proficiency in the cognitively demanding language skills that are needed if students are to understand and produce the academic language of the different school subjects (Cummins, 1979).

Code switching: The use of more than one language, or language variety, in conversation. It usually refers to the ability to switch languages or dialects depending on the context or conversational partner.

Communication system: Ways in which teachers organise the talk in the classroom to meet their pedagogic purposes.

Comprehensible input: Messages in the target language that are slightly above learners' current second language competence. Associated with the work of Krashen (1985), who claimed that comprehensible input is necessary for second language acquisition.

Comprehensible output (also 'pushed' output): Language production in which students have been 'pushed' to make their messages more precise, coherent and appropriate (Swain, 1985).

Comprehension check: A move in conversation where one speaker tries to find out whether his / her interlocutor has understood his / her message.

Content-based instruction: A form of language instruction in which academic content topics from other, non-language subjects are used to organise the curriculum and support language learning.

Continua of multilingual education: A framework introduced by Cenoz (2009) for describing how **multilingual education** programmes may vary across three dimensions: sociolinguistic, educational and linguistic distance.

Corpus: A systematic and often large collection of spoken or written texts stored in computerised form, often with the purpose of representing different contexts of language use.

Corrective feedback: A teacher's response to a learner's utterance, in which the teacher provides the learner with information about the appropriateness of their performance.

Counterbalanced approach: In content-based classrooms, a counterbalanced approach is one in which students' attention is focused on language forms as well as content-related meanings (Lyster, 2007).

Curriculum macrogenre: A sequence of classroom actvities designed to achieve a pedagogical goal, and which may stretch over a number of lessons (Christie, 2002).

Dialogic inquiry An educational approach which emphasises achieving understanding through collaboration with others in communicative interaction (Wells, 1999).

Dialogic teaching (also dialogic talk): A form of pedagogy in which classroom talk is used to establish common understanding of curricular content between teachers and learners.

Directive: This refers to uses of language which aim to get the hearer perform an action. Types of directives include requests, commands, suggestions etc.

Discourse marker: Words or phrases which have the function of connecting messages in a spoken or written text without themselves forming part of the content of the message.

Dynamic assessment: An interventionist approach to assessment which sets out to measure learners' true potential when given appropriate support in performing learning tasks.

Evaluative feedback: In classroom talk, a response by a teacher to a learner in which the content of the learner's utterance is evaluated either positively or negatively.

Field: One of the three **register** variables. It refers to the kind of activity the participants are engaged in, or to the topic of a text.

Focus on form: A type of language instruction in which teachers draw the students' attention to language form during a meaning-oriented classroom activity.

Foreign language: A language that is not generally used in the learner's community, so that the learner's contact with the language will be mainly limited to the classroom.

Formative assessment: An approach to assessment in which teachers and students use evidence of students' performance through planned assessment tasks or observation to adjust either instructional procedures or learning tactics (see also **assessment for learning**).

Four Cs approach to CLIL: A conceptual framework for CLIL, which, as described by Coyle, Hood and Marsh (2010: 41), consists of four 'building blocks': content (subject matter); communication (language learning and using); cognition (learning and thinking processes); and culture (developing intercultural understanding and global citizenship).

Functional recast: A type of **corrective feedback** in which the teacher reformulates a student's utterance to make it conform more to the **register** – in the classroom this would be to the academic language of the subject being taught.

Generic competence: The ability to participate in new **genres** to achieve particular communicative ends.

Generic structure: The functional stages through which **genres** are realised in spoken or written language.

Genre: The text types used in different academic subjects (e.g. report, procedure, explanation).

Higher-order thinking skills: Advanced cognitive abilities acquired mainly through formal education. These include critical thinking, analysis and problem solving.

Horizontal knowledge structure: Term used by Bernstein (1999) to refer to knowledge that is not rigidly structured, usually consisting of the kinds of everyday concepts that can be picked up by participating in ordinary activities (see also **vertical discourse**).

Ideational One of the three metafunctions in systemic functional linguistics. It refers to the use of language to represent experience.

IGCSE: The International General Certificate of Secondary Education, an internationally recognized qualification for secondary school students.

Immersion: Highly intensive language-learning situations in which students are exposed to the **second language** for several hours a day.

Instructional register: The classroom **register** through which the academic content and skills being learnt are communicated (see also **regulative register**).

Interactional feedback: A type of feedback in which a teacher responds to a student's utterance without evaluating or correcting their performance (Llinares, 2005). Contrasts with **pedagogic feedback**.

Interactional format: This refers to different ways of organising interaction in the classroom. These include whole-class teaching, teacher-led group work, pupil-led group work, and one-to-one pupil pairs (see Alexander, 2008: 40).

Interactional scaffolding (also 'contingent' scaffolding): Support or help provided by the teacher in an unplanned or incidental way to help students convey their messages and complete an assigned learning task.

Interlanguage: Term introduced by Selinker (1992) to describe intermediate states of a learner's language system as it develops towards the target language / L2.

Interlanguage pragmatics: This refers to learners' acquisition and use of **pragmatic competence** in the target language; for example, learning to be polite in the target language in different situations.

Intermental In sociocultural theory, this refers to processes of communication between individuals.

Intramental In sociocultural theory, this refers to cognitive processes within individuals.

IRF exchange: A common interaction pattern in the classroom described by Sinclair and Coulthard (1975). It consists of three moves: Initiation–Response–Follow-up.

Language for learning: This refers to the language required to participate in classroom learning in a foreign language (Coyle et al., 2010).

Language of learning: This refers to the language needed for learners to access subject-related knowledge and skills (Coyle et al., 2010).

Language of schooling: The academic language that students are expected to understand and use to study the different school subjects, particularly at secondary level (Schleppegrell, 2004).

Language through learning: This refers to the language which emerges through deep engagement with content and activation of thinking processes (Coyle et al., 2010).

Literacy (subject related): The ability to read and write texts in the academic **genres** which are specific to different subjects.

Logical metafunction A subcomponent of the ideational metafunction which refers to the grammatical resources used to combine different units (such as clauses) by expressing meaning relationships such as time, consequence, comparison and addition.

Mediation: A process through which a more expert person interacts with a learner to help provide the learner with the means to improve his or her performance towards learning goals.

Medium of instruction (also language of instruction): A language used for the learning and teaching of non-language subject matter.

Metacognition: The ability to reflect on one's own thinking processes with the aim of using them more strategically.

Metafunctions: This refers to the three major functions of language in **systemic functional linguistics**: to represent experience (ideational), to enact human relationships (interpersonal), and to organise texts in a meaningful and coherent way (textual).

Metalanguage: Terminology for describing linguistic phenomena. This includes terms for talking about language at all levels, including grammar and vocabulary, discourse, and language as a social phenomenon.

Modality: The linguistic category involved in the expression of possibility, probability, certainty, obligation and permission.

Mode: One of the three **register** variables. It refers to the channels of communication (e.g. speaking, writing, image).

Mode continuum: This describes how language use can be seen as moving from more 'spoken' to more 'written' forms.

Multilingual education: Similar to **bilingual education**, but involving the use of two or more languages for the learning and teaching of non-language subject matter.

Negotiation of meaning: Collaboration in interaction that helps prevent problems in communication between native speakers and non-native speakers, or between the teacher and the learners in a classroom situation.

Nominalisation The process by which nouns or noun phrases are used to express what may be expressed in a different form in more natural spoken interaction, for example, when verbs are turned into nouns.

Noticing Hypothesis: Proposed by Schmidt (1990), who stated that some features of a language cannot be learned unless the learners focus their attention on them, either voluntarily or involuntarily.

Oracy: Developing the skills to participate in talk about school subjects.

Pedagogic feedback (see interactional feedback): A type of feedback in which a teacher responds to a student's utterance by evaluating or correcting it (Llinares, 2005).

Peer scaffolding: Collaboration between learners in which they provide temporary support for each other in carrying out learning tasks.

Personal function of language: This refers to the use of language to express feelings, opinions and individual identity. It is one of the functions identified by Halliday (1975) in his study of early language use in children.

Pragmatic competence: The knowledge of the linguistic resources available in a given language for realising particular pragmatic functions (pragmalinguistics) and knowledge of the appropriate contextual use of these linguistic resources of a particular language (sociopragmatics).

Pragmatic development The process by which language learners become more skilled in using language in appropriate and communicatively effective ways.

Register: The way specific features of language vary according to the social situation, in terms of three variables: the activity participants are doing (**field**), the relationships between them (**tenor**), and the channel of communication (**mode**).

Register scaffolding: This refers to two types of intervention to support learning: the planned sequencing of learning tasks (task scaffolding) in which activity in the spoken mode supports a later written task; and more spontaneous classroom interventions in which teachers reformulate students' spoken, everyday language in more academic terms (Llinares and Whittaker, 2009).

Regulative register: The classroom **register** which allows for the management of the overall direction, goals, pace and sequence of instructional activity (Christie, 2002).

Repair: This refers to the ways in which conversational partners resolve breakdowns in communication, usually problems in understanding each other. It includes, but is not limited to, correction, either by oneself or others.

Scaffolding: Temporary support given by a tutor / teacher to a learner in order to help them perform a task which would be too difficult for them to perform alone.

Second language: An **additional language** that is generally used in the learners' community but is not the learners' first language. The learners have exposure to this language in their daily lives outside the classroom.

Second language acquisition (SLA): A discipline within Applied Linguistics devoted to the study of individuals and groups who are learning an **additional language** (second or foreign) and to the process (mental and contextual) of learning that language.

Social semiotic (language as): A view of language as consisting of a set of resources which people use to make meanings in a particular social context.

Sociocultural theory: A theory in which learning is seen as taking place through social interaction and participation in activity with more expert members of the culture. Often associated with the work of the Russian psychologist L.S. Vygotsky.

Sociolinguistic variables Different ways in which a language can be seen as having a role in a society, for example in the number of speakers, its status, its use in everyday life and the media.

Sociolinguistic status This refers to the value and prestige given to any language in a society.

Summative assessment: A form of assessment in which students' achievement of learning goals is measured at the end of a unit or course of study. Contrasts with **formative assessment**.

Systemic functional linguistics (SFL): A linguistic model which sees language as systems of choices for making meaning. It focuses on how language is used in context for different purposes. Associated with the work of Michael Halliday (Halliday and Matthiessen, 2004).

Task scaffolding: See **register scaffolding**.

Tenor: One of the three **register** variables. In a social situation, it refers to the nature of the participants and the relationships between them. This can involve familiarity, distance, and power and status differences.

Uptake: Learners' responses to their teacher's or peers' feedback, in which they attempt to correct their errors.

Vehicular language: See **medium of instruction**.

Vertical knowledge structure: Bernstein's (1999) term for knowledge which is hierarchically structured, with concepts and constructs building on one another to construct one overarching theory. Contrasts with **horizontal discourse**.

Zone of proximal development (ZPD): This refers to the difference between levels of development a person can achieve without help and what they are capable of with appropriate assistance. This concept was introduced by the Russian psychologist L.S. Vygotsky.

References

Alexander, R. J. (2008) *Towards Dialogic Teaching: Rethinking Classroom Talk* (4th ed.), Cambridge: Dialogos.

Bernstein, B. B. (1999) 'Vertical and horizontal discourse: An essay', *British Journal of Sociology of Education*, 20, 2, 157–73.

Cenoz, J. (2009) *Towards Multilingual Education: Basque Educational Research from an International Perspective*, Bristol: Multilingual Matters.

Christie, F. (2002) *Classroom Discourse Analysis: A Functional Perspective.* London: Continuum.

Coyle, D., Hood, P. and Marsh, D. (2010) *CLIL: Content and Language Integrated Learning*, Cambridge: Cambridge University Press.

Cummins, J. (1979) 'Cognitive / academic language proficiency, linguistic interdependence, the optimum age question and some other matters', *Working Papers on Bilingualism*, 19, 121–9.

Halliday, M. A. K. (1975) *Learning how to Mean: Explorations in the Development of Language*, London: Edward Arnold.

Halliday, M. A. K. (2004) and Matthiessen, C. M. I. M. (eds.) *An Introduction to Functional Grammar* (3rd ed.), London: Hodder Arnold.

Krashen, S. (1985) *The input hypothesis: issues and implications*, London: Longman.

Llinares, A. (2005) 'The effect of teacher feedback on EFL learners' functional production in classroom discourse', *Anglogermanica Online: Revista Electrónica Periódica De Filología Alemana e Inglesa*, 3.

Llinares, A. and Whittaker, R. (2009) 'Teaching and learning history in secondary CLIL classrooms: From speaking to writing', in Dafouz, E. and Guerinni, M. (ed.), *CLIL Across Educational Levels: Experiences from Primary, Secondary and Tertiary Contexts*, pp. 73–89. London and Madrid: Richmond / Santillana.

Lyster, R. (2007) *Learning and Teaching Languages through Content: A Counterbalanced Approach*, Amsterdam and Philadelphia, PA: John Benjamins.

Schleppegrell, M. (2004) *The Language of Schooling: A Functional Linguistics Perspective.* Mahwah, NJ, and London: Lawrence Erlbaum.

Schmidt, R. W. (1990) 'The role of consciousness in second language learning', *Applied Linguistics*, 11, 2, 129–58.

Selinker, L. (1992) *Rediscovering Interlanguage*, London; New York: Longman.

Sinclair, J. and Coulthard, M. (1975) Towards an Analysis of Discourse: The English Used by teachers and Pupils, Oxford: Oxford University Press.

Swain, M. (1985) 'Communicative competence: Some roles of comprehensive input and comprehensible output in its development', Gass, S. M. and Madden, C. (eds.) *Input in Second Language Acquisition.* Cambridge, MA: Newbury House Publishers.

Wells, G. (1999). *Dialogic Inquiry: Towards a Socio-Cultural Practice and Theory of Education.* Cambridge: Cambridge University Press.

Wiggins, G. P. and McTighe, J. (2005) *Understanding by Design* (2nd ed.), Alexandria, VA: Association for Supervision and Curriculum Development.

Index

Note: Page numbers in *italic* indicate Glossary entries

academic language 219
  genres 109–47
  grammar and lexis 154–81
  see also CALP
academic register 44 *see also* vertical
  knowledge
action (Mortimer and Scott
  framework) 76–102
  analysing classroom talk 15, 16, 17
additional language *331*
Alexander, Robin 53, 63, 64–5, 69, 70, 71
analysing classroom talk (Mortimer and
  Scott) 11, 15, 16–17
Applied Linguistics 188
appraisal
  attitude 223
  engagement 223–4
  graduation 223–4
  in school genres 223–7
  in students' spoken and written
    discourse 223–6
  use of modality 226–7
appraisal theory *331*
approach (Mortimer and Scott framework)
  analysing classroom talk 15, 16, 17
  communication systems in CLIL 52–72
assessment as learning 282, 301, 310
assessment as teaching 310
assessment for learning 12, 13, 18, 281,
  282, 285, 310, *331*
assessment in CLIL 15, 18–19
  assessment as learning 282, 301, 310
  assessment as teaching 310
  assessment for learning 12, 13, 18, 281,
    282, 285, 310, *331*
  backward design 18, 292, 296, 299,
    300, *331*
  case for formative assessment 285–7
  content–language integrated scale 287–99
  conventional language assessment 283–4
  dynamic assessment 301–6
  formative assessment 280, 281–2
  instructional feedback 287, 299–306
  levels of assessment 280–1
  role of language 283–5

scoring systems 287–99
  teachers' concerns 280
  use of scales for scoring achievement 287–99
  uses of formative assessment 287
  widening the range of techniques 306–9
Assessment Reform Group (UK) 282, 286,
  290–1, 300
attitude (appraisal theory) 223, *331*
audiolingual method 188
Austria
  CLIL classroom data 3
  presence of English in everyday life 6–7
authoritative communication 54–5
  classroom examples 55–63

backward design 18, 292, 296, 299, 300, *331*
Basic Interpersonal Communication Skills
  (BICS) 83, 219–20, 229, 239, 283, *331*
behaviourist theory 188
Bernstein, Basil 29, 39
bilingual education *331*
  approaches 1–2
  school factors 4–5
bridging processes 39
  interactional scaffolding 99–100
Byrnes, H. 280–1

CALP (Cognitive Academic Language
  Proficiency) 83, 219–20, 283, *331*
Canada, immersion programmes 1
Cenoz, continua of multilingual education
  3–7, *332*
Chomskian linguistics 188
clarification requests 202–7
classifications of knowledge 36–8, 39
classroom assessment *see* formative
  assessment
classroom interaction 15, 16–17
  dynamic assessment 301–6
classroom registers *see* register
classroom talk, registers 29–47
CLIL (Content and Language Integrated
  Learning)
  and everyday language 8–9
  classroom data corpus 3, 4

contexts 1–7
definition 1–2
development in Europe 1
distinction from immersion 1–3
inclusion of immigrant students 2–3
inclusiveness of programmes 7
issues on the roles of language 8–9
language competence objectives 2
language of instruction 2
multilingual competence of teachers 4, 5
origins of 1
research 3
school-based factors 4–5
search for core principles 1, 3–7
starting age 2
teachers 2, 4, 5
teaching materials 2
theoretical perspectives 9–14
code switching *331*
Cognitive Academic Language Proficiency
    (CALP) 83, 219–20, 283, *331*
cognitive development, and use of
    language 11
Common European Framework of
    Reference 284
commonsense knowledge 38–40
    see also horizontal knowledge
communication systems 17, 52–4, 70–2, *331*
    approaches in CLIL 52–72
    classroom examples 55–63
    types of approach 54–5
communicative competence 188
comprehensible input 64, *331*
comprehensible output 64, *331*
comprehension check *332*
Content and Language Integrated Learning
    see CLIL
content-based instruction 1, *332*
content-driven nature of CLIL 187
content in CLIL 14
content–language integrated scale 287–99
contexts for CLIL 1–7
contingent scaffolding 300, *333*
    see also interactional scaffolding
continua of multilingual education
    (Cenoz) 3–7, *332*
  linguistic distance 4, 6
  school-based factors 4
  school context 4, 5–6
  sociolinguistic variables 4, 6–7
  teacher continuum 4, 5

convergence, integrated framework 14
conversational repair *see* repair
corpus *332*
corpus of CLIL classroom data 3, 4
corrective feedback *332*
  clarification requests 202–7
  elicitation 202–3, 210–12
  explicit correction 202–3, 205–7, 211–12
  in student–student interactions 212–14
  metalinguistic feedback 202–3, 212
  recasts 202–3, 207–10, 212
  repetition 202–3, 211–12
  role in CLIL 202–14
counterbalanced approach 12, *332*
Coyle, Do 1, 9, 14, 34, 71, 76, 79, 87, 90,
    101, 189, 222, 227–8, 237, 238, 291,
    300, *333, 334*
curriculum macrogenre 227–8, 229, *332*

Dale, Liz 3
Dalton-Puffer, Christiane 3, 8, 9, 25, 29, 31,
    33–4, 44, 52–3, 63, 79, 82, 84, 85–8,
    117, 121, 159, 214, 220–1, 226, 229,
    234, 250, 303
declaratives 31
dialogic communication 54–5
    classroom examples 55–63
dialogic inquiry 11, 13, *332*
dialogic interaction 17
dialogic teaching (dialogic talk) 11, 53, *332*
    importance in CLIL classrooms 53,
        63–70, 71–2
dimensions of language and content
    development 15
directives 30, 31, 33, 97, 221–2, 231, *332*
discourse markers 228–9, *332*
discourse strategies for CLIL students 228–9
discourse structure 109–12
display questions 84–5
Dutch, linguistic distance from English 6
dynamic assessment 12, 15, 301–6, *332*

elicitation, corrective feedback 202–3,
    210–12
engagement (appraisal theory) 223–4, *331*
English
  as lingua franca 6
  impact on other languages 6
  shared sociolinguistic status 6
European Commission 1
evaluative feedback *332*

Index

evaluative language in school genres 223–7
everyday language and CLIL 8–9
everyday knowledge and language 38–40
   see also horizontal knowledge
explanation
  field 165–9
  grammar and lexis 163–72
  mode 170–2
  register analysis 163–72
  tenor 169–70
explicit correction 202–3, 205–7, 211–12

feedback
  assessment 18
  assessment for learning 12, 13
  role of corrective feedback in
    CLIL 202–14
  see also IRF exchange
field (register variable) 15, 26–9, 34–6, 44,
  332
  choosing the appropriate lexis 188, 190–4
  displaying knowledge in writing 257–62
  grammar and lexis required 155
Finland
  CLIL classroom data 3
  presence of English in everyday life 6–7
Finnish, linguistic distance from English 6
focus, analysing classroom talk 15, 16–17,
  25–48
focus on content and focus on language
  202–14
focus on form 188–90, 332
focus on meaning 181–90
foreign language 332
formative assessment 15, 18, 280, 281–2,
  285–7, 332–3
  content–language integrated scale 287–99
  instructional feedback 299–306
four C's approach to CLIL (Coyle) 237, 333
framework for the roles of language in
  CLIL 14–19
  assessment 15, 18–19
  classroom interaction 15, 16–17
  language development 15, 17–18
  subject literacies 15–16
  theories of learning and language 9–14
functional recasts 209–10, 300–1, 333

generic competence 111, 333
generic structure 333
genres 12, 13, 14–16, 188, 333

definition 14, 110–12
discourse structure 109–12
evaluative language in 223–7
geography 126–32
history 132–46
in CLIL subjects 109–47
science 112–26
geography genres 126–32
  causal explanations 129–30
  consequential explanations 130
  definitions in descriptive reports 127–9
  descriptive reports 126–9
  explanations 129–30
  factorial explanations 130
  reports 126–9
  sequential explanations 129
  tasks requiring 131–2
  taxonomic (classifying) reports 129
German, linguistic distance from English 6
graduation (appraisal theory) 223–4, 331
grammar and lexis in CLIL subjects 154–81
  challenges in the language of
    textbooks 172–80
  explanation 163–72
  historical account 163–72
  register analysis 155–6
  science procedure 157–60
  science report 160–3
grammatical metaphor 44, 176–80, 209–10
group work 30–3, 45–6
  language of socialising 229–31

Halliday, Michael 10, 11, 13–14, 15, 17, 27,
  249, 336
higher-order thinking skills 333
historical accounts 138–9
  field 165–9
  grammar and lexis 163–72
  mode 170–2
  register analysis 163–72
  tenor 169–70
history, features of written language 256–73
history genres 132–46
  biographical recounts 135–8
  consequential explanations 140
  discussion 142, 144–5
  exposition 142–4
  factorial explanations 140–2
  historical accounts 138–9, 163–72
  historical explanations 139–42
  period study 133–5

recounts 135–8
  tasks requiring 145–6
horizontal discourse *333*
horizontal knowledge 16–17, 29, 38–45, 54
hyponymy 36, 37
hypothesising 250

ideational *333*
ideational content 48
ideational meanings 17
  grammar and lexis required 155
ideational metafunction of language 10, 28,
    35–8, 44, 188, 190–7
IGCSE (International General Certificate of
    Secondary Education) 111, 282, *333*
  geography 131–2
  history 145–6
  science subjects 124–6
immersion technique 1, 12, 187, 239, *333*
  distinction from CLIL 1–3
  language competence objectives 2
  language of instruction 2
  research 3
  starting age 2
  teachers 2
  teaching materials 2
immigrant learners 2–3, 219
imperatives 31
inclusiveness of CLIL programmes 7
Initiation–Response–Follow-up *see* IRF
instructional feedback 287, 299–306
instructional register 16, 29–30, 34–47, *333*
interaction patterns in the CLIL classroom 76–7
  IRF exchange 77–83
  questions 83–90
  repair 90–1
interactional feedback 202, *333*
interactional formats 53–5, 71, *333*
interactional scaffolding 91–101, *333*
  bridging 99–100
  carrying out a task 97
  end-of-topic discussion 95
  peer scaffolding 100–1
  reflection on a task 98–100
  review and orientation stage 92–3
  setting up a new task 95–7
  topic introduction 93–4
interactive toolkit for teachers 68–9
interactive and non-interactive
    communication 54–5
interlanguage 164, *333*

interlanguage pragmatics 238, *334*
intermental *334*
intermental activity 26
interpersonal language in CLIL 219–39
  appraisal in school genres 223–7
  discourse markers 228–9
  evaluative language in school genres 223–7
  expanding students' linguistic resources
    236–8
  expanding students' turns in interaction
    235–6
  for operating in the classroom 227–9
  functions in CLIL classes 222–3
  language of socialising 229–32
  opportunities to develop 221–2
  range of communicative functions 233–5
  role plays for social purposes 231–2
  students' discourse strategies 228–9
  students' personal experiences 232–8
interpersonal meanings 17–18
  grammar and lexis required 156
interpersonal metafunction of language 10,
    28, 31, 33, 220–3
intramental *334*
intramental activity 26
IRF (Initiation–Response–Follow-up)
    exchange 17, 221, *334*
IRF pattern in CLIL classrooms 77–83
  expanding feedback 81–3
  student-initiated interactions 79–81

language, social-semiotic theory 13, *335*
language-bath approach 8
language competence objectives in CLIL 2
language development 15, 17–18
language-focused tasks and activities, role
    of 197–202
language for learning 9, 26, 34, 38, 71,
    227–8, 300, *334*
language of instruction 2, 4, *334*
language of learning 9, 26, 34, 38, 71, 300, *334*
language of schooling 8–9, 40, *334*
language through learning 9, 34, 38, 87, 90,
    238, *334*
learner autonomy 33
learning opportunities in CLIL 25–6, 29,
    52, 77
lingua franca, English as 6
linguistic distance 4, 6
linguistic features *see* grammar and lexis in
    CLIL subjects

Index

linguistic landscape 6
literacy (subject-related) 14, 15–16, 245, *334*
literacy pedagogical content knowledge (LPCK) 15
Llinares, Ana 79, 80, 82–3, 84, 91, 95, 101, 192–4, 195–6, 199, 202, 208, 226, 229, 231, 233, 245, 270, 272, 279, 292, 333, 335
loan words 6
logical metafunction *334*

macrogenre *see* curriculum macrogenre
macro-level sociolinguistic variables 4, 6
Marzano, R. J. 287, 288–92, 299, 300, 303
meaning-based theory of language 10
mediation 15, 18–19, *334*
medium of instruction 6, *334*
meronymy 36, 37
metacognition *334*
metafunctions of language 10–11, 28, 35, *334*
metalanguage *334*
  for classroom communication 25–6, 48, 71
metalinguistic feedback 202–3, 212
micro-level sociolinguistic variables 4, 7
modality *334*
  use by students 226–7
mode 15, 26–9, *334*
  challenges in the language of textbooks 172–80
  grammar and lexis required 156
  in historical accounts 170–2
  in life sciences 172–6
  in science procedures 159–60
  in science reports 163
  in social science 177–80
  structuring written texts 268–73
mode continuum 301, *334*
Morton, Tom 147, 292
multilingual education *334*
Musumeci, Diane 52

negotiation of meaning 47, *334*
Netherlands
  CLIL classroom data 3
  presence of English in everyday life 6–7
Nikula, Tarja 3, 9, 31, 33, 44, 78–9, 80, 81, 221, 229
nominalisation 44, 173–80, *335*
noticing hypothesis 201, 214, *335*

oracy *335*
  focus in CLIL 244
organisational aspect of learning 26

participation in CLIL classrooms 12
pedagogic feedback *335 see also* corrective feedback
peer scaffolding 100–1, *335*
personal function of language 197, 233, *335*
Popham, W. J. 281, 286
pragmatic competence *335*
pragmatic development *335*
proactive approach to instruction 12–13
pushed output *see* comprehensible output

questions 48–9
  and class activities 85–8
  and previous knowledge 85–8
  goals 85–8
  in the CLIL classroom 83–90
  referential questions 84–5
  students' questions 88–90

reactive approach to instruction 12–13
recasts 202–3, 207–10, 212, 300–1, *333*
referential questions 84–5
register 12, 13, 14–16, 26–48, 188, *335*
register analysis
  explanation 163–72
  historical account 163–72
  linguistic features in texts 155–6
  science procedure 157–60
  science repost 160–3
register scaffolding *335*
  at the micro-level 194
  for writing activities 245
register variables 26–9 *see also* field; mode; tenor
regulative register 16, 45–7, *335*
  in CLIL lessons 29–34
  use of the target language (L2) 31–4
repair (of communication) 66, 90–1, *335*
repetition (corrective feedback) 202–3, 211–12
role plays, developing interpersonal language 231–2

sampling approach to CLIL 5
scaffolding 11–12, 13, 15, 17, 76, 193–4, 300, *335*
  definitions 91–2
  types of 91–2

see also interactional scaffolding; task
   scaffolding
scales for scoring achievement 287–99
Schleppegrell, Mary 226, 255
schools
   approaches to multilingual education 4–5
   context for multilingual education 4, 5–6
science, features of written language 255–73
science genres 112–26
   causal explanations 121, 122
   classifying (taxonomic) reports 116, 117,
      119–20
   compositional reports 116–17, 120
   consequential explanations 122–3
   descriptive reports 116–18
   explanations 112, 120–4
   factorial explanations 123–4
   procedural recounts 114–16
   procedures 112, 113–14
   reports 112, 116–20
   sequential explanations 121–2
   tasks requiring 124–6
science procedures
   field 157–9
   grammar and lexis 157–60
   mode 159–60
   register analysis 157–60
   tenor 159
science reports
   field 160–2
   grammar and lexis 160–3
   mode 163
   register analysis 160–3
   tenor 162–3
scientific knowledge and language 38–9
   see also vertical knowledge
Scope and Scales tool 292–5
scoring systems 287–99
second language 335
second language acquisition (SLA) 12,
   13–14, 335
SFL *see* systemic functional linguistics
Short, D. 308
social-semiotic theory of language 13, 335
socialising
   in group work 229–31
   language of 229–32
sociocultural perspective 11–14
sociocultural theory of learning 11, 13–14,
   274, 336
sociolinguistic status 336

sociolinguistic variables
   general 336
   macro-level 4, 6
   micro-level 4, 7
Spain
   CLIL classroom data 3
   presence of English in everyday life 6–7
Spanish, linguistic distance from English 6
specific interventions 76
spoken mode in the CLIL classroom
   248–54
starting age for CLIL 2
strong bilingual education 5
Structuralism 188
student-initiated interactions 79–81
student–student interactions, corrective
   feedback 212–14
students' language development
   choosing the appropriate lexis 188, 190–4
   creating field 188, 190–4
   expression of logical relations 194–7
   focus on content/focus on language
      202–14
   focus on form/focus on meaning 188–90
   integrating form and meaning 187–215
   language-focused tasks and
      activities 197–202
   lexico-grammar in representation of
      content 190–7
   role of corrective feedback 202–14
students' questions 88–90
subject language
   genres 109–47
   grammar and lexis 154–81
subject literacy 14, 15–16, 245, 334
subject-specific terminology 34
summative assessment 281, 336
systemic functional linguistics (SFL) 10–11,
   13–14, 220–3, 255, 336

task scaffolding, for writing activities 245
taxonomies of knowledge 36–8, 39
teachers, level of multilingual
   competence 4, 5
teaching purpose, and level of focus 25–6
tenor (register variable) 15, 26–9, 31, 336
   being authoritative in writing 262–8
   grammar and lexis required 156
textual meanings 18
   grammar and lexis required 156
textual metafunction of language 10, 28, 31

Index

theories of learning and language 9–14
triadic dialogue 77

UAM-CLIL corpus 3
uncommonsense knowledge 38–9
  see also vertical knowledge
United States, content-based instruction 1
uptake 198, 203, 206–8, 213, *336*

vehicular language *see* medium of
  instruction
vertical discourse *336*
vertical knowledge 16, 29, 38–45, 54
vocabulary *see* grammar and lexis in CLIL
  subjects
Vygotsky, L. S. 11, 13–14, 26, 38, 301, 336

weak bilingual education 5
Wells, G. 11, 13, 17, 64–5, 78, 81

Whittaker, Rachel 91, 95, 101, 192–4,
  195–6, 199, 208, 226, 245, 270, 272,
  279, 335
writing
  and subject literacy 245
  being authoritative (tenor) 262–8
  developing language functions 255–73
  developing student's writing 244–75
  displaying knowledge in writing
    (field) 257–62
  register scaffolding for students 245
  role in CLIL 244–5
  roles for students in different genres 255–7
  structuring texts (mode) 268–73
written language, different uses from spoken
  language 245–8

zone of proximal development (ZPD) 301,
  303, *336*

Lightning Source UK Ltd.
Milton Keynes UK
UKHW02f1839250418
321660UK00032B/622/P